Trading Industries,
Trading Regions

PERSPECTIVES ON ECONOMIC CHANGE

Series Editors

Peter Dicken
University of Manchester

Meric Gertler
University of Toronto

TRADING INDUSTRIES, TRADING REGIONS: INTERNATIONAL TRADE, AMERICAN INDUSTRY, AND REGIONAL ECONOMIC DEVELOPMENT

Helzi Noponen, Julie Graham, and Ann R. Markusen, Editors

TRADING INDUSTRIES, TRADING REGIONS

International Trade, American Industry, and Regional Economic Development

Edited by

HELZI NOPONEN
JULIE GRAHAM
ANN R. MARKUSEN

THE GUILFORD PRESS
New York   London

© 1993 The Guilford Press
A Division of Guilford Publications, Inc.
72 Spring Street, New York, NY 10012

Printed in the United States of America

This book is printed on acid-free paper.

Last digit is print number: 9   8   7   6   5   4   3   2   1

Library of Congress Cataloging-in-Publication Data

Trading industries, trading regions : international trade, American
    industry, and regional economic development / edited by Helzi
    Noponen, Julie Graham, Ann R. Markusen.
        p.   cm. — (Perspectives on economic change)
    Includes bibliographical references and index.
    ISBN 0-89862-296-4.—ISBN 0-89862-753-2 (pbk.)
        1. Industry—Location.   I. Noponen, Helzi.   II. Graham, Julie.
III. Markusen, Ann R.   IV. Series.
HC79.D5T73   1993
338.6'042—dc20   93-19475
                                                           CIP

Acknowledgments

We would like to thank the Mott Foundation and the Center for Urban Affairs and Policy Research of Northwestern University for funding and support for the initial research. We would also like to thank the Geography and Regional Science Program of the National Science Foundation, which provided grant support for the research of Julie Graham (grant no. SES 87-07291). After 1989, the research effort was continued and completed at the Project on Regional and Industrial Economics, in the Center for Urban Policy Research at Rutgers University, with additional support from the University of Massachusetts at Amherst and the University of North Carolina at Chapel Hill. The editors would like to thank in particular Scott Campbell, Yang Chao, Karl Driessen, Rodney Erickson, Vickie Gwiasda, Candace Howes, Pierre Paul Proulx, and Larry Radbill for extensive comments and research assistance, and our series editors, Meric Gertler and Peter Dicken, for their helpful reviews. Our thanks, too, to Peter Wissoker, who migrated in the course of this project from his role as a contributor to that of an editor at Guilford Press. Kim Smith and Barbara Brunialti helped maneuver the manuscript over a series of hurdles. Carol Vogel and Ann Lucas at the University of Massachusetts provided skilled wordprocessing services at various stages of the project.

Contributors

Scott Campbell, PhD, Department of Urban Planning and Policy Development, Rutgers University, New Brunswick, New Jersey

Anthony P. D'Costa, PhD, Comparative International Development, Liberal Studies Program, University of Washington, Tacoma, Washington

Julie Graham, PhD, Department of Geology and Geography, University of Massachusetts, Amherst, Massachusetts

Candace Howes, PhD, Department of Economics, University of Notre Dame, South Bend, Indiana

Ann R. Markusen, PhD, Department of Urban Planning and Policy Development, Rutgers University, New Brunswick, New Jersey

Helzi Noponen, PhD, Department of City and Regional Planning, University of North Carolina, Chapel Hill, North Carolina

Peter Wissoker, MS, Brooklyn, New York

Preface

This book is about the impact of intensified international trade on regions in the United States. Over the past two decades, the share of GNP exported has doubled, and the share of domestic consumption met by imported goods has nearly tripled. U.S. industries previously national in scope have undergone dramatic restructuring, with some falling victim to increased international competition and others thriving on new, more extensive markets.

The consequences for regions within the United States have often been highly disruptive. Many regions, especially those with either a preponderance of mature manufacturing industries or with branch plants dependent upon low cost, relatively unskilled labor, find themselves confronting new waves of plant closings and outmigration of capital. Particularly hard hit are the interior regions, including the industrial heartland of the Great Lakes; rural areas with a reliance on branch plants; and inner cities with relatively aged capital stock. Other regions, particularly those hosting concentrations of certain high tech industries (aircraft, computers, communications equipment, pharmaceuticals, for instance) or business services (finance, legal services, management consulting) have boomed with the rapid growth of trade and the opening of new markets.

Overall, however, the growth of high-paying trade-generated jobs in the latter industries has not compensated for the loss of such jobs in the former, leading to a deterioration in the level of wages and incomes. Moreover, the spatial mismatch between new and old trade-related jobs has left the country pockmarked with sizeable pockets of unemployment. The absence of effective adjustment policies and of a coherent regional development strategy at the national level has exacerbated these problems, creating considerable social costs which must be borne by the welfare state or by individuals and their communities.

The phenomenon of trade integration and its consequences requires new methods of economic, geographic, and policy analysis. Previous methods of gauging regional development patterns which stop at the nation's borders (shift-share analysis, for instance, or location quotients) must be abandoned as industries are studied on the world rather than national scale. Location theory must be recast as an international exercise, and empirical tests of locational behavior must transcend national boundaries. Trade theory must be expanded beyond the narrow comparative advantage framework to encompass strategic economic development and trade practices of nations.

This book offers a new approach to the study of trade and its impact on industries and regions. In the first chapter, theories of international trade are reviewed and critiqued, and a method is outlined for studying industry-by-industry spatial evolution. In the case studies that follow, the contributing authors work to a common research design, analyzing a number of industries—including two in the service sector—that are prototypical yet unique. Each study interprets the international trade and locational forces that have shaped the changing geography of the industry within the United States. Since the different policy postures of national governments with respect to trade and development strategy contribute to the location and success of industries internationally, considerable emphasis is placed on analyzing the role of nation states in shaping the distribution of each industry. And, since oligopolistic multinational corporations choose to site and expand or contract activity across global space, their leadership in reshaping international industries is also considered.

The book closes with a summary chapter that compares the industries analyzed. The industry studies show that the contemporary size and location of the American steel, auto, insurance, machine tool, shipping, and pharmaceutical industries are neither the product of natural comparative advantage nor of domestic cost differentials. Together, they form a powerful indictment of the free trade prescription as a national growth and regional development strategy. Many regions and communities have been adversely affected by the policies of other national governments, as well as by the lack of a coherent trade and development policy on the part of the United States government. Thousands of workers, and entire communities, have suffered irreversible losses which are not the result of any inherent "competitiveness" problem, but of policies promoted by interests that benefit from heightened trade activity (especially commercial and financial sectors) and by those who believe in the ideologically rigid free trade prescription. The research suggests an alternative political and economic course for the United States and its trading partners, with managed trade policies tailored to the specifics of each industry under consideration.

THE EDITORS

Contents

1

Trade, Industry, and Economic Development

CANDACE HOWES
ANN R. MARKUSEN

American workers, industries, and communities are increasingly embedded in a worldwide system of trading relationships. The share of U.S. gross national product (GNP) exported rose from 7% in 1970 to nearly 12% by 1989, while the import share of domestic markets climbed from 6 to 13%. Over the past decade about 49% of growth in domestic consumption was met by imports. Americans are buying more imported goods and services than ever before, and what workers make in urban factories is more apt to be exported than it was 20 years ago. In addition, much of the new job creation in the economy is trade-generated. Compared to past decades, many more white-, pink-, and blue-collar workers are engaged in financing, accounting, marketing, shipping, wholesaling, warehousing, distributing, and retailing the enlarged volume of internationally traded goods and services.

Internationalization of trade has proven uneven and disruptive (Drache & Gertler, 1991.) Some occupations, industries, and cities have thrived because of heightened trade, while others have been net losers. In the United States semiskilled blue-collar workers who once held steady jobs and received good benefits find themselves "displaced" by cheaper third world workers or by equally skilled and well-paid workers in Europe or Japan. So do many of their middle managers. Sectors such as autos, steel, textiles, semiconductors, and consumer electronics have experienced net job and capacity losses, while others such as aircraft, computers, movies, and finance have boomed. Big cities in the industrial heartland, including Chicago, Milwaukee, Cleveland, and Detroit, and smaller ones such as Flint, Peoria, and Gary have suffered dramatic losses, while Los Angeles, Miami, and Seattle have flourished, at least until the recession of the early 1990s.

The growth of trade and its ramifications for individual regions and industries are not, however, natural or inevitable processes. Indeed, workers and communities in Europe and Japan have faced considerably less displacement from the growth of trade than have their American or Canadian counterparts. Wrenching trade-induced change versus slow, managed adaption is very much a question of public policy—the postures that national governments take toward industrial investment, trade policies, and macroeconomic management. Strategic trade and industrial policies have enabled Japan, Germany, Italy, and Korea to achieve and maintain considerable trade surpluses with cumulative and salutary effects on the growth of output, incomes, productivity, and world market shares. In contrast, countries that have relied upon free trade prescriptions have experienced deep erosion in their competitive positions.

In the United States professionals debating trade policy have given regrettably short shrift to the considerable and costly disruptions associated with adherence to the free trade formula. While denying the public sector any legitimate role other than guaranteeing open borders, free trade ideologues have admonished industries to "get competitive" or die. While concern has mounted in tandem with the size of the trade deficit, most proffered solutions are strictly macroeconomic in nature: raise the savings rate and let the dollar fall to cheapen American goods abroad and to hike up the prices of imports, a prescription that has not worked, at least not at acceptable levels of employment and inflation. Only for those industries claiming some special relationship to the national interest —aircraft because it is closely tied to military capabilities, or electronics because it is a technological leader under duress—have American presidents and the Congress been willing to engage in special trade deals or industrial policies to bolster performance. Other industries, even those with political muscle, have had to be content with far-from-satisfactory "voluntary" restraints bargained at each president's discretion or with expensive and interminable litigation charging "unfair trade" practices.

Because national policymakers in the United States have remained indifferent to the hardships suffered by widespread groups of workers, industries, and communities, the task of coping with them has fallen by default on the shoulders of unions, industrial associations, and state and local governments.[1] For these stakeholders, exhortations to become more "competitive" have proven inadequate. Job loss and plant shutdowns translate into escalating social welfare costs, a shrinking tax base, and outmigration.[2] Proving that necessity is indeed the mother of invention, those hardest hit by trade-related restructuring have been the most creative, engaging in experiments that range from the building of the new

Steel Valley Authority in the Pittsburgh area to burgeoning state programs for export promotion.[3] Unfortunately, most of the participants have neither the resources nor the expertise to confront the considerable challenges posed to them by an internationalizing world. The federal government may also lack such experience, but it certainly has the resources and the discretionary power to respond.

Increasingly, public opinion in the United States supports some version of managed trade and industrial policy despite nearly universal opposition from the economics profession. Simultaneously, a new body of literature within economics has emerged to challenge the fundamental underpinnings of the neoclassical free trade position. Ever since Georg Frederick List (1922) first argued in the 19th century that free trade worked only for the first arrival, generations of dissenting and recently even some mainstream economists have demonstrated that mercantilist policies can and have enriched some nations, perhaps at the expense of others. More recently, theorists of the "revisionist" trade school who have challenged the assumption of constant returns to scale (Kaldor, 1989; Krugman, 1991a, 1991b; Romer, 1986, 1987) stress the likelihood of increasing returns to scale and imperfect markets, which will reward those nations whose industries first successfully penetrate foreign markets while resisting market penetration at home. The assumption that sectoral mix does not matter to economic growth is contested indirectly by some and directly by others (Scott, 1992; Kaldor, 1989; Dosi, Tyson, & Zysman, 1989).

Success at international market penetration is a function both of competitive advantages in relative prices, technology, and productivity, themselves often a function of cultural and institutional factors, and of concerted government policies to pursue strategic advantages. Such policies are almost always implemented at the sectoral level—within and among a group of firms concentrating in certain industry lines. They can have a dramatic effect on the evolving location of an industry internationally, by cultivating it in one region at the expense of another. They can, in short, "construct" comparative advantages in ways not taken into account in traditional free trade theories. Recently, the spectacular performances of Japan and Korea in particular suggest that overall shifts in trade patterns are more a function of strategic trade behavior than of simple differences in factor costs.

Taking place-by-place socioeconomic costs and dynamic comparative advantage construction into account requires a different way of thinking about and researching international trade issues than is offered by the static, neoclassical general equilibrium approach. It calls for an industry-by-industry approach. The traditional orthodoxy presumes that dislocation and unemployment are temporary disequilibria en route to a new equilibrium with full employment. An alternative theory shows that not only are dislocation and unemployment the almost inevitable consequences of free trade, but that acceptable levels of growth, employment, and per capita income require sectoral policies to promote strategic industries. International trade issues must therefore be approached on an industry-by-industry basis.

This book analyzes the impact of trade on regional development and employment. It pulls together a set of industry-specific studies in location where national boundaries are not accepted as the relevant universe. The industries were selected on the basis of their significance, both internationally and regionally, across a range of sectors, including services, and from among industries in different stages in the profit cycle (Markusen, 1985a). Most have been viewed as strategic by the governments of one or more major exporting nations, offering an opportunity to compare outcomes across competing nations with different trade and investment strategies. All were written to a common research design, in an attempt to develop international industry location studies that could illuminate the experience of any one set of subregions embedded within the system—in this case, U.S. regions. Each attempts to show how the U.S. market has been served by an industry whose international locational patterns are shifting, often as the result of strategic planning by firms and even whole industries and active intervention on the part of a national, or more rarely regional, government. In order to interpret the causes and extent of the social costs imposed on the closings sites, each study links the changing pattern of trade in an industry to the geography of plant openings and closings around the globe.

Together, the case studies pose a considerable challenge to the free trade prescription. They suggest that success in trade is fundamentally shaped by governmental intervention. Governments have played a pioneering role in creating and maintaining industrial leadership in key sectors, constructing the conditions for relative comparative advantage. In a world with governments successfully conducting such industrial and trade policies, open economies without such efforts will find themselves the targets of import penetration and potential export market shrinkage.

The studies also show that entire regions can suffer severe adversities and adjustment costs that must be weighed against purported gains from free trade. They challenge the notion that cheap imports are unambiguously better for consumers, by pointing out that many of the "consumers" so served may simultaneously be workers whose incomes have been severely depressed by redundancy or plant closings. The studies do not rest their case against free trade on equity grounds alone. Together, they suggest that cumulative adjustment costs may actually contribute to laggard global growth and a net lowering of world living standards. Overall, they demonstrate that in this new, complicated, and more-interconnected world of trade, fine-grained attention to individual industries and regions calls for policy responses that are carefully attuned to basic human needs and economic development potential.

In this chapter we review the scant theoretical or empirical work on the impact of trade on regional development and the studies on international industry location. Since state and local policymakers have been left with the responsibility of trying to cope with trade-related restructuring, this intellectual deficit is particularly distressing. In the 1980s, a period when American trade patterns were changing dramatically, disparities in the economic development experience of U.S. regions were exacerbated. We draw the causal connection between the two phenomena, whereby dramatic increases in imports and a fall in exports in traditional equipment and metals industries disproportionately hurt the industrial heartland, while military-nurtured sectors like aerospace, electronics, and communications equipment and trade-associated sectors like finance and business services selectively boosted the growth rates of coastal regions. We show that such outcomes are not satisfactorily explained by orthodox trade theories, and we argue that the neoclassical inference that such outcomes are desirable is incorrect, due to a number of key problems in the theory itself.

To replace the free trade ideology with an alternative historically based and empirically testable policy approach is a daunting task. It requires a study of the specific key industries involved and of the ways in which each industry's location and character have been historically generated through deliberate policy interventions as well as through natural resource endowments and comparative advantages. In the final part of this chapter we lay out the elements of such a methodology and suggest how its use would alter the terms of the national and international debate about trade relationships.

LINKING TRADE WITH CITIES AND REGIONS

The internationalization of the U.S. economy and its consequences for domestic jobs have become hot topics in the past decades. A number of researchers have attempted to measure the employment effect of international trade at the national level. For a single year, 1982, heightened trade was estimated to have displaced 1.11 million manufacturing workers but created another 525,000 jobs, leaving a net negative impact of 584,000 (New York Stock Exchange, 1984, pp. 22–24.) These losses were heavily concentrated in four industries: apparel, autos, shoes, and steel. Between 1984 and 1987 5.1 million jobs were lost as a result of trade deficits; 60% of these were in manufacturing, and about half were jobs that paid more than $400 per week (Duchin & Lange, 1988, cited in Salvatore, 1990). At the same time, as the internationally traded component of output rises, more jobs than ever become dependent upon or vulnerable to shifts in trade. Some 4.8 million jobs were attributable to manufactured exports in 1981 (International Trade Commission, 1984).[4]

To date, little systematic research has been conducted on the employment consequences of increased trade for American cities and regions. Several recent studies chart the empirical consequences of market integration on supranational, national, or sectoral/industry bases.[5] Conceptually, several researchers have hypothesized trade-associated changes in regional industry structure (Hansen, 1979; Renaud, 1984; Markusen, 1985a). Only a few studies have been conducted on the differential effects of international trade on industries and employment at the metropolitan or regional level (Erickson, 1989; Reifler, 1990; Bauer & Eberts, 1990; Markusen, Noponen, & Driessen, 1991; Erickson & Hayward, 1991).[6] In general, they confirm distinct patterns in international trade-related growth, although domestic markets remain predominant in explaining regional growth differentials.

Disaggregated commodity trade data has been used to chart differential regional and urban growth experience as a function of trade-related industrial structure (Markusen, Noponen, & Driessen, 1991; Noponen, Markusen, & Driessen, 1992a, 1992b). In the period from 1977 to 1986, despite import vulnerability, the New England, Mountain, West North Central, and Pacific regions of the United States posted relatively high employment growth rates as a result of their industrial capacity to capture both export and domestic markets. In large part, their performance was a product of the extraordinary boom in defense spending, (up 50% in real terms) and foreign arms sales over the period (Markusen, Hall, Deitrick, & Campbell, 1991). In contrast, the East North Central region was ill-positioned to take advantage of new export and domestic markets, and its industrial structure was found to be quite vulnerable to imports as well. Two regions—the South Atlantic and West South Central—were found to have industrial structures relatively resistant to import penetration and were relatively well positioned domestically, but less so vis-à-vis export markets.

That exacerbated regional growth differentials in the United States occurred in tandem with the exploding trade deficit in the 1980s can easily be demonstrated. Of course, not all recent geographic disparities in growth rates are attributable to trade. Lopsided military spending, discriminatory macroeconomic policies, and disparities in regional business cultures are also major contributors.[7] But the fact remains that some cities and regions are predominantly host to the industries suffering stagnation in export markets and invasion of import markets, while others' fortunes wax with new opportunities in both domestic and international markets. The industrial heartland, in particular, stretching from Buffalo through Baltimore and St. Louis to Milwaukee, is home to those nonmilitary durable goods industries that have been the hardest hit by international market integration and declining relative competitiveness.[8]

Employment in the heartland, approximated by the East North Central and Middle Atlantic regions, grew at little more than one-third of the national rate between 1979 and 1992, at a time when the Pacific, Mountain, and South Atlantic regions added jobs at rates of 28%, 33%, and 33%, respectively (see Table 1.1).[9] Manufacturing job losses were the dominant contributor to this disparity. The two heartland regions lost 22% and 32% of their net manufacturing jobs over the period, far in excess of the national loss of 14%, while the South Atlantic and Pacific regions held losses to a minimum, and the Mountain region actually posted an increase (see Table 1.2). In their wake manufacturing shutdowns depressed certain regions' service sectors, so that in states like

TABLE 1.1. Regional Change in Nonagricultural Employment, in Thousands (1979–1992)

Region	1979 Number	1979 % of U.S. total	1992 Number	1992 % of U.S. total	Change, 1979–1992 Number	Change, 1979–1992 %
Northeast	20406.2	22.6	21842.1	20.5	1435.9	7.0
Mid-Atlantic	15012.7	16.6	15964.4	15.0	951.7	6.3
New England	5393.5	6.0	5877.7	5.5	484.2	9.0
Midwest	24171.8	26.7	26263.9	24.6	2092.1	8.7
West North Central	6973.4	7.7	7943.5	7.5	970.1	13.9
East North Central	17198.4	19.0	18320.4	17.2	1122.0	6.5
South	28571.1	31.6	36201.3	34.0	7630.2	26.7
West South Central	8956.5	9.9	10907.1	10.2	1950.6	21.8
East South Central	5222.8	5.8	6165.2	5.8	942.4	18.0
South Atlantic	14391.8	15.9	19129.0	17.9	4737.2	32.9
West	17276.3	19.1	22313.0	20.9	5036.7	29.2
Pacific	12862.8	14.2	16438.3	15.4	3575.5	27.8
Mountain	4413.5	4.9	5874.7	5.5	1461.2	33.1
U.S. total	90425.4	100	106620.3	100	16194.9	17.9

Source: Compiled by A. Markusen from Bureau of Labor Statistics, U.S. Department of Labor, unpublished data.

TABLE 1.2. Regional Change in Manufacturing Employment, in Thousands
(1979-1992)

Region	1979		1992		Change, 1979-1992	
	Number	% of U.S. total	Number	% of U.S. total	Number	%
Northeast	5202.6	24.7	3620.7	20.0	−1581.9	−30.4
Mid-Atlantic	3678.8	17.5	2509.1	13.9	−1169.7	−31.8
New England	1523.8	7.2	1111.6	6.1	−412.2	−27.1
Midwest	6587.1	31.3	5356.7	29.6	−1230.4	−18.7
West North Central	1448.5	6.9	1353.5	7.5	−95.0	−6.6
East North Central	5138.6	24.4	4003.2	22.1	−1135.4	−22.1
South	6140.4	29.1	5960.6	32.9	−179.8	−2.9
West South Central	1637.7	7.8	1565.9	8.7	−71.8	−4.4
East South Central	1432.0	6.8	1406.7	7.8	−25.3	−1.8
South Atlantic	3070.7	14.6	2988.0	16.5	−82.7	−2.7
West	3148.4	14.9	3161.3	17.5	12.9	0.4
Pacific	2587.3	12.3	2543.4	14.1	−43.9	−1.7
Mountain	561.1	2.7	617.9	3.4	56.8	10.1
U.S. total	21078.5	100	18099.3	100	−2979.2	−14.1

Source: Compiled by A. Markusen from Bureau of Labor Statistics, U.S. Department of Labor, unpublished data.

Illinois and Michigan services grew at only one-half to two-thirds of the national rate. Over the decade labor force growth in the heavy industrial states outpaced job creation, resulting in dramatic rates of net out-migration (see Figure 1.1 and Table 1.3).[10]

Such stunning differentials have much to do with the ways in which the dramatic growth in international trade has played itself out across the nation's terrain. While many midwestern cities have watched their local industries fall to stiff import competition, often the outcome of exchange rate policies or foreign industrial policy, they have not found themselves well positioned to increase exports or engender new economic base activities. Other cities (New York, Miami, and Seattle, for example) have revitalized, albeit spottily, because they appear to have gained a large share of trade-generated activity. And still others (Minneapolis, Los Angeles) have flourished because their economic base industries have so far managed to successfully compete internationally and/or to withstand heightened import competition.

Under the free trade regime the pressures of growing international market exposure in the United States will force both national and local

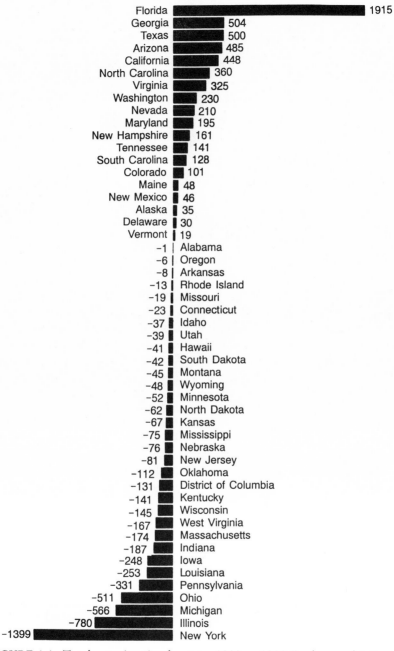

FIGURE 1.1. Total net migration by state: 1980 to 1988 (in thousands). Economics and Statistics Administration, Bureau of the Census, U.S. Department of Commerce. *Source:* "Population Trends in the 1980's," Current Population Reports, Series P-23, no. 175, p, 34. Washington, DC: U.S. Government Printing Office.

TABLE 1.3. Components of Population Growth Rates by Region (1980–1985)

Region	Total growth	Natural increase	Net migration
New England	2.5	2.3	0.2
East North Central	–0.1	3.5	–3.6
West North Central	2.2	3.7	–1.6
Mid-Atlantic	1.1	2.1	–1.0
South Atlantic	8.8	3.2	5.7
East South Central	3.1	3.4	–0.3
West South Central	11.6	5.8	5.8
Mountain	12.5	6.9	5.6
Pacific	10.2	5.3	4.9

Source: Current Population Reports, Series P-25, no. 998, p. 13.

economies to specialize even more than before. If exchange rates fluctuate considerably, as they did in the 1980s, this can happen at a brutally rapid pace. Employment in the United States has shifted toward aircraft, telecommunications equipment, computers, chemicals, pharmaceuticals, and business and financial services, while Korean workers become concentrated in export-oriented electronics, steel, autos, and consumer goods. For states and localities such exposure is a graver danger than for a large nation like the United States. For compared to the latter, regional economies are much more open. While only 7% of U.S. consumption is exported, at least 30% of the output of a large American city is exported out of its environs, and for a mining town in the Rocky Mountains probably 85%. Any change in trading patterns that diminishes what once was a regional comparative advantage will reverberate more powerfully on local economies than it does on the national economy. Some regions, of course, will flourish if they host the internationally competitive sectors, such as aircraft and telecommunications equipment. But others that specialize in industries hard-pressed by increased imports may find deep cuts in capacity and output inevitable.

Access to American markets by other countries' industries means that more domestic consumers will buy foreign goods and services if they are cheaper or of superior quality to U.S. goods and services. Every region and city, then, will be importing more than it did before. How can loealities pay for the imported clothing, toys, and cars sold at K-Mart®, Toys-R-Us®, and Toyota® dealerships? They must increase exports of goods and services in which they have a comparative advantage. Import substitution ("Buy local") and hinterland-urban dynamism (the ability of rural and small-town growth to boost economic activity in larger central places) appear to be weaker forces for growth than export-led stimuli. Such exports, of course, can be to other cities and regions, not just overseas. Indeed, other regions will constitute the bulk of the trading partners for most local economies.

But whichever the destination, a free trade regime favors those cities and regions that can increase exports and/or benefit from the increased activity that higher absolute levels of trade requires (accounting, ports, wholesaling, and so on). In the United States, regions that have developed specializations under the umbrella of agricultural, oil, and defense policies are those best positioned to succeed. But even then, fluctuations in commodity prices, political fashions, or slow market growth may render them quite vulnerable. Because of the free trade regime that has been more or less in place over the entire postwar period and because the participation of developing countries in international trade has risen during the same period, American cities and regions are increasingly tied into the international economy. At the state and local levels, where strategic trade policy is beyond the jurisdictions' capabilities, economic development agencies have increasingly engaged in export base promotion.[11] Since "imports" into local economies are growing, both from national and international sources, localities must enhance their ability to "export" in order to earn enough to finance their "imports." If they don't, plant closings, net job loss, and net outmigration will be the result.

State and local officials and their constituents are not particularly well equipped to tackle this challenge with either information or policy tools. What are their comparative advantages? In what market niches, nationally and internationally, are they well positioned? What local sectors can successfully compete with the new imports from previously unknown competitors or branches of home-based multinationals? In the 1980s most state and local efforts have been supply-side-oriented: they have tried to improve the productivity of existing local resources through small business programs, infrastructure provision, and incubators. But these efforts to revitalize local economies have not been strong enough to override the tide of restructuring forced on local economies by external factors, especially strategic trade policies on the part of competing nations and the absence of a coherent economic development policy for the United States. Thus, despite strong and innovative commitments to economic development, cities like Chicago, Flint, and Pittsburgh continue to lose their manufacturing base at rates in excess of the national average. In a recent poll the top economic development professionals around the country voted "the changing economic base" the number-one problem of the nation's cities.

EXPLAINING TRADE PATTERNS, INDUSTRIES,
AND REGIONAL GROWTH RATES

Since trade is palpably so important to the fortunes of individual regions, citizens and economic developers need to know why trading patterns are changing and what the more powerful responses to it might be. When they try to find out, they are confronted with a bewildering array of theories and ideologies about how trade operates.

In this section we present five theories that have been used to explain patterns of trade, production location, and economic growth. As we show, each theory explains some aspect of present trade patterns, but only one theory accounts for the growth experiences associated with those trade patterns. Neoclassical theory provides the theoretical framework within which U.S. trade policy, the General Agreement on Tariffs and Trade, (GATT), the United States–Canada Free Trade Agreement, and the pending North American Free Trade Agreement (NAFTA) are all justified, but fails to explain most trade flows in the late 20th century. As we also argue, the neoclassical prescription for growth through free operation of markets and free trade is theoretically unfounded. Neither does the "new international division of labor" hypothesis, which has been invoked to challenge NAFTA and European integration, provide a sufficiently accurate account of the determinants of trade and production location. "Flexible specialization" and "strategic trade theory" offer compelling explanations for the very trade anomalies that confound neoclassical theorists, but again the implications of these theories for growth strategy and economic policy leave nations undefended against rivals informed by the final theory, which we call "dynamic revisionism." Directly challenging the free trade prescription of neoclassical theory, revisionist theory argues that strong government intervention may dramatically alter the growth trajectories of some nations and regions over others.

The Static, or Neoclassical, Perspective

Neoclassical theory argues that the optimal economic strategy for a nation is to exploit its natural comparative advantages as efficiently as possible. The most effective way to do this is through the free operation of factor and product markets and open competition among firms. All economic actors will specialize in those things they do best; all resources will be allocated to their highest rate of return; and in so doing, resources will be optimally allocated. Once the most efficient or optimal allocation of resources is achieved, no one can be made better off through further exchange without making someone else worse off. Productive efficiency is also achieved as firms are forced through competition in the market to use the most efficient production techniques available. The wider the market, the greater the possibilities for specialization, and the greater the potential for efficiency.

Neoclassical trade theory extends these propositions to international trade. The international market affords enormous possibilities for specialization and greater efficiency. If nations specialize in the production of goods and services in which they have a natural comparative advantage and acquire through international trade the goods in which they do not have a comparative advantage, the optimal use of resources will prevail globally, and all nations will gain from trade.

Comparative advantage is conferred by a country's natural endowment of factors of production. The nation that has abundant labor, relative to capital, will specialize in the production of labor-intensive goods. Countries whose high savings rates make capital abundant relative to labor will specialize in the production of capital-intensive goods. Countries endowed with natural resources will produce resource-intensive goods.

Growth in the neoclassical system is a function of factor growth—growth of the labor force and capital—and the rate of labor-saving technical change. The natural rate of growth is said to be equal to the sum of the rate of growth of the labor force and the rate of technical change. Through factor substitution, the economy will adjust to the natural rate of growth. As long as markets operate freely, nations can be assured of achieving the optimal allocation of resources and their natural rate of growth.

While neoclassical theory does not explicitly suggest that trade enhances growth—since growth depends only on national rates of growth of factors of production and technical change—it does suggest that the greater specialization and allocative efficiency made possible through international trade will raise the overall productive efficiency at any given rate of growth. Neither the mix of industries nor demand affects economic growth, and there is no suggestion that there might be any conflict between short-run static efficiency and long-run economic growth (dynamic efficiency).

The theory suggests a limited role for government. Since growth is constrained only by the growth of factors of production, government should provide the conditions for the smooth functioning of markets through enforcement of trade and antitrust laws, seek to improve the quality of the labor force through education, and foster technical change through policies such as tax credits to encourage research and development (R&D). There is no role for demand. There is no role for the government in the selection of industries to promote, since the appropriate industries are defined by the relative natural factor endowments. The fact that some industries have higher rates of productivity growth, providing greater potential for per capita income growth, is irrelevant.

The theory is consumer-oriented. Real income grows not through rising productivity and wage growth, but through lower prices to consumers. It is this theoretical perspective that has shaped economic policy in the United States and Britain since the 19th century.

How, then, do neoclassical economists explain the poor performance of the United States in trade during several decades of "free trade" federal policy? They argue that market imperfections and macroeconomic policy, particularly the growing budget deficit combined with low savings rates and high interest rates, intervened to cause a trade deficit. If markets had been operating properly, the dollar would have fallen sooner and the United States, relatively capital-poor, would have shifted production specializations toward labor-intensive production while Japan exported more capital goods. The policy implication, then, is that the government should pursue even more vigorously the elimination of international trade barriers and other regulatory impediments to market adjustment.

This prescription was applied by the Reagan and Bush administrations over the 1980s, with great fanfare attending the fashioning of free trade agreements with Canada and Mexico. Meanwhile, growth in the domestic economy slowed and then turned negative by 1989. A major fall in the dollar at mid-decade was not effective in lowering the deficit substantially, suggesting that the trade problem was more complicated than simple adjustment of relative prices. Imports continued to surge and exports responded only modestly. The domestic recession was more effective at diminishing the trade gap, chiefly by cutting deeply into consumption of imports.

The New International Division of Labor

A logical extension, but with different consequences, of the neoclassical model is found in the work of a group of theorists who focus on the "new international division of labor" (NIDL) and the "globalization of production" (GOP) that began in the late 1970s. According to these theorists, the development of transportation and communications technology in the late 20th century has made possible the rationalization of production on a global scale. Firms could now transfer advanced technology to countries with low labor costs, simultaneously exploiting the advantages of cheap capital in capital-rich countries and low labor costs in labor-rich countries (Dicken, 1988). As in neoclassical trade theory, relative production costs determine the global distribution of production. As a consequence, "according to the NIDL theory, a new capitalist world economy has emerged, its main feature being a massive migration of capital from major Organization for Economic Cooperation and Development (OECD) countries to low-cost production sites in the Third World" (Gordon, 1988, p. 26).[12] The income equalization hypothesis of neoclassical trade theory is obviated by capital mobility that leaves capital-rich countries with no economic rationale for local production.

However, the evidence of a long-term structural transformation in the global economy toward a steadily increasing share of less developed country (LDC) production and trade since 1950 is not unambiguous (Gordon, 1988; Graham, 1991). Trade patterns now reflect a structural shift during the past 40 years toward Japan, Southeast Asia, and the centrally planned economies (CPEs), not a massive migration of capital from major (OECD) countries to low-cost production sites in the third world.

NIDL and GOP scholarship is primarily descriptive and not particularly prescriptive.[13] It is critical of the process of internationalization of capital, and preoccupied with the process of uneven development that ensues. Its adherents favor an industrial policy that slows down the rate of market integration and offers older, mature industries with less skilled labor a chance to modernize. With respect to trade, the growing critique of proposed free trade agreements (NAFTA, European integration) by groups in developed countries owes much to the belief that migration of capital to countries with low wages and few environmental regulations will be their chief outcome, swamping any positive effect from increased commodity and service flows.

Flexible Specialization

Over the past 8 years a body of literature grouped under the rubric of "flexible specialization" has posed a powerful challenge to both neoclassical and Keynesian (demand-based) models of growth.[14] The theory begins with the following historical observations. Capitalist economies were self-regulating, efficiently allocating resources through the market, only until roughly the middle of the 19th century. The ability of the economy to regulate itself through price competition, and small-scale entry and exit, was obviated by the growth of very-large-scale organizations in most industries for which there was a real imperative to both maintain high rates of capacity utilization and to cover costs of low capacity utilization during downturns. The imperative to regulate competition that grew throughout advanced industrial economies was satisfied by different mechanisms in each country (Best, 1990, Chapter 3; Lamoreaux, 1985; Chandler, 1990; Berk, 1993). In the United States, in the context of early antitrust regulation, firms formed oligopolies to regulate themselves. Within that industrial structure a complex regulatory system emerged, embodying a production system (fordism), an industrial relations system characterized by wage rigidity, and a macro-regulatory system that worked to dampen the intensity of recessions.

Flexible specialization theory suggests the emergence of a viable alternative to fordist production methods. A related alternative is the Japanese production system which thrives on a large but malleable firm nestled in a network of flexible suppliers. Large-scale, mass-production facilities, assembling very long runs of interchangeable parts, using relatively unskilled labor, are gradually being challenged by small-scale, flexible producers organized in industrial districts that capture many of the advantages of scale without being hampered by the inflexibility inherent in fordist methods. The alternative production methods have the advantage of being more responsive to rapidly changing tastes without the cost penalties associated with small-scale production in the fordist system.

Flexibly specialized production systems are inherently self-regulating because small scale and flexibility encourage smooth marginal adjustments to changes in demand or supply conditions. There is none of the ruinous competition and excess capacity that threatens large-scale producers during downturns. Because resources are so flexible, one expects them to be fully utilized. Hence there is no problem of unemployment, either. Competition takes place on the basis of variety and quality, and short-term monopoly profits can be realized. Cost and price, while not irrelevant—flexibly specialized firms must compare favorably with mass-production firms in terms of cost—are not primary. One politically appealing twist, however, is that the emphasis has been placed on flexible specialization in skill-intensive, high value-added production, even in traditionally low-wage industries. High fashion garments and textiles are considered with the same enthusiasm as microelectronics, telecommunications equipment, and other high technology industries. Even some segments of labor-intensive, low-wage industries are transformed into high-skill, high-wage industries. The return of 19th-century ideals of competition does not necessarily imply a return to 19th-century standards of living.

It is an essentially neoclassical vision in which competition among firms assures efficient allocation of resources and diffusion of technologies. Product and factor markets resume their proper disciplinary roles. At the same time, through the creation of "industrial districts"—groups of firms performing complementary tasks in the production of the same or similar products—many of the advantages of large-scale production are preserved. Group provision of ancillary services such as finance, marketing, insurance, transportation, research, and purchasing can still be provided at low unit cost.

Since the flexible production system is seen as a fertile environment for learning, there is some endogenous growth implicit in the model. But demand plays no explicit role. Growth in flexible specialization is a function of the growth of the (highly skilled) work force. Mix is given a special role, only to the extent that some industries require more skills and so suggest the possibility of avoiding competition with low-wage, low-skilled producers. The possibility that some industries have greater potential for rapid growth of demand is not explicitly considered.

Flexibly specialized firms are said to have a competitive advantage in industries for which demand is fragmented and volatile.[15] In a world of fragmented markets and volatile demand for *some* products, countries that can create industrial districts will have a competitive advantage over those that cannot. Furthermore, since industrial districts are believed to be better structured than fordist organizations to achieve economies of learning, it is possible that a flexible firm or industrial district that is first to enter a new, or newly fragmented, market will have a widening advantage over late arrivals as it moves steadily down a learning curve. Therefore, in a world of industrial districts, we would expect to see trade structured by relative advantages in specific products due to the existence of industrial districts and to the good luck of being first to enter the market.

In practice, and similar to neoclassical economists, adherents of flexible specialization advocate training to enhance the skill level of the labor force and infrastructure investment to smooth communication and transportation. The object in both cases is similar: to enhance the smooth functioning of factor markets. For neoclassical economists, this simply lubricates the process of substitution at the margin so critical to efficient resource allocation. For flexible specialization theorists, these policies help create an organizational form—the industrial district—that ensures that firms will remain small, and through that institutional mechanism Marshallian competition is ensured.

A Dynamic Alternative

For many decades a real alternative to neoclassical theory has been embodied in the economic development strategies of Japan, and more recently Korea, Taiwan, and Singapore. Only recently has this "revisionist" approach been codified, most notably in the work of Kaldor (1989), Johnson, Tyson, and Zysman (1989), Scott (1991), and Shinohara (1982).[16]

Four critical elements of the revisionist theory directly contradict the assumptions of neoclassical theory. First, the mix of sectors matters. Some industries grow more rapidly than others due to larger potential

markets, and in a world of less-than-full employment, offer greater potential for rapid productivity growth, rising per capita income, and overall
contribution to economic growth. Second, growth is constrained not by
factors—labor has proven to be relatively mobile and capital is created
when there is demand and a potential high rate of return—but
by demand for the product. Hence, growth is enhanced by specialization in industries in which there is a high income elasticity of demand.
Third, in some industries rapid growth leads to continued success due
to increasing returns. Hence, once a nation or firm has a competitive
advantage in an industry characterized by increasing returns, that advantage is apt to persist. Fourth, due to the existence of increasing returns,
comparative advantage can be created by strategic intervention on the
part of nation states, and conceivably of regional governing bodies.

Borrowing from Myrdal (1957), Kaldor argues that in industries in
which there are increasing returns, success breeds further success, leading to the "principle of circular and cumulative causation." First mov-
ers in an industry have the advantage of declining costs as their market
and scale of production grows. This in turn leads to a process of "po-
larization" or concentration of manufacturing production in certain
areas.[17] Once an industry has a technological lead, its market share will
continue to grow, permitting a high rate of investment that will lead to
new innovations, thereby rendering the technological lead a moving
target. That lead can be arrested only if the rate of growth of market
share, output, and investment is slowed, and that is likely to occur only
if there is an overall decline in the rate of growth of the world market,
or if access to the world market is limited by national governments
through protectionist policies.[18]

For revisionist trade theorists who rely more on empirical and historical evidence, economic growth is not a function of competitive
markets and free trade, but of strategic advantage in high-growth industries which is cumulative and which has often been created. The vocabu-
lary of revisionist trade policy, as practiced by Japan and Southeast Asian
countries, has included strategic targeting of high-growth-potential sectors, policies to force rapid transfer and control over technology—Western nations have found that they can license their technology in Japan
but are prohibited from engaging in direct investment and production—
protection of the domestic market, which has permitted firms to subsidize exports through high prices in the local market, and, frequently,
exchange rate policies to reduce the price of exports and increase the
price of imports. Strategic advantage in industries with large potential
markets leads to rapid export growth, rapidly declining costs, and rising standards of living.

In contrast to the orthodox theory, the revisionist trade theory as
practiced by Japan and other Southeast Asian countries is producer-

oriented and growth-oriented. Growth is achieved through strategic promotion of industries with high potential for productivity growth. Short-term concern for consumer prices is subverted to long-term concern for overall growth rates. Per capita income grows not due to lower prices, but due to high rates of productivity growth.

Kaldor's theory suggests the following considerations for trade-impacted regions in the United States. The competitive success of industries with high export potential is critical to the growth potential of the region, but the success of industries is in no way guaranteed by free trade. In fact, once an industry lags behind foreign rivals, its only chance for success lies in temporary protection and programs to promote innovation.

Trade Patterns and Theory

What patterns of trade do we observe, how do we explain these patterns of trade, and how do they affect growth?

In 1990 over half of all merchandise trade took place between developed countries (see Table 1.4); 29% was between developed countries and developing countries; 9% was between developing countries, and the remaining 7% involved centrally planned economies.

In the past decade the role of Japan and other Asian countries has grown. Trade among developed market economies (DMEs) as a share of total world trade has increased by 11 points or 27% in the last 10 years, but has increased most dramatically between Japan and Western Europe and Japan and North America (see Table 1.4). The share of trade between DMEs and *all* less developed countries (LDCs) has declined by 21% but the share of trade between DMEs and Asian countries has increased by 42%. The share of trade among developing countries has risen by 14% but that is due entirely to the 122% increase in the share of trade among Asian countries and between Asian and oil-producing Middle Eastern countries.

The patterns of trade described in Table 1.4 seem to reflect three underlying causalities: the rise in intrasectoral trade between DMEs of North America and Europe suggests trade based on specific competitive advantages associated with firms rather than countries; the growth and pattern of trade between Japan and North America and Europe suggests a particular advantage to Japan across a broad range of manufacturing industries; the role of relative factor endowments (or low wages) is apparent in the increased role of other Southeast Asian countries, as well as Brazil and Mexico.[19] These few developing countries have assumed increasing importance in the production of price-sensitive goods such as textiles, apparel, shoes, and furnishings.

The actual patterns of trade in the late 20th century reveal that each theory explains trade for particular sectors. The neoclassical theory had

TABLE 1.4. Shares of Regional Trade Flows in World Merchandise Trade, 1980 and 1990

	1980 (%)	1990 (%)	% change in share
Inter-developed country	42.1	53.4	+27
Developed country/less developed country (LDC)	36.9	29.2	−21
Developed/Latin America–Africa–Middle East	26.2	14.0	−47
Developed/Asia	10.7	15.2	+42
Developed country/centrally planned economy (CPE)	4.7	3.5	−26
Inter-developing countries	8.0	9.1	+14
Intra–Latin America–Africa–Middle East	3.2	1.6	−50
Asia with Latin America–Africa–Middle East	2.5	2.4	−4
Asia–Asia	2.3	5.1	+122
Developing country–CPE	2.1	1.6	−24
CPE–CPE	3.9	2.2	−44
World	100.0	100.0	

Source: Adapted by Howes from GATT (1992), vol. 2, table III. 3, p. 9, and table A17, p. 109.

strong predictive capabilities in the late 19th century when most trade was in resource-intensive goods and industrial structures were competitive. Trade in minerals and agricultural goods is adequately accounted for by relative endowments of resources necessary to the production of these goods: mineral deposits; land well suited to the cultivation of wine, wheat, bananas, and other food stuffs; and cheap plentiful labor. Even trade in some labor-intensive consumer goods, such as textiles and apparel, can be explained by factor endowments.

In the last decade industrial scholars have unearthed evidence of well-functioning industrial districts with highly successful export performance in design-intensive consumer goods: textiles, apparel, shoes, furniture, ceramics (from Italy), and engineering-intensive machinery (from Germany). Among other things, the competitive advantage of these districts derives from their capacity to respond smoothly to changes in tastes, and to continually upgrade the skills of their work force. The export prowess of Italy, reflected in its manufacturing trade surplus, is due to the effective use of flexible methods in the production of textiles, apparel, furniture, and ceramics.

Much of the trade between North America and Europe can be explained by the strategic trade theory. Specific firms on each continent have developed particular technological capabilities, or have achieved very large scales of output relative to the size of the market, that secure them an unassailable competitive advantage. Intrasectoral trade in chemicals and pharmaceuticals is due to company-specific advantages in particular products. Intrasectoral trade in aircraft and parts is due to company-specific scale advantages in aircraft assembly, or company-specific advantage in specific jet-engine technologies.

Finally, Japan and Korea's trade with North America and Western Europe illustrates the explanatory power of the "dynamic revisionist" view. Japan and Korea in its wake have successfully exported manufactured goods to these two markets, working their way gradually up the value chain to higher and higher value-added goods, through the strategic use of industrial policies to promote development of targeted industries.

EVIDENCE ON COMPETITIVENESS AND
THE ROLE OF TRADE POLICY

The United States had an $84 billion manufacturing trade deficit in 1990, equivalent to 2% of the Gross Domestic Product (GDP) (see Table 1.5). The value of imported goods was equivalent to 9.6% of GDP, and the value of exports 7.1% of GDP (see Table 1.6). U.S. exports were only 76% Of the value of imports (see Table 1.5). The U.S. trade deficit reflects four contributing factors. First, $53 billion of the trade deficit, $40 billion with Asia and $13 billion with Latin America, can be explained by neoclassical trade theory, or its modern expression in the NIDL theory. The United States was importing low-wage consumer goods and labor-intensive electronics assemblies from Southeast Asia. Much of the trade between the United States and Mexico is in automotive products and electronics that are exported to Mexico for assembly or fabrication and reimported into the United States. Consumer goods imports from Southeast Asia were the consequence of indigenous development efforts. The electronics and auto parts imports followed the search for low-wage havens for labor-intensive assembly by multinational companies.

Second, much of the trade between the United States and Canada is due to the integration of automotive production. The rest of the trade between the United States and Canada is either raw materials imports from Canada or exchange across a broad range of products reflecting merely the proximity of the two countries.

Third, balanced trade between the United States and Europe can be explained by the strategic trade theory and flexible specialization. The former emphasizes the competitive advantages that accrue to specific firms in industries due to their good fortune of being the first entrant or

TABLE 1.5. Merchandise Trade Balances of Major DMEs, by Sector and Country, 1990 (Billions of Dollars)

Sector	U.S.	EC/EFTA	U.K.	Germany	France	Italy	Japan
Primary	−41	−115	−18	−51	−13	−41	−121
Semimanu.	−7	+42	−I	+29	−2	−2	+11
Mach. & transp.	−31	+34	−9	+86	−1	+9	+167
Consumer goods	−46	−21	−12	−5	−9	+28	−3
Manufactured	−84	+55	−22	+110	−11	+35	+175
% of GDP	−2%	+1%	−3%	+10%	−1%	+4%	+6%
Merchandise	−124	−60	−40	+56	−23	−10	+52
% of GDP	−2%	−1%	−5%	+5%	−2%	−1%	+2%
Country							
North America	−10	−10	−3	+6	−6	+4	+36
Latin America	−13	−9	−1	−2	+1	−1	−2
Western Europe	0	+8	−31	+59	−8	−5	+21
CPEs	+2	−8	−1	+1	−2	−2	−1
Africa	−9	−11	+1	0	+3	−8	+1
Middle East	−8	+4	+5	+5	−1	0	−22
Asia	−40	−13	−2	−4	−1	0	+16
Japan	−44	−32	−7	−10	−5	0	—
World	−124	−60	−40	+56	−23	−10	+52
Exports/imports	.76	.96	.83	1.16	.90	.94	1.22

Source: Compiled by Howes from GATT (1992), vol. 2, tables A10, A12–A17, pp. 94–111.

a very-large-scale producer relative to the market, due either to accident or strategic government policies. The latter emphasizes the role of federal and local policies to promote the effective formation of industrial districts that achieve low unit costs through the combined advantages of scale and flexibility. The United States exports those products in which it still has a competitive advantage and in which there is not a

TABLE 1.6. Exports and Imports as Share of GDP, 1990

	Exports/GDP (%)	Imports/GDP (%)
U.S.A.	7.1	9.6
W.E., E.C.[a]	6.0	7.2
Japan	9.7	7.4

[a]For Western Europe (W.E.) and the European Community (E.C.), imports and exports are only for trade with regions outside Western Europe.
Source: Compiled by Howes based on GATT (1992), Vol. 1, Table A4; Vol. 2, Tables III.27, III.28, III.29.

significant European challenge: semiconductors, mainframe computers, telecommunications equipment, and aircraft. Imports from Europe reflect the German competitive advantage in chemicals, machine tools, and precision motor vehicles, and an Italian advantage in consumer goods, especially textiles, apparel, and ceramics.[20] Many scholars have attributed German and Italian success in these industries to the organization of production around industrial districts.

Finally, trade with Japan has changed as Japan has consistently promoted one strategic sector after another, adhering to its understanding of the factors that promote dynamic growth. The $44 billion trade deficit with Japan now reflects the Japanese competitive advantage in consumer electronics products and motor vehicles, and a growing advantage in certain aspects of semiconductor technology and computers—all considered strategic sectors. Japanese imports are only partially offset by the U.S. advantage in raw materials, some remaining parts of the electronics industry, telecommunications equipment, and aircraft. Most of the major trade conflicts between Japan and the United States in the last few years have been due to Japanese reluctance to purchase products in which the United States still has a clear advantage and in which Japan now seeks a presence—the NTT purchase of telecommunications equipment and the Japanese purchase of U.S. aircraft technology, *not* U.S. aircraft.

Contrast European trade balances and trade patterns to those of the United States. Seventy percent of European Economic Community (EEC) trade is accounted for by intraregional (Western European) trade. Measured by imports and exports as a percent of GDP, Western Europe is less integrated into world trade than Japan or the United States (see Table 1.6). Western Europe is largely self-sufficient in steel, iron, chemicals, machine tools, and automotive products. Interregional trade is concentrated in raw materials, power generation equipment, electronics, aircraft, and clothing. Only 12% of total EEC trade is with Japan and Asia, compared to 36% for the United States (see Table 1.7). Europe imports electronics from Japan and Southeast Asia and consumer goods from Southeast Asia. While the EEC also imports motor vehicles from Japan, these are offset by motor vehicle exports to Japan, so that there is only a small deficit in motor vehicle trade.

What is most striking about European trade patterns is that, in contrast to the United States, Europe appears to have rejected high-technology dependence on Japan and low-wage dependence on Asia, in favor of European self-sufficiency, except in the special case of electronics (in which they have little presence) and some consumer goods. But Europe has been able to resist Japanese domination in their automotive sector, despite a less-efficient industry than that of the United States, and Europe

TABLE 1.7. Share of Total Merchandise Trade with
Japan and Southeast Asia

	Japan	Southeast Asia
U.S.A.	16%	20%
E.C.	3%	9%
France	3%	5%
Germany	6%	6%
U.K.	4%	9%
Italy	2%	5%

Note: Total merchandise trade includes merchandise imports plus exports.
Source: Compiled by Howes from GATT (1992), Table AI0–AI4.

has also partially resisted Asian domination of labor-intensive industries, in favor of European production (mainly in Italy). This marked difference in trade patterns is entirely due to formal and informal protection of these vulnerable industries.

Japanese trade patterns reveal yet another strategy toward international integration. Less than half of Japanese imports are manufactured goods, compared to 70% for North America and Europe; 95% of its exports are manufactured goods. Japan imports only those manufactured goods in which it clearly does not have a manufacturing presence to date—mainframe computers, chemicals, and aircraft, and some specialty machine tools from Europe—and exports only sophisticated machinery and automotive products in which it has achieved world dominance. But it is able to export in volume only where import-challenged industries are unprotected. Automotive products are exported in volume to North America; in the case of electronics, Japan has access to both Western European and North American markets.

In sum, global trade patterns are now determined by multiple forces. First, some trade is still a function of absolute advantages conferred by the possession of natural resources. Second, especially for trade among European countries and between Europe and North America, patterns are explained by firm-specific competitive advantage due to scale economies or technological advantages, cumulatively reinforced by increasing market share. Third, trade is shaped by state-sponsored construction of absolute competitive advantage of Japanese and Asian firms across a range of industries considered strategic to economic development. Fourth, trade is shaped by the willingness of nation states to allow competition from Japanese automotive and electronics companies and Asian textile, apparel, footwear, and other nonelectronic consumer goods firms. Fifth, trade relations between advanced market economies and the developing countries of Africa and Latin America remain bound by ties of empire that still privilege relations between some European countries and their former colonies. Finally, geographical proximity privileges trade among European countries, among the countries of the Western Hemisphere, and within Asia.

The trade policies of the United States, Europe, and Japan reflect three different development strategies. The United States, adhering to the doctrine of free trade, has relied on growth of the domestic market. In actuality, though unacknowledged by free trade theorists, export growth has been due to superiority in products benefiting from state R&D subsidies and procurement for aerospace, electronics, communications, agriculture, and forestry. However, in the case of the military industrial sector, the technologies underwritten are often ill-suited to commercial markets, and worse, commercialization often does not take place in the United States (MIT Commission on Productivity, 1990).

The free trade doctrine has left the U.S. market open to import competition from countries that have taken a strategic approach to export promotion and/or import restriction: Japan, Germany, Italy, and Southeast Asian countries. Rather than fostering the economic growth promised by neoclassical theory, free trade has left the United States far more dependent than either Japan or Western Europe on both imports of innovation-intensive goods from high-wage countries (3.3% of GDP, compared to 2.5% for the EEC and 2.3% for Japan) and consumer goods imports from low-wage countries (2.4% of GDP compared to 1.7 and 1.2% for Europe and Japan) (see Table 1.8). Slow growth and huge trade deficits, not full employment and convergence to the natural rate of growth, are the legacy of free trade.

The second development approach, that of Europe, is to protect and nurture indigenous sectors regardless of their growth potential—as though mix didn't matter. Europe's trade is largely internal. When it does turn to external trade, it does so strategically, limiting imports to those goods that do not compete directly with European goods. Nurturing competitiveness in indigenous industries takes Europe one step beyond the free trade doctrine of North America. Large trade surpluses result from competitive success in slow-growth industries; but the cost of ignoring mix is slow overall growth and high rates of unemployment.

The third development strategy, that of Japan (and Southeast Asia) is strategic, promoting those industries that have potential for high growth. Japan imports only raw materials and exports goods that have high income elasticity of demand in export markets. Attention to industry mix rewards Japan with a range of highly competitive, high-growth industries, huge trade surpluses, and high rates of overall growth.

The incontrovertible lesson is that regions losing jobs to German,

TABLE 1.8. Manufacturing Imports from High-Wage and Low-Wage Countries as a Percentage of GDP

	High-wage			Low-wage			
	W.E. and/or U.S.	Japan	Total	S.E. Asia	Other	Total	Total
U.S.A.	1.65	1.65	3.3	1.9	0.7	2.6	5.9
E.C.	1.5	1.0	2.5	1.1	0.6	1.7	4.2
Japan	2.3	—	2.3	1.1	0.1	1.2	3.5

Source: Compiled by Howes from GATT (1992), vol. 2, Tables A11, A13, A17, and vol. 1, Table A4.

Italian, Japanese, and Southeast Asian rivals cannot seek solace in initiatives to liberalize trade. These rivals attribute their success more often than not to strategic efforts on the part of their governments to promote their success in the global market. Furthermore, that success depends on the openness of the U.S. market, the very openness that is supposed to restore U.S. competitiveness. Only those industries, and the regions they inhabit, that still face little competition from foreign rivals continue to enjoy good fortune: mainframe computers, some telecommunications equipment, biotechnology, military hardware, and commercial aircraft. In all other tradeable goods the impact of Japanese and German competition (in innovation-intensive and skill-intensive goods), and Southeast Asian and Italian competition (in consumer goods) has caused enormous dislocation in various regions of the United States.

MAPPING TRADE ONTO REGIONS

Whether managed consciously or not, then, the United States and its constituent regions are deeply involved in a fundamental shift in posture toward the international marketplace. How can we interpret these changes and the shadows they cast across the regional landscape? To begin with, each locality and its policymakers must understand the role that their respective economies have played in the larger national and increasingly international economies. Lopsided industrial experiences in international trade can be mapped back onto the regions that specialize in those sectors, explaining a large share of the differential in regional growth rates in the 1980s.

The major beneficiaries in the United States are those sectors that have a "comparative advantage"—in commodities such as arms, computing, and pharmaceuticals, and in services such as mass culture (TV, movies), finance, and business services. The advantages to services come from the centrality of U.S. banks, financial exchanges, law firms, accountants, and the like, to the process of internationalization, including the mobilization of capital and the activities of international agencies based in the United States (United Nations, World Bank, International Monetary Fund [IMF], and so on). The major losers are those sectors hard hit by vigorous competition from both developed and developing countries: consumer goods (apparel, autos, TVs and VCRs) and nonmilitary producer goods (machine tools, semiconductors, tractors).

We can hypothesize that the regional impacts of heightened international trade activity are as follows. The Great Lakes industrial heartland, stretching from Buffalo and Pittsburgh west to Chicago and Milwaukee and other industrial pockets scattered around the nation, which specialize heavily in the nonmilitary capital goods/consumer durables complex, will suffer disproportionately from the restructuring associated with growing imports. Indeed, this has been the case in the five Great Lakes states since the late 1970s. Illinois, whose experience is typical for the region, lost 325,000 heavy industrial jobs between 1978 and 1986, losses that ran between 24% and 44% of total employment in these sectors (metals, machinery, and transportation equipment). Another major export-oriented sector in the Midwest, agriculture, has also declined in net exports.

However, both machinery and agricultural industries are still large exporters in absolute terms. As a result, central business districts in cities like Chicago and Minneapolis have benefited from the enlarged role of institutions of transnational corporate management, finance, and distribution, such as corporate headquarters, grain flow management, commodities exchanges, and futures markets. Yet the growth in midwestern trade-related business services is relatively moderate and cannot overcome the negative impact on the same business service sector from the contraction of the manufacturing base. In other words, because of their interior position, these states benefit little from the heightened trade-related activity associated with shipping, warehousing, and wholesaling the increased volume of overseas trade.

The regions that have benefited from trade-induced restructuring are chiefly on the coasts. Several factors have been important here. First, the enormous increase in arms sales abroad, up from $10 billion in 1980 to nearly $40 billion in 1991 has disproportionately boosted the economies of nonheartland states, already flush from U.S. government orders. This is because the defense manufacturing complex is heavily skewed toward coastal states and away from the industrial heartland.

Second, the major centers of international commercial activity—not just the physical transshipment and storage of goods but the planning, financing, accounting, marketing, and so on, that attends trade growth—are located on the coasts. The growth of mercantilist ports was for more than a century eclipsed by the growth of industrial cities like Chicago and Detroit borne along by the dynamism of domestic industry and agriculture. The "world cities" of Los Angeles, Seattle, San Francisco, Miami, and New York have benefited from the renewed external orientation of the U.S. economy, albeit with severely uneven internal distribution of the benefits.[21]

In contrast, the predicament of Chicago, the capital city of the industrial heartland, is particularly revealing. Long the nation's principal industrial hub and still the second-largest concentration of corporate headquarters, Chicago's status is slipping rapidly. It has fallen from being the nation's second-largest city, to its third-largest, behind Los Angeles. Trade-related restructuring is a major cause. The Midwest has borne the brunt of the drying up of machinery and agricultural export markets and deep inroads into domestic markets made by foreign autos, tractors, consumer electronics, and machine tools. In the 1980s, when employment nationally grew by about 10%, the entire Chicago metropolitan area actually lost jobs, down from 3 million in 1979 to 2.9 million in 1985, a loss of almost 3%. Once a major money and banking center, serving its farm and factory hinterland, Chicago now hosts less than the nation's per capita average number of banking jobs. Despite a number of unique, world-renowned financial exchanges, like the Chicago Board of Trade and the Chicago Mercantile Exchange, jobs in finance are a minuscule percentage of total area jobs and are not expected to grow in the future.[22]

Finally, the growth and commoditization of mass culture, and its penetration of foreign markets, has favored centers of cultural production, particularly New York and Los Angeles. Advertising, television shows, and movies bring in substantial export earnings. They have helped to boost the central-city economies of these coastal world cities disproportionately. Again, cities like Chicago, whose major role is the distribution of domestically produced goods and services, have seen such business shrink with internationalization.

A special note on services trade is in order here. Much hope has been placed in the ability of service exports to replace local economic activity lost in manufacturing. Certainly, since services have been growing rapidly, it is reasonable to expect that they might account for a disproportionate share of export growth. However, this evidence, albeit difficult to marshall because of poor data, is not encouraging. The transformation of domestic and international economies from manufacturing to services, particularly to "producer services," has clearly benefited some cities at the expense of others.[23] But although service industries have contributed to economic development in the form of net job creation, the extent to which their output is exported internationally versus to their hinterlands and other regions is not clear. Recent work by Beyers (1989) shows that services are more provincially oriented than is manufacturing, on average. Cohen and Zysman (1987) argue that services have limited potential in correcting balance of payments problems.

In particular, despite the outstanding exceptions of world cities like New York and Los Angeles, services are much less apt to be traded across international boundaries. The U.S. Office of Technology Assessment (OTA) has produced two exhaustive studies (1986, 1987) on international trade and competition in services. Their findings show that while services make a significant contribution to the U.S. balance of payments, direct trade in manufacturing remains much larger.[24] The share of services in total world trade has remained constant at 17 to 18% over the past 15 years. Thus, the growing prevalence of services domestically—in terms of employment and share of gross output—has not carried over into the international trade arena. While a small and constant level of trade in services to date may not preclude future export growth, a focus on manufacturing output and trade remains defensible for the near future.

STUDYING SUBNATIONAL ECONOMIC DEVELOPMENT THROUGH INTERNATIONAL INDUSTRY STUDIES

Trade-related regional restructuring, then, is not a simple matter of impersonal market forces at work nor of capital flight to low-wage countries. Trade volumes are very much an artifact of government policy and corporate practices. In the past decade dramatic swings in trade balances have been heavily influenced by "constructed comparative advantages"—interventions to regulate the addition of capacity, block imports, expand exports, all in order to guarantee an expanding market. Although the United States does engage in such practices, especially in the areas of agriculture, aerospace, and textiles, and to a lesser extent in autos, machine tools, and steel, its trading partners have been more strategic and astute, linking them up to macroeconomic policies—such as an undervalued exchange rate, low interest rates, and strategic use of government purchases—that reinforce their positive trade consequences.[25]

This macroeconomic coordination is important. In the United States the extensive erosion of the trade position of midwestern manufacturing is in large part a function of adverse national economic policies, including high real interest rates, the persistently overvalued dollar in the first years of the decade, and the shifting composition of federal government purchases. It is also a function of the resistance to third world debt restructuring on the part of American banks, which has destroyed export markets, and of decisions by some American multinationals—encouraged by U.S. tariff laws—to close plants at home and import from new branch plants abroad. In the longer run, differentially constructed comparative advantages are the product of the disparity between the indifferent or outright adverse American government policy regarding free trade and industrial policy, and those of its trading partners, including Japan, the EEC, and developing countries. Such policies, by constructing comparative advantages, go a long way toward explaining emerging locational patterns of industries internationally.

To analyze regional economic development, then, it is no longer sufficient to study industrial location on a national scale. Yet national-level analysis is what scholarship in regional science and economic geography have almost exclusively relied upon. To interpret the impact on regional economic activity of a growing volume of international trade and its relationship to shifts in industrial location on a global scale, the studies in this book draw upon and merge the insights from three literatures.

First, there is the literature on international trade and economic development. From this body of work we see that the particular form industrial competition assumes between firms in different nations, however idealized, emerges as a dominant factor in regional growth. Theories of imperfect competition embodied in the work of Kaldor and the revisionist trade theorists introduce more realistic views of how industrial competition contributes to regional growth. Regrettably, few good cross-national empirical studies of specific sectors exist to document, particularly in an evolutionary sense, how comparative advantages have in fact evolved.

Second, institutional theories have also been employed in these studies. The insights of industrial organization theory enable the authors to demonstrate where market power, in either monopolistic or oligopolistic form, has significantly altered locational and investment strategies from what they would have been in a purely atomistic competitive market. Such market power often breeds political power. Thus institutionalist theories of the state are also helpful in the research endeavors. States shape the economic environments in which static trade decisions are made. Nation states, as a result of business power structures and/or as semiautonomous entrepreneurs, may embark upon a developmental course that diverges radically from what would be prescribed by natural comparative advantages. Both these bodies of "institutional" work are critical to explaining the contemporary array of industrial capacity internationally.

Third, there are still lessons to be learned from the more static of location and regional development theories. These offer insights into how firms make decisions regarding the siting or closings of plants, especially in the case of price-sensitive industries, and the impact of such activities on the surrounding regions. However, the prevalent practice in regional science of gauging one region's performance by using another region, or the nation, as a yardstick is increasingly problematic. Most empirical studies of shifts in industry location similarly contrast the Sunbelt with the Rustbelt, rather than brave comparisons across international borders. The studies in this book all tackle this challenge by looking at the international locational calculus of their respective industries and linking it with differential metropolitan and regional growth patterns.

Illuminating the ways in which international market integration hurts or helps the prospects for particular subregions requires a "meso-level" approach—an analysis lodged between the macro- and the microeconomic levels and one that is capable of blending in the above bodies of theory. The individual regions cannot be understood on their own—by studying their resources and industrial mix, as has been the recent tradition in the economic development field. Nor can their fortunes be simply derived from the mechanics of national trade and growth patterns. Resources, environment, industrial mix, and economic base are the key characteristics of each region, but it is increasingly useless to study these without a fine-grained appreciation of the international dynamics of the industries involved and the postures of the key players in each.

Our approach is to take a single industry and map its changing location across the globe. Take steel, for instance. Most efforts to explain the poor performance of the American steel industry and its disastrous implications for steelworkers and their communities point the finger at certain characteristics of indigenous steel capacity: the mills are old and out of date technologically; their cost structures are too high, especially in the labor, energy, and environmental areas; and market imperfections—oligopolistic market power, government quotas, and voluntary restraint agreements (VRAs)—protected their parent companies from the vigors of competition for too long.[26]

But the fate of American steel mills cannot be understood without taking into account the reasons for the addition of steelmaking capacity elsewhere in the world, especially where new mills have been expressly aimed at export markets. If one probes beyond the simple statement that imports of steel are rising to ask why it is that increments have been added in Japan, Brazil, and Korea, among other countries, with the American market in mind, then the causality becomes much more complex. Decisions by foreign banks, governments, and companies are the explicit agents behind the meteoric rise of steel imports, not some faceless, mechanical market. Steel has been one of the key sectors targeted by countries with strategic trade and industrial policies.

Each of the industry studies in this book works across international boundaries. Each follows a methodology that we, the various authors, have developed together. We offer this framework as a way of thinking about regional economic development for planners in U.S. cities and states. The changing spatial orientation of each industry, with its consequences for regions on the receiving and exiting ends, is the "dependent variable," although the massiveness of the research task resulted in our concentrating analytical attention on U.S. regions in particular. World industrial location patterns are a function of differences in natural resource endowments, human capital, and technologies, as well as the stock of human and physical capital, and the dynamics of their evolution are attributable to strategies of principal economic agents. Our approach places analytical emphasis on large corporations and governments as primary agents in locational and capacity-enhancing processes.

The methodology for our industry studies begins with a description of the changing size and location of each industry in the United States. It is this geographical record we are trying to explain. For instance, in steel, D'Costa sets out to explain the precipitous drop in overall steel employment, the shifts in the industry from the western Appalachian slope to the western Great Lakes, and the dispersion of remaining steelworker employment to smaller outlying sites. In autos, Howes analyzes the historical transition from dispersion to concentration in the rate of new plant additions, predominantly by foreign direct investors, in the east south central region, far from the industry's historic center in Detroit. In the port study, Campbell shows how new technologies that radically increased trade volumes, like containerization, simultaneously resulted in the devastation of older shipping areas and the diffusion of unbundling and warehousing jobs.

The studies then move to the international level, placing the domestic industry in context and charting the growth of capacity among major trading partners, including changing patterns of world exports and imports. This exercise helps us to move beyond the provinciality of our images of a "domestic" industry. By moving beyond borders we can detect the extent to which growth has been disproportionately located in certain countries and the extent to which new capacity has been oriented toward internal or export markets. Segmentation of the markets by sophistication of product is taken into account. For instance, in steel, traditional industrialized countries like the United States, Germany, and Japan specialize in the high-quality flat-rolled products tied in with auto and consumer appliance markets, while new third world producers have begun to export semifinished steel and the simpler fabricated products.

Each study tackles the causal factors explaining evolving world location and growth patterns. The contemporary array of plants and offices can only be explained by exploring the industry's historical origins. Each study covers the differential evolution of markets, technology, labor, and inputs in the relevant countries as well as mobility of capital, and in some cases labor. Accidents of history and differences in political regimes may play a critical role in explaining world capacity. For instance, the steel industry in Brazil and the auto industries in Japan, Mexico, and Brazil all began as nationalized companies aimed at internal industrialization. The populist regime of President Vargas had invited U.S. Steel (USS) to design and build a plant in Brazil, but as the recession in the United States deepened, USS decided not to build it but to serve the Brazilian market from underutilized domestic capacity. Vargas, an adamant nationalist, was furious, and decided to embark on constructing the mill anyway, transforming the USS site plans into a state-owned enterprise. This was to be but the first in almost a dozen steel plants that Brazil would build, most of them in the interior, as part of its industrial modernization program.

More recently, upheavals in international industrial leadership can be credited chiefly to national economic development plans and their impact on competitiveness, multinational corporate strategies, the associated increase in competition, and occasionally the consolidation of market power, changing the competitive environment. Traditional market factors like the changing location of demand and changes in factor endowments and/or costs play only a secondary role. A considerable portion of each industry study is dedicated to elucidating these causal factors, particularly over the past two decades.

Remarkable differences in strategy with respect to location are found across the industries investigated here. For instance, the leaders of the American steel industry never attempted to build plants overseas, while the auto and pharmaceutical companies moved into Europe as early as 1911. Differences in drug regulation and health profiles attracted the pharmaceuticals, while the enormous size and accessibility of the American and European auto markets explain their significance, enhanced by barriers to imports, as targets for direct investment.

Policy decisions, on market openness, voluntary restraints, and foreign direct investment, have often been a major force in shaping industrial capacity and trading patterns. Where this is the case, each industry study demonstrates the character and chronology of such policies. Each concludes with some reflection on what types of policies might ameliorate domestic regional differentials and disruptive trade-related displacement. For instance, the increments in steel capacity around the world have disproportionately been aimed at the American market, partly because low wages and heavy debt burdens do not offer sufficient stimulus from those countries' own domestic markets.

Continued low wages and poor environmental standards are part of the formula ensuring that such upstart producers can be competitive, over oceans and across national boundaries, so that the process becomes self-reinforcing. An American policy attempting to extend environmental protections globally and soften the displacement of American workers by such heavily state-subsidized imports might consider tariffs equal to the differentials in wages and in environmental protection costs, aimed at encouraging the raising of incomes for workers in the exporting nation (and thereby the expansion of their own domestic market to "absorb" steel capacity additions) and the improvement of their environment. In other words, instead of prescribing a policy that would push wages in developed countries down toward those elsewhere, the strategy would be to raise wages, and therefore living standards, worldwide.

Although trade has been a major policy buzzword in the past few years, and job loss has frequently been attributed to it, the studies also show that not all the ills of domestic industry can be ascribed to differing trade practices. On the other hand, not all internationally successful industries owe their achievements purely to inherent comparative advantage. Nor is the international arena always worthy of the attention it gets. In some cases strong domestic markets are the key to continued vitality in regional economies. As one Chicago executive put it recently, "We'd be better off if the State of Illinois closed its office in Kuala Lumpar and opened one up in Los Angeles" (quoted in Markusen, Hall, Deitrick, & Campbell, 1991, p. 72). It is precisely to separate out the hype from the reality in the pursuit of international trade by American cities and regions that these industry studies have been undertaken.

As a group, these studies constitute a critique of the free trade position. They eschew the widespread advocacy of free trade so common in the trade literature, whereby strategic trade policies as practiced by countries like Japan and Korea are deemed "unfair" and countries so engaged are exhorted to change. By inquiring about the economic development impact of trade, and by investigating a host of market and extramarket practices that have helped to create and locate each industry internationally, they illuminate both normative and positive problems with "free trade" as a national policy. Instead of accepting the ideas that growth is good and that free trade automatically means growth, they tackle the troubling issues of the differential benefits of trade, including absolute losses by some, and the prevalence of adjustment barriers that result in net losses due to resource immobility. Together, they constitute an exposé of the "growth-through-more-trade" mentality, by showing that such a formulation is indifferent to the question of whether all citizens participate in its bounty. Indeed, there is some real danger that the unfettered pursuit of free trade will actually depress wages and employment and lower world living standards. Each set of authors offers alternative directions for the United States and other nations to go, tailored to the specifics of the industry under consideration.

ACKNOWLEDGMENTS

The authors wish to acknowledge funding from the Mott Foundation in support of this research. Julie Graham and Helzi Noponen contributed substantially to the ideas presented in this chapter as well as to its form. We are grateful for the helpful comments of our editors, Meric Gertler and Peter Dicken.

NOTES

1. This indifference is in marked contrast to the concern shown for financial markets and their participants or for military markets and their constituents. While only the weakest form of plant closing legislation has been able to pass Congress, hundreds of billions are slated to bail out the savings and loan industry and will only narrowly benefit managers and shareholders, not financial sector workers.

2. On the impact of plant closings, see Howland (1988) and Shapira (1986).

3. For reviews of such innovations, see Osborne (1987), Goldstein (1986), Fosler (1986), and Markusen and Carlson (1989).

4. Losses from trade were particularly high in the early to mid-1980s. From 1973 to 1980 trade has been estimated by at least one researcher to have added 280,000 manufacturing jobs (Lawrence, 1984). Estimates of the net jobs impact of the North American Free Trade Agreement, negotiated in 1992, range widely, from a net gain of 175,000 for the United States (Institute for International Economics) to a net loss of 550,000 (Economic Policy Institute).

5. See the industry studies in Tyson, Dickens, and Zysman (1988) and Howes (1993). Davis (1983) generates estimates of export-related employment for lumpy categories like manufacturing, agriculture, and several resource categories at the national level.

6. The marked absence of a trade dimension in regional analysis has been noted by Tervo and Okko (1983), especially with respect to possible trade policy effects on regional growth performance. Two recent articles have made some headway in this area. Henderson, McGregor, and McNicoll (1989) derive a technique for taking account of changing import coefficients in the calculation of employment multipliers based on input-output data. They find that changes in import coefficients over time accounted for more than 25% of the change in employment-generation potential in 5 of 12 major sectors in Scotland from

1973 to 1979. Sihang and McDonough (1989) place regions in an international context by elaborating an international shift share formula with world growth and world industry mix effects; however, their work has no empirical counterpart. Coughlin and Cartwright (1987a) show that national manufacturing exports do bear a positive relationship to state-level employment, but do not investigate disaggregated industry groups.

7. For an elaboration of these arguments, see Markusen and Carlson (1989).

8. The durables industries in the heartland, like farm machinery and autos, have a number of features that render them particularly vulnerable to heightened international competition. They behave as though they are technologically mature industries (unlike their counterparts in Japan); are saddled with oligopolistic industry structures; are not favored by defense research, development, or procurement patronage; and produce relatively expensive items, rendering them quite sensitive to exchange rate distortions. See Howes on the auto industry in this volume.

9. The New England case is more complicated. In the early part of the decade, spurred on by defense spending, it distinguished itself from its heartland neighbors by posting both employment and manufacturing growth rates superior to the national average. All that has come undone since defense cuts have begun to take hold, so that by 1992 New England's job losses for the decade were actually more severe than were those for the Great Lakes region.

10. Not all of the displacement occurred within the heartland, however. Plant closings were widespread in California, where deep cuts occurred in autos, steel, and related industries, despite the boost in aerospace from defense spending. In many southern states plant closings in textiles were more common than in the older New England region. See Shapira (1986) on California plant closings and Bluestone and Harrison (1982) on southern textile mill closings.

11. Despite a proliferation of interest and programs, few evaluative studies have been done of state and local trade-oriented policy's impact on economic development. An exception is the area of state government export promotion, where several excellent surveys have been conducted (Posner, 1984; Goldberg, 1987). One empirical effort, correlating state output data with state government promotional expenditures, suggests that such efforts have paid off (Coughlin & Cartwright, 1987b). See also Erickson (1989) and Zech (1986).

12. Gordon claims the NIDL hypothesis is best represented by Froebel, Heinrichs, and Kreye (1980); he attributes the GOP perspective to Bluestone and Harrison (1982), United Nations Centre on Transnational Corporations (1983), Piore and Sable (1984), and Harrison (1987).

13. A related concern is how international capital mobility and foreign direct investment shape regional and metropolitan economies. Here, the recent literature is better developed (Howes, 1993; Bluestone & Harrison, 1982; Glickman, 1980; Glickman & Woodward, 1989; Cohen, 1979).

14. This literature finds its first U.S. expression in the work of Piore and Sabel (1984). A large literature describes location trends in various industries—electronics, filmmaking, autos—as a reflection of this alternative organization

of production (Sabel, 1989; Goodman & Bamford, 1989; Saxenian, 1989, 1990, 1991; Storper, 1989; Scott, 1988a, 1988b, 1988c; Storper & Scott 1988; Schoenberger, 1988; Glasmeier, 1988).

15. To some extent the existence of flexibly specialized firms and industrial districts, by creating the possibility of small, but economical, scales of production, creates fragmented demand.

16. Certain elements of the approach are also recognized in the strategic trade theory literature associated with Krugman (1986), Brander and Spencer (1985), and Helpman and Krugman (1989). Bruce Scott groups strategic trade theory under the "revisionist trade theory" rubic. However, the dynamic aspects that are essential to the development strategy of Japan are missing in strategic trade theory. These "new international economists" have theorized that nations might strategically exploit product market imperfections to their advantage. Attempting to remedy the failure of neoclassical trade theory to explain intrasectoral trade, strategic trade theorists raised the theoretical possibility that economies of scale could be so large relative to the size of the market that an early entrant might successfully discourage any competitors from entering the market. It is a theory that recognizes the benefits of "misallocation" due to monopoly but that fails to link these static phenomena to economic growth.

17. As Kaldor (1989) points out, however, for those products in which innovation and technical change are far less important (and for which technology is easily transferable)—consumer goods such as garments, textiles, shoes, home furnishings, and toys, and even some standardized semiconductor chips—price elasticity is still important. These are the industries in which developing countries achieved rapid gains because they were able to imitate or copy technologies, but had the advantage of lower wages.

18. Kaldor points out that all countries that industrialized after Britain, including the United States, did so *only* with the aid of protective tariffs. What distinguished the successful industrializers were relatively moderate tariffs, just high enough to make the domestic industry profitable, and duties favoring industries that could be exports, not just import substitutes.

19. More important seems to be the stability of these developing countries relative to other lower wage countries (Gordon, 1988).

20. Germany has an advantage in chemicals and many machinery industries, especially machine tools for the production of chemicals and motor vehicles and other industry-specific tools. Michael Porter (1990) attributes German superiority in metalworking tools, precision autos, writing implements, and chemicals to a host of institutional factors including regionally based and industry-specific R&D centers and training institutes. One could credibly argue that Germany had an early start and ideal institutional environment for continual improvement ("continual upgrading of factors" is Porter's terminology), all of which was enhanced by its capacity to export.

Italy has an advantage in consumer goods and machinery used in the production of those consumer goods. Italy developed its competitive superiority in textiles, apparel, ceramics, and furniture beginning in the postwar period.

Cooperative institutions for R&D, finance, and marketing, as well as industrial parks providing low rent, all sponsored by local Communist parties, are
said to have given a tremendous advantage to these industries, especially beginning in the 1960s (Best, 1990). The products were targeted to middle-class and
European tastes which gave them a special advantage in the European market
as per capita income rose. By the 1970s the consumer goods industry was a
powerful exporter. Italy is said to have transformed low-wage, low-technology
industries into high-wage, innovative industries.

21. Those metropolises heavily favored by internationalization have been
dubbed "world cities," and the shape of trade-led development elucidated in
several excellent case studies (Friedmann, 1986; Friedmann & Wolff, 1982;
Sassen-Koob, 1987; Soja, 1987). This body of work suggests a spatial concentration of economic benefits derived from the emergence of worldwide financial markets in particular, although it concentrates on the service and financial
sectors and addresses only the largest cities in the most advanced market economies.

22. The four major Chicago exchanges together employ only 3,600 people,
and with related organizations account for 33,000 jobs. Even if a multiplier of
3 is used to measure total employment impact, the total comes to merely
110,000 out of an area work force of 2.9 million, or less than 4% (see Financial Services Task Force of the Civic Committee of the Commercial Club of
Chicago, *The Economic Impact of the Chicago Exchanges* [Chicago: Cresap,
McCormick & Paget, 1987]; D. Elsner, "City Financial Climate Cooling,"
Chicago Tribune, May 3, 1987, p. 1).

23. See Noyelle & Stanback (1983), Beyers (1986), Lakshmanan (1987).
For a skeptical view of the role of services to promote metropolitan growth
independently of manufacturing, see Markusen and Gwiasda (1993) and Patton
& Markusen (1991).

24. However, OTA is careful to note that data on trade in services is
inadequate and lacks the detail on spatial, temporal, and industrial disaggre-
gation available for manufacturing, mining, and agricultural commodities.

25. See, for instance, Amsden (1989) on the way in which the Korean
government bolstered its import protection and export promotion strategies
with macroeconomic policies that defied World Bank austerity prescriptions
and smoothed out disruptive cyclical impacts.

26. See Markusen (1985b) for an extended discussion of these factors and
general references to the literature.

REFERENCES

Abegglen, J. C., & Stalk, G., Jr. 1985. *Kaisha: The Japanese Corporation.* New
    York: Basic Books.
Amsden, A. 1989. *Asia's Next Giant.* New York: Oxford University Press.
Bauer, P., & Eberts, R. 1990. Exports and Regional Economic Restructuring,
    Regional Science Perspectives, 20(1), 39-53.

Berk, G. 1993. *Alternative Tracks: The Constitution of the American Industrial Order, 1905-1916.* Baltimore: Johns Hopkins University Press.

Best, M. 1990. *The New Competitors.* Cambridge: Harvard University Press.

Beyers, W. G. 1986. *The Service Economy: Understanding Growth of Producer Services in the Central Puget Sound Region.* Seattle: Central Puget Sound Economic Development District.

Beyers, W. G. 1989. *The Producer Services and the Economic Development in the United States: The Last Decade.* Final Report to the U.S. Department of Commerce, Economic Development Administration, Department of Geography, University of Washington, April.

Bluestone, B., & Harrison, B. 1982. *The Deindustrialization of America: Plant Closings, Community Abandonment, and the Dismantling of Basic Industry.* New York: Basic Books.

Bowles, S., Gordon, D. M., & Weisskopf, T. E. 1983. *Beyond the Waste Land: A Democratic Alternative to Economic Decline.* New York: Basic Books.

Brander, J., & Spencer, B. 1985. Export Subsidies and International Market Share Rivalry. *Journal of International Economics, 18*(1), 83-100.

Chandler, A. 1990. *Scale and Scope: The Dynamics of Industrial Capitalism.* Cambridge: Harvard/Belknap.

Cohen, R. 1979. *The Impact of Foreign Direct Investment on U.S. Cities and Regions.* Washington, DC: U.S. Department of Housing and Urban Development.

Cohen, R. 1981. The New International Division of Labor, Multinational Corporations, and Urban Hierarchy. In M. Dear & A. J. Scott, eds., *Urbanization and Urban Planning in Capitalist Society,* pp. 287-315. London: Methuen.

Cohen, S., & Zysman, J. 1987. *Manufacturing Matters.* New York: Basic Books.

Coughlin, C., & Cartwright, P. 1987a. An Examination of State Foreign Exports and Manufacturing Employment. *Economic Development Quarterly, 1*(3), 257-267.

Coughlin, C., & Cartwright, P. 1987b. An Examination of State Foreign Export Promotion and Manufacturing Exports. *Journal of Regional Science, 27*(3), 439–449.

Davis, L. 1983. *Domestic Employment Generated by U.S. Exports.* Washington, DC: International Trade Administration, U.S. Department of Commerce.

Dicken, P. 1988. *Global Shift: Industrial Change in a Turbulent World.* London: Paul Chapman.

Dore, R. 1986. *Flexible Rigidities.* Stanford, CA: Stanford University Press.

Dosi, G., Tyson, L. D., & Zysman, J. 1989. Trade, Technologies, and Development: A Framework for Discussing Japan. In C. Johnson, L. D. Tyson, & J. Zysman, eds., *Politics and Productivity: How Japan's Development Strategy Works,* 3-30. New York: Harper Business.

Drache, D., & Gertler, M. 1991. *The New Era of Global Competition.* Toronto: McGill–Queen's University Press.

Duchin, F., & Lange, G.-M. 1988. "Trading Away Jobs: The Effects of the U.S. Merchandise Trade Deficit on Employment." Working Paper no. 102. Washington, DC: Economic Policy Institute.

Erickson, R. 1989. Export Performance and State Industrial Growth. *Economic Geography, 65*(4), 280–292.

Erickson, R., & Hayward, D. 1991. The International Flows of Industrial Exports from U.S. Regions. *Annals of the Association of American Geographers, 81*(3), 371–390.

Fosler, R. S., ed. 1986. *The New Economic Role of the States.* New York: Oxford University Press.

Friedmann, J. 1986. The World City Hypothesis. *Development and Change, 17*(1), 69–83.

Friedmann, J., & Wolff, G. 1982. World City Formation: An Agenda for Research and Action. *International Journal of Urban and Regional Research, 6*(3), 310–343.

Froebel, F., Heinrichs, J., & Kreye, O. 1980. *The New International Division of Labor.* London: Cambridge University Press.

Galbraith, J. K. 1991. *A History of Economics: The Past as the Present.* London: Penguin Books.

GATT (General Agreement on Tariffs and Trade). 1992. *International Trade 90–91.* Vols. 1 and 2. Geneva, Switzerland: GATT.

Glasmeier, A. 1988. Factors Governing the Development of High Tech Industry Agglomerations: A Tale of Three Cities. *Regional Studies, 22*(4), 287–301.

Glickman, N. J. 1980. *International Trade, Capital Mobility, and Economic Growth: Some Implications for American Cities in the 1980s.* Report to the President's Commission for a National Agenda for the Eighties. Working Paper no. 32. Department of Regional Science, University of Pennsylvania.

Glickman, N. J., & Woodward, D. 1989. *The New Competitors.* New York: Basic Books.

Goldberg, R. 1987. *Federal Programs for the Promotion of Manufactured Exports.* Draft. Washington, DC: U.S. Office of Technology Assessment.

Goldstein, H. 1986. The Changing International Division of Labor and Regional Employment Cycles in the U.S. *Review of Regional Studies, 16*(1), 31–43.

Goodman, E., & Bamford, J., eds. 1989. *Small Firms and Industrial Districts in Italy.* London: Routledge.

Gordon, D. M. 1988. The Global Economy: New Edifice or Crumbling Foundations? *New Left Review,* no. 168, 24–64.

Gordon, D. M., Edwards, R., & Reich, M. 1982. *Segmented Work, Divided Workers: The Historical Transformation of Labor in the United States.* New York: Basic Books.

Graham, J. 1991. "Multinational Corporations and the Internationalization of Production: An Industry Perspective." Working Paper. Department of Geology and Geography, University of Massachusetts, July.

Hansen, N. 1979. The New International Division of Labor and Manufacturing Decentralization in the United States. *Review of Regional Studies, 9,* 1–11.

Harrison, B. 1987. Cold Bath or Restructuring? *Science and Society, 51*(1), 72–81.

Helpman, E., & Krugman, P. 1989. *Trade Policy and Market Structure*. Cambridge: MIT Press.

Henderson, D., McGregor, P., & McNicoll, I. 1989. Measuring the Effects of Changing Structure on Employment Generation Potential. *International Regional Science Review*, 12(1), 57–65.

Howes, C. 1992. "Mix Matters and It Doesn't Just Happen: What the U.S. Must Learn From Japan, Germany and Italy About Trade, Growth and Industrial Policy." Notre Dame, IN: Department of Economics, University of Notre Dame.

Howes, C. 1993. *Japanese Foreign Direct Investment in the U.S. Auto Industry*. Washington, DC: Economic Policy Institute.

Howland, M. 1988. *Plant Closings and Worker Displacement: The Regional Issues*. Kalamazoo, MI: Upjohn Institute.

International Trade Commission. 1984. *1981 U.S. Manufactured Exports and Export-Related Employment*. Washington, DC: International Trade Administration, U.S. Department of Commerce.

Johnson, C., Tyson, L. D., & Zysman, J., eds. 1989. *Politics and Productivity: How Japan's Development Strategy Works*. New York: Harper Business.

Kaldor, N. 1989. The Role of Increasing Returns, Technical Progress and Cumulative Causation in the Theory of International Trade and Economic Growth. In F. Targetti & A. P. Thirwall, eds., *The Essential Kaldor*. London: Duckworth.

Krugman, P. 1984. Import Protection as Export Promotion: International Competition in the Presence of Oligopoly and Economies of Scale. In H. Kierzkowski, ed., *Monopolistic Competition and International Trade*. Cambridge: MIT Press.

Krugman, P. 1991a. History and Industry Location: The Case of the Manufacturing Belt. *American Economic Review*, 81(2), 80–83.

Krugman, P. 1991b. Increasing Returns and Economic Geography. *Journal of Political Economy*, 99(3), 483–499.

Krugman, P. 1992. *The Age of Diminished Expectations*. Cambridge: MIT Press.

Krugman, P., ed. 1986. *Strategic Trade Policy and the New International Economics*. Cambridge: MIT Press.

Kuttner, R. 1984. *The Economic Illusion: False Choices between Prosperity and Social Justice*. Boston: Houghton Mifflin.

Kuttner, R. 1989. *Managed Trade and Economic Sovereignty*. Washington, DC: Economic Policy Institute.

Lakshmanan, T. R. 1987. "Technological and Institutional Innovations in the Service Sector." Paper presented at the Symposium on Research and Development, Industrial Change and Economic Policy, University of Karlstad, Sweden, June 24.

Lamoreaux, N. R. 1985. *The Great Merger Movement in American Business, 1895–1904*. Cambridge: Cambridge University Press.

Lawrence, R. Z. 1984. *Can America Compete?* Washington, DC: Brookings Institution.

List, G. F. 1922. *The National System of Political Economy*. London: Longmans, Green.

Maddison, A. 1991. *Dynamic Forces in Capitalist Development: A Long-Run Comparative View.* Oxford: Oxford University Press.

Markusen, A. R. 1985a. *Profit Cycles, Oligopoly, and Regional Development.* Cambridge: MIT Press.

Markusen, A. R. 1985b. *Steel and Southeast Chicago: Reasons and Opportunities for Industrial Renewal.* Evanston, IL: Center for Urban Affairs and Policy Research, Northwestern University.

Markusen, A. R., & Carlson, V. 1989. Deindustrialization in the American Midwest: Causes and Responses. In L. Rodwin & H. Sazanami, eds., *Deindustrialization in the U.S.: Lessons for Japan.* Boston: Unwin Hyman.

Markusen, A. R., & Gwiasda, V. In press. Multi-Polarity and the Layering of Functions in World Cities: New York City's Struggle to Stay on Top. *International Journal of Urban and Regional Research, 17,* 2.

Markusen, A., Hall, P., Deitrick, S., & Campbell, S. 1991. *The Rise of the Gunbelt.* New York: Oxford University Press.

Markusen, A. R., & McCurdy, K. 1989. Chicago's Defense-Based High Technology: A Case Study of the "Seedbeds of Innovation" Hypothesis. *Economic Development Quarterly, 3*(1), 15–31.

Markusen, A., Noponen, H., & Driessen, K. 1991. International Trade, Productivity and Regional Growth. *International Regional Science Review, 14*(1), 15–39.

Markusen, A., & Yudken, J. 1992. *Dismantling the Cold War Economy.* New York: Basic Books.

MIT Commission on Productivity. 1990. *The Working Papers of the MIT Commission on Productivity.* Cambridge; MIT Press.

Myrdal, G. 1957. *Economic Theory and Underdeveloped Regions.* London: Duckworth.

New York Stock Exchange. 1984. *U.S. International Competitiveness: Perception and Reality.* New York: Office of Economic Research, New York Stock Exchange, August.

Noponen, H., Markusen, A., & Driessen, K. 1992. "Trade and American Cities: Who Has the Comparative Advantage?" Working Paper. Project on Regional and Industrial Economics, Rutgers University, August.

Noponen, H., Markusen, A., & Shao, Y. 1992. "Is There a Trade and Defense Perimeter? The Geographical Impacts of Trade and Defense Spending in the United States, 1977–1986." Working Paper. Project on Regional and Industrial Economics, Rutgers University, August.

Noyelle, T. J., & Stanback, T. 1983. *The Economic Transformation of American Cities.* Totowa, NJ: Rowman & Allenheld.

Osborne, D. 1987. *Economic Competitiveness: The States Take the Lead.* Washington, DC: Economic Policy Institute.

Patton, W., & Markusen, A. 1991. The Perils of Overstating Service Sector Growth Potential: A Study of Linkages in Distributive Services. *Economic Development Quarterly, 5*(3), 197–212.

Piore, M., & Sabel, C.. 1984. *The Second Industrial Divide.* New York: Basic Books.

Porter, M. 1990. *The Competitiue Advantage of Nations.* New York: Free Press.

Posner, A. 1984. *State Government Export Promotion.* Westport, CT: Quorum Books.

Reich, R. 1984. *The Next American Frontier.* New York: Basic Books.

Reifler, R. 1990. Regional Implications of the International Economy. *Regional Science Perspectives,* 20(1), 5–17.

Renaud, B. 1984. Structural Changes in Advanced Economies and Their Impact on Cities in the 1980s. *Research in Urban Economics, 4,* 1–10.

Romer, P. 1986. Increasing Returns and Long Run Growth. *Journal of Political Economy, 94,* 1002–1038.

Romer, P. 1987. Growth Based on Increasing Returns Due to Specialization. *American Economic Review,* 77(1), 56–62.

Sabel, C. 1989. Flexible Specialization and the Reemergence of Regional Economies. In P. Hirst & J. Zeitlin, eds., *Reversing Industrial Decline.* New York: St. Martin's Press.

Salvatore, D. 1990. *The Japanese Trade Challenge and the U.S. Response.* Washington, DC: Economic Policy Institute.

Sassen-Koob, S. 1987. Growth and Informalization at the Core: A Preliminary Report on New York City. In M. Smith & J. R. Feagin, eds., *The Capitalist City.* New York: Oxford University Press.

Saxenian, A. 1989. A High Technology Industrial District: Silicon Valley in the American Context. In P. Perulli, ed., *Cittaq della Scienza e della Technologia.* Venice, Italy: Arsenale Editrice.

Saxenian, A. 1990. Regional Networks and the Resurgence of Silicon Valley. *California Management Review,* Fall, 89–112.

Saxenian, A. 1991. "Contrasting Patterns of Business Organization in Silicon Valley." Working Paper No. *535.* Institute of Urban and Regional Development, University of California at Berkeley, April.

Schoenberger, E. 1988. From Fordism to Flexible Accumulation: Technology, Competitive Strategies, and International Location. *Environment and Planning D: Society and Space,* 6(3), 245–262.

Scott, A. 1988a. Flexible Production Systems and Regional Development: The Rise of New Industrial Space in North America and Western Europe. *International Journal of Urban and Regional Research,* 12(2), 171–186.

Scott, A. 1988b. *Metropolis: From the Division of Labor to Urban Form.* Berkeley and Los Angeles: University of California Press.

Scott, A. 1988c. *New Industrial Space.* London: Pion.

Scott, B. 1987. "U.S. Competitiveness in the World Economy: An Update." Paper presented at the Workshops on Competitiveness, Harvard Business School, July 12–18.

Scott, B. 1991. "Economic Strategy and Economic Policy." Paper presented at the World Bank, Washington, DC, November 21.

Sen, A. 1970. *Growth Economics.* Harmondsworth, England: Penguin Books.

Shapira, P. 1986. "Industry and Jobs in Transition: A Study of Industrial Restructuring and Worker Displacement in California." Unpublished doctoral dissertation, University of California, Berkeley.

Shinohara, M. 1982. *Industrial Growth, Trade and Dynamic Patterns in the Japanese Economy.* Tokyo: University of Tokyo Press.

Sihang, B., & McDonough, C. 1989. Shift–Share Analysis: The International Dimension. *Growth and Change, 20*(3), 80–88.

Singh, A. 1992. "'Close' vs. 'Strategic' Integration with the World Economy and the 'Market-Friendly Approach to Development' vs. an 'Industrial Policy': A Critique of the World Development Report 1991 and an Alternative Policy Perspective." Faculty of Economics, University of Cambridge, April.

Soja, E. 1987. Economic Restructuring and the Internationalization of the Los Angeles Region. In M. Smith & J. R. Feagin, eds., *The Capitalist City.* New York: Oxford University Press.

Stegemann, K. 1989. Policy Rivalry among Industrial States: What Can We Learn from Models of Strategic Trade Policy? *International Organization, 43*(1), 73–100.

Storper, M. 1989. The Transition to Flexible Specialization in Industry: External Economies, the Division of Labor and the Crossing of Industrial Divides. *Cambridge Journal of Economics, 13,* 273–305.

Storper, M., & Scott, A. 1988. The Geographical Foundations and Social Regulation of Flexible Production Complexes. In J. Wolch & M. Dear, eds., *Territory and Social Reproduction.* Hemel Hempstead, England: Allen and Unwin.

Tervo, H., & Okko P. 1983. A Note on Shift–Share Analysis as a Method of Estimating the Employment Effects of Regional Economic Policy. *Journal of Regional Science, 23*(1), 115–121.

Tyson, L. D., Dickens W., & Zysman, J. 1988. *The Dynamics of Trade and Employment.* Cambridge, MA: Ballinger.

United Nations Centre on Transnational Corporations. 1983. *Survey on Transnational Corporations: 1983.* New York: United Nations.

U.S. Office of Technology Assessment. 1986. *Trade in Services, Exports, and Foreign Revenues.* Washington, DC: U.S. Government Printing Office.

U.S. Office of Technology Assessment. 1987. *International Competition in Services.* Washington, DC: U.S. Government Printing Office.

Womack, J., Jones, D. T., & Roos, D. 1990. *The Machine that Changed the World.* New York: Rawson Associates.

Zech, C. 1986. Sub-National Foreign Export Development and Its Impact on Productivity. *Growth and Change, 17*(3), 1–12.

2

Constructing Comparative Disadvantage: Lessons from the U.S. Auto Industry

CANDACE HOWES

In 1925 90% of all motor vehicles were produced in North America; by 1955 the North American share had declined to 73%, as European production reached 24% of global output. By 1978 Europe and Japan were responsible for 35 and 25% of world vehicle production, respectively, leaving only 32% to North America (Motor Vehicle Manufacturers Association, 1989). Nonetheless, in that same year more vehicles were produced in North America than had ever been produced before, or would ever be produced again, creating 2.1 million jobs—10% of all manufacturing jobs in the United States—directly associated with auto production; by 1992 that number had fallen to 1.7 million. In the last few decades dozens of plants have closed from California to Massachusetts. Michigan, once the heart of automotive production, has lost 200,000 auto jobs since 1978, while new plants have opened in Tennessee, Kentucky, Louisiana, and Oklahoma.

Such large-scale restructuring in autos is always a source for concern, especially for those nations and regions on the losing end. The auto industry is a strategic industry, not only for its employment capabilities but also because it is the downstream customer for many other critical industries. It is the largest consumer of robotics, and a very large consumer of electronics equipment, including audio electronic and engine control equipment. It absorbs many of the commercial spin-offs from aerospace technology, and is a leader in the development of new production technologies, including new flexible methods of mass production and cellular batch production. All developed and most developing countries acknowledge that the auto industry is critical to industrial development, and all countries engaged in auto production have at some time consciously designed policies to develop or preserve auto production within their national boundaries. Therefore, what determines the location of auto production is of central concern to planners and policymakers, worldwide.

The purpose of this chapter is twofold: first, to explain the locational patterns of auto production since the turn of the century, a story that mainly assigns new weights to factors that have been identified by previous authors but does not differ in substance from already accepted explanations; second, to offer a corrective to what is becoming accepted wisdom regarding future patterns of production location.

Production location from the turn of the century until approximately 1980 can be explained within a theoretical model of capitalist production that generally regards 20th-century organization as rooted in the "fordist" production principles described by the French "regulationists" (Aglietta, 1979; Lipietz, 1982), the American "social structure of accumulation" school (Bowles, Gordon, & Weisskopf, 1983; Gordon, Edwards, & Reich, 1982), and theorists of its possible successor, flexible specialization (Piore & Sabel, 1984; Sabel, 1982). Large-scale mass production, which greatly reduced unit costs in manufacturing, and its necessary complement, mass markets, defined the logic of production organization, industrial relations, and location under fordist regimes.

Declining profit rates across fordist regimes, beginning in the 1960s, first called forth a theory of "fordism" in order to explain its demise. Joining the theorists of fordism were new groups who tried to explain "restructuring," that is, the changing organization of production, new spatial patterns, new systems of industrial relations, as desperate efforts to maintain profit rates in the face of failing structures of accumulation (Froebel, Heinrichs, & Kreye, 1980; Bluestone & Harrison, 1982; Wilkinson, 1983).

Beginning with the work of Sabel and Piore in the United States, production organized within flexibly specialized firms producing complementary goods has been posited as a viable alternative to fordism, especially in the context of fragmenting markets in the late 20th century. Several scholars, turning their focus on the auto industry, have theorized the implications for the spatial organization of North American production (Glasmeier & McCluskey, 1987; Florida & Kenney, 1992; Florida, Kenney, & Mair, 1988; Holmes, 1988, 1992; Schoenberger, 1987). All have concluded that the intense division of labor and decentralization that characterized fordism and saw its most extreme expression in the 1970s' efforts to relocate production to low-wage areas in the face of declining profits, is being reversed as European and North American producers meet the competitive challenge offered by Japanese producers using new flexible production methods. These authors conclude that the spatial concentration required by Japanese production methods will overwhelm the tendency to dispersion witnessed in the 1970s.

Given the current popular understanding of the Japanese production system, this is a logical conclusion to draw, and given that the actual restructuring process is ongoing and incomplete, these writers have by necessity turned to logic rather than to fact. But drawing on more detailed information now available about the actual patterns of Japanese investment and a somewhat different perception of Japanese production methods, I offer a corrective to these initial impressions.

This chapter begins with a brief overview of various theories that have been used to explain global spatial organization of production and the associated trade patterns, drawing from competing trade, industrial organization, and growth theories.[1] The main difference underlying all these theories is whether they start with the premise that competition—the motive for location—is based on cost and price, suggesting competitive markets, or on strategic advantage due to scale or innovation, which implies imperfect product markets. The second order of differentiation concerns whether strategic advantage is static—due to some absolute cost advantage—or dynamic, due to steadily declining costs and increasing capacity for innovation. Location and trade patterns in a fordist system reflect strategic advantage due to static economies of scale that have an absolute limit. Fordist firms' spatial adaptation to declining profit rates seems to reflect an effort to undergird that scale advantage with lower factor costs. On the other hand, in the 1970s, it was the confrontation between the fordist and the flexible fordist system, with its dynamic economies, that called forth spatial reordering. However, at every point where production organization offers the theoretical possibility of strategic advantage, that advantage and its spatial logic is only realized because of the intervention of the state. Either one's own state helps foster strategic advantage or foreign states do not frustrate it. Either way, strategic advantage is constructed by the policies of nation states.

In the third section, I discuss the four distinct periods of global spatial organization in the light of these theories. At every historical marker answers to the following questions offer a plausible explanation for locational patterns. What national industry or set of firms has the superior production system and why? What is the ideal locational manifestation of that production system? Can that production system be successfully transferred to other nations or regions and how? To what extent is the leader in that production system free to exploit its productive superiority? In every period, whichever national firms enjoy productive superiority, it is shown that that superiority is exploited only due to state policies.

Section four takes a closer look at spatial organization within the United States, concluding that until 1975 it reflects the rationalization required by fordist production principles. Section five explores the effect on spatial organization of the confrontation between fordism and flexible fordism after 1975, which led to efforts at further fordist-type rationalization as well as to the appearance in the United States of some spatial organization apparently based on flexible fordist principles. But as I show in the sixth section, the apparent transfer of Japanese production organization to the United States masks a more-insidious appropriation of U.S. production sites to exploit low-wage labor, while maintaining the bulk of production in Japan. Furthermore, efforts by U.S. firms to meet the Japanese challenge with Japanese-style reorganization are hampered by the very process of Japanese investment. The final section reviews the employment, location, and trade effects of this restructuring and suggests some policy implications.

THEORIES OF LOCATION

Orthodox economic theorists would argue that in a world free of market imperfections, production location would be determined by the relative comparative advantage of producing nations in the production of particular goods. Comparative advantage is in turn a function of relative factor endowments. The more land one has relative to labor, the cheaper land is, and hence the greater one's relative advantage in the production of land-intensive goods, for example, agricultural products. A country endowed with mineral deposits will obviously have an advantage in the production of that mineral and possibly all goods that use that mineral intensively. A country better endowed with labor relative to capital will specialize in the production of labor-intensive goods. Under conditions in which labor-rich countries specialize in the production of labor-intensive goods and trade their goods for goods from capital-rich countries, according to the theory, all countries will be better off. The greatest possible output will be produced at the lowest possible cost.

We should expect automotive production, by that logic, to take place in capital-rich countries, it being a relatively capital-intensive industry. Certainly, this orthodox theory can superficially explain the development of the auto industry in the United States in the early part of this century. The extraordinarily high savings rates in Japan (which is the measure of capital endowment in orthodox theory) would explain the apparent relative advantage of Japan over North America and Europe in the late 20th century. Orthodox economists conclude that we should relinquish auto production and jobs to countries that now have the comparative advantage and move our resources into areas in which we still enjoy a comparative advantage, namely, services and some knowledge-intensive industries.

A logical extension of orthodox theory is found among the theorists of the new international division of labor (NIDL) and globalization of production (GOP), who tried to account for the apparent large-scale movement of production facilities from developed to developing countries beginning in the 1960s (Froebel, Heinrichs, & Kreye, 1980; Bluestone & Harrison, 1982). With improvements in telecommunications and transportation technology, capital became sufficiently mobile to seek the lowest cost production sites worldwide. Comparative advantage due to a high savings rate merely meant that multinational firms would have their headquarters in capital-rich regions, but production would take place wherever labor was cheap.

But the orthodox theory and the NIDL only *seem* to explain production location and trade with Japan and they completely fail to explain trade with Europe. In fact, very little trade and production location has been based on relative factor endowments since the end of the 19th century. Orthodox trade theory best fits a world in which competitive advantage is really based on relative factor costs—a world in which most trade is in raw materials and materials-intensive manufactured goods, the world of the 19th century in which 80% of trade was in agricultural products.

But in the late 20th century, we find that 80% of trade is in manufactured goods and that competitive advantage in many manufactured goods is now based not on relative costs and relative factor endowments, but on strategic advantage due to scale or the capacity to innovate. U.S. firms enjoyed unrivaled economies of scale and low unit costs until the late 1960s. But since some of their large-scale plants were in Canada, the volume of automotive trade between Canada and the United States was enormous. Specific German and British firms have developed the capacity to design and produce high-quality luxury vehicles that they export throughout Europe and all over the world. But motor vehicles are not only Germany's largest export, they are also its largest import; and textile machinery, its second-largest export, is also its second-largest import. Similar trade patterns exist across most industrialized countries. The prevalence of such intrasectoral trade is completely inconsistent with any theory of trade based on relative factor endowments. But it is consistent with a theory of competitive advantage based on widespread imperfections in product markets due to increasing returns to scale or firm-specific, nontransferable innovative capabilities, or both. So the existence of firm-specific competitive advantages provides a first clue to the mystery of auto geography.

If competitive advantage is based on firm-specific capabilities, under what conditions are those capabilities created? What conditions promote national competitive advantage and hence local production and employment? Two related bodies of theory have helped to explain these trade patterns in the last decade, the first based on static models of imperfect product markets, the second with roots in the dynamic growth theories of Cambridge economics. The new "strategic trade theory" most closely associated with Krugman (1986), Brander and Spencer (1985), and Helpman and Krugman (1989), suggests, in its simplest form, that for product markets in which there are significant scale economies, there may be excess profits associated with being a first mover. Under such circumstances, it may be in the interest of a nation to subsidize and/or protect an indigenous industry in order to achieve a global competitive advantage from which the nation will reap excess profits. In other words, the economic welfare of the nation with first-mover firms is improved at the expense of other nations. Just as neoclassical trade theory explains trade of the 18th and early 19th century when competitive capitalism prevailed, strategic trade theory helps us to better understand the trade between 20th-century nations organized on fordist principles. It shows that free trade may not be the optimal policy when product markets are imperfect.

But even more problematic for the free trade orthodoxy is the obvious challenge raised by the development policies of Japan and Southeast Asia.[2] In contrast to the "new trade theory" perspective, which suggests mainly the advantages of promoting industries in which there are static economies, the Japanese recognized the importance of promoting industries with strong growth potential due to dynamic economies of learning.[3] Competition is sought on the basis of innovation in product, process, and organization; unit costs decline steadily and are not limited by the extent of the market, as with static scale economies. Nonetheless, productivity growth is enhanced by market growth, which affords the opportunity for continuous investment and reorganization (Kaldor, 1989). Growth also seems to be a necessary condition for the effective functioning of the incentive systems that enhance flexibility and innovation (Aoki, 1990). The country that creates the conditions for continuous innovation embarks on a virtuous circle of growth and innovation that leads to flexibility that leads to further growth. Flexibility cannot be separated from growth, but it also enhances growth.[4]

Japan has chosen with surgical precision to nurture industries with high growth potential at the time—textiles, steel, shipbuilding, autos, electronics, aircraft—climbing progressively up the industry hierarchy to those with greater potential for productivity and wage growth. Unburdened by the ideological constraint of orthodox trade theory, Japan (and now Korea, Hong Kong, Singapore, Taiwan, and Malaysia) have successfully created comparative advantage in industry after industry. In fact, defying economic orthodoxy, the Japanese have shown that most comparative advantage in industry is or can be created. Nurturing high-growth industries requires creating the conditions for demand growth. In the early stages this may mean protection of the domestic market from superior foreign rivals (as was done in the auto industry), and then in the later stages the promotion of exports, through subsidies and exchange rate policies designed to lower export prices.

What do these "new" theories tell us in the end about trade and employment patterns? Strategic trade theory tells us that much of manufacturing trade is based on firm-specific competitive advantages associated with being the first mover in an industry in which optimal scale is large relative to the size of the market. The United States had scale advantages in the production of most vehicle types until the late 1960s. Germany seems to have cornered a relatively small market for high-performance luxury cars, and Sweden has an advantage in high-performance family vehicles. This explains intrasectoral trade and suggests that while current trade patterns may simply be accidents of history, such accidents can be made to happen through explicit policies to subsidize early entry or protect local markets. But the dynamic perspective suggests that strategic advantage comes from promotion of an industry with economies of learning and that such industries can be carefully targeted to promote long-term growth and employment opportunities. It is precisely this kind of strategic targeting that explains the pattern of Japanese exports, not only of motor vehicles, but also of consumer electronics, computer equipment, telecommunications equipment, and in earlier times, of steel and textiles. Though Japan, a resource-poor country, has been forced to import all raw materials, it has carefully planned the development of its manufacturing sector to ensure almost complete self-reliance in manufactured goods. Japan has in effect ensured that the right accidents will happen to Japanese firms.

Finally, if we look at the history of production location, we find that over time, government policies, either to create national strategic advantage or to stymy the strategic advantage of other nations, have done far more to shape the international distribution of employment than relative factor costs.

GLOBAL AUTOMOTIVE PRODUCTION

Drawing on these three theories, we are able to explain patterns of automotive trade and production location over the last century. In every major epoch, we ask, what firms have the best production techniques? Those firms will have the competitive advantage that privilege domestic production, if required by the spatial logic of the production system.

Can that production system be imitated? If so, that suggests that it will be replicated by other countries seeking auto production. Is the superior producer free to exploit its advantage, that is, free to export to or to invest in regions that do not have competitive industries?

Strategic trade theory gives us insight into the distribution of auto production from about 1913 to the mid-1970s. The fordist production system, which was first developed by Henry Ford at the turn of the century and slowly improved by U.S. producers throughout the next 50 years, was internationally unrivaled. Long production runs manufacturing and assembling interchangeable parts conferred enormous economies of scale. Only in the United States, because of the enormous internal market, was it possible to achieve the full potential of these scale economies. The system could only be imitated if large unfragmented markets were available, a condition that did not arise in Europe until the late 1960s. U.S. firms had no serious challengers for 60 years.

The location logic of the fordist system in a sufficiently large market required centralization of parts production and, until the 1950s, decentralization of assembly, to achieve minimum production and transportation costs. And these are the factors that determined production location in the United States. But based on economic incentives, one would have expected to see exports from the United States to foreign markets until those markets were large enough to support assembly plants at which point parts or knockdown kit exports would be substituted for fully built-up vehicles. But protective policies—mainly high tariff rates —in foreign markets prevented U.S. firms from fully exploiting their superior production system. Inefficient plants were built and parts sourced locally in the European market.

In the late 1960s, when fordism began to show early signs of wear— declining profit rates across a broad range of fordist industries—new patterns of location began to emerge at the margin, patterns that seem to conform to more-neoclassical explanations. Seeking to bolster narrow profit margins, U.S. (and European) auto firms began to build assembly and parts plants in low-wage regions of the United States, Europe, Latin America, and Southeast Asia. Theorists of the new international division of labor saw this activity as the beginning of a large-scale move of production to low-wage countries, made possible by advances in specialization and the division of labor and in transportation and communications technologies. Movement of labor-intensive production—wire harness assembly, textile assembly, and brake assembly—to low-wage countries grew as U.S. firms faced the first competition from Japanese firms with huge labor cost advantages.

By the late 1970s the internal problems of the fordist system were overwhelmed by the external threat of competition from a superior production system: the flexible fordist system of Japanese firms. Japanese imports flowed into the U.S. market especially after the second oil price shock. Between 1978 and 1986 Japanese imports doubled. Beginning in 1982 the United States imposed some mild restrictions on Japanese imports, but not enough to keep Japanese market share below 22% by 1986. Japanese imports flowed into Europe at a slower pace due to more-aggressive protection, capturing no more than 10% of that market by 1986. Japanese firms also captured significant positions in Southeast Asia. The volume of Japanese production doubled between 1973 and 1986; its global share of production rose from 18 to 27%.

Only dynamic trade theory can explain this success. Japan targeted its auto industry beginning after World War II. The Japanese auto industry grew on licensed foreign technology and a protected domestic market. Growth was rapid and productivity growth was sensational. By 1979 Japanese firms had surpassed the U.S. auto industry in absolute productivity (Howes, 1991b). Access to the second-largest market in the world—North America—and limited access to the largest market, Europe, provided the steady growth necessary to develop the industrial relations, supplier, design, and finance systems that make Japanese firms so flexible and competitive.

The evolution of the global auto market can be divided into roughly four periods. Until about 1955 the United States was the unchallenged leader in world auto production. The U.S. market grew rapidly from less than 5 million units just before World War II to over 9 million in 1955. Worldwide, most vehicles were built and sold in North America (see Figure 2.1). The second period, the decade after 1955, witnessed Europe's ascendence to a close second place as a world power in the motor vehicle industry. The European market and European production tripled, reaching a scale almost comparable to that of the United States. Japan emerged as a contender in the third period, after 1965. Japanese production more than tripled between 1965 and 1973, rapidly narrowing the gap with slow-growing European and North American producers. Since 1973 Japanese production, fueled almost entirely by export growth, has again doubled, reaching parity with North American production by 1986.

North American Preeminence, World War I–1955

Automotive production was begun in the 1890s both in North America and Europe by many small manufacturers engaged in craft-style production. This period stretches from the beginning of auto production until about 1913. In both Europe and North America small manufacturers

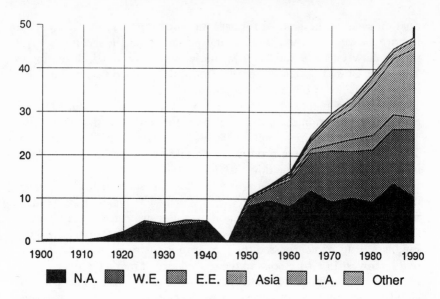

FIGURE 2.1. World motor vehicle production by region, 1900–1990 (in millions). *Source*: Compiled by author from Motor Vehicle Manufacturers Association, *World Motor Vehicle Data*, 1989 edition, and *Ward's Automotive Yearbook*, 1992.

located at sites formerly dedicated to carriage or bicycle manufacture. But because U.S. manufacturers developed a system of large-scale mass production using standardized parts, by the beginning of World War I they had a significant cost advantage over European firms. Whereas European firms produced more than half of all motor vehicles until 1906, by 1925 the European share had dropped to 10% of world production. With the exception of a Ford branch plant established in the United Kingdom in 1911 to assemble knockdown kits, U.S. firms exported only built-up vehicles to Europe in the first two decades of this century. This was probably the last time free trade and comparative advantage determined trade patterns in the auto industry.

Following World War I, when Britain, France, Germany, and Italy erected 30 to 50% tariff rates, Ford and General Motors (GM) began to build or acquire European factories. Soon European firms were adopting some U.S. mass production techniques and competing with the European operations of U.S. firms (Bloomfield, 1978). By 1937, the last peak year before WWII, U.S. firms had settled into the 25 to 30% share of the then 1.1 million unit Western European market that they still hold today. Also in the 1920s Ford and GM, again to circumvent import restrictions, established branch plants in other parts of the world including Brazil, Argentina, and Mexico. By 1937 only 78% of worldwide vehicles were produced in North America, compared to 17% in Western Europe (see Table 2.1).

The European industry was a collection of small national industries. High tariffs prevented trade between countries, thereby restricting production of each vehicle model to a scale that could be supported by the national market. Unable to realize the scale potential of fordist production methods, high unit costs kept prices high and the industry grew slowly from 1.1 million vehicles in 1937 to 3.8 million in 1955. Though by 1955 Europe had a much larger population than the United States, the United States and Canada still produced (and consumed) 73% of all world vehicles, compared to Europe's 24%.

Europe's Decade, 1955–1965

In the 10 years between 1955 and 1965 European production grew threefold. Recovery from World War II and a huge spurt of income growth accounted for rising demand. On the supply side, significant changes in

TABLE 2.1. Regional Production of Motor Vehicles, 1925–1986[a]

	U.S.	N.A.	E.Eur	W.Eur	Europe	Japan	Other	World
	Millions of units							
1925	4.3	4.4	0.0	0.5	0.5	0.0	0.2	4.9
1937	4.8	5.0	0.0	1.1	1.1	0.0	0.2	6.4
1955	9.2	9.7	0.5	2.7	3.2	0.1	0.3	13.2
1965	11.1	12.0	1.0	8.6	9.6	1.9	1.1	24.6
1973	12.7	14.3	2.3	13.3	15.6	7.1	2.3	39.2
1986	11.3	13.2	3.4	13.3	16.7	12.3	2.9	45.1
	Regional share							
1925	88%	90%	0%	10%	10%	0%	0%	100%
1937	75%	78%	0%	17%	17%	0%	4%	100%
1955	69%	73%	4%	20%	24%	1%	2%	100%
1965	45%	49%	4%	35%	39%	8%	5%	100%
1973	32%	36%	6%	34%	40%	18%	6%	100%
1986	25%	29%	8%	29%	37%	27%	6%	100%

[a]To avoid distortions due to business cycles, regional production shares are calculated for peak industry production years: 1925, 1937, 1955, 1965, 1973, and 1986. Until the 1970s global production was cyclical only because North American production was cyclical. Western Europe began to experience cycles comparable to those of North America after 1973. Japanese production has grown steadily, unperturbed by cyclical behavior, due partly to its reliance on exports for the past 40 years.
Source: Compiled by author from Motor Vehicle Manufacturers Association, *World Motor Vehicle Data*, 1989 edition.

the structure of the industry lead to rising productivity and falling prices. In 1957, with the establishment of the European Economic Community (EEC), the process of intraregional trade liberalization began. By 1967 intracommunity tariffs were eliminated. Within a few short years the automotive firms were finally able to exploit the potential of mass production, consolidating and rationalizing dozens of firms and production facilities, centralizing production in areas convenient to supply the whole European community.

In the decade after 1955 the Japanese industry also began to take off. The U.S. decision to procure military vehicles from Japan during the Korean War provided stimulus to an industry that had been so moribund by 1950 that the president of the Bank of Japan said it should be phased out (Ono, Odaka, & Adachi, 1988). Throughout the 1950s, behind a protective wall of 40% tariff rates on small cars, and an absolute prohibition on foreign direct investment in Japan, Japanese firms undertook technical tie-ups with European firms to learn product design and production techniques. The Japan Ministry of International Trade and Industry (MITI) issued strict guidelines for the joint ventures, enforced by rigid foreign exchange allocation in order to force rapid localization. Nissan achieved complete localization of Austin production within 4 years (Ono, Odaka, & Adachi, 1988; Cusumano, 1985). High import duties were maintained thoughout the 1960s. Japan produced 500,000 vehicles in 1960 and 1.9 million by 1965. Most of these vehicles were produced for the domestic market, though by 1965 approximately 10% were exported.

Latin American countries also pursued policies in the 1950s to promote local auto production. Unlike Japan, however, inward foreign direct investment was permitted. In Brazil, beginning in 1956–1957, companies that accepted plans for local manufacturing were granted various incentives, including favorable tariffs on imported equipment, and tax benefits. Within 4 years 95% of the weight of each vehicle was being produced locally (Jenkins, 1987). Tariffs as high as 200% were imposed on imported vehicles to protect the fledgling industry. Similarly in Mexico, under the Auto Decree of 1962, firms were required to source 60% of the value of production locally (Bennett & Sharpe, 1985). Between 1955 and 1965 Latin American production, largely by North American and European multinational firms seeking new profit centers, rose from about 70,000 units to almost 500,000 units.

During the decade after 1955, despite the fact that U.S. producers were still the most efficient in the world, the U.S. share of world production shrunk to 45% while the European share rose to 39% and the Japanese share to 8%. High tariffs in Japan and Latin America, and continuing high external tariffs for the EEC, kept the technically superior U.S. firms from exporting to these markets. On the other hand, Germany, which had developed specializations in luxury vehicles and in small inexpensive cars, exported about 10% of its vehicles to the open U.S. market, beginning in 1957. Nonetheless, since all markets were growing during the period, most auto-producing countries experienced rapid growth of production and employment in the industry.

Japan Enters the World Market, 1965–1973

During the third period, 1965 to 1973, Japanese production tripled, European production increased 62%, and U.S. output rose only 14%. By 1973 Japan produced 18% of the world's vehicles, Europe maintained a constant share of 40%, and the U.S. share fell to 32%. Since U.S. production in Europe continued to expand at the same rate of growth as the European market, U.S. firms retained a 25% share of the Western European market. Total Western European exports to the United States never accounted for more than about 7% of European production or 8% of the U.S. market. However, between 1968 and 1973 Germany exported about 20% of its production—mainly its specialty luxury and low-cost Volkswagens—to the United States.

Though Japanese companies had cost problems until the late 1960s, due mainly to low volumes and high material and components prices, by the late 1960s most firms, benefiting from low labor costs, were able to improve quality and lower production costs to international levels. In the early 1970s Japanese firms found an unexploited niche in the North American market: mini and subcompact cars.

Until 1973, then, U.S. firms were still the most productive in the world, but trade patterns reflected three other factors. First, German firms had developed a specialization in two niches that other countries had not dared to enter until Japan began to export small cars. Second, Japanese productivity growth, low wages, and specialization in the small car niche gave them a competitive advantage in one market segment. Third, the protective policies of Japan and Europe kept imports out of those markets and chaneled exports toward the U.S. market. By 1973, after 2 decades of growth within a protected domestic market, Japanese firms were sufficiently competitive to export 31% of total production, or 2 million units, half to North America. The three largest firms, Mazda, Toyota, and Nissan, were each exporting nearly half of their total output.[5] Japan's car exports to the United States increased 14-fold between 1967 and 1973. By 1973 28% of Japanese vehicles were exported, nearly half to the United States, where they captured a 5% share of the market.

Export-Led Growth and Beyond, after 1973

The final period stretches from 1973 to the present.[6] Japanese production, similar to Europe in the 1950s and 1960s, grew 72% over 13 years. Japanese firms continued to base their growth strategy on exports to North America, Europe, and some markets of Oceania. Japanese firms exported half of their output; 50% of Japanese exports went to the U.S. market in 1986, 25% to the European market. Slow market growth and heightened foreign competition slowed output growth in Europe to 7%, and in the same period U.S. output fell 11%.

Five factors during this period accounted for the change in the global distribution of automotive production and employment and the trade patterns that distribution reflected. First, Japanese firms produced a product line that was not produced in the United States: the minicompact and subcompact car. Strategic segment targeting allowed them to enter the market in the late sixties and gave them a particular advantage following the 1973 and especially the 1979 oil crisis. Second, the oil crisis (through a complex chain of feedbacks through the lending institutions of developed countries) led to debt crises in developing countries. The developing countries undertook export promotion programs, including promotion of automotive exports, to earn the foreign currency necessary to pay interest on their debt. Profit-squeezed multinational firms seeking new sites for low-cost production were often the agents of export promotion in developing countries. Third, despite these changes in export behavior, the United States adhered to a relatively open market policy, only putting limited controls on Japanese vehicle imports beginning in 1981. Fourth, as their export volume grew, Japanese firms moved rapidly out along a learning curve, ultimately developing a productive system that proved superior to the U.S. productive system in terms of quality and productivity by the late 1970s. Japanese firms were then able to compete head on with U.S. firms in their primary market segments. Overlaying changes in relative costs and levels of productivity, government policies in both Japan and the United States effectively aided the development of the Japanese industry at the expense of U.S. firms.

Coming out of the recession induced by the first oil crisis, as motor vehicle sales resumed at a healthy pace, Japanese exports to the United States increased from 1 million in 1973 to 1.7 million, 11% of the U.S. vehicle market, in 1978. But while Japanese firms had made sizeable inroads into the U.S. market, it took a second oil crisis in 1979 to create a large and permanent shift in consumer demand toward smaller vehicles. By 1981, though total sales in the United States had declined 30% to 11 million units, Japanese imports had risen 600,000 units to 2.3 million, capturing 21% of the total vehicle market. Despite the more than doubling of Japanese imports between 1973 and 1981, the United States had not considered any restrictions on Japanese imports.

In contrast, Japanese exports to Europe were less successful. In a market as large as North America's, Japanese imports reached only 1.2 million units or 10% of sales in 1981. The European market, despite the tariff-free policy for trade among EEC nations, had a complicated pattern of protective practices toward nonmember trading partners. All the auto-producing countries, with the exception of Sweden and Belgium, maintained some form of barrier to Japanese imports, either through tariffs or explicit quotas. Italy permitted only 2,500 Japanese passenger cars to be directly imported from Japan annually. Britain restricted Japanese firms to 11% of the market. France had a 2% quota, Germany an informal 11 to 15% quota. Portugal and Spain had very high tariffs. There was an informal agreement among the members of the EEC that Japanese car imports should not exceed 11% of the total market.

All Latin American and some Southeast Asian producers had erected trade barriers to protect their fledgling industries well before the upheavals of the 1970s, but the debt crisis, resulting from the oil price hikes of the 1970s and the interest rate appreciations, renewed their commitment not only to develop their local industries but also to use them as prime sources for export earnings. These efforts contributed to further erosion of North American production.

Export requirements were added to the Mexican Auto Decree in 1969. The Mexican government added several provisions over the next 10 years designed to bring the value of exports in line with the value of imports. In a policy meant to encourage multinational production in Mexico for export to U.S. markets, multinational firms were given greater flexibility to import parts as long as imports were compensated by exports (Jenkins, 1987). The peso devaluation of 1980 coupled with existing U.S. trade regulations which facilitated low-wage (*maquiladora*) production on the Mexican border, made Mexico a desirable production location for U.S. parts manufacturers. In 1980 Ford, Chrysler, and GM all built or expanded engine capacity in Mexico, both to serve the Mexican market and for export to the United States. By 1984 Chrysler and GM were both exporting small volumes of vehicles from Mexico to the United States. In 1988 Ford began assembling large volumes of small cars in a new plant producing exclusively for export to the United States. The Mexican export strategy was executed entirely by foreign multinational firms, including Ford, Chrysler, GM, Volkswagen, and Nissan.

South Korea's even more ambitious export strategy put their auto industry at the center of an economic development strategy modeled on past Japanese practice. In the face of the external shocks of the 1970s, Korea borrowed its way out of balance of payments problems and subsidized its strategic auto sector, a strategy that was rewarded by market growth and rapid productivity growth (Amsden, 1989). Between 1980 and 1987 Korean motor vehicle production rose from 100,000 units to 1 million. In 1987 half of Korean production was exported, 90% to North America. Again the offshore production strategies of U.S. firms contributed to the Korean export strategy. Half the vehicles produced by two Korean firms were exported to the United States as the Ford Festiva and the Pontiac Le Mans. But unlike the Mexican industry, there is also a large Korean national manufacturer—Hyundai—which in 1987 accounted for 75% of all exports.

In contrast to Japan, Mexico, and Korea, European exports slowed during this period. The exchange rate did not work in favor of European exports, except in the case of Germany, but German volume exports—the Volkswagen—were badly battered by competition from the Japanese. After 1973 the share of total German production going to the United States fell to 10%; on average, 5 to 6% of European production is now exported to the United States.

In 1981 the imposition of some limited import restraints in the U.S. market altered the Japanese strategy slightly. The early 1980s was also the period when Japanese firms were beginning to reap the rewards of their rapid move down the learning curve toward a production system that was superior to the United States in terms of quality, productivity, and the speed with which new products were brought to the market. Just as the Japanese manufacturers were in the position to challenge the U.S. firms in the heart of their product market, they faced the possibility of restricted access.

Anticipating protectionist legislation, due to the very large market share they had captured, the Japanese agreed to a Voluntary Restraint Agreement (VRA) (initiated by MITI) to begin in 1981. The VRA limited the volume of Japanese imports to 1.68 million passenger cars annually, to be divided among the Japanese companies by MITI. In theory, the VRA was meant to encourage Japanese firms to invest in local production if they wanted to sell vehicles in the U.S. market.[7] While the VRA restricted the level of car imports, no such volume limitations were put on truck or parts imports.[8] The VRA was renegotiated annually and the minimum level gradually raised at an annual average rate of about 8.6% to 2.3 million units by 1985. Total Japanese imports to the United States peaked at 3.4 million units in 1986 (see Figure 2.2).

Following the imposition of the VRA Japanese firms did invest in U.S. production. In 1982 Honda built the first automotive assembly plant

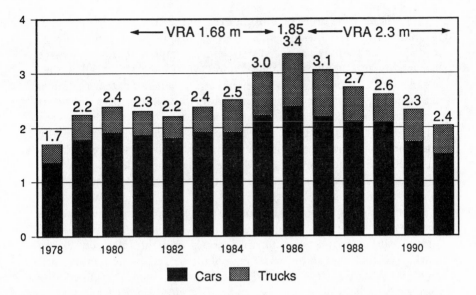

FIGURE 2.2. Japanese imports, 1978–1991 (in millions). *Source*: Compiled by author from *Ward's Automotive Reports.*

in Ohio. Nissan and Toyota (in a joint venture with GM) followed in 1984. Most of the plans to build 13 plants in North America have now been locked in with completion scheduled for the end of 1993. Three hundred parts plants have also been planned or already built. By 1986 4 million Japanese cars and trucks were being sold in the United States, 3.4 million imports and 0.6 million transplant vehicles. So while the VRA with the United States altered the form, it did not reduce the overall level of Japanese access to the U.S. market. Japanese firms still had considerably more access than to the European market where only 1.6 million vehicles were sold in 1986, or to any of the markets of developing countries with motor vehicle industries.

As the preceding discussion shows, global trade patterns and employment have not been governed by natural comparative advantage since the 1920s. Once mass production gave them a cost advantage over European firms, U.S. firms experienced a brief period of unrivaled supremacy. But soon European nation states created high tariff walls behind which less-efficient local producers were protected from low-cost imports. U.S. firms were obliged to build small-scale production facilities in several European countries to serve the local markets.

Japanese firms grew behind an even tighter protective shield that precluded *any* competition, either from imports or foreign direct investors. For decades they produced vehicles for a captive market that were low quality and high cost by world standards. By the 1970s, when they began to export to the North American and to a lesser extent the European market, low labor costs, improved quality, and increased productivity made them competitive in some segments of their export markets. Rapid growth through exports over the next 10 years allowed them to fine-tune what was becoming a superior productive system, so that by the 1980s the policies of the past 30 years had succeeded in constructing a solid dynamic comparative advantage for Japanese firms vis-à-vis their rivals in the global market.

Today the superior production system of Japanese firms, and the uneven opportunities to exploit the benefits of that superiority in the relatively open markets of North America and the relatively closed markets of the other auto-producing countries, largely determines current patterns of global production and employment. Dynamic trade theory offers the tools to comprehend the development of that Japanese superiority in which market growth permits firms to move rapidly down a learning curve. It also helps to explain the declining relative competitiveness of U.S. producers. Insights from the "new international division of labor" theory lead us to conclude that foreign investment by profit-squeezed U.S. firms explains much of the growth of imports from developing countries.

Automotive trade has grown enormously since the early 1970s. In contrast to the minimal role played by trade in the world motor vehicle market previous to 1973, approximately 15% of vehicles are now exported. (This figure does not include intraregional trade in North America or Europe.) Figure 2.3 illustrates the lopsided nature of this trade. Most of the volume has been generated by Japanese exports to North America, Europe, and developing countries.

As a consequence, there is now a huge global imbalance between production and consumption of motor vehicles. While North America produced only 19% of world motor vehicles in 1990, it consumed 30%; Japan, which produced 28%, consumed only 16% (see Figure 2.4).

Whether these trends will continue depends on whether the Japanese will retain their superior productive position in the global market, whether the United States will continue to maintain a relatively liberal attitude to Japanese imports and foreign direct investment, and whether other major markets, such as Europe, will continue with their current restrictive policies.

In the next two sections I look at the determinants of investment and employment location within the United States. I will show that until

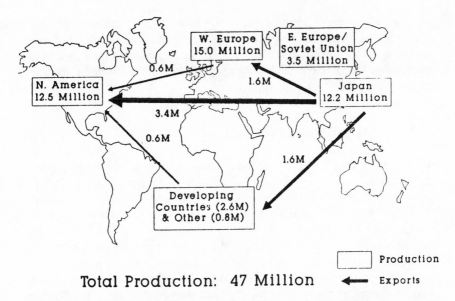

Total Production: 47 Million

FIGURE 2.3. World vehicle production and exports, 1987. *Source:* Compiled by author from Motor Vehicle Manufacturers Association, *World Motor Vehicle Data*, 1989 edition.

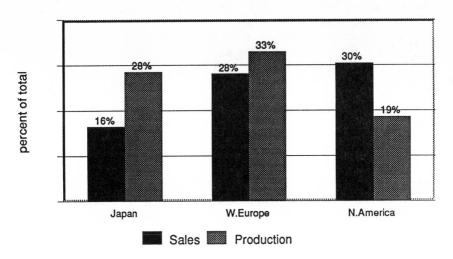

FIGURE 2.4. Domestic share of world sales and production, 1990. *Source:* Compiled by author from *Ward's Automotive Yearbook*, 1992.

the late 1970s spatial patterns were determined by the locational imperitive of fordist production which changed several times with new developments in technology. After about 1975 trade began to influence auto geography. I will also explore expectations for the continued effects of trade on auto location.

TECHNOLOGY AND U.S. AUTO GEOGRAPHY

Since the beginning of the century there have been several reconfigurations of auto geography within the United States.[9] We will concern ourselves with three periods of reorganization that have occurred since World War II. Within the United States, site-factor costs and technology played a large role in the location of auto production until the mid-1970s. The first two periods of spatial reorganization were made largely in response to slight changes in production organization—still within a fordist system—and/or in transportation technology and the interaction with site factors. The first reorganization resulted in greater dispersion of automotive assembly facilities, but greater concentration in ownership. The second phase of reorganization led to a reconcentration of assembly facilities in the Midwest and further concentration in ownership. Until the mid-1970s the location of auto production was unrelated to world trade patterns.[10] Since then, however, the tremendous increase in import and transplant competition and the response of U.S. firms has provoked *both* geographic decentralization and recentralization as well as deconcentration in ownership. This period will be discussed in the fifth section of this chapter, Trade and U.S. Auto Geography.

Space, Decentralization, and the Rise of Oligopoly

The early 1950s marked the first wave of restructuring, when many smaller companies, known as the independents, were driven out of business by their high-volume, low-cost domestic competitors. Ford, motivated by the high damage costs associated with long-distance transportation, had, prior to World War II, pioneered regionally dispersed branch plants to assemble knockdown vehicles for sale in local markets. By the 1950s pure transportation costs were sufficient motivation for Ford and other successful firms to build plants up and down both the East and West Coasts, in Texas, in Georgia, in the plains states, and in Michigan and other Great Lakes states. The cost of shipping a completed Dodge from Detroit to Chrysler's Los Angeles assembly plant in 1955 was almost $300—25% of the average price of a car. The estimated cost of shipping the same vehicle in the form of components was $124 (Edwards, 1965).

There was a volume constraint on the establishment of branch plants, however. Since the minimum volume required for low-unit-cost branch assembly at the time was 60,000, only the large firms like Ford, GM, and Chrylser had the volume necessary for the regional markets. Consequently, the smaller independent companies with inadequate volume to sustain branch plants were at a tremendous disadvantage supplying the more-distant markets. As the independent companies succumbed to the cost disadvantages associated with small size, numerous firms merged or were bought up by larger firms, and many plants were shut down in the rationalization process. Thus the spatial enormity of the U.S. market contributed to the oligopolization of the industry.

As Figure 2.5a shows, there were 13 assembly plants on the West Coast in 1950. Each firm wanted a plant in Los Angeles and another in the San Francisco area. Between 1951 and 1956 Kaiser-Fraser, Nash, Studebaker, and Willys each shut down plants in Los Angeles, and Dodge shut a plant in the San Francisco area. Studebaker shut a plant in New Brunswick, New Jersey, in 1955, and Crosley closed a plant in Marion, Indiana, in 1952.[11]

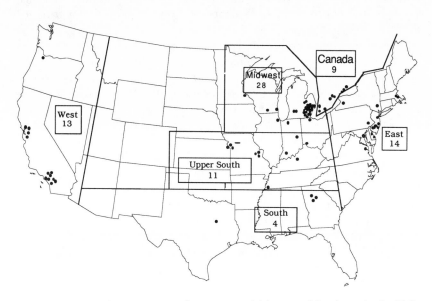

FIGURE 2.5a. U.S. auto geography, motor vehicle assembly plants in the U.S. and Canada, 1950. *Source*: Compiled by author based on plant location data from *Ward's Automotive Yearbook*, 1950.

Technology and Geographic Recentralization

The late 1950s brought, too late for most independents, an innovation in transportation technology that nearly eliminated the cost disadvantage of centralized assembly. Oversized railroad flatcars allowed for the "piggyback" and "rack car" method of shipping automobiles. The cost for Studebaker or American Motors to transport vehicles from their South Bend or Kenosha plants to Los Angeles was now almost comparable to the cost of transporting parts. Though there may still have been some advantages to regional assembly plants, especially for the high-volume producers, there was no longer an imperative (Edwards, 1965). Furthermore, since plants could now specialize in a single vehicle for distribution to the national market, they could be built to larger scale.

Production was rationalized in larger, specialized assembly plants, and recentralized in the Midwest. Ford and Plymouth each closed plants in Los Angeles. Ford closed three plants on the East Coast and one in Memphis, the Chevrolet division of General Motors closed one in the East, and Chrysler's Plymouth division closed a plant in Evansville, Indiana. By 1978, through the process of mergers, consolidation, and recentralization in the wake of altered transportation costs, the regional landscape of the auto industry had been greatly compressed toward the middle. As Figure 2.5b shows, the assembly plant population on the East Coast had fallen from 14 to 9 plants, and on the West Coast from 13 to 5.

One additional event, the enactment of the Automotive Products Trade Act (APTA) which eliminated tariffs on most automotive products trade between the United States and Canada, contributed to this rationalization and recentralization of auto geography before the mid-1970s. Until 1964 Canada had a wholly integrated, low-volume, high-cost industry, owned by U.S. firms. APTA allowed the U.S. firms to integrate Canadian production into their U.S. operations. Canadian plants could now become specialized high-volume, low-cost plants and the full range of product offerings could be supplied to the Canadian market from both Canadian and U.S. plants (Holmes, 1983). While the number of assembly plants in Canada did not increase significantly (from 9 to 11), the volume of Canadian production increased almost fivefold and the Canadian share in North American production rose from 5% in 1950 to 12% in 1978 (Motor Vehicle Manufacturers Association, 1989). Further, Canadian content provisions, required by Canada as a condition of its participation, created an incentive for U.S. volume parts manufacturers to establish plants in Canada to supply the U.S. market.

Because Canadian labor compensation was 30% lower than U.S. compensation (Holmes, 1988), for the first time since the establishment

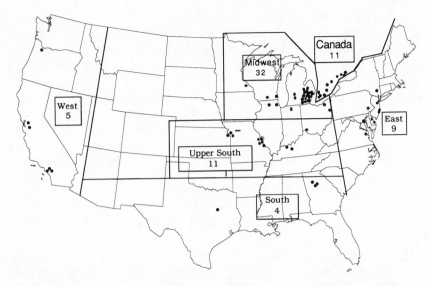

FIGURE 2.5b. U.S. auto geography, motor vehicle assembly plants in the U.S. and Canada, 1978. *Source*: Compiled by author based on plant location data from *Ward's Automotive Yearbook*, 1951–1978.

of pattern bargaining in the auto industry wage differentials at the assembly level also became a potential locational factor.[12] Virtually all Canadian production takes place in Ontario, most within a few hours' drive of Detroit. Therefore, APTA served as an additional incentive to rationalize production into specialized plants and recentralize production in the Midwest. The Canadian share of North American auto employment grew from about 7% in 1964 to 15% by 1988 (United Auto Workers Research Department, 1987).

Until about 1975 auto geography was shaped by a rationalization process within a fordist production system. The imperative of standardization, mechanization, and high fixed costs demanded large markets to achieve economies of scale. Firms within the industry sought low unit costs through large-scale production facilities and consolidation to reduce transportation costs. Competition was between firms shaped by the same industrial logic and those firms that best conformed to that industrial logic became the dominant firms. Ultimately, concentration in the industry increased to the point where oligopolistic coordination of prices and output became possible. But it was also true that firms had more or less achieved the pinnacles of rationalization within the framework of fordist production.

Location and employment patterns were derived from this rationalization framework. Within the context of a growing mass market, plants were closed in some regions, reopened in others. Concentrations of production workers moved between regions. Often it was the same workers, moving from a closing assembly plant in Hamtramck, for example, to a new plant in Oklahoma City, under some provision of the contract between the United Auto Workers (UAW) union and the company. Since the market was growing, the total number of people employed in the industry was also growing. While entire cities or regions might be devastated by the rationalization process, the jobs themselves were not. The players were simply shifted around on the chess board.

TRADE AND U.S. AUTO GEOGRAPHY

After approximately 1975 the determinants of auto geography changed dramatically. Rather than reflecting a rationalization process within a productive system, auto geography would henceforth be shaped by a confrontation between two productive systems, the traditional fordist system of the U.S. producers and the flexible fordist system of the Japanese producers. The confrontation between productive systems of unequal strength will inevitably result in the displacement of the weaker by the stronger. The old system may live alongside the new for a period of time. It is also possible that the firms wedded to the old productive system will be able to adopt the new productive techniques and become part of the new productive system (Wilkinson, 1983). But the speed with which the new system overwhelms the old, the degree to which the old system persists, the extent to which the new system replaces the actors in the old system with new actors, is partly determined by the regulatory environment in which the rationalization process takes place.

Trade and investment policies play a crucial role in that regulatory system. They define the rules of the game. If trade policy allows only a slow influx of imports from firms with superior production systems, the adjustment process may be slow, indigenous firms may be able to adopt the new productive system, and the impact on employment and even plant location may be small. But a rapid influx of imports will drive domestic firms, facing an ever-shrinking market and unable to finance new production techniques, out of business.

U.S. auto geography since the mid-1970s has been shaped by three factors. First, the existence of a superior production system in the hands of foreign competitors seeking access to the U.S. market; second, the regulation of that access in the form of trade and investment policies;

third, the response of U.S. firms to the competitive challenge, given the regulatory environment in which they have been operating.[13]

The restructuring process has seen three distinct periods since the mid-1970s. First, when profit rates began to fall in the 1960s and 1970s, U.S. assemblers put pressure on their suppliers to lower prices. Parts suppliers, focusing mainly on labor costs, moved plants to nonunion areas and sought reforms in the terms of employment, for example, two-tier contracts and fringe-benefit reductions. By the second period in the late 1970s, at the same time they were heading into a recession, assemblers were confronting competition directly from imports. The result was excess capacity, which the firms correctly perceived as structural rather than cyclical. They responded by shutting down some of that capacity. The third phase has seen enormous investment by foreign manufacturers in new capacity in the United States.

Shakeout in Parts—1970s

U.S. assemblers experienced steadily declining profit rates beginning in the late 1960s as the growth rate of the domestic market began to slow and competition from foreign firms was first experienced in overseas markets. U.S. firms tried to reduce costs through their suppliers. Labor costs in parts firms average about 32% of the value of shipments, compared to 13% in assembly (*Survey of Current Business*, 1985). Because there were both union and nonunion firms in the parts industry, labor cost–based competition increased during this period. Within companies, one began to see unionized plants in North-Central urban locations closing while new plants were opened in the southern states, or in Mexico or Brazil. Parts employment in the North-Central region as a percentage of national employment in parts declined from 73 to 56% between 1974 and 1983 while the percentage in the South increased from 14 to 32% (Herzenberg, 1989, Table 46B).

Imports and Assembly Plant Closings—1980s

A major shakeout began among assemblers after 1979 when the industry, already pressed by import competition and an overvalued dollar, went into a deep recession for 4 years. Domestic output fell by more than 30% between 1978 and 1982. While there was already evidence that Japanese manufacturers were producing superior products in the small-size classes, the appreciation of the dollar relative to the yen by about 50% between 1978 and 1982 greatly increased their advantage in the U.S. market.

The response of U.S. firms to import competition critically affected the spatial location of production and employment. By the time U.S. firms recognized the need for fundamental changes in their product line they were already headed into a deep recession. Faced with record losses during the 1980s, the companies lacked the resources to make necessary changes in production and distribution. And the tremendous fluctuations in the market left them with little confidence that they would be able to sell what they built. U.S. firms chose a defensive strategy: they closed plants, outsourced parts, and reduced their work forces, hoping to ride out the recession on lower costs.

By 1982 U.S. manufacturers, struggling under the weight of excess capacity and high fixed costs, began to shut some of the older plants. Over the next 2 years Ford and Chrysler both shut a number of assembly and parts plants and reduced their work forces by close to 40%. GM postponed the adjustment process, reducing its work force by only 17% by 1984. Ford and GM each shut two assembly plants in California in the early eighties (one GM plant was later reopened in a joint project with Toyota). Ford and GM each shut a plant on the East Coast, and GM shut one in the upper South. Seven plants were shut in Michigan and one in Kenosha, Wisconsin (see Figure 2.5c). Total auto jobs

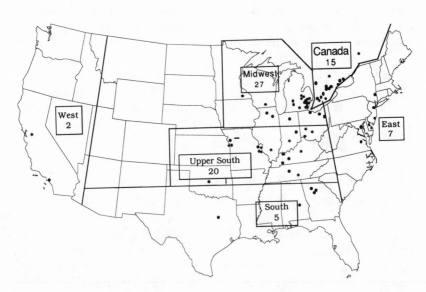

FIGURE 2.5c. U.S. auto geography, motor vehicle assembly plants in the U.S. and Canada, 1989 (* = transplants). *Source:* Compiled by author based on plant location data from *Ward's Automotive Yearbook,* 1979–1989.

fell by 390,000 between 1978 and 1984. Two hundred thousand UAW jobs were lost.

The results of these cost-cutting efforts were mixed. Ford combined efforts to cut costs sharply by paring down the work force to a bare minimum, outsourcing and increasing the intensity of work in their plants with changes in product and production techniques. Ford was able to regain market share lost during the early 1980s. GM and Chrysler (which had acquired excess capacity when it bought American Motors), closed plants and continued to lose market share and so closed more plants.

U.S. firms would inevitably have faced competition from superior Japanese products and production techniques. However, U.S. trade and macro policies exacerbated the force and suddenness with which they were confronted. Since Japanese firms faced import restrictions in the other large market—Europe—they concentrated their export strategy on the U.S. market. But the tight money policies of the United States, following the oil price shock in 1979, which raised the value of the dollar, meant that not only were Americans suddenly seeking fuel-efficient vehicles, they were also presented with Japanese imports that were considerably cheaper than they had been a few months earlier.

Import competition and U.S. trade and macro policies in the 1980s helped shutter 14 North American auto plants in the Midwest and on the East and West Coasts, and cost 390,000 jobs over a 6-year period. Perhaps if the process had been slowed somewhat, the dislocation would have been mitigated.

Transplants—1980s and 1990s

The sudden growth in the Japanese import share and the wave of plant closings caused sufficient alarm in Congress by 1980 to raise the specter of protectionist legislation. Concerned that their access to U.S. and Canadian markets would be curtailed by the VRA or other, more-restrictive regulations, Japanese firms quickly responded with plans to build plants in North America.

Honda was the first to build a U.S. plant, in 1982; Nissan opened a plant in 1983; and GM and Toyota undertook a venture to jointly assemble vehicles beginning in 1984. These plants were built at a time when the dollar was still very high relative to the yen and it was widely believed that Japanese firms sacrificed their cost advantage when they produced in the United States. However, for Honda, Nissan, and Toyota, which were by then selling about 500,000 units each in the U.S. market, fear of exclusion motivated their decision to invest. Soon after, all but one of the remaining Japanese producers announced plans to follow the leaders into the U.S. market.

Most observers conclude that the latecomers decided to build plants in the United States after the appreciation of the yen in 1985 made it more expensive to export to the United States. It is more likely that the latecomers feared that early arrivals would build so much capacity in the United States that there would be no room left. Most firms had announced plans to expand before the yen appreciated. Given firm-specific quotas, the only way to expand market share in the United States was to build local plants. Once some firms had declared their intentions, all firms followed suit. Knowing that there would be intense rivalry for the U.S. market, each Japanese firm was eager to capture market share, even before their U.S. plants were built. The huge growth of imports in 1985 and 1986 should be seen as a scramble to secure share of the U.S. market for their forthcoming local production before other Japanese competitors became entrenched. After 1986, as transplants came on-line, Japanese imports slackened somewhat. Total Japanese sales, however, continued to grow. By the mid-1990s Japanese firms plan to sell almost 5 million vehicles in the U.S. market—3.2 million transplants (see Figure 2.6) and 1.8 million imports.

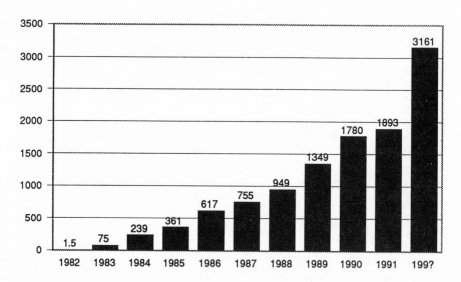

FIGURE 2.6. North American transplant production, 1982–1993 (in thousands). While 3.161 million units of capacity are planned for 1993, the current recession may lead firms to ramp up production more slowly; however, no changes in planned capacity have been announced. North America includes here only the United States and Canada. *Source:* Compiled by author from *Ward's Automotive Reports*—author's projections.

Japanese assemblers are being followed to the North American market by their parts suppliers. By the end of 1989 there were nearly 300 Japanese parts plants in or planned for North America, the great majority located in Kentucky, Tennessee, southern Ohio, Illinois, and Indiana.

The recent growth of Japanese automotive production in the United States raises a new set of issues for planners and policymakers. Economists, planners, and policy analysts, representing a broad political spectrum, have advocated unrestricted Japanese investment in U.S. manufacturing facilities.[14] The argument is as follows. First, it is fairly commonly accepted that Japanese firms have a superior production system that cannot be easily transferred to U.S. firms, either because the learning nature of the system precludes instantaneous transfer, or because U.S. firms do not have the political will or organizational capacity to adopt the system. Therefore, in a world of unrestricted competition, U.S. firms are expected to steadily lose market share to Japanese firms. The inevitable outcome will be declining employment and a deteriorating sectoral trade balance. However, if Japanese firms are willing to build plants in the United States, U.S. competitiveness can be restored (even if it is Japanese firms doing the production, it is still being done on U.S. soil), employment can be preserved, and the trade imbalance mitigated.

This argument requires two necessary underlying assumptions. First, since the U.S. market is not growing, any increase in Japanese volume must come at the expense of other vehicles. Most analysts argue that Japanese transplants are mainly displacing Japanese imports rather than U.S. vehicles. Second, as Womack, Jones, and Roos (1990, p. 200) have argued, it is inevitable that Japanese firms will build "top-to-bottom, paper-concept to finished-car manufacturing systems in the three great markets of the world—North America, Europe, and East Asia" because "this mode of production achieves its highest efficiency, quality and flexibility when all activities from design to assembly occur in the same place." In other words, Japanese firms can ultimately be expected to build the whole car in the United States.

Supporting and extending these conclusions, Florida and Kenney (1992) argue that

> The location choices of the Japanese industrial transplants reflect a new spatial division of labor which is coincident to this new model of production organization. Under this model, both internal and external factors in the division of labor are located close together in an agglomerated production complex. The glue that holds the complex together is the requirement for tightly networked, just-in-time production. . . .

Simply put, Japanese manufacturing investment is creating a Japanese-style production complex on American soil, establishing a new landscape of steel-rubber-automobile production. This complex is integrated across the entire production chain providing the steel, automotive parts, tires, glass, and even some of the machines used to manufacture automobiles. (p. 29)

Following that logic, most analysts now assume that Japanese trans-plants will have a very high proportion of North American–built parts in them. Hence, if a Japanese transplant replaces a Japanese import, there is a large net increase in jobs. When a Japanese transplant displaces a Big Three vehicle, there may be a net loss of jobs but that will be because the Japanese car is built more efficiently not because the parts are imported. In theory, that means resources released from inefficient U.S. car production can be put to more efficient use.

In contrast, drawing on a somewhat different understanding of the logic of the Japanese production system, I expect the outcome to be quite different.[15] While it is true that the Japanese system achieves the high-est efficiency, quality, and flexibility when all activities from design to final assembly occur in one place, as I show in the next section, the Japanese firms have been able to successfully cut off some final assem-bly from Japan, as long as most of the rest of the value chain remains in Japan. In fact, the logic of the Japanese system is that most activities *must* remain in Japan. The locational logic of Japanese production flows directly from that production logic. The outcome of unrestricted Japa-nese investment will be a significant decline in U.S. automotive employ-ment and a steadily deteriorating automotive trade deficit.

JAPANESE INVESTMENT—TECHNOLOGY TRANSFER OR SOCIAL DUMPING?

A brief discussion of the Japanese production system is required before explaining why there is neither an incentive nor a necessity to transfer the full system to the United States in order to reap the benefits of their superior system in the U.S. market.[16]

It seems that much of the enthusiasm for the system is based on interpretation of only part of the system. The Japanese production sys-tem is a finely balanced blend of two diametrically opposed incentive systems. One, the system that has so enthused Western writers, draws on community values and common interests to forge a consensus around corporate strategy. But this incentive structure, embedded in large manu-facturing firms, appears to depend on a surrounding structure of con-tingent workers and secondary suppliers whose behavior is motivated by more traditional economic incentives. Students of Japanese industry have concentrated on the large manufacturing firms (Dore, 1973, 1986, 1987; Aoki, 1990; Abegglen & Stalk, 1985). Less is known about the secondary markets for parts and labor.

The success of the Japanese production system, and much of its appeal, can be traced to its superior capacity to contain the competitive forces of the market where they have proven destructive, for example, in suppressing innovation, while promoting the constructive effects of cooperation that can elicit innovation and effort (Dore, 1986; Aoki, 1990; Abegglen & Stalk, 1985). This is apparent in the industrial relations system for large firms, in the relationship between assemblers and first-tier suppliers, and in the relationship of large firms to their banks and stockholders. Many of the exchanges that would be mediated by the market in a Western firm seem to be affected through negotiation and mutual agreement in large Japanese firms. Japanese firms, for historically specific reasons, entered into relations with workers, suppliers, and financiers that entailed a greater sharing of power than is characteristic of Western firms. The result is an incentive structure better suited to the needs of contemporary markets.

For example, the permanent employment system in large firms, which was initiated in the 1950s to retain scarce skilled labor, is part of an incentive system that now draws a high level of commitment from employees. The technological and commercial dynamism of the system— new products are brought to market in half the time required of Western firms (Clark & Fujimoto, 1991)—is frequently credited to the scope and sophistication of the permanently employed work force.

The majority of the workers in the top-tier firms in the industry face a labor market only for entry-level positions in the firm. Once the worker joins the firm, there is virtually no lateral mobility outside the company. Workers expect to spend their lifetime (until 55) in a single firm. Workers are rewarded through promotion and both group and individual performance-based productivity bonuses. Promotion is based on performance criteria that include some measure of the workers' ability to handle a broad range of tasks and work collectively in groups. Broadly defined tasks and job rotation relieve the traditional boredom of the assembly line while raising the employees' awareness of the objectives of the firm. Dore (1986), Aoki (1990), and Abegglen and Stalk (1985) all suggest that this incentive system successfully encourages employees to view their interests in common with the firm.

First-tier suppliers are part of the "team" as well, contributing to the design of the product from the early stages. Unlike Detroit-based firms which traditionally organize relations with suppliers through a competitive bidding process, Japanese firms maintain very long-term, frequently exclusive relations with suppliers (Helper, 1991; Asanuma, 1988; Takeishi, 1990; Cusumano, 1985). Because suppliers and assemblers often hold stakes in the equity of one another's firm, they are conscious of their common fortune (Aoki, 1990). Consequently, the Japanese assemblers have been able to exploit the design and engineering capabilities of their suppliers. The just-in-time system of inventory and parts delivery and statistical quality control build quality and efficiency into the production process without costly inspection.

But the consensus forged from job security and sharing the benefits of prosperity depends on two things: first, growth that ensures that loyalty will be rewarded with more shared benefits than shared losses; second, cost flexibility built into the system through the use of contingent workers and secondary and lower-tier suppliers. This is the level of the system where more familiar relations of power between capital and labor and between monopoly or oligopoly capital and competitive capital prevail.

Robert Cole (1979, p. 61) estimates that only about 32% of Japanese employees in all industries enjoy the benefits of lifetime employment. In the auto industry, it is those working in assembly plants or first-tier suppliers who are offered lifetime employment. There are approximately 500,000 people employed in the auto parts industry in Japan (Japanese Automobile Manufacturers Association, 1987, p. 18). Using Toyota as an example, I calculated that about 40% of parts workers in the auto industry were employed by third- and fourth-tier suppliers where there is no permanent employment and where wages are about 67% of the level of wages among assemblers and first-tier suppliers (Howes, 1991a, pp. 9–10).

There exists an army of third- and fourth-tier suppliers that is never involved in planning, that does not have exclusive relations with any assembler, and that wins contracts through a cost-based bidding process. These contingent workers and suppliers build cost flexibility into a system otherwise characterized by high fixed costs. This too is a crucial part of the Japanese system.

There is no reason why the creative parts of the system should be transferred and a lot of reasons why the exploitative parts of the system would fit well in the United States. Toyota employs 65,000 people in Japan designing, manufacturing, and assembling 3.6 million vehicles (Toyota Motor Corporation, 1987). Among its assembly plants are Takaoka, which produces the Corolla (the same vehicle assembled at NUMMI, the GM–Toyota joint venture in California), and Tsutsumi, which assembles the Camry (also assembled at the Toyota plant in Kentucky). In the United States, Toyota ultimately plans to directly employ approximately 5,500 people when it reaches full production of 550,000 cars in the mid-1990s.

Each Toyota employee in Japan produces 55 cars annually. Each Toyota employee in the United States will produce 100 cars annually. The difference in cars per worker is not a measure of productivity differences. Japanese assembly workers in the Takaoka plant in Japan and American assembly workers in the NUMMI plant in California both require roughly the same number of hours in direct assembly of a car (Krafcik, 1987). Rather, it is clear evidence of the difference in levels of integration between U.S. and Japanese operations. For each vehicle produced, there must be substantially more labor involved in the "system" work—design, engineering, high technology parts fabrication, research, and development—in Japan than in the United States. The apparent difference in productivity really reflects the difference in the role of Japanese and U.S. production in the Toyota production system. The U.S. operations are simply branch assembly plants. While U.S. production is a marginal part of the "Toyota production system," employing less than 10% of Toyota's worldwide work force, U.S. sales which account for 25% of Toyota worldwide sales, certainly are not marginal.

Toyota can fully realize much of the strength of the Toyota production system—the close relationship between assemblers and suppliers, the team approach to design, the troubleshooting role played by production workers—through its operations in Japan. Since it produces the same vehicles in Japan, it can eliminate any of the problems in the production process there. If the synergy with suppliers can take place in Japan, if all the parts are designed there, there is little need for these relations in the United States. In fact, if Toyota dismantled its system and moved parts to the United States, it would weaken the system.

On the other hand, it can transfer a "debugged" assembly line to the United States and use production workers in fairly traditional ways (as it did at NUMMI). Since the assembly process is among the most mechanized and hence immutable parts of the production process, there is less room for worker input into the production process than is the case in the design process or batch production. If the Japanese assembly workers make necessary changes during the start-up process in the sister plant in Japan, then the work of American production workers can be reduced to machine tenders.

Since teams are used, some authors have argued that the industrial relations system is being successfully transferred (Florida, Kenney, and Mair, 1988). But teams serve a range of functions from integrative to supervisory. Teams are a cost-effective system for monitoring workers (Dohse, Jurgens, & Malsch, 1988; Parker & Slaughter, 1988). If the reward structure is even partially based on team performance and if workers monitor one another, they can eliminate the need for a supervisor. But that does not mean they have the kind of broadly defined discretionary roles attributed to Japanese workers.

Nor can the fact that transplants source parts just-in-time from hundreds of U.S.–based suppliers be taken as evidence of a transfer. In the United States, transplants buy low value-added, standardized parts from nonunion transplant suppliers who pay an average hourly compensation rate 40% below the average for the auto parts sector as a whole (Howes, 1991a). These are "third-tier" suppliers; they do not work closely with assemblers in the design and development of parts; their function is to absorb the costs and risks of holding inventory and supplying just in time.

Japanese investment in the U.S. auto industry does not fit the profile of foreign direct investment that has been described by Graham and Krugman (1991), Reich (1990), Lawrence (1990), and Florida, Kenney, and Mair (1988). In fact, the investment practice of Japanese automakers differs little from imports. Japanese firms have circumvented the restrictions of the Voluntary Restraint Agreement without really abandoning integrated production in Japan. The "Japanese production system" remains in Japan while something very close to the end product is exported to the United States. Furthermore, it appears that Japanese firms have not sacrificed the factor cost advantages associated with the dualistic structure in Japan when they come to the United States. Japanese firms are not engaged in the transfer of technology to the United States. Instead they are dumping some of the social problems of their dualist production structure—low wages and employment insecurity—in the United States.

In the next section I suggest that the location decisions of Japanese firms in the United States is motivated more by a desire to preserve factor cost advantages than by efforts to achieve economies of agglomeration. There are real differences in factor costs facing U.S. and Japanese firms. The factor cost differences are based primarily on benefit cost differences that occur when new greenfield plants are built in an industry that is populated by older plants and an aging work force. Japanese firms are able to employ a segment of the labor force not available to the Big Three. There are additional advantages derived from the tax system and from low wage rates in the secondary sector of the industry.

Factor Costs and Location Decisions

In an industry where wage rates were taken out of the calculus of assembly plant location decisions long ago, Japanese firms are successfully bringing compensation back into competition. The location policies and hiring practices of some transplants seem to be designed to avoid employing minorities, women, older workers, and people with union experience. Plants have been located in rural areas, far from traditional manufacturing centers, far from concentrations of minorities, and where wage levels are well below those of midwestern auto communities. Transplants have been shown to have hired blacks in proportions substantially below their population ratios (Cole & Deskins, 1988), and have been successfully charged with age discrimination by the Equal Employment Opportunity Commission (EEOC) (Tolchin & Tolchin, 1988).[17]

The location strategies of the transplants were also politically motivated. One assembly plant was placed in each of the states that would potentially suffer the most dislocation from transplant production: Michigan, Ohio, Illinois, and Indiana. With the exception of Mazda, however, the plants have been put in the less-developed, low-wage, and nonunion areas of these states. Other plants can be located in areas not traditionally considered automotive centers—Kentucky and Tennessee —but have been located along Interstate Highway I-75 which connects the upper South to the rest of the country.

While the new concentration of automotive production in the upper South has suggested an economies-of-agglomeration motive to some researchers (Florida & Kenney, 1992; Florida, Kenney, & Mair, 1988; Glasmeier & McCluskey, 1987), as important seems to be the fact that suppliers have been located at sufficient distance from the assembly plants and from one another to avoid the concentration that has traditionally facilitated unionization in this country. As a consequence of their location strategies, Japanese firms have been able to partially reconstruct their lower-tier supplier chain in the United States and preserve the advantages of their dualistic structure in Japan. Further, the location strategy has allowed them to achieve significant labor cost advantages at the assembler level over their North American competitors.

There are three sources of the cost advantage: first, a minor but much publicized advantage comes from the tax breaks and subsidies offered by localities in the bidding war for Japanese investment, subsidies that are not available to the Big Three to upgrade their existing facilities. The second and far greater advantage comes from the tremendous savings in fringe benefit costs associated with the use of a youthful nonunion work force. The third factor cost advantage comes from traditional dualist use of low-wage third- and fourth-tier suppliers.[18]

In order to attract new assembly plants, state governments have engaged in an elaborate bidding war. Typical incentives have included job training money and infrastructure improvement—roads, sewers, and bridges have been built and plant sites have been purchased by the state;

up to 100% tax abatements for 15 to 20 years, and in one case 40 years, have been offered. The typical direct incentive is now averaging $50 to $100 million; Indiana spent $85 million to get the Fuji-Isuzu plant. The indirect incentives such as tax abatements and loans can reach $50 to $100 million. Kentucky offered Toyota a total package of direct and indirect incentives worth more than $300 million (Glickman & Woodward, 1989).[19] A state subsidy of $200 to $300 million is a hefty subsidy for the typical greenfield investment of $500 million. Some of the states are paying as much as $100,000 per job. That is equivalent to paying the entire wage bill for 2 to 3 years.

State subsidies, however, are a relatively small part of the cost advantage on a per vehicle basis, averaging about $50 to $75 per car annually over a 10-year period. The real advantage associated with greenfielding is the opportunity it affords to use a young nonunion labor force. Even if the transplant pays UAW-level assembly base wages—and most of the transplants are paying close to that—there is a tremendous savings in benefit costs, especially for pension and medical insurance.

As the domestic industry has declined, an ever-smaller base of workers has funded, through their hourly compensation, a pension fund that must support an ever-larger pool of retirees. The companies did not anticipate in the 1970s that they would be supporting a retiree population as large as their active work force by the mid-1980s. As a consequence, the cost of supporting those funds has escalated over the last 10 years. Because of the particular form of pension plan that many transplants are adopting, and because they have young work forces and no retirees, most transplants will never face these problems. The cost of pensions at a typical transplant are one-fifth to one-half those at the Big Three.

The costs of supporting a large number of retirees from an ever-shrinking base of active workers is even more staggering in medical insurance. Pension funds are just that, funds that are in the best of cases prefinanced. But medical insurance is costed on a pay-as-you-go basis. The savings in medical insurance costs associated with a young labor force are spectacular. Even if the transplants have exactly the same medical benefits as a typical Big Three firm, for a work force with an average age of 25, the cost will be half that of a work force with an average age of 45. In 1989 the average age at Honda was 30 years after 7 years of operation, the average age at Mazda was less than 30, while the average age of the Ford production work force was 48 years.

The cost differential between transplants and the Big Three, based solely on benefits, could run as high as $400 per vehicle. The state subsidies add another $75. But, for the transplants, the benefits of greenfielding do not stop at state subsidies and assembly labor costs. Transplants also face lower purchased materials costs that can range from 65 to 80% of the cost of a vehicle.

First, about 50% of their purchased components are still imported from Japan (McAlinden, Andrea, Flynn, & Smith, 1991), where all the cost advantages of the Japanese system, including dualism, are operative. Second, those components that are purchased in the United States come almost exclusively from Japanese suppliers operating in new greenfield plants themselves. Greenfield suppliers enjoy similar cost advantages to greenfield assemblers: state subsidies to attract the investment, young work forces, and potentially lower benefit costs. But transplant suppliers also have labor costs that may range from 26 to 50% below other parts suppliers in the industry. Some of that cost difference is due to lower wage rates, which are about 50% of UAW rates, and benefits that are about 25% of UAW costs (Howes, 1991a, pp. 12–13). The cost advantage associated with the use of transplant suppliers may be over $400. The total greenfield cost advantage associated with state subsidies, lower assembly labor costs, and lower supplier costs could be close to $900.

As we can see, this is hardly a location strategy motivated solely by a more efficient spatial arrangement that renders economies of agglomeration. Nor is it a locational strategy that will have minimal net employment implications. The transplant location strategy has greatly enhanced their ability to transfer exploitative components of their production system to the United States while preserving the creative integrated part of the system—and most of the jobs—in Japan.

An advocate of unrestricted investment would argue that the U.S. firms could and should meet the competitive challenge of the Japanese system by building more new productive facilities, exploiting the possibilities of more efficient spatial arrangements practiced by Japanese firms. But the real implication is that competition should now be based on emiserating older workers, gutting their pensions, and lowering the long-term living standards of workers in the auto industry as a whole. It is hardly a formula for revitalization.

Unfortunately, because the Japanese have pursued this dualist strategy and have eroded for the first time since the 1940s the pattern of wages and fringe benefits in the U.S. assembly sector, U.S. firms are now more likely than ever to adopt the compensation-cutting strategy as well.[20] Furthermore, the fact that this process has taken place within a very narrow time frame, in a period when the U.S. industry was in recession, profit rates over the cycle have been very low, and when there was no reason to believe that major investment in new technology and new forms of organization would actually regain sufficient market share in time to recover investment costs, the U.S. firms have had little incentive to undertake such investment. It's easier just to squeeze labor.

Geography and Jobs in the 1990s

If the preceding accurately describes the competitive trends in the U.S. auto industry, by the middle of the decade we will have witnessed a spectacular spatial reorganization of the auto industry. Japanese vehicle sales in the United States will have increased by about 3.2 million units since 1978, displacing a similar volume of U.S. parent–produced vehicles as overall market growth stagnates. Nearly 16 North American assembly plants will have been rendered obsolete and undoubtedly closed, largely in the urban areas of the Midwest including Flint, Lansing, and Detroit. Hundreds of small parts plants that supplied these assembly plants will lose business and close. Thirteen new Japanese plants will have been built mainly in the upper South and in rural regions of the Midwest and Ontario. Hundreds of Japanese transplant parts suppliers will gather around (but not too close) to the new assembly plants.

Proponents of unregulated inward foreign direct investment contend that Japanese transplants create jobs. Calculations by Robert Lawrence (1990, p. 58) "suggest the transplants will raise U.S. auto-related employment opportunities by 1992 by between 41,000 and 196,500." Calculations of this nature vary according to the two basic assumptions mentioned earlier: first, Japanese transplants will displace more imports than traditional U.S.-built vehicles; and second, Japanese firms will use North American parts in the transplant vehicles. While all of these questions are open to speculation, research done by this author (1988, 1993) and by McAlinden, Andrea, Flynn, and Smith (1991) suggest that transplant volume will be close to 3.2 million (1 million units more than Lawrence assumed), will displace considerably more U.S.-built cars than imports, and that domestic content levels will not exceed 50% (25 points lower than Lawrence's assumption). Netting out the effect of productivity increases, by middecade there will be 165,000 fewer U.S. auto jobs opportunities than in 1978 as a consequence of transplants and imports.[21] Moreover, more than twice as many people will have lost their jobs. By 1993 365,000 high and medium wage assembly and parts workers will have been displaced by transplants and imports, whereas transplants will contribute only 200,000 new jobs.

Approximately $10 billion in gross income will be lost annually. If these jobs are lost to young people in auto plants in the upper South, earning comparable wages in assembly plants but much lower wages ($8 an hour) in parts plants, only $3.8 billion in new income will be generated. There will be a net annual loss of $6.2 billion to workers in the industry. If the value of benefits (measured by cost to the employer) is added, the net loss would be $8.97 billion. It is a redistribution from the older Rustbelt cities of the north central region of the country to the new autobelt of the upper South, and from older white and black workers to younger, largely white, male workers. But most importantly, it is a redistribution from auto workers to transplant auto company profits.

EMPLOYMENT, LOCATION, TRADE, AND POLICY

Finally, we return to our original concern. Because the auto industry is so central to manufacturing strength, what determines the location of auto production—and how to affect those decisions—is of central concern to planners and policymakers. To date, many scholars who have studied trends in the auto industry have weighed in in favor of encouraging Japanese investment in the United States. Their argument is based on the generally accepted premise that "the real problem is the outmoded "fordist" organization and what is needed in new economic development approaches which recognize the new realities of a new model of production organization" (Florida & Kenney, 1992, p. 37).

"Our conclusion is simple," write Womack, Jones, and Roos (1990, p. 225), "lean production is a superior way for humans to make things. It provides better products in wider variety at lower cost. Equally important, it provides more challenging and fulfilling work for employees at every level, from the factory to headquarters. It follows that the whole world should adopt lean production, and as quickly as possible." They conclude that there are only two ways for lean, that is, Japanese, production techniques to be transferred to the United States: through Japanese investment or adoption by U.S. firms. But since they have little confidence that U.S. firms will do so without external competitive pressure, they suggest that every mass producer needs a lean producer across the road.

While this argument is true, most of these analysts have failed to understand two of the most important realities of the new model of production. First, Japanese firms have no incentive to transfer a full-scale production system to the United States in order to meet demand in the U.S. market. To do so would weaken the integrity of the design, development, sourcing, and industrial relations system in Japan, where most production still takes place for their worldwide sales. Therefore, if the United States is counting on Japanese firms to rescue it from its outmoded production system and declining competitiveness, there will have to be inducements that do not currently exist.

Second, and perhaps more important, much of the analysis to date has focused on the supply-side weaknesses in U.S. production. U.S. firms are using the wrong production, sourcing, and industrial relations techniques; if they were compelled to adopt Japanese production techniques, competitiveness might be restored. But the conditions under which Japanese firms adopted Japanese production techniques, and the macroeconomic conditions still necessary for the proper functioning of the system, are largely ignored. The Japanese auto industry grew behind a solid wall that protected it from the competition of still-superior fordist producers until the 1970s. Guaranteed their domestic market, Japanese producers enjoyed the kind of rapid growth experienced by U.S. firms beginning in the 1920s. As production scale rose, costs and prices fell dramatically, generating new demand. Then, with their internal market still protected, Japanese firms were able to subsidize exports in the 1960s and 1970s from profits in the domestic market. The protected domestic market, subsidized exports, and very large unprotected foreign markets ensured rapid growth of production volume, productivity, and geometrically declining unit costs until the 1980s.

Rapid growth provided the economic environment necessary to develop the types of organization that are so appreciated by Womack, Jones, and Roos (1990), Florida and Kenney (1992), and Lawrence (1990). These writers have missed the argument made so clearly by Japanologists (Aoki, 1990; Dore, 1986) that the collaborative relations enjoyed between Japanese employers and their employees requires continual opportunities for promotion, which in hierarchical structures requires continuous lateral growth. The same is true for the relations with suppliers and with financial backers.

The unavoidable implication is that even if U.S. firms wanted to adopt Japanese production techniques, supply methods, and industrial relations customs, so long as they are facing steady competition from Japanese rivals they do not operate within an economic environment conducive to developing Japanese-style production systems. The Japanese government understood this fact when it protected its producers from U.S. competition for almost 40 years.

We cannot conclude that the kind of low-content Japanese investment that is currently taking place will revitalize the U.S. auto industry. Furthermore, if U.S. firms are going to adopt Japanese production strategies, they cannot do so without policies to guarantee a stable and perhaps growing market for a sustained period of time. If Japanese investment is going to contribute to growth, prosperity, and industrial development in the United States, high-content, fully integrated production must be made a condition of access to the U.S. market.[22] If U.S. firms are going to adopt Japanese production techniques, the U.S. market must be protected from excessive foreign competition, in exchange for which U.S. firms would be required to meet performance criteria, including standards of productivity growth, investment, and innovation.

Auto geography is not constructed by comparative advantage. But comparative advantage is constructed by auto policy and auto policy therefore constructs auto geography. The history of the location of auto production and jobs over the last 90 years suggests that auto-producing countries construct their own fates.

The U.S. industry, the technological leader for 7 decades, was constrained largely to the growth of its own market by the auto policies of foreign countries. The Japanese industry emerged as the technological leader by the end of that seventh decade because Japan dutifully nurtured and protected its industry from premature competition. But Japan's success is also explained by the United States's failure to defend its own industry and its own market, allowing Japanese firms to grow at spectacular rates through export, primarily to the U.S. market.

We see the consequences today: less than two-thirds of the value of vehicles consumed in the United States is actually produced here; hundreds of thousands of jobs have been lost in the United States and the conditions that foster innovation and productivity growth have been eroded. Factories could be rebuilt and jobs recovered but not without an auto policy and a trade policy that acknowledges that comparative advantage must be constructed, and recognizes the terms of that construction in the era of lean production. Until that time hollow Japanese assembly plants will proliferate in rural low-wage areas of this country, assembling technologically superior vehicles from imported parts and forcing U.S. firms along technologically inferior paths of retrenchment in a futile effort to meet the competition. More jobs will be lost, more integrated plants closed.

NOTES

1. A more complete discussion is offered in Chapter 1 of this volume.
2. See Kaldor (1989), Dosi, Tyson, and Zysman (1989), Singh (1992), Scott (1991), and Howes (1992) for discussions of this theoretical perspective embodied in Japanese development policy.
3. Contrast Germany and Japan, both of which are said to have created institutions conducive to innovation and growth. While Germany's regional research and training institutions contribute to the competitive success of German mechanical engineering products, chemicals, and precision instruments, and hence to Germany's strong trade position, these are not growth industries generating increasing employment opportunities. In fact, in 1991, Germany had

the distinction of having both a huge trade surplus and a 10% rate of unemployment.

4. See Howes (1992) for a discussion of the combination of macroeconomic and microeconomic factors that contribute to the success of the Japanese system.

5. Toyota began efforts to export to the United States as early as 1957, after witnessing the growing popularity of Volkswagen Beetles in the U.S. market. Both Toyota and Nissan, fearful that U.S. firms would develop their own small vehicles and preclude late entry into the market, showed vehicles in the Los Angeles imported car show in 1958. Both vehicles performed badly in road tests and the companies suspended export efforts for a few years (Cusumano, 1985).

6. Since this is an analysis of market share changes between peak years of output, this section covers the period 1973 to 1986, the most recent peak year.

7. Interested parties and their supporters in Congress recognized that local assembly did not necessarily guarantee high levels of local parts production. So in 1981, and again in 1982, some members in Congress attempted to enact legislation that would require minimal levels of domestic content. The bill passed twice in the House but was defeated in the Senate.

8. There was a 25% tariff on truck imports. Since Japanese production costs were lower than U.S. production costs, it was not an enormous barrier. After the dollar began to appreciate, it was no barrier at all.

9. The periodization for U.S. auto geography differs from the periodizaton for global auto production because the factors determining global and U.S. spatial epochs differ. It is only in the final epoch of global production that factors affecting global distribution begin to affect internal U.S. auto geography. Though Japanese exports grew rapidly after the first oil crisis in 1973, it is mainly after 1979, when the United States went into another energy-related recession and renewed demand for fuel-efficient vehicles created a permanent opening for Japanese cars, that the Japanese export strategy began to reconfigure U.S. auto geography.

10. The one exception is that the elimination of tariffs on automotive trade between the United States and Canada after 1964 led to the integration of U.S. and Canadian production.

11. Data on plant locations is culled from various issues of *Ward's Automotive Yearbook*.

12. Though by the 1970s Canadian contracts were bargained jointly with U.S. Big Three contracts, exchange rate differentials meant that Canadian wage rates continued to be effectively lower than U.S. rates.

13. See Howes (1991a, 1992a) for a more detailed discussion of this period of restructuring in the auto industry.

14. Among this group I count Reich (1991), Florida and Kenney (1992), Florida, Kenney, and Mair (1988), the MIT International Motor Vehicle Project (IMVP) from which comes the recent book, *The Machine that Changed the World* (Womack, Jones, & Roos, 1991), Morris (1991), Graham and Krugman (1991), and Lawrence (1990).

15. Also supporting this view are Williams and Haslam (1991, 1992) for Europe and North America, Economic Strategy Institute (1992), and McAlinden, Andrea, Flynn, and Smith (1991).

16. A more complete version of this argument is found in Howes (1991a, 1992a).

17. Robert Cole, who published the initial study alleging possible discriminatory practices, believes the situation is now improving. "You're seeing substantial change in minority hiring at the transplants," Cole told *Automotive News* (4 April 1990). "It's largely because of all the negative public attention they received."

18. See Howes (1991a, 1992a) for a more detailed treatment of the role of Japanese fringe benefit policies and the cost advantage in the restructuring of the U.S. motor vehicle industry.

19. Canada provides similar incentives. One Canadian auto analyst claimed that with the incentive package it received, Hyundai could have built the plant, never produced a vehicle, and still made money.

20. It is not really the first case of pattern erosion, but rather the first case that seems likely to be permanent. In the early 1980s when Chrysler was on the verge of bankruptcy, it broke from the pattern of wage rates in the industry for a few years. But the gap was closed again by 1987 (Katz, 1985, p. 55).

21. This is an estimate of lost employment "opportunity." It is based on the assumption that sales remain at the same level as 1978. If sales are higher, 165,000 jobs will not have been lost because more people will be working, but on the other hand, absent transplants, there would be 165,000 more people working.

22. A more detailed discussion of proposals to regulate Japanese investment and revitalize the U.S. industry are found in Howes (1993).

REFERENCES

Abegglen, J. C., & Stalk, G., Jr. 1985. *Kaisha: The Japanese Corporation.* New York: Basic Books.

Aglietta, M. 1979. *A Theory of Capitalist Regulation: The U.S. Experience.* London: New Left Books.

Amsden, A. 1989. *Asia's Next Giant.* New York: Oxford University Press.

Aoki, M. 1990. Toward an Economic Assessment of the Japanese Firm. *Journal of Economic Literature,* 28(1), 1–27.

Asanuma, B. 1988. Manufacturer–Supplier Relationships in Japan and the Concept of Relation-Specific Skill. *Journal of the Japanese and International Economics,* 3(1), 1–30.

Bennett, D. C., & Sharpe, K. E. 1985. *Transnational Corporations versus the State: the Political Economy of the Mexican Auto Industry.* Princeton: Princeton University Press.

Bloomfield, G. 1978. *The World Automobile Industry.* North Pomfret, VT: David and Charles.

Bluestone, B., & Harrison, B. 1982. *The Deindustrialization of America.* New York: Basic Books.

Bowles, S., Gordon, D. M., & Weisskopf, T. E. 1983. *Beyond the Wasteland: A Democratic Alternative to Economic Decline.* New York: Basic Books.

Brander, J., & Spencer, B. 1985. Export Subsidies and International Market Share Rivalry. *Journal of International Economics, 18*(1), 83–100.

Clark, K. B., & Fujimoto, T. 1991. *Product Development Performance: Strategy, Organization and Management in the World Auto Industry.* Boston: Harvard Business School Press.

Cole, R. 1979. *Work, Mobility and Participation: A Comparative Study of American and Japanese Industry.* Berkeley and Los Angeles: University of California Press.

Cole, R. E., & Deskins, D., Jr. 1988. Racial Factors in Site Location and Employment Patterns of Japanese Auto Firms in America. *California Management Review, 31*(1), 9–22.

Cusumano, M. A. 1985. *The Japanese Automobile Industry.* Cambridge: Harvard University Press.

Dohse, K., Jurgens, U., & Malsch, T. 1988. From "Fordism" to "Toyotism"? The Social Organization of the Labor Process in the Japanese Automobile Industry. *Politics and Society, 14*, 115–146.

Dore, R. 1973. *British Factory/Japanese Factory.* Berkeley and Los Angeles: University of California Press.

Dore, R. 1986. *Flexible Rigidities.* Stanford, CA: Stanford University Press.

Dore, R. 1987. *Taking Japan Seriously: A Confucian Perspective on Leading Economic Issues.* Stanford, CA: Stanford University Press.

Dosi, G., Tyson, L. D., & Zysman, J. 1989. Trade, Technologies and Development: A Framework for Discussing Japan. In C. Johnson, L. D. Tyson, & J. Zysman, eds., *Politics and Productivity: The Real Story of Why Japan Works.* New York: Harper Business.

Economic Strategy Institute. 1992. *The Case for Saving the Big Three.* (Interim Report.) Washington, DC: Economic Strategy Institute.

Edwards, C. E. 1965. *Dynamics of the United States Automobile Industry.* Columbia: University of South Carolina Press.

Florida, R., & Kenney, M. 1992. Japanese Transplants, Production Organization and Regional Development. *Journal of the American Planning Association, 58*(1), 21–38.

Florida, R., Kenney, M., & Mair, A. 1988. The Transplant Phenomenon: Japanese Auto Manufacturers in the United States. *Economic Development Commentary, 12*(4), 3–9.

Froebel, F., Heinrichs, J., & Kreye, O. 1980. *The New International Division of Labor.* London: Cambridge University Press.

Glasmeier, A. K., & McCluskey, R. E. 1987. U.S. Auto Parts Production: An Analysis of the Organization and Location of a Changing Industry. *Economic Geography, 63*(2), 142–159.

Glickman, N. J., & Woodward, D. P. 1989. *The New Competitors: How Foreign Investors Are Changing the US Economy.* New York: Basic Books.

Gordon, D. M., Edwards, R., & Reich, M. 1982. *Segmented Work, Divided*

Workers: The Historical Transformation of Labor in the United States. New York: Basic Books.

Graham, E. M., & Krugman, P. 1991. *Foreign Direct Investment in the United States.* Washington, DC: Institute for International Economics.

Helper, S. 1991. An Exit-Voice Analysis of Supplier Relations. In R. Coughlin, ed., *Morality, Rationality, and Efficiency: New Perspectives on Socio-Economics.* Armonk, NY: M. E. Sharpe.

Helpman, E., & Krugman, P. 1989. *Trade Policy and Market Structure.* Cambridge: MIT Press.

Herzenberg, S. 1989. *The Internationalization of the Auto Parts Industry: 1958–1987 and Beyond.* Washington, DC: Bureau of International Labor Affairs, Office of International Economic Affairs, U.S. Department of Labor, January.

Holmes, J. 1983. Industrial Reorganization, Capital Restructuring and Locational Change: An Analysis of the Canadian Automobile Industry in the 1960s. *Economic Geography, 59*(3), 251–271.

Holmes, J. 1988. Industrial Restructuring in a Period of Crisis: An Analysis of the Canadian Automotive Products Industry, 1973–1983. *Antipode, 20,* 19–51.

Holmes, J. 1992. The Continental Integration of the North American Automobile Industry: From the Auto Pact to the FTA and Beyond. *Environment and Planning A, 24*(1), 95–119.

Howes, C. 1988. *Transplants and Job Loss: The UAW Response to the GAO.* Detroit, MI: UAW Research Department, May 10.

Howes, C. 1991a. The Benefits of Youth: The Role of Japanese Fringe Benefit Policies in the Restructuring of the U.S. Motor Vehicle Industry. *International Contributions to Labour Studies, 1,* 113–132.

Howes, C. 1991b. "Total Factor Productivity in the U.S. and Japanese Motor Vehicle Industries, 1965–1985: A Firm Level Comparison." Unpublished Ph.D. dissertation, University of California, Berkeley.

Howes, C. 1992. *Mix Matters and It Doesn't Just Happen: What the U.S. Must Learn from Japan, Germany and Italy about Trade, Growth and Industrial Policy.* Notre Dame, IN: Department of Economics, University of Notre Dame.

Howes, C. 1993. *Japanese Auto Transplants and the U.S. Automobile Industry.* Washington, DC: Economic Policy Institute.

Japan Automobile Manufacturers Association. 1987. *The Motor Industry of Japan.* Washington, DC: JAMA.

Jenkins, R. O. 1987. *Transnational Corporations and the Latin American Automobile Industry.* Pittsburgh: University of Pittsburgh Press.

Johnson, C., Tyson, L. D., & Zysman, J. 1989. *Politics and Productivity: How Japan's Development Strategy Works.* New York: Harper Business.

Kaldor, N. 1981. The Role of Increasing Returns, Technical Progress and Cumulative Causation in the Theory of International Trade and Economic Growth. In F. Targetti & A. P. Thirwall, eds., *The Essential Kaldor.* London: Duckworth. (First published in *Economie Appliquee,* no. 4, 1981.)

Katz, H. C. 1985. *Shifting Gears: Changing Labor Relations in the U.S. Automobile Industry.* Cambridge: MIT Press.

Krafcik, J. F. 1987. *Trends in International Automotive Assembly Practice*. Cambridge: International Motor Vehicle Project, MIT, September.

Krugman, P., ed. 1986. *Strategic Trade Policy and the New International Economics*. Cambridge: MIT Press.

Lawrence, R. 1990. *Foreign-Affiliated Automakers in the United States: An Appraisal*. Private study done for the Automobile Importers of America, Washington, DC, January.

Lipietz, A. 1982. Toward a Global Fordism? *New Left Review*, 132, 33–147.

McAlinden, S. P., Andrea, D. J., Flynn, M. S., & Smith, B. C. 1991. *The U.S.–Japan Automotive Bilateral 1994 Trade Deficit*. Report for the Automotive Parts Advisory Committee, Report Number: UMTRI 91-20. Ann Arbor: University of Michigan Transportation Research Institute, May.

Morris, J. 1991. Globalization and Global Localisation: Explaining Trends in Japanese Foreign Manufacturing Investment. In J. Morris, ed., *Japan and the Global Economy*. London: Routledge.

Motor Vehicle Manufacturers Association. 1989. *World Motor Vehicle Data*. Detroit: Motor Vehicle Manufacturers Association.

Ono, K., Odaka, K., & Adachi, F. 1988. *The Automobile Industry in Japan: A Study of Ancillary Firm Development*. Oxford: Oxford University Press.

Parker, M., & Slaughter, J. 1988. Management by Stress. *Technology Review*, October, 37–44.

Piore, M., & Sabel, C. 1984. *The Second Industrial Divide*. New York: Basic Books.

Reich, R. 1991. Who Do We Think They Are? *American Prospect*, 1(4), 49–53.

Sabel, C. 1982. *Work and Politics: The Division of Labor in Industry*. Cambridge: Cambridge University Press.

Scott, B. 1991. "Economic Strategy and Economic Policy." Paper presented at the World Bank, Washinton, DC, November 21.

Shoenberger, E. 1987. Technological and Organizational Change in Automobile Production: Spatial Implications. *Regional Studies*, 21(3), 199–214.

Singh, A. 1992. "'Close' vs. 'Strategic' Integration with the World Economy and the 'Market-Friendly Approach to Development' vs. an 'Industrial Policy': A Critique of the World Development Report 1991 and an Alternative Policy Perspective." Faculty of Economics, University of Cambridge, April.

Survey of Current Business. 1985. Employment and Employee Compensation in the 1977 Input-Output Accounts. November, 11–25.

Takeishi, A. 1990. "A Study of Supplier Relationships in American and Japanese Automotive Industries." Unpublished M.B.A dissertation, Massachusetts Institute of Technology.

Tolchin, M., & Tolchin, S. 1988. *Buying into America: How Foreign Money Is Changing the Face of Our Nation*. New York: Basic Books.

Toyota Motor Corporation. 1987. *The Automobile Industry: Japan and Toyota* (1987 ed.) Public Affairs Department, Toyota Motor Corporation.

United Auto Workers Research Department. 1987. *The U.S.–Canada Auto Pact*. *UAW Research Bulletin*, September, 5–7.

Wards Communications. Various Years. *Ward's Automotive Yearbook*. Detroit: Wards Communications.

Ward's Communications. Various Issues. *Ward's Automotive Reports*. Detroit: Wards Communications.

Wilkinson, F. 1983. Productive Systems. *Cambridge Journal of Economics*, 7(3–4), 413–429.

Williams, K., & Haslam, C. In press. Against Lean Production. *Economy and Society*.

Williams, K., & Haslam, C. 1991. *Factories or Warehouses?: Japanese Foreign Manufacturing Direct Investment in Britain and the United States*. Polytechnic of East London Occasional Papers on Business, Economy and Society, no. 6.

Womack, J., Jones, D. T., & Roos, D. 1990. *The Machine that Changed the World*. New York: Rawson Associates.

3

State-Sponsored Internationalization: Restructuring and Development of the Steel Industry

ANTHONY P. D'COSTA

The development of the global steel industry since World War II has been very uneven. The international division of labor emerging from this development has resulted in heavy losses in production and employment in the United States and Western Europe. Japan, Brazil, South Korea, India, and Taiwan, among others, have gained a significant share of capitalist world production. Most of these newcomers are also responsible for the dramatic increases in international steel trade.

Contrary to those who promote free trade, I will argue that the recent internationalization of steel production and trade is less an outcome of resource endowment and proximity to markets and more a result of state policies and business behavior. Fundamentally, heightened international competition weakened the spatial and firm monopoly power of the U.S. industry. As governments in other countries targeted the steel industry for economic development, they began exporting a significant share of their steel output. Their new mills were built using state-of-the-art technology, while U.S. mills increasingly relied on outdated technology. Other countries, such as those of Western Europe, for political expediency were reluctant to reduce excess steel capacity and relied on export markets to complement shortfalls in domestic demand. With the onslaught of imports, the U.S. industry sought market protection, shut down plants, and diversified into other activities. The U.S. government's ad hoc response to increasing steel imports by and large failed to encourage investments in new production sites and modern technology.

As a result, the burden of trade-related adjustments fell squarely on the workers and their communities.

What went wrong? What options are open to the U.S. steel industry? Emulating foreign industrial policies, such as export aggressiveness, and practices, such as state ownership, may not be a panacea for the industry's problems, although certainly there are some lessons to be learned from the experience of other steel-producing countries. One major policy implication evident from the internationalization of steel production is that the state cannot leave industrial restructuring to market forces alone. Both building up new capacity and phasing out obsolete facilities must rest on an active state involvement and cooperation with business and labor. However, the degree and form of state intervention will depend on the specific socioinstitutional contexts, circumscribed not only by larger social goals such as employment and equality, but also by the anticipated changes in the global steel industry. Thus industrial policies to revive a mature and *aging* U.S. steel industry will be different from positive policies that have nurtured the steel industry from its conception in Japan and South Korea. The continental size of the U.S. economy is an additional factor that must be taken into account. Understanding the dynamics of the industry as charted by the changing geography of steel production, and identifying the policies and actors of competing nations, are likely to provide a valuable guide for U.S. policymakers concerning the range of options for sector-specific policies, to minimize regional differentials and disruptive trade-related displacement.

STEEL ECONOMIES IN THE UNITED STATES

The steel industry played a key role in American industrialization well into the post–World War II period. Historically, steel production has been concentrated in the nation's industrial heartland. Mills lay along an arc stretching from Buffalo through Pittsburgh, Youngstown, Cleveland, Detroit, and Gary/Chicago, the centers of gravity between Appalachian coal and Marquette-to-Mesabi iron ore production. On this iron base, an elaborate durable industrial complex grew, encompassing the heavy industries of farm equipment, industrial machinery, automobiles, and trucks. The rooting of steel-using industries in the Great Lakes states reinforced the comparative advantage of industrial heartland steel, while the oligopolistic nature of the industry suppressed the development of competing steel centers in the periphery.[1]

Until the 1960s a number of cities depended heavily upon steel for their livelihoods. Within these areas, certain districts and working-class suburbs were even more heavily specialized in steel—the Monongahela

Valley communities of Homestead and Munhall in the Pittsburgh region, for instance, and the south side of Chicago and the communities of Gary, Hammond, and East Chicago in Indiana. Not all were in the Great Lakes states. Some, like Geneva, Utah, Pittsburg, California, and Birmingham, Alabama, had large steel-dependent enclaves far from the industrial heartland. Other towns, like Georgetown, South Carolina, relied on new postwar minimills to provide blue-collar jobs.

Since the turn of the century distinct changes in this internal distribution of steel production have taken place (see Table 3.1). During this period the major steel-producing states in the Great Lakes region saw their share of national raw steel output decline from 90 to 70%, due mainly to competition from the new minimills located outside the Great Lakes region. During the period 1954–1970 several southern states, including Missouri, Virginia, South Carolina, Florida, Texas, and Alabama, and western states such as California and Oregon, emerged as important minimill centers (Markusen, 1985, pp. 87–89). In the postwar period the center of gravity of production has gradually shifted from the old resource-oriented core in Pittsburgh, Pennsylvania, toward a new steel user–oriented one at Gary/Chicago, a shift that accelerated in the 1980s. Pennsylvania's share of the national output dropped steadily from 51% in 1910 to 14% in 1988. Michigan, Indiana, and Ohio registered slight gains in the 1980s, as just-in-time inventory systems for automobile production were implemented. As a result of new automobile production in these areas, demand for high-quality sheet steel expanded steel-producing capacity in their environs.

TABLE 3.1. Distribution of U.S. Steel Output by States, 1910–1988 (% of National Output)[a]

State	1910	1930	1950	1970	1980	1982	1988
Indiana/Illinois	15	21	20	25	26	26	29
Pennsylvania	51	35	28	23	21	15	14
Ohio	19	23	20	18	14	16	18
Michigan	0	1	6	7	7	8	8
New York	5	4	5	3	2	2	[b]
Total of Great Lake States	90	84	79	76	70	67	69
California	0	1	3	3	2	2	[b]

[a]Figures have been rounded.
[b]Negligible.
Source: American Iron and Steel Institute, *Annual Statistical Reports*, various dates.

Despite relative gains in steel output, cities like Gary and Detroit experienced plummeting employment rates among steelworkers throughout the postwar period. The United States had about 169,000 steelworkers in 1988, down by two-thirds since 1958 (American Iron and Steel Institute, various dates). These job losses were unevenly distributed across the steel states. Rates of displacement ran particularly high in cities such as Buffalo, Pittsburgh, Youngstown, and Chicago, and in areas of West Virginia. In the last 3 decades major steel-producing states witnessed varying rates of job displacement, ranging from over 40% to 60% (Bureau of Census, U.S. Department of Commerce, various dates). More recently, between 1982 and 1985, steel cities such as Chicago, Birmingham, Youngstown, and Pittsburgh lost basic steel jobs at rates ranging from slightly under 30% to over 50% (Patton & Markusen, 1990, p. 39). Only a relatively small portion of this job loss was due to improved technology and automation—perhaps one-third.[2] A major share of the job loss was the fallout from dramatic increases in imports in the 1980s, as steel imports gained ever-greater shares of the domestic market. Imported steel displaced domestic production not only directly, but also indirectly, through expanded imports of auto parts, machinery, and consumer goods made from foreign steel. Steel exports also languished. While U.S. production declined, mills in Japan, South Korea, and Brazil reached far outside their own national borders to serve export markets in the United States and elsewhere.

What factors contributed to the changing location of steel production? Have workers and communities from Pittsburgh, Pennsylvania, to Pittsburg, California, lost jobs because of some irreversible comparative advantage evolving in the world economy? Who are the major actors in this process: American multinationals, American trade policymakers, new entrepreneurs, international financing agencies, or national governments abroad? What influenced the siting of new plants and at what markets are they aimed? What role have changes in consumption, technology, and resources played? What role have the concerted efforts of governments, capital, labor, and communities played? Answering these questions is the task of this study.

THE INTERNATIONALIZATION
OF STEEL PRODUCTION

Until the 1960s the U.S. steel industry maintained control over the U.S. market and contributed nearly 40% of capitalist world production. But symptoms of its relative decline were apparent as early as the mid-1950s. Production in 1955 was 106.2 million tons (mt). Imports contributed a little more than 1% of U.S. consumption. In 1959 total imports exceeded total exports for the first time in the industry's history. Over the next 3 decades the U.S. industry's share of world output was halved (see Table 3.2). Imports in 1988 accounted for 20% of U.S. consumption.

The postwar reconstruction of Western Europe and Japan posed a serious challenge to the U.S. steel industry. As a group, Western European countries increased their output of raw steel by over 70% from 1960 until the end of 1974, the peak production year Organization for Economic Co-operation and Development (OECD, 1985, p. 52). However, from the mid-1960s and through the 1970s hasty state investments in most European countries created massive overcapacity and huge financial deficits. The depressed steel-consuming sectors aggravated the European steel industry crisis (Mény & Wright, 1987, pp. 1–14). As a result, European firms have been forced to reduce production and output has declined by more than 30%.

Perhaps the most dramatic development has been Japan's fivefold increase in production from 1960 to 1980. In 1980 Japan accounted for almost a quarter of the capitalist world's output. Brazil, South Korea, Taiwan, and India have also increased steel production in the postwar period (see Table 3.2).[3] Their combined share of over 2% in 1960 increased to over 13% by 1988, nearly twice the share of all the remaining nonsocialist developing countries.

Dramatic growth in steel trade followed increases in global steel production. The volume of international trade grew from 10% of world steel production at the beginning of the 1950s to nearly 30% by the end of the 1970s (Yachir, 1988, p. 19). By the 1980s the ratio of exports to production of some countries was higher than 30%. Most prominent

TABLE 3.2. Geography of Global Steel Production, 1960–1988 (Percentage Share of Capitalist World Total)

Country	1960	1970	1980	1988
United States	37.36	28.51	22.00	18.77
Brazil	0.95	1.29	3.32	5.10
Western Europe	45.22	38.59	35.04	33.93
India	1.36	1.50	2.06	2.94
Japan	9.18	22.30	24.16	21.88
South Korea	[a]	0.11	1.86	3.96
Taiwan	0.05	0.07	0.92	1.72
Rest of capitalist developing countries	2.13	1.54	5.49	7.18
World capitalist production (mt)	241.06	418.44	461.05	482.95

[a] Negligible.
Source: American Iron and Steel Institute, Annual Statistical Reports, various dates.

TABLE 3.3. Major Exporters of Steel Products to the United States
(% Share of Total Imports)[a]

Country	1964	1970	1980	1988
Canada	10.75	8.27	15.29	15.19
Brazil	b	b	2.95	6.55
Mexico/Argentina	b	b	0.55	4.81
E.E.C.	47.58[c]	34.21	25.08	29.80
Other European Countries	n.a.	8.22	5.53	8.61
Japan	37.99	44.41	38.77	20.54
South Korea	b	b	6.71	6.26
Taiwan	b	b	0.55	1.13
U.S. imports (mt)	5.84	12.12	14.06	18.95

[a]Percentages do not add up to 100 because many countries exporting small quantities of steel are excluded.
[b]Negligible.
[c]Total Western Europe.
Source: Compiled from American Iron and Steel Institute, *Annual Statistical Reports*, various dates.

among these countries have been Japan, South Korea, and Brazil. These three countries along with Canada and the European Economic Community (EEC) are the major suppliers to the U.S. market, and together accounted for nearly 80% of U.S. steel imports in 1988 (see Table 3.3).[4]

DYNAMICS OF THE CHANGING GEOGRAPHY OF STEEL PRODUCTION

Several interrelated factors have influenced the changing geography of steel production. In the 1980s the center of gravity of steelmaking capacity moved away from the older industrialized countries. In the United States the legacy of an oligopolistic structure in the steel industry facilitated significant market control. Furthermore, the nature of financial markets discouraged firms from taking advantage of changing technology. Unchallenged by competition, U.S. firms declined to make large financial commitments for new methods of production and continued to invest in tried-and-true technology. U.S. government policy was inadequate to address the steel industry's investment problem. In the meantime, governments of other countries invested heavily in modern technology for their steel industries and actively promoted their nation's steel industry for economic development. As a result, the gaps in production costs and productivity between U.S. and foreign firms widened. Foreign firms found not only a lucrative direct export market for steel in the United States but also a profitable indirect market through the sale of such steel-using commodities as automobiles and machinery. In the 1980s the U.S. industry was challenged by low-cost, high-quality imports. By that time banks were unwilling to lend for long-term investment, and interest rates were prohibitively high. As a result, the U.S. industry found investments in new technology beyond its reach.

The rapid increase in imports of steel by U.S. steel-using firms weakened many U.S. steel producers. This allowed U.S. competitors to gain and consolidate their foothold in market regions underserved by U.S. producers. As U.S. steel companies abandoned construction of new mills, the U.S. government, at the behest of the industry, reacted to the surge in imports with import quotas. This government–business action stemmed market penetration by foreign firms. It also reinforced a market-control and market-sharing strategy on the part of both domestic and foreign producers. Several important exporters to the U.S. market shifted to high-value exports, and later some of them avoided the quota limits by setting up joint ventures in the United States. The collaborations between U.S. and foreign firms in the steel industry certainly shored up particular markets in the United States and helped the technologically and financially weak U.S. integrated producers to modernize some steel-finishing facilities. However, most of these joint ventures were more of an outcome of the needs of American and Japanese automobile plants sited in the United States for high-quality finished steel. Hence no new steelmaking capacity in locations that are particularly vulnerable to imports has been created. How the erstwhile powerful U.S. steel industry attained its current unenviable status and in what ways the U.S. industry has been restructured are discussed below.

U.S. Industry Strategy and Industrial Structure

Traditionally, most steel plants in major producing countries have been located near iron ore or coal sources, or near centers of steel consumption. Thus in the mid-1800s coal fields in Pennsylvania, Ohio, New York, and New Jersey influenced the siting of major iron works. Similarly, the availability of iron ore and coal around Birmingham, Alabama, served a spatially distinct market (Markusen, 1985, p. 78). The gradual expansion of steel plants to the Great Lakes region in the late 19th century was dictated by the discovery of new ore and coal sites in Minnesota and Michigan and expanding markets in the Chicago region. The emergence of new steelmaking locations was encouraged by the dynamic growth of railroads, manufacture of agricultural machinery, and construction activity accompanying the general population movement westward (Agnew, 1987, pp. 48–49). The Chicago region benefited from this synergistic relation between steel-producing and steel-consuming industries. As production shifted westward, the small iron works in the northeastern states declined in importance.

Despite these changes in the industrial landscape, the spatial expansion of new steel mills was limited. Three factors were responsible. First, the highly fragmented U.S. industry was consolidated after the "merger movement" of the 1890s. In 1901 a series of mergers involving over 160 separate companies resulted in the U.S. Steel Corporation (USS), the world's first billion-dollar firm. U.S. Steel Corporation at that time controlled over 60% of the U.S. market (Edwards, 1979, p. 42).[5] Second, crucible technology suited for small-scale production was replaced with large-scale production technology, thereby limiting the geographical spread of steel plants. Third, the consolidation of the industry with fewer firms and larger production units encouraged collusive pricing schemes, such as the Pittsburgh Plus system in use in the early part of this century.[6] This pricing strategy gave tremendous market power to steel firms and eliminated any advantage that northern plants might have in serving southern or western markets. The few regional centers that did exist, such as Fairfield, Alabama, resulted from a preemptive strategy to limit competition rather than a move to locate production near underserved markets.

Thus neither industry strategies nor technological change since the turn of the century until the early 1960s appreciably altered the geographical location of steelmaking plants in the United States. Pennsylvania remained the most important steel-producing state.[7] In 1910 it produced 51% of national output while Ohio, Illinois, and Indiana together contributed 34% (American Iron and Steel Institute, various dates). By 1930 Pittsburgh, Pennsylvania, and Youngstown, Ohio, together controlled over 42% of total steelmaking capacity (Warren, 1988, p. 243). Despite the massive growth of the auto industry, Detroit did not attract its first major steel mill until 1922 (Markusen, 1985, p. 80).

During the World War II period the U.S. government financed steel plants to aid in the war effort, investing $2 billion in the industry (Scheurman, 1986, p. 47). The industry had strongly resisted this expansion for fear of postwar overcapacity (Tiffany, 1988, pp. 17–18). Most of the investments benefited the existing steelmaking belt, extending from the Northeast to the Midwest. The northeastern region garnered nearly 75% of war-related new capacity due to low construction costs at existing plant sites and the availability of skilled labor. The more-remote and obsolete plants in the Pittsburgh region were not phased out despite underutilization of capacity.[8] Only four major new integrated steel plants were established in nontraditional areas. Two of these were sited in Texas and one each in California and Utah.[9] Some of these were later purchased by existing firms, reinforcing the oligopolistic structure of the U.S. industry.[10] This structure continues to characterize the U.S. steel industry today in which approximately 70% of national production is accounted for by just eight firms (see Table 3.4).[11] The presence of just a few firms discouraged the massive investments required for new plants in the postwar period and focused managerial attention on controlling market shares, policing their oligopolistic partners, and disciplining labor.

The addition of war-related steel-producing capacity in California, Utah, and Texas did not keep pace with growing civilian demand nor were the new mills well suited to serve postwar consumption patterns.[12] For the war effort these plants were designed to produce slabs, plates, and heavy structurals for shipbuilding. In the postwar period these items were less in demand. Moreover, of a total of 43 new open hearth furnaces constructed from 1950 to 1953, Pennsylvania, Ohio, Indiana, and Illinois absorbed 39 of them (Hogan, 1971, p. 1321). The inland location of these mills was unattractive, making delivery of iron and coal difficult. Population and industrial growth in California created heavy demand for steel products which these mills could not meet. In a shortsighted move, private U.S. firms shied away from investing in the West Coast market. U.S. Steel, Bethlehem, and National Steel abandoned postwar plans for constructing new plants in the West Coast region.[13] Only Kaiser Steel had a major facility in California.[14] However, Kaiser failed to make timely investments for modernization which resulted in the plant's quick obsolescence.

Steel Industry Promotion by Foreign Governments

Unlike the limited involvement of the U.S. government in the American steel industry, the Japanese state was actively involved in developing the industry to fulfill national economic development goals. Steel industrial policies were not dictated by short-term profit outlook or by existing comparative advantage. Rather, the anticipated impact of steel on the development of steel-using industries formed the basis of intense state intervention (Shinohara, 1982).[15]

The Japanese government carefully orchestrated the development of a technically efficient steel industry. Production and investment cartels were encouraged and mergers were engineered to exploit economies of scale. At the beginning of this century Japan's first modern facility, the Yawata Iron Works, was established by the government.[16] In 1934 Yawata was merged with the top six mills to form Nippon Steel Company, producing over 95% of the pig iron and nearly 45% of all Japa-

TABLE 3.4. Concentration Ratios of Top U.S. Steel Firms (% of Total U.S. Production)

	1947	1975	1985
Top 2 firms	46.53	37.64	33.76
Top 4 firms	61.15	52.55	51.64
Top 8 firms	77.12	73.63	68.96
U.S. total (mt)	82.77	105.82	80.10

Sources: Metal Statistics, various dates; U.S. Federal Trade Commission, 1948, p. 14, for 1947 data.

nese steel products (Yamazawa, 1990, pp. 87–92). The Japanese finance ministry held 82% of its shares (Yamazawa, 1990, p. 91). This control was retained until the end of World War II (Kaplan, 1972, pp. 138–139), after which ownership passed to private hands. In 1970 it was reformed into Nippon Steel Corporation (NSC), today the largest steel firm in the world. In 1987 the top six Japanese firms produced 71% of the nation's output.[17]

In Canada also there has been a close interaction between Canadian steel-producing companies and the state (Masi, 1991, pp. 197–198), ultimately creating a highly profitable industry (Hogan, 1991, p. 34). Until the late 1970s business–government consensus in Canada allowed the expansion of modern steelmaking capacity, reducing Canada's import dependence. Imports in 1958 stood at 25% of consumption. By 1981 this had declined to 16% (Barnett & Schorsch, 1983, p. 218). During the same period Canada's exports of steel increased from 9.8% to 24% of domestic shipments. With increases in modern steelmaking capacity since the 1970s, Canada became a net exporter. A large share of these exports is being directed to U.S. markets.

Since the 1950s informal institutional linkages between the Canadian state and steel companies has forged a policy consensus regarding the steel industry in Canada. The government recognized Canada's small market and the importance of high-capacity utilization to maintain competitiveness. Hence the government promoted, and the industry accepted, product specialization to capture the benefits of economies of scale. The government flexibly interpreted its antitrust laws and facilitated market-sharing arrangements among Canadian producers (Masi, 1991, p. 197). Trade laws, however, were strictly applied whenever imports posed a serious threat. Other policy instruments included favorable tax policies (quick depreciation schedules), state investments in the energy sector, high tariffs, and a cap on wages (Masi, 1991, pp. 191,

197–198). Today Canada has four firms with integrated steelmaking mills. The industry is highly concentrated, with Stelco, the largest producer, accounting for nearly a third of Canada's steel production (U.S. International Trade Commission, 1988b, p. 6-4). The top three firms together account for about 90% of national hot rolling capacity (U.S. International Trade Commission, 1988b, p. 6-2). Sidbec-Dosco, the fourth-largest steel firm, however, has been a loss-maker for many years. Since the late 1960s Sidbec in Quebec and Sysco in Nova Scotia have been owned by provincial governments. The government of Quebec has been subsidizing the losses of Sidbec for several years.

The EEC as a whole also emerged as a major producer of steel in the world economy. Similar to the Japanese government, EEC member governments viewed their industry as strategic for sustaining well-paying jobs. However, the rapid postwar reconstruction and large-scale, often uncoordinated, investments based on optimistic steel demand projections created massive steel capacity in the region (Ballance, 1987, pp. 216–217). By the early 1980s the EEC's steel industry, despite significant government ownership and subsidies, confronted problems similar to that of the United States: excess capacity, downward pressure on prices, obsolete facilities, secular decline in demand, high transportation and input costs, and increased competition from new low-cost producers.[18] Mounting losses, indebtedness, and rising interest payments in almost every steel-producing EEC country called for huge state subsidies (Mény & Wright, 1987, pp. 17–23).

The ensuing steel crisis reinforced the traditional involvement of the state in each member country. Despite major layoffs and labor concessions, restructuring was slow and politically difficult to sustain. This was especially true for state-owned firms. Many European firms were compelled to export at prices below cost of production. A large share of exports was directed to the U.S. market, a strategy that prompted the U.S. government to limit such exports. Meanwhile, European governments also limited Japanese exports to the EEC through its own quota systems, and firms both private and state-owned continued to seek state financial assistance. Consequently, the EEC attempted to eliminate some of its excess capacity through production and market-sharing arrangements, mergers, privatization, and plant shutdowns, among other actions (Hogan, 1991, pp. 51–71).

While the degree and nature of state intervention varied significantly among member states, most took an active role in their industry, separately as well as in conjunction with the European Commission on Steel and Coal (ECSC). The French government has been the most interventionist. France, through its 5-year indicative plans, systematically established a national steel industry, often with state-sponsored mergers. Since the mid-1960s, through successive plans, the French state has established significant steelmaking capacity. This ultimately contributed to European overcapacity and their financial difficulties of the 1970s. Aiming to restructure the industry and stem the financial hemorrhaging, in 1981 the French government nationalized the steel industry and in 1988 merged two firms, Usinor and Sacilor.[19] This entity accounted for over 90% of French steel production and ranked second in the world after Nippon Steel Corporation of Japan.

In contrast to France, the postwar history of state intervention in West Germany has been limited. There was very little government funding for the industry prior to 1981. However, like its European counterparts, West Germany was also saddled with excess capacity. Inland location of mills, high costs of transportation and coal, and the rising deutsche mark created severe problems for the industry. The reorganization and consolidation of the industry became an economic and political necessity, making the West German state bear a significant portion of the social costs of restructuring and retrenchment (U.S. International Trade Commission, 1988b, pp. 7-18–7-19). Most other steel-producing EEC members confronted similar problems and called for state intervention. European governments assisted the restructuring of the industry through state ownership, forced mergers, infusion of investment capital, output control, and pricing decisions. However, aggressive exports remained the pillar for maintaining capacity utilization, revealing the vulnerabilities associated with excess capacity.

The governments of Brazil, India, and South Korea have gone beyond Japan's strategy by monopolizing a large share of their national steel production capacity. In the 1920s Brazil's heavy reliance on imported steel and on the foreign-owned and powerful steel firm of Belgo Mineira paved the way for the military-dominated minister of war to establish a large integrated mill. The National Steel Company (CSN) was set up in the early 1940s. To date, the Brazilian government has constructed five integrated mills, representing over 60% of national crude steel output.

After gaining independence in 1947, the newly constituted "nationalist" Indian government effectively demarcated the boundaries of industrial activities between the state and private capital. All new capacity in the iron and steel industry was reserved for the state. The government of India embarked on its heavy industrialization program by constructing three steel plants, accounting for about 70% of output by the early 1970s.

In South Korea, building a world-class steel industry was a major objective of President Park Chung Hee who came to power through a military coup in 1961. The "Steel Industry Promotion Law" passed in

1970 channeled relatively scarce capital resources to South Korea's steel industry. Government targeting ultimately created the highly successful Pohang Iron and Steel Company (POSCO), one of the world's largest steel firms. Low prices for electricity, discounted costs for rail transport, and limits on steel imports assisted in the completion of South Korea's first integrated plant at Pohang.[20]

These so-called developing countries, which by definition are capital-scarce, are today's emerging producers. Despite the absence of any natural comparative advantage in steel production, the governments in these countries have aggressively targeted the steel industry to fulfill economic development goals. Despite the enormous financial and technological requirements of steelmaking, governments in these countries have mobilized resources that even long-established private firms in the United States find difficult to raise. In the United States, in contrast, short-term profit considerations and high investment requirements have made new plants unattractive, especially given anticipated low rates of return on new steel projects. Foreign governments, on the other hand, pooled investment resources from steel corporations, multinational banks, and nongovernmental international lending agencies. These loans were tied to technology acquisition and often underwritten by developed countries.[21] Finding U.S. firms unwilling to invest in their operations in the 1970s, the top six Japanese firms secured nearly $1.5 billion in loans from more than a dozen U.S. banks, several of them Pittsburgh-based (Shapiro & Volk, 1979, p. 15). Major Japanese and West European companies, financial institutions, and their corresponding governments provided both capital and knowhow for the construction of new steel mills in Brazil, India, and South Korea.[22]

This government involvement commonly results in state monopolies in developing countries. Typically state enterprises control over 60% of a country's domestic production. In 1986 five state-owned mills produced 62% of Brazil's total steel output (Instituto Brasileiro de Siderúrgica, 1987, p. 1-10). South Korea's two government-owned integrated mills produced nearly 80% of that country's annual steel output. Government-owned China Steel produces nearly 70% of Taiwan's output.

Governments monopolize this industry because of its strategic importance. As a result, foreign equity participation in steel plants around the world is marginal, as states have refused to hand over management or ownership control to foreign enterprises. In addition, firms from industrialized countries have been reluctant to build new mills in foreign countries because of the high investment requirement. Also, building a new facility abroad would then undermine their exports to those countries from their original mills. U.S. Steel's participation in the 1930s in Brazil's first integrated steel mill failed because USS did not want to relinquish a growing export market and undermine its own plants in the United States (Baer, 1969, pp. 72–75). Instead it sought to expand its ore holdings in Brazil.[23] Much later, in India, U.S. Steel insisted on the management of the would-be Bokaro plant for at least 10 years. This was unacceptable to the government of India and the project was then implemented by the Soviet Union (Krishna Moorty, 1984).

Changes in Steelmaking Technology

The general trend in postwar steelmaking technology has favored very large-scale integrated plants built from scratch at coastal sites. An integrated plant, now the established state of the art, uses both a blast furnace (BF) and a basic oxygen furnace (BOF). Older technology depended on a combination of a smaller BF and an open hearth (OH) furnace. In most cases continuous casters (CC) are also used.[24] Given the very high minimum efficient scale of integrated steel plants, generally ranging anywhere from 2 mt to greater than 10 mt of annual capacity, greenfield investments are correspondingly high, from $2 billion to $15 billion after completion (see Table 3.5). Not a single integrated greenfield plant is currently being constructed or even contemplated either in the United States or in other advanced capitalist countries. However, a few newly industrialized countries are pursuing an expansion of capacity in new integrated steel mills (see Table 3.6).

The basic oxygen furnace was an Austrian innovation, first developed and adopted in 1950 by Voest-Alpine. In North America, Dofasco,

TABLE 3.5. Investment Costs for Integrated Steel Plants[a]

Plant, country	Capacity (mt)	Total cost[b] ($billion)	Year of estimate
Kwangyang, South Korea	5.4	6.113	1983
Tubarâo, Brazil	3.0	3.000	1988
Açominas, Brazil	2.0	6.100	1988
Vishakapatnam, India	1.2	3.600	1986
Trengganu, Malaysia	2.5	3.200	1990[c]

[a]The plants presented in Table 3.5 do not account for future expansions.
[b]Total construction costs, among others, vary with levels of infrastructure availability, technology adopted, scale of operations, product mix, foreign exchange component and interest rates, project delays, construction wages, and graft (see D'Costa, 1989, pp. 45–50).
[c]Estimated investment costs.
Sources: Plant visits at Kwangyang, South Korea, October 1987, and at Açominas, Brazil, December 1987; personal communication from Tubarâo; United Nations Industrial Development Organization, 1986; *Metal Bulletin*, 10 May 1990, p. 31.

TABLE 3.6. Major New Integrated Plants: 1985–1995 (Actual and Potential Capacity after Planned Expansion)

Plant	Country	Current capacity	Technology[a]	Potential capacity
Açominas	Brazil	2.0 mt	BF/BOF	10.0 mt
Ajaokuta	Nigeria	1.3 mt	BF/BOF	n.a
Vishakapatnam	India	1.2 mt	BF/BOF/CC	4.0 mt[b]
Kwangyang	South Korea	8.1 mt	BF/BOF/CC	11.4 mt

[a]BF = Blast Furnace, BOF = Basic Oxygen Furnace, CC = Continuous Caster.
[b]At the end of 1995.
Source: Paine Webber Inc. (1987), p. 26, and field research in India, Brazil, and South Korea, June–December 1987.

a Canadian firm, was first to install the new technology (Masi, 1991, p. 191). In the United States, the small firm of McLouth was the first to put the BOF into commercial application. Only since the mid-1960s have the large integrated firms in the United States begun to adopt the most recent steelmaking technology (Adams & Mueller, 1990, p. 89). However, it was Japan that took the lead in adopting the new technology in constructing greenfield plants on a large scale. Other countries such as South Korea and Brazil followed suit. The adoption of BOF technology was already biased toward increasing scale of operations. As Japanese firms wanted to maintain market shares, each firm found it in its own interest to adopt the most modern BOF technology and the largest blast furnaces, resulting in a highly efficient industry.

In the 1950s, while Japan opted for the innovative BOF technology, the U.S. steel industry chose to invest in marginal improvements on a proven but increasingly obsolete OH system. By 1960 the BOF rendered the OH furnaces obsolete. In that year the share of Japanese output produced in BOF was 11.9% while that of the United States was only 3.4% (Barnett & Schorsch, 1983, p. 55). For the EEC (nine members) and Canada, their respective BOF shares were 1.6% and 28.1%. The U.S. industry reacted to increased competition from overseas firms by investing $16.5 billion during the period 1961–1970 in modern equipment. Open hearths were replaced with basic oxygen furnaces and continuous hot strip mills were added (Barnett & Schorsch, 1983, p. 53). However, by 1981, after significant expansion in steel capacity, BOF shares stood as the following: United States: 60.6%; Japan: 75.2%; EEC (nine members): 75.1%; and Canada: 58.6% (Barnett & Schorsch, 1983, p. 55). In most of these countries most of the remaining output was produced by electric furnaces.[25] The recent increase in the proportion of U.S. output using BOF technology was due more to the phasing out of

OH plants than to any absolute increase in BOF capacity. Similarly, West Germany since 1979 has phased out OH capacity, with a total reduction of capacity of nearly 47%. Today 80% of West German steel is made by the BOF process.

South Korea and Brazil also adopted the BOF rapidly. Their respective proportions of output using BOF technology in 1987 were 67.9% and 75.2%. In 1960 the United States and Japan used continuous casting for 4% and 11% of their respective output. By 1987 these shares stood at 59% and 93%. Brazil and South Korea each had approximately 33% of total output continuously cast in 1980. At the end of 1987 their corresponding shares were 45.5% and 83.5%. France, from a mere 13% in 1975, raised its rate of continuous casting to nearly 90% by 1986. West Germany and other major EEC steel-producing countries also have very high rates of continuous casting. EEC firms, despite experiencing problems, have been relatively quick to introduce new technologies and today along with the Japanese remain at the forefront of steel technology. Even in the mid-1980s Japan and the EEC had higher levels of investment spending than the United States (U.S. International Trade Commission, 1990, p. 51). More importantly, U.S. firms have generally lagged behind other countries in computerization and process control.[26]

One effect of the uneven adoption of modern technology has been different rates of productivity growth.[27] Using more advanced technology, Japan surpassed U.S. productivity rates in steel production, while South Korea narrowed the gap. In 1980 it took 9.8 personhours to produce a ton of steel in the United States. In Japan it took 7.1 personhours, and in South Korea 10.3 personhours. By 1986 Japan was the most efficient producer, taking 6.0 personhours to produce a ton of steel. In the United States it took 6.4 personhours, and in South Korea 7.4 personhours.[28]

These figures show that the percentage increase in physical productivity for the United States has been the highest and more recently U.S. physical productivity appears to have exceeded the Japanese (see *New York Times*, March 31, 1992; U.S. International Trade Commission, 1990, p. 52). However, productivity gains in the United States in the 1980s have come about through modernization of selected facilities and primarily by phasing out old and marginal capacity. The narrowing of productivity between Japan and the United States is also due to different product mixes and operating rates. Japan, with larger and newer capacity than the United States, has been facing the problem of excess capacity, making high-capacity utilization difficult. The focus of Japanese companies on high value-added products, such as cold-rolled and coated sheets in greater quantities than their U.S. counterparts, is another contributing factor for the narrowing of the productivity gap. In

1989 the United States produced about 15 mt of such products (U.S. International Trade Commission, 1990, p. 4), whereas Japan produced nearly 20 mt (Japan Iron and Steel Federation, 1991, p. 6). The operating rates for the United States and Japan were 95% and 85%, respectively (U.S. International Trade Commission, 1990, p. 52).

A departure from large-scale integrated technology has been the expansion of the minimill segment of the steel industry. A minimill recycles steel scrap rather than making it from scratch using iron ore and coal. Since 1960 minimill capacity in the United States has increased sevenfold, to about 28% of U.S. crude steel production (calculated from U.S. International Trade Commission, 1990, p. 4). Minimills have three basic advantages over integrated mills. First, minimills allow small-scale operation, hence greater flexibility. Second, these mills require much lower capital investment per ton of capacity. Third, minimill operators have exhibited adaptability to new technologies (Acs, 1984, pp. 98–104; Barnett & Crandall, 1986; Barnett & Schorsch, 1983, pp. 83–101). However, minimills have one serious drawback: they are not generally equipped to produce most flat products. An additional disadvantage of minimill production is that it is dependent on the scrap generated by integrated production. The integrated production process yields prime scrap as a by-product. As the technology for integrated production is improved, home scrap generation is reduced, and as ingot casting is replaced with continuous casting, prime scrap availability declines as well. Morever, the price of scrap is volatile.

The recent experience of minimills indicates a definitive shift in steel production away from the industrial heartland. As of 1987 half a dozen southern states had 42% of national minimill capacity. Texas and South Carolina had the largest shares with 19 and 7%, respectively, whereas seven states, typically considered to be industrial states, accounted for only a quarter of total minimill capacity. More recently Arkansas, southern Indiana, and South Carolina have emerged as important minimill sites using state-of-the-art technology. However, the concentration of key inputs such as scrap and electric power in urban areas is likely to retard further decentralization of steel capacity in the United States. Furthermore, markets for minimill products are uncertain. In traditional long products, typical minimill products, there is already excess capacity, while the demand growth for flat-rolled products, produced by a few innovative minimill firms, may not materialize in the medium term (Hogan, 1991, pp. 33–34).

In the postwar period dramatic changes in steelmaking technology and different rates of adoption contributed to the changing pattern of global steel production. In the absence of foreign competition the U.S. industry chose a conservative technology strategy, thus avoiding the massive investments required for modern large-scale plants. This strategy ultimately resulted in technological obsolescence with serious consequences for productivity. Japanese firms, as well as companies from developing countries, often with the aid of their government, invested in modern greenfield plants. In addition to being compatible with national long-term economic development goals, these investments also created a highly productive steel industry.

U.S. Market Penetration by Foreign Producers

The technological conservatism of U.S. producers combined with aggressive expansion by foreign firms introduced unprecedented competition in the U.S. market. This competition was especially keen in the West Coast region, where growing demand for high-quality steel products could not be met efficiently by mills located in the traditional industrial belt because transportation across the Rockies was too expensive.[29] National consumption increased by 68% from 1960 to 1973. National consumption peaked in 1973, thereafter declining by over 30%.[30] The western market, however, continued to expand. California accounted for approximately 75% of the western states' demand (Warren, 1988, p. 275). For the period from 1983 to 1988 the average consumption in the western states was 10% higher than in 1970, while the corresponding national figure had dropped by almost 34% (U.S. International Trade Commission, 1989b, 4-1).[31]

Nationally, imports of steel increased by over 200% from 1959 to 1970, and the western region absorbed a disproportionate share of that increase. During the same period import penetration (imports as a share of apparent consumption) for the United States as a whole increased from 6% to over 14%. However, for the western region the increase was far greater, jumping from 12% to 28%. Import penetration in the western region peaked in 1984. It has since declined but remains above the national average. Almost one-half of the region's steel demand is met by U.S. suppliers in the East and by imports (U.S. International Trade Commission, 1989b, p. 4-1). From 1959 to 1970 Japan's share of imports in this region increased from 39% to 83%. In 1970 Japan supplied 21% of the West Coast market (Hogan, 1971, p. 1471). By 1988 the Japanese share of this market fell to about 13%, comprising about 30% of total imports to the western region (U.S. International Trade Commission, 1989b, p. 3-1, p. D4).

These U.S. imports were surplus output arising from global expansion of steelmaking capacity. From 1960 to 1980 Japanese steelmaking capacity increased by 462%, while domestic consumption more than tripled.[32] The excess was directed to the underserved U.S. West Coast market. Surplus output from other new producers also found a market in the United States. This surplus output permitted higher rates of utilization of plant capacity. Given the large scale of operations, the higher the utilization of plant capacity, the lower the cost per unit. For example, South Korea in the 1980s operated its coastal mills in Pohang and Kwangyang at or near 100% utilization rates, thereby enabling it to meet the cost-price challenge.[33] Despite higher energy and materials costs in East Asia, lower wage rates and high-capacity utilization of new plants allowed Japan and South Korea to further consolidate their competitive position in the U.S. market.[34] Similarly, the large U.S. market was a natural outlet for European overcapacity, estimated at 50 mt in 1981 (Howell, Noellert, Kreier, & Wolff, 1988, pp. 55–57).

While high-capacity utilization, high productivity, and favorable wage rates in several countries facilitated the direct export of steel products, the production of low-cost steel in these countries has also allowed critical segments of their domestic manufacturing industries to compete successfully in the world market. Following Japan's lead, South Korea and Brazil have specialized in the production of ships, automobiles, machinery, and appliances. These steel-intensive products now compete with these same goods produced by U.S. industry. Net indirect imports amounted to –3.0 mt in 1980 and 4.2 mt in 1984. By 1986 they had risen to 9.3 mt (*Iron Age*, 1988, p. 28). Motor vehicles, stampings, and parts and accessories comprised 62% of this total. By shifting their strategy from direct exports of steel to indirect exports, overseas producers have exposed other U.S. industries to import penetration. Thus steel-consuming industries in the United States, such as transportation and consumer durables, have confronted increased international competition, depressing the demand for steel. As steel plants were shut down U.S. self-sufficiency in steel was further eroded.

During the 1980s U.S. dependence on steel imports of quality semi-finished products also increased considerably, jumping more than five-fold. Imports of other intermediate goods—pipes and tubes, galvanized sheets and strips, and other coated products—were also significant (see Table 3.7).[35] In 1988 the United States imported nearly 2 million tons of galvanized and over 4 million tons of hot and cold rolled sheets/strips, suggesting the technological weakness of U.S. producers.[36] These products are largely consumed by the energy, automobile, appliance, and other manufacturing industries.

Exports by foreign producers to the United States have also been strengthened by the dramatic changes in bulk transportation and coastal siting of plants. Coastal locations of steel mills in Japan, South Korea, Taiwan, and Brazil allow imports of high-volume and relatively low-cost raw materials from far-flung sources and exports of finished products to distant markets. As a result, the cost of shipping products from

TABLE 3.7. U.S. Imports of Iron and Steel Products (Percentage Share of Total Steel Imports)

	Semifinished	Plates	Pipes & tubes	Sheets & strips[a]
1979	1.96	11.32	16.67	39.11
1983	4.81	6.46	16.76	41.05
1988	13.62	10.44	15.71	32.39

[a]Includes HR/CR, galvanized, and other metallic coated products.
Source: American Iron and Steel Institute, *Annual Statistical Reports*, various dates.

one coast to another *within* the United States is higher than that *between* East Asia and the West Coast of the United States.[37]

Foreign producers prefer to ship products and choose destinations that minimize the share of transportation costs to total landed costs. This lowers costs of high-grade steel products and intensifies import penetration in certain U.S. regional markets. In 1986 both South Korea and Japan shipped 47% of their U.S. exports to the West Coast, with the average shipping cost varying between 7 and 8% of total costs.[38] Brazil shipped a large fraction of its products to the East Coast of the United States, with shipping costs averaging 6% of total costs.

As a development strategy, many developing countries use their export revenues to pay for raw material and technology imports, finance economic development, and repay foreign debts. Export markets are very attractive, especially when there are large foreign debts to service. One example is South Korea. Although the South Korean government has large foreign debts, its steel industry has performed extremely well and South Korea's creditworthiness is excellent. It has reduced its per capita foreign debt and is soon expected to become a net *creditor* nation.[39] In part this has been made possible by the establishment of the steel industry in South Korea which has acted as an anchor for other metalworking industries, such as shipbuilding, machinery, automobiles, and appliances. The expanding internal market and an aggressive export drive in steel and steel-using products have enabled the South Korean steel industry to earn foreign exchange and finance national economic development.

This situation sharply contrasts with Brazil's unresolved debt crisis and the inability of the Brazilian steel industry to generate adequate internal funds. Brazil has a foreign debt of more than $110 billion, $12 billion of which is owed by the state steel enterprise (SIDERBRAS). To create niches in the world steel market Brazil has sought external financing.[40] The lackluster performance of SIDERBRAS has been compounded by inefficiency, domestic economic crisis, and the power exercised by transnational auto enterprises. These foreign firms successfully kept domestic steel prices low, apparently 40–45% below mills' production costs, and lower than world prices (personal interviews with SIDERBRAS staff, Brasilia, December 1987).[41] The resulting huge losses of the state enterprise have merely aggravated the vicious debt cycle, making foreign steel markets the natural outlet.

Just as Japanese steel products entered the West Coast market, Canadian exports made their way into the Great Lakes region, despite Canada's total steel output and exports being only a small fraction of Japan's. However, the factors conditioning Canada's exports to a regional market in the United States were qualitatively different from that of Japan's exports to the West Coast market. Whereas Japanese firms maximized production and capacity utilization to reap the advantages of economies of scale, the Canadian firms attained high-capacity utilization by specializing in a few products (Barnett & Schorsch, 1983, p. 262). Unlike the Japanese, Canadian companies did not rely on an aggressive export strategy. Instead they used the export markets only when domestic demand fell. By balancing steelmaking-capacity expansion with the growth in markets, Canadian firms were able to attain international cost competitiveness.

However, the addition of new capacity during economic slowdowns created the burden of excess capacity (Barnett & Schorsch, 1983, p. 225), making nearby U.S. markets natural targets. There are several interrelated reasons for this outcome. First, four major steel plants are sited in Ontario, with three in the southern part of the province, making U.S. markets in the Great Lakes area easily accessible. Second, the proximity of the U.S. market has allowed Canadian producers to treat non–U.S. markets as less important, making the U.S. market particularly vulnerable to Canadian exports during times of recession. Third, a significant portion of Canadian output is destined for the automobile sector in Canada and the United States. Canadian steel exports to the United States are often processed further in the United States, reexported back to Canada, and finally exported out of Canada to the United States (Masi, 1991, pp. 194–195). Fourth, the decline in the Canadian dollar and relatively low labor costs in Canada make Canadian steel products competitive in the U.S. market. Fifth, the liberal trade relations between the United States and Canada facilitates interregional trade that reinforces Canada's competitive advantage vis-à-vis the United States.

U.S. Government Policy

Most governments are sensitive to steep increases in their imports. Historically, the threat of imports has been countered by industry protection, a worldwide practice that is not particularly well understood nor appreciated by the American public and policymakers. To counter the surge in imports and alleged unfair trading practices of the late 1960s, the U.S. government in alliance with major steel companies imposed Voluntary Restraint Agreements (VRAs) beginning in 1969. The VRAs, or import quotas, are quantitative limits placed on steel imports. Later, VRAs included automobile imports. They were designed specifically to provide U.S. firms some respite from foreign competition. VRAs are negotiated bilaterally on a country-by-country and product-by-product basis between the U.S. executive branch and governments of exporting countries. In 1977, under the Carter administration, another policy to protect the domestic steel producers was introduced. The Trigger Price Mechanism (TPM) established a minimum floor price for imports.[42] This policy was short-lived.

The government through the VRAs and the TPM provided some respite to the steel industry from foreign competition. By limiting imports, the government allowed domestic producers to generate additional revenues. The government expected the industry to utilize these additional resources for modernization. The principal effect of such protectionist policies was an increase in domestic steel prices. The initial set of VRAs was effective from 1969 until 1974. During this period prices of U.S. steel products rose dramatically. In the period preceding the VRAs, from 1960 to 1968, steel price increases averaged a mere 0.45% a year, whereas in the first 4 years of the VRAs prices increased by nearly 7% a year (Adams & Mueller, 1990, p. 85). Trade restrictions allowed foreign firms to export high value-added products. For example, in 1968 the value of 18 mt of total imports into the United States was $1.976 billion, whereas in 1970 the value was $1.967 billion for 13.4 mt (Hogan, 1991, p. 144).

Similarly, the TPM, effective from 1978 to 1982, allowed U.S. steel makers to raise their prices. As a result many steel consumers were forced to look for foreign sources of steel. During the TPM period indirect imports of steel also increased. The Reagan administration imposed similar quotas. During this period U.S. price increases were moderated by a depressed economy, imports, and competition from minimills. However, with many plants closed market shortages of several steel products surfaced. Because blast furnace technology in integrated steel production is well suited to the production of quality semifinished steel products, such as slabs, the phasing out of all integrated steelmaking capacity on the West Coast created supply bottlenecks. By 1988 shortages of semifinished steel products were acute in the West Coast region. Between 1983 and 1988 the western region's share of U.S. imports of semifinished steel doubled from 15% to 32% (U.S. International Trade Commission, 1989b, p. 5-2).

For free trade advocates, particularly U.S. multinational corporations, the VRAs have the advantage of protecting specific industrial sectors without resorting to protectionist legislation. However, as a policy to reduce imports and thereby aid the U.S. steel industry, the VRAs have definite shortcomings. The periodic extension of VRAs has helped foreign firms export higher grade steel products to the United States because the agreements are based on tonnage, not value. Thus, in dollar terms, imports have increased despite recent declines in tonnage. Effectively, the VRAs constitute a market-sharing arrangement.

Ironically, the limits have backfired for steel companies, especially those on the West Coast, that buy semifinished steel. As most foreign producers attempt to meet their domestic demand first, some are unable to meet their quota, introducing occasional scarcities of critical steel products in the United States. Steady supplies therefore are not always assured. As a result, U.S. steel companies recently demanded that imports of semifinished products be increased above the quotas.[43]

An interesting outcome of the VRAs in the automobile sector, and certainly a welcome change for the steel industry, has been foreign participation in U.S. steel firms. Both U.S. and Japanese automakers in the United States could not rely on the low quality of steel produced by existing U.S. firms. Given local content requirements, several U.S. and Japanese companies established joint ventures to produce high-quality coated sheets for the automotive segment. Selective investments with Japanese technology and finance for steel rolling were made in the United States (personal interview with Nippon Steel staff, Tokyo, October 1987; see also Table 3.8 below). Unlike the auto industry, however, Japanese investments in the U.S. steel industry tend to be made jointly with existing U.S. big steel firms and tend to reinforce existing locations. Nippon Kokan of Japan is the only foreign steel company that has a majority stake in the integrated firm of National Intergroup. This is likely to be a test case for a foreign company modernizing *steelmaking* facilities in the United States, revamping of which will entail significant investments in environmental cleanup.[44] While the VRAs in general may have encouraged selective modernization and stemmed the decline of the U.S. steel industry into total collapse, in effect, the VRAs have not addressed the U.S. industry's two main problems: lack of investment for upgrading/modernizing crude steel production and inappropriate plant siting.

U.S. Industry Rationalization and the Strategies of Foreign Firms

Since the late 1970s U.S. firms operating integrated plants have faced increased competition from foreign producers and minimills in non-flat-rolled products. As a result, these firms have abandoned major invest-

TABLE 3.8. Major Foreign Participation in U.S. Steel Companies

U.S. firms	Partnerships	% of Ownership
California Steel Industries (California)	CVRD, Brazil	50
	Kawasaki, Japan	50
USS-POSCO (Pittsburg, California)	POSCO, Korea	50
	U.S. Steel, United States	50
National Intergroup	National, United States	40
	Nippon Kokan, Japan	60
Wheeling-Pitt (Steubenville, Ohio)[a]	Wheeling-Pitt, United States	90
	Nisshin Steel, Japan	10
Inland Steel, Indiana (cold reduction mill)[b]	Inland Steel, United States	60[c]
	Nippon Steel, Japan	40
LTV Steel (continuous electrolytic galvanizing line, Indiana Harbor plant)	LTV Steel, United States	60[c]
	Sumitomo Metals, Japan	40
Armco Steel (Middletown, Ohio, and Ashland, Kentucky)[d]	Armco, Inc., United States	55
	Kawasaki Steel, Japan	45
U.S. Steel (Lorain, Ohio)	U.S. Steel, United States	50[c]
	Kobe Steel, Japan	50

[a]Nisshin Steel of Japan also owns two-thirds of a coating line.
[b]Nippon Steel owns 14% of Inland Steel as a whole.
[c]A second venture between the same companies with equal shares in specific steel finishing facilities.
[d]Kawasaki's 45% represents Armco's carbon steel facilities at Middletown, Ohio, and Ashland, Kentucky.
Sources: U.S. International Trade Commission, 1988b, pp. 11-13, 1990, pp. 30–32 and Appendix G; personal interviews in Tokyo, October 1987, December 1991; *New York Times*, 22 November 1988, 21 December 1989; *Metal Bulletin*, 5 June 1989, p. 26; Adams & Mueller, 1990, p. 78; Hogan, 1991, pp. 11–48.

ments, shut down several mills, and diversified into nonsteel activities. In addition, U.S. firms sought out foreign technology and capital to modernize their plants. However, these efforts resulted in piecemeal modernization, creating serious equipment imbalances in many U.S. integrated plants, making the U.S. industry as a whole technologically deficient. In addition, U.S. firms have lost their competitive advantage in steel engineering services.[45] Their lack of technological capacity to undertake the production of high value-added products has opened the door to foreign firms and increased their stake in the U.S. industry.

The effects of an aging less-than-optimally sited capacity, coupled with the rationalization strategy of U.S. firms under competitive pressure, and the expansion strategies of foreign governments bent on economic development, can clearly be seen in the West Coast region. Consider the joint venture between USS and POSCO of South Korea. U.S. Steel owns rolling mills in Pittsburg, California, and once owned the slab-producing Geneva unit in Utah, one of the World War II–built inland mills. Both are technologically obsolete. USS found the cost of transporting hot rolled bands from Utah to Pittsburg prohibitive. Just prior to the shutdown of the Geneva Works U.S. Steel negotiated with POSCO for the supply of hot bands (a semifinished product) from South Korea for the Pittsburg Works in California, effectively replacing the Geneva plant. POSCO and USS have each contributed $150 million to get the aging Pittsburg plant operating again. In a second example, Kaiser Steel's Fontana Works in California, another of the World War II newcomers, also became obsolete and was purchased by Kawasaki Steel of Japan and CVRD, the state mineral corporation of Brazil, and renamed California Steel Industries. Because integrated production could not be undertaken at this plant, the new owners imported slabs from Brazil. Brazil was producing these slabs at its modern Tubarâo plant, in part financed by Japan's private Kawasaki Steel and Italy's state-owned Finsider Group. So by 1988 all integrated capacity on the West Coast had ceased to exist, and the only steel produced there came from multinational joint ventures dependent on imported semifinished steel.

The new partnerships avoided expensive outlays for steel production by relying on the production capacity of aspiring states such as South Korea and Brazil. Unable to secure loans from domestic sources and lacking modern technological knowhow, U.S. firms sought foreign capital and technical assistance from the Japanese for modern steel-finishing facilities. Now major Japanese firms, POSCO, and the Brazilian state have gained a foothold in the quasi-protected U.S. market, in alliance with domestic producers (see Table 3.8). These alliances in finishing steel facilities in lieu of direct imports of semifinished steel certainly increase local content. However, value-added and investment per ton are higher for steelmaking than for steel finishing. Paradoxically, this change in the international division of labor within the steel industry compels debt-ridden and capital-scarce countries, such as Brazil, to focus on the capital-intensive part of steel production while subsidizing U.S. consumption.

The new joint arrangements reflect the inability of U.S. firms to supply quality steel to the growing Japanese auto sector in the United States, their lack of liquid capital, and the close relationship between U.S.-based Japanese steel and auto plants. Almost all of these joint ventures involve the finishing of steel and its conversion to galvanized and other coated sheets. These coated products are primarily destined for the automobile industry, and specifically for the Japanese-owned auto industry in the

United States (personal interview with Japan Iron and Steel Federation [JISF] official, Tokyo, December 1991). The 1989 U.S. Steel's joint venture with Japan's Kobe Steel has been specifically targeted for these Japanese auto plants. A second joint venture between USS and Kobe Steel was reportedly set into motion by Toyota and Honda of America (U.S. International Trade Commission, 1990, p. 32). It has been estimated that in the next few years 28% of U.S.–based auto production will be in the hands of foreign firms (*Metal Bulletin*, 5 June 1989, p. 26).

On a smaller scale, the French government-owned steel company Usinor-Sacilor, through its subsidiary Unimetal, is planning a joint venture with Georgetown Steel Corporation. Georgetown, a minimill, produces bars and wire rods. The venture will supply high-quality wire used in the production of tires. The underlying motive for Usinor-Sacilor is to hold on to its traditional clients in the United States, French-owned Michelin and Bekaert (U.S. International Trade Commission, 1990, p. 31).

The joint ventures demonstrate the importance of the strong positive relationship between steel and steel-using industries and manufacturing in general as evident from the large number of Japanese-owned auto parts and accessories suppliers (see Howes, Chapter 2, this volume). The joint ventures in the area of steel finishing have certainly contributed to local jobs and income and injected desperately needed investments and technology at a critical juncture (U.S. International Trade Commission, 1990, pp. 12, 30–32). The presence of large Japanese financial institutions in the United States adds to the impetus for new industrial joint ventures. However, most Japanese investments in the steel industry have been confined to brownfield sites, geared toward finishing mills. They have not altered the dispersion of steel industry capacity in any fundamental way. Nor have they addressed production capability for high-quality semifinished slabs. In the absence of a coherent industrial policy for steel-consuming industries and in the event of a downward turn in vehicle production, investments in finishing facilities could lead to future excess capacity.

INTERNATIONALIZATION AND THE IMPACT ON U.S. LABOR

Since the creation of the United Steel Workers of America (USWA) in 1936, American labor has made substantial gains in wages and benefits. The USWA has also effectively negotiated work rules and limits on subcontracting. In the 1980s, however, international competition and the lack of major investments by U.S. firms put American workers on the defensive (Moody, 1988, pp. 1–5, 177–178, 312–313). Under the threat of plant closings concessions on wages, benefits, work rules, and the increased hiring of nonunion labor have been extracted from steel unions. USWA, contrary to previous practice, no longer bargains with the industry as a whole, but negotiates contracts with each company separately.[46] This has weakened pattern bargaining, a process that provided some security to steelworkers as a whole.

In the post–World War II period growth in domestic demand in an insulated market with oligopolistic profits enabled steel companies to settle for relatively high wages. Labor peace was bought with high wages and liberal pension schemes.[47] The U.S. government also played a role in setting the pattern for high wages. To prevent disruptions in supply and dampen inflationary pressures, the government often sided with labor to settle labor disputes quickly. However, in the 1980s the shift in government policy favored management in all industries over their unions. As a result, wage concessions became the industry's strategy to increase competitiveness.

At the same time the government, under the Reagan administration, relaxed antitrust legislation and pollution standards, reduced depreciation schedules for new plants and equipment, and established loan guarantee programs. These measures were intended to increase U.S. competitiveness by improving the cash flow for investments in modern technology. Paradoxically, they encouraged "rationalization," a euphemism for reducing production capacity, stabilizing market shares, and shifting capital to other sectors. Rationalization was speeded up without tangible resistance. In part the internal weakness of U.S. labor unions, the conservative shifts of the U.S. state toward a more-liberal economic environment, and the increasing military buildup were all responsible for the continued erosion in the manufacturing base (see Bellon & Niosi, 1988). Saddled with obsolete plants and faced with massive replacement costs, the industry viewed steel production as unprofitable. For several integrated producers, nonsteel businesses became important for financial success. Perhaps the most important diversification has been U.S. Steel's acquisition of Marathon Oil in 1982 for nearly $6 billion. Over 50% of this amount was borrowed to finance the purchase. Ironically, the depressed oil market had a damaging impact on its cash flows.[48]

Industry rationalization undertaken by U.S. firms has directly affected workers and their communities. First, there has been a drastic and dramatic decline in steel employment. Although estimates vary, most of the 300,000 jobs lost since 1980 were due to the industry's conservative response to foreign competition. Second, with the loss in steel jobs, and manufacturing jobs in general, workers' health care benefits have been cut back and in many cases eliminated. Third, increased unemployment in the steel and manufacturing sectors has not been compensated by growth in the much touted service economy. The service sector has not been able to absorb all the unemployed. Furthermore, these new jobs have been mostly at low wages. Thus many affected workers have remained unemployed for prolonged periods or they have been unable to find full-time jobs. Those who did find jobs outside the steel sector have tended to earn far less than their former wages with fewer or no benefits (Deitch, 1987; Harrison & Bluestone, 1988, pp. 63–64).

In the first 2 years after being permanently displaced, workers in the steel and auto industries experienced a decline of more than 40% in their annual incomes (Bluestone & Harrison, 1982, p. 57). In the subsequent 4 years lost incomes of displaced workers remained at about 15%. For minorities, finding alternative jobs has been more difficult than for white blue-collar workers (Markusen, 1989, pp. 38–40). Plant closings and declines in incomes have resulted in what Bluestone and Harrison (1982, p. 15) call "social trauma," suggesting that "social, medical, and psychological costs may even outweigh direct economic costs in severity."

Those workers who escaped the layoffs have been forced to make various concessions. The industry claimed that it needed capital to modernize its plants. Thus during the 1980s U.S. steel companies demanded changes in wage, benefits, and work-rule structures. Workers obliged in good faith. Labor granted substantial corporate give-backs with the hope that their jobs would be retained. However, steel firms not only sought wage cuts but shut down plants (Markusen, 1989, p. 28; Moody, 1988, pp. 312–313). In the mid-1980s Wheeling-Pitt and LTV Steel first extracted concessions from labor, then filed bankruptcy, and subsequently sought additional wage and benefit cuts.

Under intense international competition some cuts in wages were necessary. Although productivity increased, it grew slower than wage rates. From 1950 to 1980 U.S. wage rates in the steel industry grew much faster than productivity—208% versus 72% (with 1950 as the base year). However, since then productivity growth has outpaced wage growth. From 1980 until 1987 the hourly wage rate in real terms *decreased* by 7%, while physical output per worker improved by 95% (computed from American Iron and Steel Institute, various dates).[49] At the same time, the number of hours worked per week has increased by 15%. Thus the decline in wages has been accompanied by the intensification of work. This near-doubling of productivity in the 1980s has been a result of large-scale rationalization of the industry and the selective infusion of new technology in existing steel production facilities.

Some workers voluntarily chose and others were forced into early retirement. However, many of these employees found that their companies could not honor their pensions and other benefits. LTV Steel has 75% of the industry's underfunded pension claims, amounting to $2.3 billion and affecting nearly 152,000 workers (U.S. International Trade Commission, 1987, p. 30).[50] LTV Steel, the second-largest U.S. steel producer, lost over $3 billion in 1986 and is currently under bankruptcy proceedings. In the event that LTV's pension obligations are taken up by the Pension Benefit Guarantee Corporation, the federal agency overseeing pension funds, taxpayers will be forced to bail out the company.[51]

LTV's huge debts and pension claims resulted from its mergers and nonsteel acquisitions.[52] LTV acquired two Ohio-based plants, one each in Youngstown and Midland, as part of these mergers. Although employees and community organizations offered to purchase these plants, LTV shut them down permanently. Recent efforts by the Steel Valley Authority, an organization that brings together local, state, labor, and community groups in Pittsburgh, attempted but failed to purchase and reopen LTV's Southside Works in Pittsburgh.

Plant shutdowns as part of the rationalization strategy of U.S. firms have intensified production and increased the hiring of contract labor at the remaining plants. Contract labor tend to be nonunionized. The 1986 labor dispute at USX, culminating in the industry's longest work stoppage (technically a lockout) was precisely on the issue of contract labor. However, workers failed to keep nonunionized labor out of predominantly unionized facilities. With a profit squeeze in the industry, management increased the use of overtime. This allowed management to avoid paying costly benefits, control the size of the labor force, and depress wages as laid-off workers were not generally recalled. The unionized work force must now not only compete with nonunion labor (contract labor) in integrated plants but also in minimills. Wage rates for nonunion labor are considerably less than for unionized labor.[53]

Workers and their unions now struggle to maintain obsolete plants that are less profitable than those in other parts of the world. Plants under employee/community ownership, such as Weirton Steel (formerly owned by National Steel), Geneva Works (formerly a USS plant), and Copperweld (formerly of LTV), are under more pressure to protect jobs and remain competitive than corporately owned plants. When a corporately owned plant loses competitiveness, shareholders can sell their steel stocks with little concern for the workers. However, these employee-owned plants have retained jobs and preserved incomes in a number of communities. Paradoxically, workers in these plants have been forced to impose layoffs and wage cuts to remain viable and to protect jobs.

At the corporate level, U.S. steel companies have found joint ventures with foreign partners to be beneficial. These joint ventures have also protected some jobs, introduced new methods of production and industrial practice, and contributed to increasing productivity. However, in the long run these ventures may also weaken worker solidarity. For example, during the long steel strike of 1986–1987, the USS–POSCO venture was allowed to function because it was considered a separate company while the rest of USS's plants were closed (Moody, 1988, pp. 103–104). The internationalization of production, poor performance of the industry, and weak labor movements have put workers in general on the defensive. Unlike in the past, employers now have greater leeway in bargaining with local unions and each local may vie with each other for retaining jobs. With Japanization of the workplace, that is, the introduction of flexible work rules, bonus and profit-sharing schemes, and teamwork, unionized workers are being increasingly differentiated on the basis of old facilities and new shops under joint ventures. Despite some of the merits of Japanese flexible practices, the possibility of two sharply contrasting work cultures coexisting in the same industry and often in the same company and plant can be a potential source of tension.[54]

Workers and their steel-dependent communities in one location now must compete with other communities to attract foreign investments, create employment, and rely on local state funds in the same industrial activity (Clark, 1989, pp. 45–87). With the general decline in manufacturing industries in many communities, the tax base of local governments is too weak to maintain even some of the most basic services. Workers on the whole are geographically balkanized and sectorally isolated and are unable to achieve their objectives of job preservation and a decent standard of living (Clark, 1989, pp. 67–87). Steel corporations have been quick to exploit the divisions in the work force. Corporate management has extracted concessions from labor and sought the support of labor to keep their aging facilities open.

In the meantime, layoffs through plant closings and diversification have gone unimpeded. From 1975 to 1987, out of a total of 47 mills operated by companies owning integrated plants, 24 have been shut down with three integrated companies permanently closing. Three other companies have ceased to be integrated (Hogan, 1987, p. 45). Many other units have been sold only to be shut down. Several existing facilities have been rounded out by partially phasing out various steelmaking and finishing facilities. Thus regionally the impact of plant shutdowns and employment cuts has been very uneven. Major metropolitan areas as well as steel towns in Pennsylvania, Ohio, Texas, New York, Illinois, and Michigan witnessed significant reduction in integrated steelmaking capacity. In addition, electric arc mills, in cities such as Los Angeles and Seattle, were also phased out, leaving the West Coast virtually without any steelmaking facility. The complex calculus of the internationalization of steel production prompted a conservative response by domestic firms, generated lopsided supplies of steel, and reduced the options available to workers, their communities, and their local governments.

A GLIMPSE INTO THE FUTURE OF THE INTERNATIONAL STEEL INDUSTRY

The evolving internationalization of steel production is likely to put the U.S. steel industry in an increasingly weak position to meet U.S. demand. Growth in U.S. consumption of steel will be minimal in this decade. However, U.S. capacity is expected to decline faster than consumption. Imports of steel products by the United States may reach an all-time high of 30% by the end of the century.[55] The potential this raises for serious international conflict is apparent. Shortages in the United States may appear as the U.S., Japan, and Western Europe continue to restructure their industries and reduce capacity. With no plans for creating new integrated capacity in these countries—either at existing locations or at greenfield sites—the United States will depend more on production by Brazil, South Korea, and others. Contrary to the assertion that minimills will assume a major role in U.S. production, minimills are unlikely to have a significant impact on the industry because of technological limitations in producing flat products.[56]

Steel production has been proven to be a cornerstone of national economic development programs for a number of countries. Hence several new steel-producing countries such as Brazil,[57] South Korea,[58] and India[59] continue to plan expansions of their respective steel industries at a time when the United States has abandoned efforts to expand.

The expansion in steel capacity is closely related to expected increases in demand in developing countries. Consumption by these countries has increased more than fourfold since 1960 (Howell, Noellert, Kreier, & Wolff, 1988, p. 29). However, only a small number of countries is responsible for most of the increase. With the intensification of international trade some of these countries are also expected to export significant amounts of steel, both directly and indirectly, to the world market. For example, in recent years the foreign-owned auto industry in Brazil has become export-oriented. South Korea has emerged as one of the world's largest shipbuilders, controlling a sizeable share of the global market. South Korea's auto industry has emerged as a major force in the U.S. market. By the early 1990s it is likely to be an important producer in the global subcompact market.[60]

In the changing geography of steel production Southeast and East Asia will be the growth centers for both steel production and consumption. Due to the recent increases in domestic demand Japanese firms have postponed planned shutdowns. The government of South Korea is conducting a feasibility study for a cold rolling mill in Malaysia. In addition, firms from South Korea and Taiwan are independently exploring the possibility of constructing tidewater integrated mills in Malaysia. The value of the two projects is estimated to be $11 billion. A rolling mill is under construction by a private-sector steel firm in Taiwan, using semi-finished slabs from Taiwanese and Brazilian plants.

WHAT CAN U.S. POLICYMAKERS DO?

Clearly, the internationalization of steel production has shifted a significant portion of production away from the United States. This process has been going on for decades but it has never been addressed adequately. So far the U.S. steel industry has made very shortsighted decisions while government policy has been too weak to reverse the decline of the industry. Typically, steel and steel-using manufacturing industries, such as automotive, machinery, and appliance sectors, constitute the fundamental building blocks of any developed industrial society. With dense intersectoral linkages among these industries the spin-offs on jobs, income, and regional development are very large. If linkages are to be retained and strengthened, workers' jobs preserved, and their communities stabilized, some form of a long-term comprehensive industrial policy must address the problems of siting, investment, and technological weakness. The steel industry, its unions, and the government could play an active role in reversing this trend and revitalizing the steel industry and its dependent communities.

The oligopolistic nature of the U.S. steel industry has greatly influenced its siting strategy. At the behest of the industry, seeking protection from foreign competition, the government sponsored VRAs. This policy reveals the industry's penchant for market-sharing arrangements, dividing the shrinking market among a small number of steel companies. The steel industry has not constructed an integrated steelmaking facility at a new site for more than 20 years. The existing plants as they are currently located in the United States cannot meet the needs of new growth centers. Foreign producers, often with the assistance of their governments, have strategically stepped in to fill this void. This problem is acute in the U.S. West Coast region.

With rising imports the U.S. government has responded to the imbalances in steel trade in an ad hoc manner by imposing import quotas. However, import quotas have not addressed the U.S. industry's investment and technology problems. The problem is not just one of *trade* but of *production capability*. Plants and equipment in the United States are dated and inappropriately sited, such as the Geneva plant in Utah. All other plants are away from the West Coast region. They need immediate, wide-ranging modernization. Piecemeal modernization cannot capture economies of scale nor increase long-term productivity. Recent joint ventures between U.S. and foreign firms in the midwestern states are insufficient to meet the growing need for high-quality steel products, particularly those demanded by the auto industry, and especially the automobile sector owned by Japanese corporations. Japan continues to lead the United States, by a wide margin, in research and development expenditures in the steel industry, making it even more difficult to match the future quality of Japanese steel.

To meet these challenges the U.S. government must promote steel and other manufacturing industries and not rely solely on the growth of the service sector as a panacea for the nation's economic ills. The steel industry must also move now to tackle the widening technological gap with foreign producers. The rationale for these steps is quite straightforward: First, manufacturing activity generates a substantial number of well-paying jobs. Second, services cannot replace manufacturing since both of these sectors are tightly integrated (Cohen & Zysman, 1987, pp. 3–58). Moreover, to a significant degree, the growth in the service sector is a statistical artifact. Many services that were provided by workers under manufacturing enterprises are now increasingly performed by contract workers and thus counted as service jobs (Markusen, 1989, pp. 30–32). Third, steel production has significant intersectoral linkages. Abandoning the steel industry implies weakening the linkages to related industries. Fourth, manufacturing industries encourage the development and diffusion of new technologies throughout the economy.

Thus national economic development, employment generation, and technological progress would be best achieved if national steel demand were to be met through efficient domestic production. The dependence of the United States on imported slabs, a necessary input for a variety of flat products, can be reversed by creating new capacity.[61] This new steelmaking capacity should be part of a state-of-the-art integrated facility so that slabs can also be converted into various coated sheets. These products can be easily absorbed by the automotive, machinery, and appliance sectors.[62]

The construction of a modern integrated mill at a tidewater location in the West Coast region would significantly address many of these problems. One potential setback to the construction of a tidewater location would be the U.S. public's concern about the threat to the environment. Thus a tidewater plant would require extensive and costly pollution control equipment. Most existing steel plants around the world are subjected to fewer environmental controls. The expensive pollution control processes that would likely be required for a new U.S. plant would substantially raise the investment and production costs. However, if pollution and other environmental concerns are viewed as global issues and not solely as America's problems, then the potential differences in costs due to lax pollution standards elsewhere could be narrowed. International cooperation to promote pollution control programs is one way to solve the dilemma of high cost of production in a new U.S. mill using state-of-the-art pollution control technology.

The federal government, together with key firms, could initiate the mobilization of investment resources and spread the ownership among employees, the industry, and government, complementing this investment by undertaking research and development. Research should be aimed at improving the quality of raw materials, innovating new process technologies, applying extensive computerization to steel production processes, and developing new steel-based materials.

Government policy can also create new steel markets and regain old ones by repairing and rebuilding the dilapidated U.S. infrastructure, including the railroad system. Rebuilding the infrastructure will raise capacity utilization of steel mills and may even encourage investments in additional capacity. Some Japanese officials have suggested that the United States adopt precisely this step as an industrial policy. Such advice most likely stems from Japan's own experience. Its recent public spending program for infrastructure development coincided with low capacity utilization of Japanese steel plants.

Although such a comprehensive industrial policy would require substantial investments, the long-term benefits in terms of production capability, technological development, and employment generation are significant. The cost of the suggested integrated greenfield in the West Coast region is likely to be under $15 billion. This amount pales into insignificance when other spending priorities by the U.S. government are considered, such as the bailout for savings and loan institutions (over $200 billion), and the Stealth B-2 Bomber program ($70 billion). Spending on military high technology is unlikely to replicate the spin-offs generated by the civilian industrial and infrastructural sectors.

Domestic initiatives such as the ones suggested above should be complemented by a foreign policy that constructively promotes growth and genuine development in developing countries. In nearly all Latin American countries spiraling inflation rates and massive foreign debts have shut off most avenues for economic development. Unable to finance imports, these countries pursue an aggressive export strategy to service their debts. The Brazilian steel industry, deep in debt, often exports steel below the cost of production.[63] Brazil, along with many other developing countries, relies on very low wages to penetrate the U.S. steel market. Wages and the standard of living in these countries could be raised by imposing an import tax—what Markusen calls a "worker exploitation tax" (Markusen, 1986a, pp. 75–76). This tax is based on the difference in wages between overseas and U.S. workers. The revenues collected could then be redistributed to workers in developing countries.

It is clearly not in the interest of the Brazilian public to subsidize American and foreign consumption of steel through cheap exports. Nor do U.S. steelworkers benefit from such a strategy, for it undermines their job security. Therefore, the U.S. and foreign governments, along with American and other foreign banks, not only must find a solution to end the debt crisis but they must also address the gross inequality that persistently characterizes the global economy. As one step, international partners should work toward stimulating domestic demand, addressing economic and social equality, and reinvigorating a stalled democratic development program in countries such as Brazil.

CONCLUSION

Notwithstanding the complex process conditioning the internationalization of steel production, it has been shown that competitiveness or comparative advantage is not determined by market forces alone. Rather, state actions and business behavior, premised on long-term ideologies of industrialization and short-term goals of market shares and profits, significantly influence locational decisions. The alliances between capital and state determine where production will take place, how it will be organized, and who will shoulder the adjustment costs for restructuring. In the postwar period the fortunes of U.S. steelworkers were inextricably tied to how the industry performed. Boom times meant job security and good wages, while internationalization of the industry was associated with job redundancies, wage and benefit concessions, fragmentation of labor, and collapse of communities. The vulnerabilities associated with internationalization are real. The question is how to deal with them in an era of globalization.

Restructuring of economic activities is nothing new to capitalism. Internationalization has simply exacerbated it. However, the social impact on workers wrought by the changes in production calls for proactive policies. One place to begin would be state-sponsored sector regulation that would reduce, if not eliminate, the hegemony of private capital. Greater involvement of the state in industrial affairs would be necessary to counteract the unilateral business decisions regarding restructuring. Shouldering the cost of disruptive economic restructuring is much too high for workers and their communities to bear alone. Socializing some of these costs through additional redistributive measures would be deemed necessary. At the industry level, laws pertaining to plant closure notice, unemployment, pension, and health care benefits, reduction of the work week, training and retraining programs, employee ownership, among others, are additional avenues to mitigate trade-related disruptions.

The integration of the global economy is now a historical fact. The internationalization of commodity, finance, and technological flows is also a reality. The direction and the magnitude of these flows are extremely uneven and structurally unfavorable to most developing countries. The postwar experience of industrialization has been limited to only a handful of countries. Yet the ideology of industrialization and modernization is sufficiently internalized by states and ruling classes. Despite the limited success of a few developing countries, industrialization will continue to be seen as a panacea to economic development problems and an end in itself. The question for most developing countries is how to set the terms of integration and industrialization without undermining national sovereignty. The inherent danger of this approach is mercantilist and beggar-thy-neighbor policies.

The internationalized steel industry is a good example of the ideology of industrialization and mercantilism. The decision to locate modern steel mills outside the United States has not been based on resource endowment, as seen in the case of the East Asian countries, or on the proximity to markets, as exemplified by Brazil. Rather, the anticipated developmental impact of steel production on national or regional economies has motivated the siting of plants. The aggressive export drive into certain niches of the U.S. market has been a product of foreign debts, domestic recessions, and import dependence. While industry strategy, foreign government policy, and technological change around the world contributed to the erosion of U.S. steel capacity, competitiveness in the United States has been reintroduced through restructuring. The cost to workers, however, has been very high. Workers in this instance have also internalized the mercantilist tendencies underlying competitiveness as they staunchly support corporate profitability and engage in bread-and-butter issues. To be sure, the fragmentation of the steel industry, into steelmaking and steel finishing, across national boundaries creates interdependencies, necessary for corporate survival. However, the spatial and class inequalities in the world economy indicate that these relationships are not necessarily symmetrical.

While specific policies for the U.S. steel industry have been suggested, by themselves they are not a guarantee for industrial renewal. Much would depend on world economic conditions and the actions of other nations. However, in the United States the absence of a long-term vision of meaningful economic development would be akin to courting social and ecological disaster. Economic leadership, embedded in "competitiveness" and "growth," may have to be abandoned if the pitfalls of hegemonic control of the world economy and nature are to be avoided. In the meantime, however, serious attention needs to be paid to U.S. working-class communities. The steel industry has traditionally formed the backbone of the U.S. industrial structure, employing hundreds of thousands of workers. This structure historically has generated employment of skilled workers, provided decent incomes for workers and their communities, ushered in technological change, and contributed significantly to regional and national income. Internationalization and the mobility of capital have reduced these benefits drastically. To revitalize the steel and related manufacturing industries labor groups, the industry and the government must cooperate to formulate a coherent industrial policy. The labor movement must also move away from narrow economic goals to larger social goals. At present, these actions seem unlikely, but the alternative is further industrial decline, erosion of living standards, and worsening social inequality.

ACKNOWLEDGMENTS

I wish to thank Ann Markusen for involving me in this project. She along with Julie Graham and Helzi Noponen made substantive comments throughout the draft stage. Bob Erickson of Tri-State Conference on Steel in Pittsburgh was always ready to provide some "inside" stories on the steel industry. Valuable publications were provided by Nancy Fulcher of the U.S. International Trade Commission. Janette Rawlings, very generous with her time, meticulously combed through the final version of this chapter and made significant editorial suggestions. The chapter was also improved by the comments of two anonymous reviewers at Guilford Press. Thanks also to the numerous steel companies and government officials in India, Brazil, South Korea, Japan, and the United States. The usual caveats apply.

NOTES

1. For an historical account of the evolution of the steel industry's location pattern in the United States, see Markusen (1985, 1986a).

2. See Markusen (1985, pp. 86–94) for a discussion of relative contributions of automation, trade penetration, steel substitutes, and decentralized minimills to steel unemployment in the Midwest.

3. It was only in 1973 that South Korea constructed a major mill. From 1975 until 1987 South Korea increased its steel output by 563%.

4. In 1988 the United States imported an additional 13.16% from Romania, Poland, Austria, Turkey, Sweden, Finland, Mexico, Argentina, and Australia.

5. In 1898 there were over 200 establishments with a total capacity under 15 mt.; see Gold, Peirce, Rosegger, and Perlman (1984, pp. 490, 580).

6. The Pittsburgh Plus system priced all products as if the products had originated in Pittsburgh, regardless of their true origin. This system obviously eliminated any advantage some producers may have had if they were located near their markets. Customers also had no incentive to seek the nearest or the least-cost producers.

7. Only three greenfields were constructed away from traditional sites between 1906 and 1952. The last integrated greenfield plant in the United States was begun in 1962 by Bethlehem Steel at the Burns Harbor Works in Indiana near Chicago.

8. The mismatch between production and consumption in Pittsburgh resulted in a surplus exceeding 16.6 mt in 1951, whereas Michigan had a deficit of 5.3 mt (Warren, 1988, p. 305). In Michigan the Ford automotive company had its own steel plant while General Motors had shares in several steel companies in the state.

9. These were designed to produce plates and structurals for shipbuilding and were located inland so as to avoid aerial bombing by the Japanese.

10. The Geneva plant in Utah, which cost the U.S. government over $191 million to build, was sold to U.S. Steel Corporation for under $50 million (Hogan, 1971, pp. 1460–1462). Another plant, the South Chicago Works, was sold to Republic Steel.

11. Despite reshuffling of individual firms through mergers, spin-offs, diversification, and plant shutdowns, the top eight firms have maintained their relative market shares since World War II. The U.S. Census of Manufactures also shows relative stability in concentration ratios. In specific products such as sheets, strips, pipes, and tubes, concentration ratios actually increased during the 1958–1982 period (U.S. Department of Commerce, 1986). In 1986 nearly 56% of strip and sheet shipments was controlled by four firms and over 86% by the top eight firms (U.S. International Trade Commission, 1988b, p. 11-2).

12. The prewar western market demand was approximately 3.5 mt, whereas production capacity was only about 2 mt. The shortfall was met by Bethlehem's Sparrows Point plant in Maryland and Tennessee Coal and Iron in Birmingham, Alabama.

13. California did have some steelmaking capacity. In 1929 U.S. Steel acquired a plant in Pittsburg, California, which it never integrated. As a strategy it dismantled the small steelmaking capacity and retained only the rolling mills. It used the Pittsburg plant to finish slabs shipped from the new war-vintage plant it purchased in Utah. Bethlehem Steel purchased land for a greenfield in the San Francisco area to meet the booming California demand while at the same time it phased out steelmaking plants in Los Angeles and San Francisco. National Steel also had a plant site in California but never built a plant there.

14. Kaiser was a relatively new entrant to steelmaking. It purchased the government-constructed Fontana, California, plant. It obtained a loan from the Reconstruction Financing Commission and by 1960 had raised the plant's capacity from 0.75 mt to 3 mt.

15. A weak capital market and an about-face in the U.S. attitude toward Japan in the immediate postwar period, from one of potential threat to that of an Asian ally, strengthened the state's role in the industry. American policies instituted under the Occupation to break up the industrial conglomerates and reduce state control were dismantled. Liberal, but highly selective, technology import policies, state control over credit, and low-interest financing for steel investments enabled Japan to enter the league of world producers. The state–industry–bank nexus formed the critical institutional arrangement for rapid development of the industry (Nakamura, 1985, pp. 56–57).

16. Since the Meiji Restoration and until the end of World War I the Japanese state owned and operated much of the industry, albeit a small one, with virtually no serious contenders. The industry was controlled for "nation building" as well as for its imperial ventures. The industry was regulated and fostered by the state with the aid of the pre–World War II *zaibatsu* (privately owned industrial conglomerates).

17. In 1987 Nippon Steel produced 41% of the total output of Japan's five largest producers, down from 44% in 1972. In high-value products such as cold rolled sheet and strips, the top six companies produced over 90% of total Japanese output (U.S. International Trade Commission, 1988b, p. 9-2).

18. In 1870 Britain produced 37% of global production. In 1980 it was struggling to maintain its 2.7% share (Mény & Wright, 1987, p. 4).

19. Average losses for 1983 and 1984 amounted to $1.6 billion (U.S. International Trade Commission, 1987, p. 8-3).

20. Similarly, the government in Taiwan established China Steel Corporation (CSC) through its Ten Major Projects of 1973–1974.

21. For the first Brazilian steel project in Volta Redonda, the U.S. government, through its Export-Import Bank, provided a sizeable share of the initial investment (Baer, 1969, p. 76). U.S. steel and other equipment companies, such as Mesta Machine, Koppers, and Kaiser, were involved in the construction of the Brazilian plant.

22. Under the second 5-year plan of India (1955–1956 to 1960–1961) British, West German, and Soviet companies participated in the construction of the three 1-million-ton plants. Similarly Japan and Western Europe provided capital and state-of-the-art technology to South Korea and Brazil.

23. In the 1960s U.S. Steel accidentally discovered the rich iron ore deposits in the Carajas region of Brazil. It formed a joint venture with CVRD, the Brazilian state mining company. Later, however, in a very shortsighted move, U.S. Steel sold its 50% stake for a "generous" $50 million (Treece, 1987, p. 12). Today Brazil is one of the cheapest sources for high-quality ore.

24. In this technology iron ore and coal are the principal raw materials. The BF is a very large vessel in which coal, iron ore, and other inputs are melted to form liquid iron. The BOF is a much smaller vessel in which the molten

iron is converted to liquid steel by injecting oxygen at very high pressure. Continuous casting permits the production of semifinished products from molten steel by eliminating several steps usually involved in the conventional ingot casting process. The advantages of continuous casting are energy savings, increased productivity, and better quality products. Alternative production units are minimills that produce steel by melting ferrous scrap in an electric arc furnace. Directly reduced iron (DRI) can be used in place of scrap. However, the process of converting iron ore into DRI pellets is very energy intensive. Minimills are relatively small operations. The major shortcoming of minimills is that their product range is still confined to lower grade (low value-added) steel, primarily long products such as bars and rods destined for the construction industry.

25. The United States still produced 5% of national output by open hearths.

26. Only minimills, which generally rely on continuous casting, have more computer-controlled operations.

27. Productivity figures must be treated with caution as information is generally incomplete. Most often such figures represent averages, hiding the diverse range of steel products and technologies in use. Capacity utilization rate also determines productivity—high utilization typically results in high productivity while low utilization implies surplus workers who cannot be retrenched in the short term. Also subcontracting generally increases output per worker.

28. Of the three countries, South Korea made the greatest gains in productivity. In 1973, on the average, it took 14.1 personhours to produce a ton of steel. Figures on productivity are compiled from Paine Webber Inc. (1987, Tables 5, 6, and 17).

29. The western states have only 13.4% of national minimill capacity and a little over 3% of total national steel capacity.

30. In the European Community and Japan consumption also peaked in 1973. However, their declines in demand were less sharp, at 20% and 11%, respectively. On the consumption side, substitutes such as plastics, aluminum, lighter but stronger steels, and the reduced size of automobiles had a marginal effect on demand for steel in the United States. The overall consumption of steel in the United States, including indirect trade in steel, remained relatively stable in the 1980s. Barring 1982, a major recession year, total usage of steel averaged 98.5 mt in from 1980 to 1985 (Locker/Abrecht Associates, 1985, p. 51). In 1986 this figure rose to 113 mt.

31. In 1988 construction and containerization absorbed 73% of domestic steel shipments to the western region.

32. Information obtained from Japan Iron and Steel Federation, Tokyo, October 1987.

33. The Pohang mill has an annual capacity of 9.1 mt. Kwangyang has an annual capacity of 5.4 mt, with a slated capacity of 11.4 mt.

34. In 1964 the Japanese wage rate in the industry was only 21% of the U.S. rate and by 1987, despite the steep climb in the value of the Japanese

yen, it remained under 75% (Barnett & Schorsch, 1983, p. 64; personal communication with Japan Iron and Steel Federation, July 1988). More recently, South Korean wage rates have been under one-fourth that of the United States.

35. In 1987 Japan supplied nearly 28% of total U.S. imports of sheets and strips, of which the more-expensive products, galvanized and other coated sheets, amounted to 30% of Japan's total exports to the United States. In value terms, based on the weighted average of net price for April–June 1987 for U.S. importers, these products represented 68.2% of these items. By tonnage they were only 60.8%.

36. The decline in domestic shipments of plates and tubular products is also indicative of the decline of the U.S. shipbuilding industry and the collapse of the oil industry.

37. Coast-to-coast shipping costs range between $35–70 per ton (U.S. International Trade Commission, 1988b, p. 3–46). In contrast, the average shipping cost per ton among various exporting countries has ranged from $35–39/ton (United Nations data base generated by U.S. International Trade Commission, 1988b, p. 3-47). Although the United States has several port-based mills (in the Great Lakes and northeastern regions) they are not as modern as those found in East Asia. The transfer of raw materials and finished products in these U.S. mills requires several stages in handling via smaller barges and interplant railroads.

38. POSCO at both Pohang and Kwangyang built harbors and other infrastructural facilities, and at Kwangyang constructed wharfs with a berthing capacity for five large ships, including one 250,000 ton ship. The plant has been built on land reclaimed from the bay (Shin, 1986, p. 17; plant visit by author at Kwangyang, October 1987). Despite the higher cost for site preparation for coastal plants than for noncoastal ones, the expenditures on port, rail, roadways, and material-handling facilities have been justified on the basis of creating growth poles and for long-term positive effects on development.

39. In 1990 its foreign debt was reduced to $34 billion from $47 billion since mid-1986. Its international reserves stood at $15 billion in 1990 (World Bank, 1992, p. 253).

40. Brazil's debt has reached crisis proportions, leaving it no other choice but to accept large investment funds from the EEC for the development of the rich Carajas ore project. Contracts have been signed for supplying 13.6 mt per year for 15 years at the 1982 bargain price of only $270 million. Such favorable pricing for high-quality ore is expected to offset the poor performance of the European steel industry (Treece, 1987, p. 21). The ecological and human devastation in the Amazon is almost a foregone conclusion.

41. The automotive industry consumes about 18% of Brazil's uncoated flat products and exports a third of its output (*Metal Bulletin*, June 15, 1989, p. 22).

42. The TPM was based on the Japanese cost of production plus some markup for profits and shipping costs. Since no Japanese producer would ever divulge its cost of production most of the antidumping suits filed by U.S. firms relied on arbitrary and often complex methods of computing costs. The Euro-

pean exporters, being less cost-efficient than the Japanese but more efficient than their U.S. counterparts, could conveniently undersell U.S. producers. The signing of the U.S.–European Community Steel Pact in 1982 (essentially VRAs) attempted to resolve this problem.

43. The ineffectiveness and the ad hoc nature of the VRAs is evident in efforts by U.S. steel companies to circumvent them. For example, Tuscaloosa Steel in Alabama has a supply contract for slabs with British Steel. However, this contract lies outside the purview of the VRAs. In a second example, a USS–POSCO collaboration will entail imports of South Korean semifinished steel which USS is attempting to import outside of the VRAs.

44. In 1987 one Nippon Steel Corporation staff member confided that Nippon Kokan made a big mistake in purchasing National's crude steel facilities (personal interview with Nippon Steel staff, Tokyo, October 1987).

45. The development of the technological expertise of U.S. firms has been limited because U.S. firms have not significantly participated in any greenfield projects since the mid-1970s. In addition, low profitability and erosion of production at home have squeezed R & D expenditures. In 1984 the industry spent $390 million on R & D, approximately 0.6% of sales, whereas the manufacturing average was 2.6% (Congressional Budget Office, U.S. Congress, 1987, p. 31). Japanese R & D expenditures have been 1.5% of sales, a far greater absolute outlay as its production exceeded that of the United States by 21.7 mt (Japanese Iron and Steel Federation, 1987, pp. 18, 29). In 1988 the gap in R & D expenditure between the United States and Japan widened even further, 0.6% versus 2.9% (U.S. International Trade Commission, 1990, p. 55). Even South Korea spent a larger fraction of its sales on R & D than the United States in that year. As an indication of the seriousness of United States lack of participation, ironically, U.S.–owned Mesta Machine, a world-renowned supplier of steel technology, had set up rolling facilities in Nippon Kokan's Keihin Works in collaboration with Mitsubishi of Japan (plant visit by author, Keihin Works, October 1987). Mesta Machine went bankrupt and is currently owned by a firm from China.

46. In 1986, for the first time, rank-and-file members voted on their contracts. Previously this was not the case: only union leaders voted on the contracts. L-S Electrogalvanizing Co., owned by LTV and Sumitomo of Japan, had a separate labor agreement resulting in only three job classifications.

47. More recently, since the Vietnam War boom, wage demands have increased. From 1973 onward, a 3% increase in *real* wages was granted each year (Barnett & Crandall, 1986, pp. 40–41).

48. Armco is also a highly diversified firm with major holdings in oil and exploration, real estate, and other services. National Intergroup has a large stake in financial services. LTV Corporation was and continues to be principally an aerospace and energy-related firm. Today only four of the top eight firms have steel production as their main activity. Changes in the corporate names of steel firms reflect their disengagement from steel production. Armco has dropped "steel" from its name, while USS has become USX. Today USX earns about 30% of its revenues from steel.

49. From 1980 until 1989 real wages declined by over 10% (calculated from U.S. International Trade Commission, 1990, p. 5). Real compensation cost for production workers as a result *fell* to $23.49 per hour in 1989 from $26.27 per hour in 1980 (U.S. International Trade Commission, 1990, p. 5). This decline narrowed the gap between steel wage rates and the average manufacturing wage rate.

50. The steel industry as a whole represents 79% of all underfunded pension claims.

51. Recently the French state-controlled Usinor expressed an interest in buying parts of LTV. But Usinor is not willing to take on LTV's underfunded pension liability, creating additional uncertainties for workers and retirees.

52. Since 1978 LTV has bought and shut down several plants. These include the purchase of two Youngstown plants and a merger with Lykes Corporation in 1978. Another important merger was with Republic Steel in 1984.

53. In the early 1980s minimill workers earned about 77% of the wages of integrated producers (Barnett & Crandall, 1986, p. 22). Today the ratio is 92% (U.S. International Trade Commission, 1988a, p. 59), reflecting wage concessions on the part of unionized labor. Organizing labor in minimills has been difficult, in part due to their location primarily in smaller towns that have been historically weak in labor organization.

54. See Drache (1991) and Morris (1991) for a discussion on the potential impact on the relationship between Japanese flexible industrial practices and Canadian labor.

55. Computed from Barnett and Schorsch (1983); National Academy of Engineering (1985, Table 5-5, p. 93). More recently, projected imports were slated at 27% (see Hogan, 1991, p. 148).

56. An official at the Japanese Iron and Steel Federation unequivocally pointed out that minimills will be inadequate to supply large quantities of steel (personal interview, Tokyo, December 1991). At the moment Nucor Corporation has the only minimill in the world with a thin slab caster that allows the production of flat products. The plant is capable of producing about 1 million tons annually. The plant is located in the industrial belt of the Great Lakes region at Crawfordsville, Indiana. There is a possibility that third world countries will initiate similar production. Taiwan has already evinced interest in the technology. It is working with equipment suppliers from Japan and West Germany, and international banks including Chase Manhattan (*Metal Bulletin*, 13 March 1989, p. 41). Nucor has little control over the technology as SMS Schloeman of West Germany supplied the caster.

57. The Second National Steel Plan of Brazil has projected a demand of 50 mt by the year 2000 (personal interview with CONSIDER and SIDERBRAS staff, Brasilia, December 1987). This plan includes the construction of an export-oriented greenfield with 3 mt of hot rolled coil aimed primarily at the U.S. market. However, the ongoing economic crisis in Brazil has compelled the government to shelve the plan for the time being.

58. South Korea anticipates a significant increase in demand. By the year 2000 the demand for steel is expected to be nearly 38 mt annually (personal interview with Ministry of Trade and Industry staff, Seoul, October 1987).

Forecasts show that South Korea will confront supply shortages throughout the 1990s, reaching 15.3 mt in the year 2000 (*Metal Bulletin*, 29 June 1989, p. 19). If this demand materializes South Korea will require another mill equivalent to Kwangyang Works in 5 or 6 years. Such strong domestic demand will mean that South Korea will not be a major supplier to the world market. The continuing struggle by South Korean workers over increased wages and benefits means that South Korean steel prices will probably rise.

59. Despite the expansion plans made by the Steel Authority of India Ltd. (SAIL) (1987), the increase in India's total steel capacity will be modest. India's domestic requirement by 1999–2000 is projected to be only about 25 mt of finished steel which the domestic industry will supply. India is unlikely to be a major contender in the international market.

60. The Hyundai in 1986 became the highest selling car of any new model in U.S. history (over 168,000 units). In addition, new Korean-produced small cars were introduced by both Ford and General Motors.

61. In 1988 California Steel Industries (CSI) requested the import of slabs above the quota limit. The U.S. Commerce Department turned the request down on the grounds that Geneva Steel in Utah and Bethlehem Steel could meet its requirement. However, CSI had bitterly complained about the poor quality of U.S. slabs. They are not continuously cast. Later, when the market for slabs firmed up, U.S. producers not only raised their prices but also reneged on their supply contracts.

62. These sectors use high-quality coated sheets. The auto industry relies more on electrogalvanized steel, a product that even Japan cannot supply in sufficient quantities to the United States (U.S. International Trade Commission, 1989a, p. 3–5).

63. In 1988 Brazil exported 40% of its domestic production. Exports from Tubarâo and Açominas were nearly 70%. In the same year, while Brazil boasted that it was the sixth-largest steel producer in the world, SIDERBRAS, the state holding company, incurred a net loss of $2.32 billion, exceeding the 1987 loss of $2.05 billion. In 1990 SIDERBRAS was dismantled but its debt still remains.

REFERENCES

Acs, Z. J. 1984. *The Changing Structure of the U.S. Economy: Lessons from the Steel Industry.* New York: Praeger.

Adams, W., & Mueller, H. 1990. The Steel Industry. In W. Adams, ed., *The Structure of American Industry* (8th ed.). New York: Macmillan.

Agnew, J. 1987. *The United States in the World Economy: A Regional Geography.* Cambridge: Cambridge University Press.

American Iron and Steel Institute. Various dates. *Annual Statistical Reports.* Washington, DC: American Iron and Steel Institute.

Baer, W. 1969. *The Development of the Brazilian Steel Industry.* Nashville, TN: Vanderbilt University Press.

Ballance, R. H. 1987. *International Industry and Business: Structural Change, Industrial Policy and Industrial Strategies.* London: Allen and Unwin.

Barnett, D. F., & Crandall, R. W. 1986. *Up from the Ashes: The Rise of the Steel Minimill in the United States.* Washington, DC: Brookings Institution.

Barnett, D. F., & Schorsch, L. 1983. *Steel: Upheaval in a Basic Industry.* Cambridge, MA: Ballinger.

Bellon, B., & Niosi, J. 1988. *The Decline of the American Economy.* Montreal: Black Rose Books.

Bluestone, B., & Harrison, B. 1982. *The Deindustrialization of America: Plant Closings, Community Abandonment, and the Dismantling of Basic Industry.* New York: Basic Books.

Bureau of Census, U.S. Department of Commerce. 1986. *Census of Manufactures, 1982: Concentration Ratios in Manufacturing.* Washington, DC: U.S. Government Printing Office.

Bureau of Census, U.S. Department of Commerce. Various dates. Washington, DC: U.S. Government Printing Office.

Clark, G. L. 1989. *Unions and Communities under Seige: American Communities and the Crisis of Organized Labor.* Cambridge: Cambridge University Press.

Cohen, S. S., & Zysman, J. 1987. *Manufacturing Matters: The Myth of the Post-Industrial Economy.* New York: Basic Books.

Congressional Budget Office, U.S. Congress. 1987. *How Federal Policies Affect the Steel Industry.* Washington, DC: U.S. Government Printing Office.

CONSIDER. 1987. *Anuário Estatístico, Setor Metalurgico.* (Statistical Yearbook.) Brasilia, Brazil: CONSIDER.

D'Costa, A. P. 1989. "Capital Accumulation, Technology, and the State: The Political Economy of Steel Industry Restructuring." Unpublished Ph.D. dissertation, University of Pittsburgh.

Deitch, C. 1987. "Displaced Workers and Labor Market Restructuring." Unpublished manuscript, Department of Sociology, University of Pittsburgh.

Drache, D. 1991. The Systematic Search for Flexibility: National Competitiveness and New Work Relations. In D. Drache, & M. S. Gertler, eds., *The New Era of Global Competition: State Policy and Market Power.* Montreal: McGill-Queen's University Press.

Edwards, R. C. 1979. *Contested Terrain: The Transformation of the Workplace in the Twentieth Century.* New York: Basic Books.

Gold, B., Peirce, W. S., Rosegger, G., & Perlman, M. 1984. *Technological Progress and Industrial Leadership: The Growth of the U.S. Steel Industry, 1900–1970.* Lexington, MA: D. C. Heath.

Harrison, B., & Bluestone, B. 1988. *The Great U-Turn: Corporate Restructuring and the Polarizing of America.* New York: Basic Books.

Hogan, W. T. 1971. *Economic History of the Iron and Steel Industry in the United States.* Vol. 4, part 6: *The Steel Industry in a Period of World-Wide Challenge and Fundamental Change, 1946–1971.* Lexington, MA: D. C. Heath.

Hogan, W. T. 1987. *Minimills and Integrated Mills: A Comparison of Steelmaking in the United States.* Lexington, MA: D. C. Heath.

Hogan, W. T. 1991. *Global Steel in the 1990s: Growth or Decline?* Lexington, MA: D. C. Heath.

Howell, T. R., Noellert, W. A., Kreier, J. G., & Wolff, A. W. 1988. *Steel and the State: Government Intervention and Steel's Structural Crisis.* Boulder, CO: Westview Press.

Instituto Brasileiro de Siderúrgica. 1987. *Anuário Estatístico da Indústria Siderúrgica Brasileira.* Rio de Janeiro, Brazil: Institutio Brasileiro de Siderúrgica.

Iron Age. January 1988.

Japanese Iron and Steel Federation. Various dates. *Monthly Report on the Iron and Steel Industry Statistics.*

Japanese Iron and Steel Federation. 1987. *The Steel Industry of Japan.* Tokyo: Japanese Iron and Steel Federation.

Kaplan, E. 1972. *Japan: The Government–Business Relationship.* Washington, DC: U.S. Department of Commerce.

Krishna Moorty, K. 1984. *Engineering Change: India's Iron and Steel.* Madras, India: Technology Books.

Locker/Abrecht Associates, Inc. 1985. *Confronting the Crisis: The Challenge for Labor.* Report to USWA, AFL-CIO-CLC. New York: Locker/Abrecht Associates, Inc.

Markusen, A. 1985. *Profit cycles, Oligopoly, and Regional Development.* Cambridge: MIT Press.

Markusen, A. 1986a. Neither Ore, nor Coal, nor Markets: A Policy-Oriented View of Steel Sites in the USA. *Regional Studies,* 20(5), 449–462.

Markusen, A. 1986b. The New International Division of Labor: The Changing Relationship of Brazilian and American Steel. In E. W. Gondolf, I. M. Marcus, & J. P. Dougherty, eds., *The Global Economy: Divergent Perspectives on Economic Change.* Boulder, CO: Westview Press.

Markusen, A. 1989. City on the Skids. *Reader,* 19(9), 1, 22, 24, 26, 28, 30, 32, 34, 36, 38, 40–42.

Masi, A. C. 1991. Structural Adjustment and Technological Change in the Canadian Steel Industry, 1970–1986. In D. Drache & M. S. Gertler, eds., *The New Era of Global Competition: State Policy and Market Power.* Montreal: McGill-Queen's University Press.

Mény, Y. & Wright, V. 1987. "Introduction: State and Steel in Western Europe." In Y. Mény & V. Wright, eds., *The Politics of Steel: Western Europe and the Steel Industry in the Crisis Years, (1974–1984).* Berlin: Walter de Gruyter.

Metal Bulletin. Various dates.

Metal Statistics. Various dates.

Moody, K. 1988. *An Injury to All: The Decline of American Unionism.* New York: Verso.

Morris, J. 1991. A Japanization of Canadian Industry? In D. Drache & M. S. Gertler, eds., *The New Era of Global Competition: State Policy and Market Power.* Montreal: McGill-Queen's University Press.

Nakamura, T. 1985. *Economic Development of Modern Japan.* Tokyo: Ministry of Foreign Affairs.

National Academy of Engineering. 1985. *The Competitive Status of the U.S. Steel Industry.* Washington, DC: National Academy Press.

New York Times. Various dates.

Organisation for Economic Co-operation and Development. 1985. *World Steel Developments, 1960–1983: A Statistical Analysis.* Paris: Organisation for Economic Co-operation and Development.

Paine Webber Inc. 1987. *World Steel Dynamics,* "Steel Strategist #14." New York: Paine Webber Inc.

Patton, W., & Markusen, A. 1990. "The Development Potential of Distributive Services: A Case Study of Steel Service Centers." Working Paper no. 18. Piscataway, NJ: Center for Urban Policy Research, Rutgers University.

Scheurman, W. 1986. *The Steel Crisis: The Economics and Politics of Declining Industry.* New York: Praeger.

Shapiro, H., & Volk, S. 1979. Steelyard Blues: New Structures in Steel. *NACLA,* 13(1), 2–40.

Shin, Y. K. 1986. A Steel Plant for the '90s: The Kwangyang Works of POSCO. *I & S M,* December, 15–20.

Shinohara, M. 1982. *Industrial Growth, Trade, and Dynamic Patterns in the Japanese Economy.* Tokyo: University of Tokyo Press.

Steel Authority of India Ltd. (SAIL). 1987. *Corporate Plan for SAIL Up to 2000 A.D.* New Delhi: SAIL Corporate Planning Directorate.

Tiffany, P. A. 1988. *The Decline of American Steel: How Management, Labor, and Government Went Wrong.* New York: Oxford University Press.

Treece, D. 1987. *Bound in Misery and Iron: The Impact of the Grande Carajas Programme on the Indians of Brazil.* London: Survival International.

United Nations Industrial Development Organization Secretariat. 1986. *Financial Problem and the Development of the Iron and Steel Industry.* New York: UNIDO Secretariat.

U.S. Federal Trade Commission. 1948. *Report to the Federal Trade Commission on International Steel Cartels.* Washington, DC: U.S. Goverment Printing Office.

U.S. International Trade Commission. 1987. *Annual Survey Concerning Competitive Conditions in the Steel Industry and Industry Efforts to Adjust and Modernize.* Publication no. 2019. Washington, DC: U.S. International Trade Commission.

U.S. International Trade Commission. 1988a. *Annual Survey Concerning Competitive Conditions in the Steel Industry and Industry Efforts to Adjust and Modernize.* Publication no. 2115. Washington, DC: U.S. International Trade Commission.

U.S. International Trade Commission. 1988b. *U.S. Global Competitiveness: Steel Sheet and Strip Industry.* Publication no. 2050. Washington, DC: U.S. International Trade Commission.

U.S. International Trade Commission. 1989a. *The Effects of the Steel Voluntary Restraint Agreements on U.S. Steel-Consuming Industries.* Publication no. 2182. Washington, DC: U.S. International Trade Commission.

U.S. International Trade Commission. 1989b. *The Western U.S. Steel Market: Analysis of Market Conditions and Assessment of the Effects of Voluntary Restraint Agreements on Steel-Producing and Steel-Consuming Indus-*

tries. Publication no. 2165. Washington, DC: U.S. International Trade Commission.

U.S. International Trade Commission. 1990. *Steel Industry Annual Report: On Competitive Conditions in the Steel Industry and Industry Efforts to Adjust and Modernize.* Publication no. 2316. Washington, DC: U.S. International Trade Commission.

Warren, K. 1988. *The American Steel Industry, 1850–1970: A Geographical Interpretation.* Pittsburgh: University of Pittsburgh Press.

World Bank. 1992. *World Development Report 1992: Development and the Environment.* New York: Oxford University Press.

Yachir, F. 1988. *The World Steel Industry Today.* Tokyo: United Nations University.

Yamazawa, I. 1990. *Economic Development and International Trade: The Japanese Model.* Honolulu, Hawaii: East-West Center, Resource Systems Institute.

4

Firm and State Strategy in a Multipolar World: The Changing Geography of Machine Tool Production and Trade

JULIE GRAHAM

The machine tool industry is often characterized as the heart or "master industry" of an industrial economy. It produces the tools used in all industries that cut and form metal, including the durable consumer goods industries and capital goods and defense-related industries such as shipbuilding and aerospace. It also produces the machines that are used in making machine tools themselves. As the primary supplier of fixed capital to itself, the machine tool industry enjoys a certain status as a self-generating, self-perpetuating industry. At the same time, and despite its perceived importance, it is a small industry, accounting for less than 2% of manufacturing value added.

In part because of its unique position as the self-starter of an industrial economy, observers often use the machine tool industry as an indicator of a country's industrial development, or conversely, of its decline. Recent geographical shifts in the machine tool industry have therefore attracted considerable attention, focusing on the decline of the United States and the concomitant rise of Japan. Over the last decade the United States has moved from number-one producer, producing almost 20% of world output in 1981, to number-four producer, producing less than 10% in 1991. The Japanese now produce almost 30% of the world's machine tools and enjoy a much higher share of world's exports than the United States. Still a major machine tool–consuming nation, the United States now imports nearly 60% of its machine tools, primarily from Japan.

Less noticeable perhaps than the dramatic shift in the relative positions of the United States and Japan is the growing internationalization of the machine tool industry. This internationalization involves both an increase in the number of countries that are engaged in machine tool production, as developing countries begin to industrialize, and a rapid expansion in the volume of international trade, as countries become increasingly specialized and/or export-oriented. It also involves an increase in international joint ventures and foreign direct investment. Both are generally intended to establish footholds in major markets, safe from currency fluctuations and trade barriers and close to networks of customers and suppliers.

This chapter examines the process of internationalization, emphasizing its implications for the United States branch of the world machine tool industry. An inward-looking producer dependent on a large domestic market, the United States has recently become the target of the marketing and investment strategies of other machine tool–producing nations. U.S. machine tool builders, accustomed to offering the full spectrum of products, now find themselves in a low-volume, high-tech corner of the market, involuntarily participating in the international trend toward product specialization.

Though many factors have contributed to the repositioning of the U.S. industry on the international scene, in this Chapter I will emphasize the active roles played by firms and national governments. My interventionist orientation is intended as an antidote to the images of "forces beyond our control" that characterize certain analyses of the internationalization process. But it should not be taken as implying that firm strategies and government policies have determinate or predictable outcomes. Rather, my goal is to lay out the international terrain of the machine tool industry and to analyze the activity of players on that terrain, attempting to extract from the recent past some hints for interventions in the future.

A GEOGRAPHICAL/TECHNOLOGICAL HISTORY OF MACHINE TOOLS

A machine tool is usually defined as a power-driven tool that is not hand-held and that is designed to cut or shape metal. Most industrial classifications divide the machine tool industry into two subsectors producing metal-cutting and metal-forming tools. In the United States these are known respectively as SICs 3541 and 3542, the machine tool "building" subsectors of the metalworking machinery industry (SIC 354).

Metal-cutting machines perform operations like turning, boring, drilling, milling, tapping and threading, planing and shaping, sawing, grinding, honing, polishing, and gear making; metal-forming machines bend, press, punch, forge, rivet, and stamp (United Nations Industrial Development Organization [UNIDO] 1974). Approximately 75% of the value of world machine tool output is accounted for by metal-cutting tools (UNIDO, 1984, p. 59).

Machine tools are differentiated not only by function but by control type (conventional, numerical, computer numerical); by degree of integration with other machines (stand-alone, flexible manufacturing cells, flexible manufacturing systems); by functional capacity (turning lathes, milling machines, machining centers); by degree of dedication (special purpose or general purpose); by type of design (standard or custom); and by scale (small, medium-sized, or large).

Both shops and countries tend to specialize, producing a type and scale of machine that reflects their capabilities or the requirements of their customers (UNIDO, 1974). Thus the U.K. produces standard machines suitable for export to the former Commonwealth countries, which were traditionally a captive source of demand, while Germany produces sophisticated machines appropriate to its technically advanced metalworking sector, and the Swiss tend to specialize in highly accurate small-scale machines used in manufacturing precision equipment (United Nations Industrial Development Organization, 1984, p. 63).

Almost all machine tools (97%) are purchased by what the British call the "engineering" industries and what U.S. industrial analysts call the "metalworking" industries. These include fabricated metal products, the machinery sectors, and the transportation equipment sectors. Of the latter, automobiles and aerospace are the primary consumers (National Machine Tool Builders' Association [NMTBA], 1985, p. 1).

The machine tool industry developed during the Industrial Revolution, when the demand for machines that could make machines first arose. In the early phases of industrialization machinists were employees or independent contractors hired by shops and large mills that required their services in the making of custom machines and replacement parts. As the industry began to mature, independent machine tool companies developed. In the United States there were approximately 72 machine-tool-building companies by the 1870s, extending from New England where the industry originated to the Middle Atlantic states (Machine Tool Panel, 1983, p. 13).

The United Kingdom dominated world markets in machine tools until the end of the 19th century. U.K machine tool builders tended to specialize in large-scale custom-designed machines for the railway, shipbuilding, and industrial machinery industries (UNIDO, 1984). Historians of the machine tool industry usually identify this specialization as both a source of 19th-century strength and a cause of 20th-century decline in the U.K. machine tool industry.

In the early 20th century the United States and Germany emerged as industrial leaders. The U.S. industry in particular had become a large producer of special-purpose machines suitable for the mass production of durable consumer goods such as bicycles, automobiles, and appliances. These machines, with their standardized interchangeable parts, generated considerable export as well as domestic demand (UNIDO, 1984, p. 66).

As consumer durable industries grew in the post–World War II era, the U.S. machine tool industry grew as well, with domestic producers satisfying almost all domestic demand (94% in 1960, 90% in 1968) (UNIDO, 1974, p. 37). Situated in the enormous U.S. market, U.S. producers—despite their considerable share of world exports—did not develop an export-oriented marketing strategy. European countries, however, being smaller, tended to specialize in particular products that they would export as well as consume, while relying heavily on imports of all other machine tool products.

The Japanese, from the mid-19th century until 1945, imported most of the tools required for their industrial and military development from the United States and Britain, producing their own only when the supply of imports was cut off during the two world wars. After World War II, when the government abolished the arsenals and thereby eliminated a major source of demand, Japanese machine tool producers found themselves in a highly competitive situation. Like other Japanese manufacturers, known worldwide during the 1950s as producers of low-quality goods, machine tool builders embarked on a concerted and successful effort to improve product quality (Chokki, 1986).

For much of the postwar period Japanese machine tool exports were directed toward other Asian countries. In the 1970s, however, there was a massive surge in domestic and foreign demand for Japan's manufactured goods, and Japanese machine tool builders found themselves in an enviable position—producing high-quality, small and medium-scale numerically controlled machine tools at competitive prices. These tools flooded the United States and world markets in a manner similar to the American invasion of the European market at the turn of the century (Fransman, 1986b), when standardized U.S. machines pushed aside custom-built U.K. machines by virtue of their lower unit cost (Floud, 1976).

The developed market economies, of course, have not been the only producers and consumers of machine tools. Though most historians of machine tools ignore the growth of the industry in the former Soviet Union and other socialist countries, their output and consumption of machine tools in this century has been considerable. In 1987, for example, the USSR was the third-largest producer of machine tools (the United States was fourth) and by far the largest consumer.

The other participants in the global machine tool industry are the newly industrialized countries (NICs), most prominently China, Taiwan, and South Korea. Their history as machine tool producers is relatively short and their share of world output small, but they play an important and specialized role in the industry's international division of labor, producing low-cost conventional machines—once produced by the United States—for their own use and to some extent for export.

Over the course of its history two innovations in control systems have revolutionized the machine tool industry and the metalworking industries that are its customers. The first, developed in the second half of the 19th century, involved an upgrading of manual control through the application of fixtures and jigs specially designed to hold the workpiece and allow the standardized replication of a particular design (Rosenberg, 1976). A similar breakthrough occurred in the post–World War II period, when the development of numerical control (NC) and the application of computer technology to machine tools enhanced their accuracy and flexibility to an extraordinary degree.

Numerical control involves the use of a punchcard, magnetic tape, or other medium to control timing, sequencing, tool selection, set up, counting, and other functions of production. NC can replace jigs and fixtures, the staples of mechanical control for more than a century, and at the same time eliminate the need for skilled machinists to read complex blueprints or to design and set up fixtures for less-experienced workers (Noble, 1979).

In the past two decades NC technology has been upgraded through the development of programmable NC units and systems, including computer numerical control (CNC), which gives the machinist or other controller the capability of editing and storing programs created in the process of work. With this innovation, electronic control itself has become more flexible and easily modifiable.

Programmability has more recently been extended beyond the control function to the integration function. Large-scale flexible manufacturing systems (FMS) incorporate a number of machine tools, automated materials handling and transfer systems, and a computer control integrating these components, which takes charge of such functions as routing and scheduling. When one machine in a system is down, for example, the system controller may be programmed to route the workpiece to another machine or to move on to another operation that does not require that machine.

Flexible manufacturing systems and their smaller siblings, CNC stand-alone machines and flexible manufacturing cells (FMC) incorporating several machines, represent different scales of the solution to the problem of minimizing the cost and time involved in changing the production process. For small-batch producers like the machine tool builders themselves, the new technology is the long-awaited key to automation. For high-volume producers like the automobile industry, which has historically automated its mass-production process through the use of dedicated machines and transfer lines, the new technology represents an opportunity to increase the efficiency of automated operations—reducing downtime, avoiding bottlenecks, cutting set-up costs, and so forth.

THE CHANGING GEOGRAPHY OF MACHINE TOOL PRODUCTION AND TRADE

Perhaps the most obvious geographic characteristic of the machine tool industry is its locational conservatism. Machine tool production is historically and currently concentrated in the world's major industrial centers. Geographic change in the industry usually involves shifts in position, specialization, and trade among the major producing regions rather than locational reorientation.

Figures 4.1 and 4.2 show that the machine tool industry is geographically concentrated in those countries (or regions) where industrial development is most advanced. According to most industry analysts, this is because these areas have the skilled labor force, appropriate supplies of materials and equipment, and proximate market that the industry traditionally requires.

In 1955 the top four countries accounted for 77% of total output. In 1987 the top four accounted for 65%, while the top six countries accounted for over 75%. (Lest we see this as a unidirectional trend toward geographic deconcentration, it should be noted that in 1976 the top four countries accounted for only 57% of the world's output.) Since the major producers of machine tools tend also to be the major consumers, trade in machine tools is geographically concentrated as well, taking place largely among the top producer countries.

Up until the time of World War II the United Kingdom, Germany, and the United States were the major producers and exporters of machine tools (United Nations Industrial Development Organization, 1984, p. 66). Since World War II, the rise of Japan has been the most significant new development in the industry. Though its output was negligible in 1955, Japan was the largest producer by 1982, with the major growth spurt taking place in the past 12 years (see Figure 4.2). Other important producers throughout the postwar period include the U.S.S.R., the German Democratic Republic, Switzerland, Italy, and France. Although

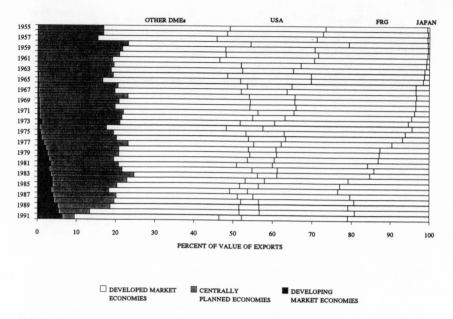

FIGURE 4.1. World production of machine tools, 1955–1991. *Source: American Machinist*, various years.

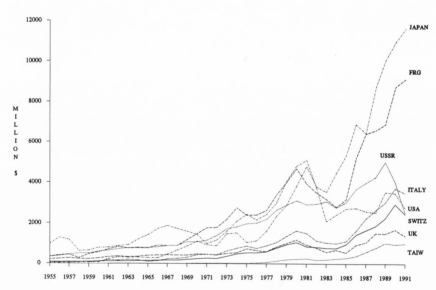

FIGURE 4.2. Production of machine tools, selected countries, 1955–1991 (in $millions). *Source: American Machinist*, various years.

the NICs—most notably Brazil, China, India, South Korea, and Taiwan— are not particularly significant in terms of overall production, they have shown impressive rates of growth and should continue to account for an increasing share of world output (see Figure 4.1).

Since 1970 international trade in machine tools, like that in many other manufactured products, has grown faster than production (see Figure 4.3). The distribution of world exports has been substantially affected by the rise of Japan, which shows a rapidly increasing share of exports while other countries or country groupings (with the exception of the NICs) show shrinking or stable shares (see Figure 4.4).

The very low export share of the United States can be attributed to a variety of factors, the most visible being the strong dollar of the early 1980s. Traditionally the United States has been able to rely on exports to take up any slack in the domestic market. But even with the dollar down to acceptable levels, U.S. producers have found it difficult to re-gain access to world or even to domestic markets. With Japan and Tai-wan pursuing an export strategy focused on the U.S. market and with traditional producers like Germany, Italy, and Switzerland vigorously

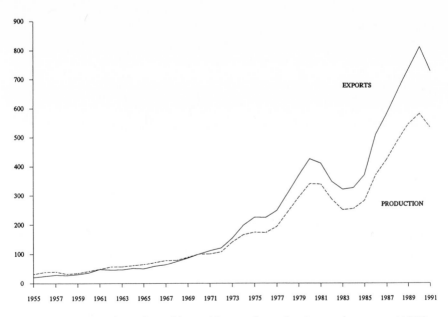

FIGURE 4.3. Value of world machine tool production and exports (1970 = 100). *Source: American Machinist*, various years.

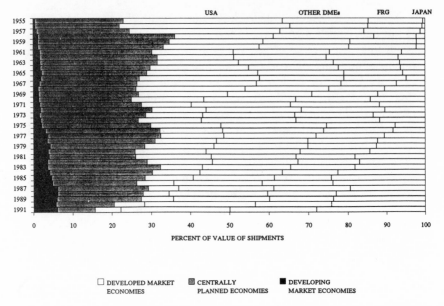

FIGURE 4.4. World machine tool exports, 1955–1991. *Source: American Machinist*, various years.

maintaining their long-term export orientation (see Figure 4.5 and Table 4.1), the United States is squeezed competitively at home and abroad.

The International Division of Labor in Machine Tools

At present the division of labor between the developed and the developing countries is clearly demarcated along technological lines, with NC/CNC machine tools as the boundary marker. NC/CNC machine tools are more expensive and more complex to produce and market than simpler, low-tech machines. Their production requires greater inputs of R & D, electrical and electronic as well as mechanical engineering, and software development and interfacing. Their marketing often involves the provision of design and applications engineering to the industrial consumer. It is not surprising, then, that third world countries are only minimally engaged in producing NC/CNC machines, either for the local or for the world market. Rather, they produce and export the less-sophisticated, standard, universal machine tools that are still extensively used in both the developed and the developing worlds and that they can sell at extremely competitive prices.

On the other side of the technological gap created by the conjoining of computer technology to machine tools, the developed countries are ranged in specialized niches in the mid-tech (small- and medium-scale NC/CNC machines and flexible manufacturing cells) and high-tech (large-scale flexible manufacturing systems) markets. Japan is the acknowledged leader in the production and export of NC/CNC machines, and in industrial automation technology in general (United Nations Industrial Development Organization, 1984, p. 121). U.S. producers have concentrated on large-scale, integrated, highly automated flexible manufacturing systems (FMS) for the defense industries and major transportation equipment manufacturers. In doing so, they have lost out in the market for smaller standard NC/CNC and conventional machines. This situation represents a major change since 1980, when the United States was still a full-spectrum producer able to satisfy every type of machine tool demand in the national and world markets.

The growth of machine tool exports relative to production reflects, among other things, increased international interdependence and product specialization in the industry. As Table 4.1 indicates, Japan is the one major producer/consumer country that is not heavily dependent on

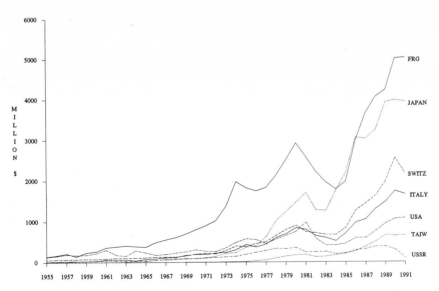

FIGURE 4.5. Machine tool exports, selected countries, 1955–1991 (in $million). *Source: American Machinist,* various years.

TABLE 4.1. Indicators of International Specialization in Machine Tools, 1991[a]

Country	Exports as % of country production	Imports as % of apparent comsumption[b]	Net trade as % of gross trade[c]
Leaders			
Japan	33.9	7.7	72.0
FRG	55.2	34.1	40.9
Italy	47.7	37.8	20.1
USA	39.4	58.5	−36.8
USSR	4.0	41.5	−88.9
Switzerland	88.6	75.7	42.7
Significant OECD			
UK	54.2	59.3	−10.4
France	41.0	72.7	−58.6
Spain	48.4	55.2	−13.6
Sweden	107.1	104.4	−22.3
Principal Developing Countries			
Taiwan	66.9	52.7	29.1
China	25.7	46.8	−43.6
South Korea	11.3	53.9	−80.3
Brazil	15.4	10.6	21.3
India	10.9	35.9	−64.2
Mexico	66.7	98.1	−92.5

[a]Data for 1991 is estimated.
[b]Imports divided by production plus imports less exports.
[c]The difference between exports and imports divided by their sum; a positive sign indicates a positive balance of trade.
Source: American Machinist, February 1992; O'Brien, 1987, Table 3, p. 28.

machine tool imports (Jablonowski, 1992). This suggests that the Japanese industry is the only national machine tool industry that produces for almost all aspects of the market. Thus we should not see national-level product specialization as a necessary outcome of industry development, even though increasing geographic specialization in particular products has characterized the world industry as a whole (UNIDO, 1984, p. 63). Nor should we see specialization and export orientation as necessarily linked. The NICs are relatively specialized producers of low-tech tools but continue to be net machine tool importers (see Table 4.2).

It is likely that the geographic concentration of the industry will continue, though the international division of labor may change. The orientation of the industry toward markets and expertise (technological depth and skilled labor) gives it a degree of geographic stability. Major industrial markets—though plagued by cyclicality—do not appear or disappear at any great rate, nor do geographic concentrations of high technology and machining skill spring up over night. On the other hand, as the growth in exports relative to production seems to suggest, markets may be losing their pull. Even at the high end of the market, where producer–consumer interaction is increasing, that interaction often involves the system or cell rather than the actual machine tool itself, which could be imported (Alexander, 1990). Conceivably, then, a major consuming nation such as the United States could become a minor producer, as other countries replicate its technological strength.

U.S. Industry Geography

The geographic concentration that characterizes the world industry also characterizes the U.S. industry (see Table 4.3 and Figure 4.6). Machine tool producers are clustered in the Midwest around the automobile in-

TABLE 4.2. Machine Tool Production, Comsumption, and Trade, 1991[a] (in $millions)

Country	Production	Comsumption[b]	Exports	Imports
Leaders				
Japan	11617.7	8316.7	3941.8	640.8
FRG	9123.8	6204.3	5032.9	2113.4
Italy	3468.4	2915.5	1653.6	1100.7
USA	2740	4000	1080	2340
USSR	2500	4100	100	1700
Switzerland	2441.3	1147.3	2162.3	868.3
Significant OECD				
UK	1370.3	1543.4	742.6	915.7
France	1081.6	2335	443.3	1696.7
Spain	798.6	919.9	386.3	507.6
Sweden	231.4	373.3	247.9	389.8
Principal Developing Countries				
Taiwan	981.5	685.6	657.1	361.2
China	837.6	1170.6	215	548
South Korea	790.8	1521.4	89.4	820
Brazil	350	331	54	35
India	230	319.6	25	114.6
Mexico	15	263	10	258

[a]Data for 1991 is estimated.
[b]Consumption = (Production − Exports) + Imports.
Source: American Machinist, February 1992.

TABLE 4.3. Machine Tool Employment in the Top
12 States, 1989

United States	49,430
Top 12 States	41,304
Ohio	8502
Michigan	8074
Illinois	7228
New York	4493
Connecticut	2420
Wisconsin	2189
California	2021
Pennsylvania	1621
Indiana	1414
Massachusetts	1383
Minnesota	987
Rhode Island	972

Source: County Business Patterns, 1989.

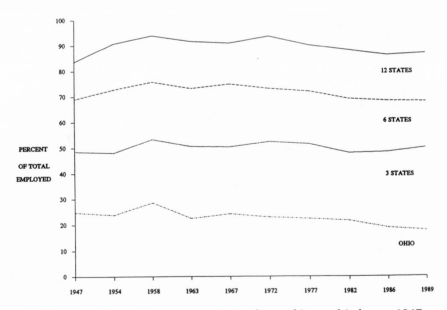

FIGURE 4.6. Geographic concentration in the machine tool industry, 1947–
1989. *Source: Census of Manufacturers, County Business Patterns.*

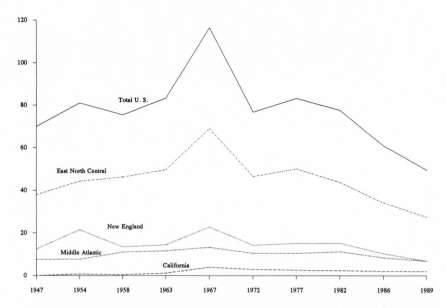

FIGURE 4.7. Employment in machine tools, 1947–1989 (in thousands). *Source: Census of Manufacturers, County Business Patterns.* (For certain years, values for ME, NH, RI, and VT were selected from a range provided by the census.)

dustry, with some smaller concentrations in New England and the Middle Atlantic states. In addition, California is a center of aerospace manufacture and boasts a small machine tool industry (see Figure 4.7).

Machine tools were first produced in New England, where some large firms and many smaller ones are still located. Toward the latter part of the 19th century the industry spread to the Middle Atlantic states and to the east north central region, its geographic center today. In the 20th century output grew rapidly in Michigan, spurred by the growth of the auto industry, and Illinois, where the expansion of the farm and construction machinery industry created a growing demand for machine tools. Currently, Ohio, Michigan, and Illinois are the major centers of machine tool employment (see Table 4.3 and Figure 4.7). Because of recent plant closings in the Great Lakes states, the center of gravity of the industry shows a slight shift to the south (U.S. Department of Commerce, 1992).

During the 1980s employment in the industry fell off steadily, though not as precipitously as it did between 1967 and 1972 (see Figure 4.7). Employment has continued to decline in the 1990s, dropping to 40,500 in 1992 (U.S. Department of Commerce, 1992). It is now considerably lower than it was in the late 1940s, when the cancellation of government contracts and the concomitant dumping of machine tools no longer needed in the war effort caused a wave of layoffs that was only reversed by the Korean War buildup in the early 1950s. The recent decline in employment has been steepest in the Midwest but New England has also experienced a significant drop. This may reflect its particular product mix. While suppliers to the local weapons and aerospace industries prospered during the defense buildup of the late 1970s and early 80s, New England machine tool builders have historically tended to produce a diverse line of general purpose tools with no particular geographical orientation (except to centers of metalworking such as the industrial Midwest and the Northeast) (Wagoner, 1968). This distinguishes them from firms in the Midwest, which tend to be producers of special-purpose machine tools clustered around particular user industries, and it also makes them particularly vulnerable to the foreign competition that has hit hardest in the market for small- and medium-scale conventional and NC/CNC machines.

Clearly, the United States experienced a major—though not unprecedented—setback in its machine tool industry during the 1980s. This was reflected in a 50% decrease in output and a somewhat smaller percentage decrease in employment over the course of the decade. At the same time many European producers have held their own, in output if not in market share, and the Japanese have expanded rapidly in both. A new international division of labor is in place, in which Taiwan (and the other Asian NICs) are increasingly supplying low-cost conventional machine tools while the Japanese have largely captured the market for high-quality small- and medium-scale NC/CNC machines.

The causes of the geographic shifts in machine tool production and trade are, of course, infinitely complex. But the interventionist orientation of this chapter dictates an emphasis on the activities of organizations, in particular those of firms and governments. After a brief discussion of technological development in user industries, the rest of the chapter will explore the impact of firm strategies and government policy on the geography of the global machine tool industry, in an attempt to signal some of the processes that have contributed to its recent transformation.

TECHNOLOGICAL DEVELOPMENT IN MACHINE TOOLS AND USER INDUSTRIES

Centering the discussion of geographic change in the machine tool industry on first, the rapid shift in relative position of the Japanese and U.S. industries, and second, the dramatic absolute decline in U.S. output and employment, several things stand out as contributing factors. One important factor is the orientation toward user industries and the way in which that orientation has shaped technological and organizational development (Rosenberg, 1976).

The machine tool industry in most countries has been guided in its technological development by the government's involvement in and planning for war. In the early days of the industry the British and U.S. governments nurtured the fledgling industry because it could create machines for mass-producing weapons. During the American Civil War, a well-timed event from an industrial development perspective, government calls for armaments gave the industry a major boost. Similarly World War I and World War II prompted massive investments in machine tools by the industries building weapons, tanks, aircraft, ships, and other war-related transportation equipment (Machine Tool Panel, 1983, p. 14).

Though historians of the U.S. industry disagree over whether the military connection produced innovation or just growth and dependency (see, for example, DiFilipo, 1986; Melman, 1983), it is certainly true that the development of numerically controlled machine tools was an outgrowth of postwar U.S. Air Force contracts to MIT and large machine tool builders. The Air Force sought highly accurate, automated machine tools that could contribute their deadly precision to the management of the cold war and its hot spots. What they got, in addition, was the beginning of a technological revolution.

NC was expensive to institute in the 1950s when it first became available commercially, but it was often cost-effective for defense contractors and aerospace firms that required high-quality, precision machining. These firms became the primary consumers of the technically advanced machine tools and they tended to order large, custom-built equipment at the high end of the price and technology spectrum. Their suppliers among U.S. machine tool builders became proficient in producing NC technology in its most complex, technically rarefied, and expensive form.

The U.S. automobile industry, the other major consumer of U.S. machine tools, was not an early user of NC technology. In the 1950s and 1960s this oligopolized industry operated in a growth market and pursued an entrenched strategy of mass production with dedicated equipment. Thoroughly committed to mechanical automation, auto firms purchased huge customized installations integrating machine tools and transfer systems. After the crisis of the mid-1970s when the automakers decided to retool, they ordered large-scale, custom-designed NC equipment like their aerospace counterparts.

In postwar Japan the nature of demand was entirely different (Watanabe, 1983). The highly competitive auto industry and the extensive subcontracting network with which it is associated represented an extremely demanding market in terms of both price and quality (Fransman, 1986b, p. 29). Since NC machine tools can deliver greater accuracy than their conventional counterparts, Japanese machine tool builders began very early on to produce low-cost NC machines. Only later, when they perceived the lack of such machines in the United States, did they hit on the strategy of capturing the U.S. market for small- and medium-scale CNC machines.

Their opening came in the second half of the 1970s, when U.S. automobile and aerospace manufacturers underwent their massive retooling programs and U.S. machine tool builders were preoccupied and backlogged. By the time orders dropped off again in the early 1980s, the Japanese were firmly entrenched in the U.S. market for CNC machines. Though European producers and even Taiwan are currently giving the Japanese some stiff competition in this market, U.S. machine tool builders have not recovered from the Japanese onslaught. This can be explained, in part, by their user-oriented specialization in high-end custom products (Raia, 1985) and by technological stagnation in firms producing standardized tools.

FIRM STRATEGY AND INDUSTRY STRUCTURE

Although every major producing nation has some large machine tool firms with thousands of employees, the machine tool industry has traditionally been characterized by family-owned firms operating small, craft-based job shops in a highly competitive environment. This is especially true in the United States. According to the 1982 Census of Manufactures, 93% of U.S. machine tool firms were single-establishment firms and two-thirds of machine tool establishments had fewer than 20 employees. As the NMTBA (1985, p. 60) points out, however, these figures should be taken with a grain of salt. Many of the establishments counted by the census are engaged in the production of machine tool accessories rather than machine tools per se, and thus should not be included in SICs 3541 and 3542.

Table 4.4 lists the large firms that dominated the U.S. machine tool industry in 1988. This list should help to dispel the miniaturized image of the U.S. machine tool producer, which is only partially correct. A more accurate image would portray a small pond with a few large fish, more medium-sized ones, and hundreds of minnows.

In other countries the tendency toward small- and medium-sized firms and small shops is observable but less extreme. In Japan, for

TABLE 4.4. Major U.S. Machine Tool Builders, 1988

Firm or Division[a]	Sales ($million)	Employees
Cincinnati Milacron	850	9,600
GTE Precision Materials	645	9,000
Cross & Trecker	418	4,300
Ingersoll International	380	5,000
Kennemetal	355	4,800
Lamb Technicon	350	2,200
Gleason	252	3,400
Sandvik Coromant	220	3,400
Bridgeport Machines	200	900
Acme-Cleveland	191	2,400

[a]Only companies that produce machine tools as their primary type of output are included in this list. Some major machine tool builders whose primary output is another product are therefore excluded. *Source: Ward's Business Directory*, Vol. 3. Belmont, CA: Ziff-Davis, 1988.

example, firms tend to be larger and more vertically integrated ("Holding the Lead," 1987). Almost one-quarter of Japanese firms have more than 1000 employees and are engaged in producing other products in addition to machine tools. In Germany independent, medium-sized firms predominate. And in Italy the industry is characterized by the peaceful coexistence of large and very small but versatile firms (Harrop, 1985).

Small size is not necessarily associated with backwardness or weakness in the machine tool industry. In the United States, however, small- and medium-sized firms appear to be weaker than they are in other countries. Whereas other countries have provided government support and other social infrastructure for the machine tool industry, U.S. firms have had to be more self-sufficient. As a result, they have tended to internalize functions like R & D, training, and finance through vertical integration and concentration (Herrigel, 1988). This has contributed to a lopsided dualism in the industry, where the large firms have access to resources in the form of skilled labor, R & D capability, and capital that are not readily available to small firms.

The market for machine tools is extremely sensitive to fluctuations in demand for the output of the metalworking industries, some of which themselves are capital goods industries with highly cyclical markets. These industries do not undertake major investments in capital goods in a bad year, nor do they do so in every good year. When conditions are right, however, the machine tool industry is flooded with orders, most of which have to be backlogged. These may turn into cancellations as conditions change or as other suppliers are found. The intense cyclicality of the industry exacerbates the weakness of the smaller firms, which survive precariously on the orders that spill over from backlogged large firms during booms.

The strong dollar of the early 1980s and the growth of foreign competition in both NC/CNC and conventional machine tools have had a profound effect on the size and, to a lesser extent, the structure of the U.S. industry. Historically, four- and eight-firm concentration ratios have been relatively low (see Figure 4.8). But in the 1980s mergers and acquisitions as well as closures radically reduced the number of firms operating in the industry. Nine of the top twelve machine tool builders merged or were purchased by conglomerates in the first half of the decade (Raia, 1985). Of the 800 firms in SICs 3541 and 3542 that were really producing machine tools in 1982, only 500 were left in 1986 (O'Brien, 1987, p. 24). Among the U.S. firms that have emerged from the 1980s as survivors committed to the continued manufacture of machine tools, the largest are Cincinnati Milacron, Cross and Trecker, Litton Industries, Ingersoll Milling Machine, and Giddings & Lewis. The first three are

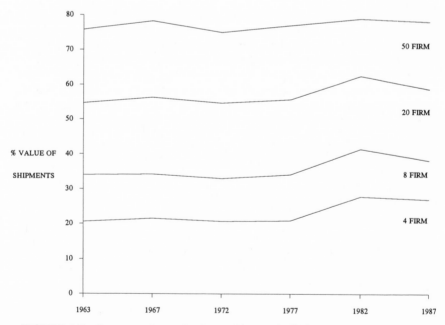

FIGURE 4.8. Concentration ratios in machine tools (SICs 3541, 3542). *Source: Census of Manufacturers*, 1987.

multiunit firms while the last two are machine tool-producing units within larger firms (R. E. Winter, 1987). Other firms, including large conglomerates like Textron and small, family-owned machine tool builders, are getting out of the machine tool business altogether. Though they are accustomed to the cyclicality of the industry, the lengthy order drought of the 1980s was too long for these firms to weather.

The computer revolution in machine tools has also had a decided impact on the structure of the industry. Analysts perceive a distinct split between those firms that are engaged in the production of computerized machine tools and those that are not. Many of the latter do not even use the new technology in their own shops (Rohan, 1986). The small size of these firms and the cyclicality of the industry has limited their ability to invest in the new generation of tools (Marx, 1979, p. 43). They also cannot afford the increasing R & D costs associated with producing NC machines, cells, and systems. The owner of one company, diagnosing its failure, encapsulated the problem in these words: "We got into projects where the engineering hours were greater than the direct labor hours" (quoted in Levinson, 1987, p. 48).

Companies that can afford large initial investments in design and technology can enter the high-tech market in which the U.S. machine tool industry is still competitive. These companies tend to be either the industry giants or the medium-sized firms in specialized niches. For the remaining firms, the question of the appropriate strategy for survival and growth seems to be an open one. In the world machine tool industry, however, certain strategies stand out for their popularity among machine tool firms interested in improving their position. These include investment strategies, export orientation, product development and specialization, and interfirm cooperation. Interestingly enough, these diverse strategies are all geographically conservative, in the sense that they have little impact on the location of the industry. Many of them, however, contribute to the internationalization of the industry, that is, to greater international interaction and interdependence among geographically stable clusters of firms. They also contribute to the rapid shifts in relative position that characterize the international division of labor in machine tools.

Investment Strategies

The investment strategies that figure most prominently in the machine tool industry are acquisition, divestment, and foreign direct investment (FDI). Much of this activity is focused on the United States where few new plants are being built by domestic machine tool producers: "Many of us . . . are being very careful about building brick and mortar"

(Schiller, 1989, quoting a vice-president of Ingersoll-Rand). Instead, domestic and foreign machine tool builders looking for ways to expand their markets or develop new products have increasingly pursued a strategy of acquisition. Even a failing company has a network of suppliers and customers that has taken many years to develop. And an undercapitalized firm in a growth area of the high-tech market is ripe for takeover.

Though there is no available quantitative data on the purpose of mergers and acquisitions, it appears that most are extensively oriented (expanding into new product or new national markets) rather than intensively oriented (deepening or vertically integrating in the existing product market). According to some analysts, in fact, the industry trend is toward vertical disintegration (Alexander, 1990), reflecting the impact of electronic technology (Rendeiro, 1985). Companies that formerly relied on proprietary mechanical technology as the basis of their market are now developing NC/CNC machines and systems. They prefer to outsource to highly specialized "niche" firms their demand for certain increasingly standardized mechanical components of machine tools. To some extent, this new trend toward outsourcing is responsible for indigenous start-ups in this country, usually in older regions of machine tool production where machinists and machine tool plants are available. In Grafton, Wisconsin, for example, Ozaukee Tool was started in 1982 by a machinist at Milwaukee Gear. Three years later, when he moved the operation out of his house and quit his job to devote full time to the business, he was producing parts for machine tools at "unbelievable tolerances" for customers like General Motors and Briggs & Stratton (Spivak, 1987).

While foreign direct investment is on the rise in the industry (O'Brien, 1987), it has a long history with U.S. firms, which expanded into Europe and Asia in the post–World War II period. Then, as now, most FDI is market-oriented and much of it involves the acquisition of existing plants rather than the construction of new ones. This is especially true of recent inward investment to the United States, through which foreign firms acquire existing U.S. facilities and the distribution network that goes with them. Of the top 12 U.S. machine tool builders, several were purchased by foreign firms in the 1980s (U.S. Department of Commerce, 1985).

Though most FDI is market-oriented, it still contributes to the internationalization of production (as well as marketing and ownership.) Mazak of Japan uses its plants in Britain and the United States primarily for access to the U.S. and European markets but also for export (even to Japan) (Weiss, 1987). Hueller Hille fulfilled its recent contract with General Motors using machines built both in its Troy, Michigan, plant and its plant in Germany (Wrigley, 1988b). Makino acquired Cincinnati-based Le Blond so they could ship knocked-down machine tools from Japan to be assembled in Le Blond plants (Raia, 1985).

The Japanese are the most vigorous pursuers of the FDI strategy, with Germany close behind. FDI in the United States was speeded up in the late 1980s by the weakened dollar, the threat and reality of protectionist measures such as Voluntary Restraint Agreements (VRAs) and domestic content regulations, and the increased interaction between machine tool producers and consumers required by the modular development of flexible manufacturing cells and systems. While larger Japanese firms like Mazak and Toyoda tend to operate full-scale plants in the United States, others like Okamoto, Kitamura, and Miyano in Illinois have started small with assembly or "screwdriver" plants intended to circumvent VRAs and provide a base for later increases in domestic content (Giesen, 1987).

Investment strategies seem basically to be responsible for growth (or decline) of the industry in established locations rather than generating a new industry geography. Major U.S. machine tool producers, such as Cincinnati Milacron, which have been almost entirely dependent on contracts from U.S. automobile and aerospace manufacturers undergoing retooling since the 1970s, found themselves forced to rationalize by closing plants as retooling wound down (Weiss, 1988). In addition, large conglomerate firms have milked and subsequently shut down the marginal machine tool plants within their corporate structure. But the remaining plants as well as any new plants built by more-successful or more-dedicated firms are generally concentrated in the industrial Midwest or its immediate periphery. Moreover, indigenous start-ups, such as those recorded in Precision Valley in northern New England (Gabriele, 1988), tend to rise from the industrial ashes of larger, failed firms. Overall, then, investment-related geographic change is relatively subtle in the machine tool industry.

Export Orientation

Though foreign machine tool builders have generally been oriented toward the world market, U.S. firms have traditionally been more inward-looking, concentrating on satisfying an enormous U.S. appetite for all sizes and types of machine tools (Real, 1980). Only the very large firms have made sustained efforts to enter foreign markets, either through FDI or the export of machines and service. In general, the export market has been used as a buffer against bad times at home, rather than a target of a well-developed marketing effort. The fact that the United States was until recently a major exporter of machine tools had more to do with its position as a major producer of the full spectrum of machine tool products rather than with any particular interest or capability in overseas markets.

The opposite is the case for Japan, Taiwan, and the major European producers. The latter have long concentrated considerable energy on the U.S. market in particular, while the first two have more recently made it the target of concerted export campaigns. In addition to attempting to develop price competitiveness and a reputation for high quality, foreign producers have also tended to offer customer service programs that are better than those offered by U.S. machine tool builders. Japanese overseas sales and service representatives in particular are known for their attentiveness, availability, and high levels of technical expertise.

While Japanese machine tool exporters concentrated on providing high-quality, low-cost NC/CNC machine tools to the United States and increasingly to the European markets, the Taiwanese developed an export-oriented strategy principally focused on selling low-priced conventional machines in the United States. In the 1980s, however, certain Taiwanese firms attempted to enter the world market for CNC machines, continuing the strategy of price competition that has been so successful for their conventional machines. By building "low-performance" CNC lathes, for example, they hoped to break into the CNC market, selling cheaper, less-durable, less-accurate machines to schools, first-time users, and small subcontractors in the United States, and to metalworking firms in the NICs that do not require sophisticated equipment (Chudnovsky & Nagao, 1983). Thus the division of labor that has been in place may soon be radically modified, as the NICs increasingly enter the NC/CNC market.

Of course, an export strategy is not enough to guarantee success in the world market, as Japanese producers have found out recently with the imposition of VRAs in the United States and "antidumping" duties in the EC. Exporters are also vulnerable to currency fluctuations, which may not only price their tools out of foreign markets but make foreign tool producers more competitive at home. With the rise in the value of the yen in the latter part of the 1980s, Japanese machine tool builders ceded a small but growing share of their domestic market to U.S., European, and Taiwanese producers. They also began to import and distribute foreign machine tools themselves, including those made in their overseas plants and even some made by competitors (Chatterjee, 1988). At the same time U.S. producers, long cut out of foreign markets by the strong dollar and the perception that their competitors made higher quality machine tools, experienced a welcome surge in foreign orders, especially from Europe (Holstein, 1988; Schiller, 1989).

Product Development and Market Orientation

Though many years intervened between their invention and their wide-spread adoption, the place of electronically controlled NC machine tools in the pantheon of industrial technology is now secure. Their ascendancy, however, has substantially redefined the product market and the strategic opportunities for firms to relate to that market.

At the moment large U.S. producers are alive and well in the market for NC/CNC machine tools but they are most successful in the large-scale, high-tech, low-volume experimental end of that market. Even in this market, where they are currently preeminent, U.S. firms are not secure. Rohan (1986) indicates that foreign machine tool builders, including Japanese, Italian, and West German firms, are beginning to penetrate the U.S. market for FMS and large cells. In addition, the industry and its customers seem to be pulling back from the "grand FMS" and reorienting themselves to the smaller flexible manufacturing cells (Huber, 1988). The fully automated "factory of the future" has been a disappointment to many of its former boosters. Cross and Trecker, one of the two largest machine tool builders, dismantled their FMS, constructing out of its remains a number of multimachine cells (Giesen & Weiss, 1988). Other machine tool builders have never even installed FMS, creating suspicion among their potential customers that the systems are risky and unwieldy. Only Ingersoll Milling Machine and Mazak seem to be sticking with the big systems through the current wave of disillusionment.

With the advent of NC/CNC product technology in its various incarnations, traditional machine tool producers have moved into new areas of production. Many have become producers of computer software or of automated materials handling and transfer systems like precision pallets or robots. Kearney and Trecker, for example, has "unbundled its technical capability from its machine tools and control business," selling software and systems to new customers without the "iron" (Rohan, 1987b). Furthermore, the new technologies, and especially the complex systems, require an ongoing relationship with the customer, beginning with the design phase and continuing throughout the life of the infinitely modifiable product. This means that machine tool producers are increasingly involved in service provision as well as manufacturing (Wilson, 1987), belying the vision of a unidirectional trend toward vertical disintegration. In a contract with Boeing, for example, Ingersoll Milling Machine designed and developed an entire parts production system rather than just building a preengineered system to customer-provided specifications. Ingersoll also contracted to assist Boeing with installation and provide long-term consultancy necessary to achieve guaranteed productivity gains (Winter & Stricharchuk, 1987).

As industry technology becomes ever more complex and expensive, even manufacturing is becoming a service. Thus, for example, a machine tool producer of laser-cutting machines may provide high-tech cutting services to customers who cannot afford to buy these state-of-the-art machine tools themselves (Jones, 1988).

Machine tool producers have also changed their product mix in order to deal with the competitiveness and cyclicality of the machine tool market. In the mid-1980s Browne and Sharpe, a major Rhode Island machine tool manufacturer since the 19th century, cut back its machine tool production to 35% of total output, redirecting its energies to the manufacture of precision measuring instruments (McLaughlin, 1987). In 1987 machine tools accounted for only 45% of Cincinnati Milacron's sales (R. E. Winter, 1988). This trend toward diversification among major builders has increased their resemblance to Japanese firms in the machine tool industry, 29 of which are large-scale machinery manufacturers with over 1000 employees that produce machine tools as one of several products ("Holding the Lead," 1987). It may reflect a concern for evening out the effects of the business cycle within particular firms.

In general, analysts agree that U.S. producers of small- and medium-sized machine tools have tried to market a high-volume, standardized product that the customer would customize, sometimes with the assistance of the producing firm. These producers have had difficulty meeting the challenge of Japanese firms, which were used to operating in a highly competitive market and to offering customers a large array of different products, all of which could be adjusted by the producer to meet the customer's highly specific needs.

Firm Partnerships

One of the major impacts of the introduction of electronic controls is a redefinition of the industry itself. This has been manifested on a number of levels. There is, for example, no SIC code for a flexible manufacturing system. An FMS combines technology from the machine tool, materials handling and robotics, and computer (hardware and software) industries. Since each FMS is custom designed and manufactured, firms in any of these industries may take the lead as installer. The user firm itself may even be the builder of the FMS. For the most part, however, U.S. suppliers of FMS are the large machine tool builders (U.S. Department of Commerce, 1985, p. 16) like Cincinnati Milacron and Cross and Trecker.

Nevertheless, the industry redefinition described above is reflected in a variety of new types of interfirm relationships. Increasingly, machine tool producers of FMS are engaging in joint ventures, partnerships, or subcontracting arrangements with other firms—which may or may not be machine tool firms and which may or may not be U.S.–owned—to provide the engineering, computer technology, materials handling system, or some other component of the FMS. One version of this strategy involves a partnership arranged by the customer. Ford Motor Company, for example, engaged two major machine tool producers (Cross and Trecker and Hueller Hille, U.S.- and German-owned, respectively) in the simultaneous engineering program for its modular engine production line. Though both companies contributed design work, only one was awarded the contract to build the system, while the other was paid for engineering services (Wrigley, 1988a).

There is also a trend toward customer–builder partnerships, reflected in long-term contracts that involve both parties in the coengineering of complex custom systems. While machine tool builders and their customers have always maintained close ties, these new relationships call for ongoing interaction with respect to applications engineering, maintenance, and upgrading, as well as the initial design and installation of the system (Wrigley, 1988c). Such partnerships have long been common in Japan, where suppliers and customers in the machine tool industry have historically maintained close and continuous relations (Fransman, 1986a), but are a relatively recent development in the United States.

Finally, there are partnerships arranged by the builders themselves, the most innovative of which involve the joint acquisition of production facilities. Some smaller firms interested in utilizing large-scale FMS but unable or unwilling to install such systems on their own are examining the feasibility of establishing joint facilities for parts manufacture (Rohan, 1986).

The development of service provision as a new product line of machine tool firms and the increased interaction with customers required by flexible manufacturing cells and systems both tend to reinforce geographic concentration in major metalworking centers, as does the increasing incidence of firm partnerships. The latter, however, also contribute to the internationalization of the industry, in the form of international joint ventures that provide access to a foreign market or a foreign technology. Perhaps the most prominent of these in the machine tool industry is the celebrated teaming up of General Electric (GE) and Fanuc, the major Japanese supplier of computer numerical controls. GE Fanuc Automation Corporation provides Fanuc with an invulnerable position in the U.S. market and GE with an interest in the major CNC producer in the world (Pond, 1988).

THE ROLE OF NATIONAL GOVERNMENT POLICY

According to most historians of the machine tool industry (e.g., O'Brien, 1987), the U.S. government has usually left the industry to its own devices. This does not mean that it has had no impact on its development, but rather that its impact—which at times has been massive—has usually been unintentional or indirect. Thus, for example, U.S. wars on other countries or on inflation were not specifically designed with the machine tool industry in mind, but they have sub-stantially affected the direction of industry growth (or decline), as have capital consumption allowances directed at U.S. capital in general (NMTBA, 1985).

An examination of national government intervention in the Asian NICs and Japan (Fransman, 1986a) produces a very different picture. There the state has been directly and intentionally interventionist in a number of ways—as procurer, protector, provider of subsidies, and as regulator of product and market orientation, among other things. In postwar Japan, for example, when military demand for machine tools dried up, the Japanese national railroad pursued a policy of purchasing locally produced machine tools. This was an extraordinary boon to the floundering domestic machine tool industry, in which business failures were rampant. In 1948 54% of Japanese machine tool output was pur-chased by Japan National Railways (Fransman, 1986a, p. 192).

While the railroads contributed to the survival of the postwar indus-try, government action focused on its development has been equally important. From the early 1950s on, the Ministry of International Trade and Industry (MITI) policy involved promoting the transfer of foreign technology without allowing firms to come under the control of foreign interests. The Law on Temporary Measures for the Development of the Machinery Industry targeted 21 industries for special subsidies, includ-ing subsidized credit (a disproportionate share of which went to machine tool producers). The law, formulated and administered by MITI, also attempted to develop Japan's competitiveness as an exporter of machine tools by facilitating collaborative research on technology and encourag-ing rationalization of the industry, both within and between firms (Chokki, 1986). Firms were encouraged to increase their degree of spe-cialization by eliminating product lines produced more efficiently by other producers. MITI also attempted, with dubious success, to increase industry concentration by eliminating small and presumably inefficient producers and to "seek centralization of companies by mergers" (Fransman, 1986a, p. 193). Throughout the postwar period the govern-ment frequently imposed tariffs to protect the domestic market in spe-cific machine tools. CNC machine tools, which were favored as a central element in the machine tool export strategy, were specially targeted for various forms of subsidy and protection.

Among the Asian NICs, the machine tool industry has also been a priority target of government intervention. South Korea has vigorously promoted an export strategy while keeping a tight control on imports. Taiwanese producers have been oriented by the machine tools center in the state-owned Mechanical Industrial Research Laboratories (MIRL) toward developing CNC capability for export and manufacture of a variety of products that compete with imported machine tools. Protection has been more selectively applied in Taiwan than in Korea, but it is still an important tool, second only to support and subsidies for modernization and rationalization (Fransman, 1986b).

Interestingly enough, the industrial development agencies in most countries have noted the small size of many machine tool firms and have associated that factor with backwardness and low productivity, among other problems. They have therefore generally attempted to get small firms to merge, and have often encountered stiff resistance from the firms in question, most notably in Japan and Taiwan. In Britain, where it was also seen as desirable to increase the size of firms to capture economies of scale, the major subsidized enlarged venture went into receivership within a few years (Daly & Jones, 1980). Industry analysts (for example, Alexander, 1990) have generally seen such government attempts as misguided. They point out that the industry is not really characterized by economies of scale, at least in the manufacturing end of the business.

In the United States the tendency of the government to ignore or subsume the industry is more pronounced than in other countries, despite the perceived importance of machine tools to "national security." Analysts also perceive a distinct and long-standing distrust of the government among machine tool builders, stemming in part from government dumping of machine tools after World War II (Machine Tool Panel, 1983). Nevertheless, industry advocates like the NMTBA continually solicit government support, most recently requesting the institution of VRAs, import quotas, and domestic content regulations. The ostensible effect of these would be to increase the viability of domestically produced machine tools in the domestic market and also to promote inward FDI, which might utilize existing capacity and skills that are currently underemployed. Of course, such policies have no single or simple outcome. Alexander (1990) notes that they have already prompted Japanese firms to diversify into machine tools that are not covered by the VRAs. Thus, to some extent VRAs are not deflecting imports so much as redistributing their impact on U.S. firms. They may also increase the market penetration of foreign firms, albeit from a U.S. base (Alexander, 1990, p. vii). Some producers are afraid that VRAs increase the risk of retaliation in their export markets. This may be the reason that Ingersoll Milling Machine, which exported the world's largest machining center (93 by 40 by 48 ft) to Japan, withdrew from the NMTBA in protest over their lobbying efforts on behalf of quotas (Rohan, 1987b). In any case, the VRAs do not seem to have addressed the problem of decline in the U.S. industry. Though Japanese imports have dropped, the output of U.S. firms continues to fall.

In a diverse industry like machine tools, characterized by a wide variety of products and competitive strategies, it is difficult to come up with policy measures that have a uniformly positive effect. But the recent history of the international machine tool industry suggests that there are certain things governments can do. They can promote sharing of resources among small, geographically concentrated firms in an industry like machine tools. They can also support R & D and employee training and retraining that is industry specific, just as they support more generic R & D and training through universities and schools. They can foster the development of specialized financial organizations that provide the sort of credit needed by small firms in an intensely cyclical industry. Finally, as European and Asian experience has shown, governments can be of substantial assistance to firms attempting to sell their goods in overseas markets. In the United States the NMTBA signed an agreement with the Export-Import Bank to obtain credit for machine tool builders interested in increasing their exports ("Machine Tool Builders Sign," 1987).

One area in which U.S. policy could be more effective has to do with the recruitment and retention of labor. Firms almost universally complain about the shortage of skilled machinists in this country (the same complaints are used to explain the problems of the British machine tool industry), yet at the same time many of them engage in union-busting or union-avoiding activities (see, for example, McLaughlin, 1987; Landry, 1986). Government could promote labor retention by supporting unionization within the industry and encouraging worker participation in decision making rather than condoning the adversarial labor relations that currently prevail. Given the composition of the U.S. government and the U.S. machine tool industry, this scenario is unlikely, of course, but it should be regarded as a missed opportunity rather than a natural or social impossibility.

CONCLUSION

The geography of the machine tool industry is a faint image of the geography of industrialization. In other words, most industrialized nations have machine tool industries, though most of the latter account for a very small share of manufacturing value added. To a large extent, then, the geographical expansion of the machine tool industry is associated with the geographical expansion of industrial production.

In addition to spreading slowly over a larger number of nations, the machine tool industry is becoming increasingly internationalized, in a variety of ways. International interdependence has increased, as product specialization and international trade have grown. International outsourcing is becoming a familiar practice among previously self-sufficient firms. Foreign direct investment is also rising, though its extent has not been assessed.

In this internationalized environment the Japanese have become the largest consumers of machine tools and also the most self-sufficient. Japan's imports account for only 8% of its huge demand. By contrast, the U.S. market, once the largest in the world and the exclusive preserve of U.S. machine tool builders, has now become the prime target of every exporting nation.

Over the 1980s the U.S. machine tool industry has contracted radically in both output and employment. Analysts ascribe this change to a variety of weaknesses of the U.S. industry: its unhealthy dualism, which left smaller firms unable to respond to competition and larger firms unaccustomed to its exigencies; its military connection, which encouraged the development of large firms at the high end of the market to the detriment of other market segments; its lack of government support; and the absence of a social infrastructure of institutions specific to its needs such as apprenticeship programs or cooperative banks. They look to Japan, Europe, and the NICs for examples of growing or stable machine tool industries that do not have these weaknesses and privations.

Researchers looking at Germany and Japan, for example, have stressed the embeddedness of the machine tool industries in these societies, which support them with R & D, training and apprenticeship programs, financial assistance and credit, export promotion, import restriction, and a variety of other government and industry-sponsored programs and institutions. This kind of support allowed the German industry in the early 1980s, for example, to extricate itself from technological stagnation and enter the market for CNC tools in a dramatic turnaround that took only 3 or 4 years (Herrigel, 1988). Analysts also report different forms of competitive behavior among firms in other countries: cooperation in R & D, finance, and marketing; flexibility in product technology; onsite, ongoing customer service; attention to both price and quality; and so forth.

Examining the recent history of the machine tool industry in other countries is one good way of generating ideas about what can be done for and within the U.S. machine tool industry. It is also important, however, to look at the survival strategies the U.S. industry is currently pursuing and to identify areas of strength and success as well as areas for possible intervention. Many firms, for example, are hesitant to construct new plants, preferring the cheaper alternative of acquiring existing plants from flagging competitors. If they are large firms, they may diversify their product orientation away from the highly cyclical and competitive machine tools. If they are small, they may hone in on a highly specialized "niche." To maintain or increase their sales in the face of an increasingly competitive domestic market, they may pursue an active export strategy. And to operate in the market for complex technology, they are likely to enter into cooperative relationships with customers, suppliers, and other builders.

All these strategies for survival could be assisted by national and state government. The U.S. government, for example, could aggressively support R & D and exports in growth areas of the world market, to wean the U.S. industry away from its orientation to the domestic market for FMS. Alternatively, however, policy initiatives could attempt to mitigate the conditions of uncertainty that have produced the various strategies. Government-subsidized credit and worker training could help smooth out the effects of demand cycles. U.S. economic diplomacy could contribute to an environment of managed trade, balancing each nation's interest in maintaining a machine tool industry against the desire of foreign firms to capture a growing share of the world market.

At the same time that it is important to take inspiration from the success of other countries and industries, and to support and foster successful strategies of U.S. firms, it is also important not to imbue policy and strategy with ultimate power to control events. Just as the fate of industries is not governed by an invisible hand or a natural law, it is not governed by government policy or firm strategy. The strategies and policies that we have identified as successful (or unsuccessful) in the past were embedded in an infinitely complex web of causation and a particular historical moment that will never return. Not only is it impossible to assign particular firm strategies and government policies a definite rank in a causal hierarchy, it is also impossible to predict their effects in the future.

Changes such as those experienced in the 1980s are an ongoing and perhaps inescapable part of industrial life. It is therefore important to design government policies that are oriented to dealing with difficulty and decline as well as policies oriented to promoting strength and success. In a global economy, national government policy could attempt to address the negative experience of industrial change by mitigating its social and economic impacts. The meaning of decline could be assessed in terms of domestic adjustment instead of in the context of a narrative of competition among warring nations, or of aggregate indicators and international rankings. Such a response to industrial change could be just as important for the economic health of a society and labor force as the restoration of international preeminence to the industry itself.

ACKNOWLEDGMENTS

I would like to acknowledge the able research assistance provided by Nina Laurie and Kevin St. Martin, without whom this chapter could not have been written. Peter Dicken, Meric Gertler, Kathie Gibson, Ann Markusen, and Helzi Noponen provided helpful comments on earlier drafts.

REFERENCES

Alexander, A. J. 1990. *Adaptation to Change in the U.S. Machine Tool Industry and the Effects of Government Policy*. Santa Monica, CA: Rand Corporation.

Chatterjee, S. K. 1988. Overseas Machine Tool Makers Gain Impressive Entry into the Japanese Market. *Modern Machine Shop*, June, pp. 136–137.

Chokki, T. 1986. A History of the Machine Tool Industry in Japan. In M. Fransman, ed., *Machinery and Economic Development*, pp. 124–152. London: Macmillan.

Chudnovsky, D., & Nagao, M. 1983. *Capital Goods Production in the Third World: An Economic Study of Technology Acquisition*. New York: St. Martin's Press.

Daly, A., & Jones, D. T. 1980. The Machine Tool Industry in Britain, Germany and the United States. *National Institute Economic Review, 92(5)*, 53-63.

DiFilipo, A. 1986. *Military Spending and Industrial Decline: A Study of the American Machine Tool Industry*. New York: Greenwood Press.

Floud, R. 1976. *The British Machine Tool Industry, 1850-1914*. Cambridge: Cambridge University Press.

Fransman, M. 1986a. International Competitiveness, International Diffusion of Technology and the State: A Case Study from Taiwan and Japan. In M. Fransman, ed., *Machinery and Economic Development*, pp. 153–214. London: Macmillan.

Fransman, M. 1986b. Machinery in Economic Development. In M. Fransman, ed., *Machinery and Economic Development*, pp. 1–53. London: Macmillan.

Gabriele, M. C. 1988. As Larger Firms Fade, Precision Valley Looks to New Job Shops. *Metalworking News*, 25 April, pp. 4, 24.

Giesen, L. 1987. Japan Tool Firms Eye Growth in U.S. *Metalworking News*, 4 May, pp. 5, 57.

Giesen, L., & Weiss, B. 1988. Cross and Trecker Dismantle Landmark FMS. *Metalworking News,* 5 September, p. 1.

Harrop, J. 1985. Crisis in the Machine Tool Industry: A Policy Dilemma for the European Community. *Journal of Common Market Studies, 24,* 61–75.

Herrigel, G. 1988. "Industrial Order in the Machine Tool Industry: A Comparison of the United States and Germany." Unpublished manuscript, Massachusetts Institute of Technology.

Holding the Lead in the Machine Tool Industry Proves Tough. 1987. *Business JAPAN, 32,* 95, 97, 101, 103–104.

Holstein, W. 1988. Should Small U.S. Exporters Take the Big Plunge? *Business Week,* 12 December, pp. 64, 68.

Huber, R. F. 1988. Machine Tools: A Global View. *Production,* September, pp. 40–45.

International Trade Administration, U.S. Department of Commerce. 1992. *1992 U.S. Industrial Outlook.* Washington DC: U.S. Government Printing Office.

Jablonowski, J. 1992. Machine Tool Production Drops. *American Machinist,* February, pp. 59–63.

Jones, S. L. 1988. Ebtec Shops Expanding High-Energy-Beam Market. *Metalworking News,* 30 May, p. 6.

Landry, D. 1986. "Union/Butterfield: Portrait of a Plant Closing." Unpublished undergraduate research paper, University of Massachusetts at Amherst, MA.

Levinson, M. 1987. Trying to Survive in a Changing World. *Business Month,* March, pp. 46–48.

Machine Tool Builders Sign Export Agreement. 1987. *Association Management,* April, p. 168.

Machine Tool Panel, National Academy of Engineering and the National Research Council. 1983. *The Competitive Status of the U.S. Machine Tool Industry.* Washington, DC: National Academy Press.

McLaughlin, M. 1987. The Stormy Decade. *New England Business,* 21 September, pp. 12, 16, 18, 23–24.

Marx, T. G. 1979. Technological Change and the Structure of the Machine Tool Industry. *MSU Business Topics, 27,* 41–47.

Melloan, G. 1987. Companies Team Up to Develop Better Tools. *Wall Street Journal,* 1 December, p. 37.

Melman, S. 1983. *Profits without Production.* New York: Knopf.

National Machine Tool Builders' Association. 1985. *1986–1987 Economic Handbook of the Machine Tool Industry.* McLean, VA: National Machine Tool Builders' Association.

Noble, D. F. 1979. Social Choice in Machine Design: The Case of Automatically Controlled Machine Tools. In A. Zimbalist, ed., *Case Studies on the Labor Process,* pp. 18–50. New York: Monthly Review Press.

O'Brien, P. 1987. Machine Tools: Growing Internationalisation in a Small Firm Industry. *Multinational Business, 4,* 23–34.

Pond, J. B. 1988. U.S. Acceptance of Computer Numerical Controls Slowly Edging Upward. *Metalworking News,* 25 April, pp. 17–18.

Raia, E. 1985. Japanese Grab Machine Tool Market With Low-Cost, Mass Production. *Purchasing,* 11 July, pp. 23, 29.

Real, B. 1980. *Technical Change and Economic Policy: Sector Report on the Machine Tool Industry.* Paris: Organization for Economic Cooperation and Development.

Rendeiro, J. O. 1985. How the Japanese Came to Dominate the Machine Tool Business. *Long Range Planning, 18,* 62–67.

Rohan, T. M. 1986. Split Personality: Machine Tool Industry Is Study in Contrast. *Industry Week,* 4 August, pp. 33–36.

Rohan, T. M. 1987a. Maverick Makes Out: Ingersoll Counters the Industry's Malaise. *Industry Week,* 18 May, p. 21.

Rohan, T. M. 1987b. Will Unbundling Work for Bill Fife? *Industry Week,* 15 January, pp. 44, 46.

Rosenberg, N. 1976. *Perspectives on Technology.* New York: Cambridge University Press.

Schiller, Z. 1989. Machinery Makers Enjoy the Ride—While It Lasts. *Business Week,* 9 January, p. 71.

Spivak, G. 1987. Basement Machine Tool Business Rises to Fill Profitable Niche. *Business Journal,* 13 April, p. 23.

United Nations Industrial Development Organization. 1974. *The Machine Tool Industry.* Vienna, Austria: United Nations.

United Nations Industrial Development Organization. 1984. *World Non-Electrical Machinery.* New York: United Nations.

U.S. Department of Commerce. 1985. *A Competitive Assessment of the U.S. Flexible Manufacturing Systems Industry.* Washington DC: U.S. Government Printing Office.

VRAs: The White House Answer to Imports Touches the Machine Tool. 1986. *Purchasing,* 24 July, p. 23.

Wagoner, H. D. 1968. *The Machine Tool Industry from 1900 to 1950.* Cambridge: MIT Press.

Watanabe, S. 1983. *Market Structure, Industrial Organization and Technological Development: The Case of the Japanese Electronics-Based Machine Tool Industry.* Geneva: International Labor Organization.

Weiss, B. 1987. Mazak Focuses on UK Plant, US Expansion. *Metalworking News,* 20 July, pp. 5, 19.

Weiss, B. 1988. Milacron Plans Six "Focus Factories." *Metalworking News,* 22 February, pp. 5, 16.

Wilson, K. L. 1987. The Cutting Tool Market: Growth Is Slow but Service Soars. *Purchasing,* 10 September, pp. 68, 69, 71.

Winter, D. 1988. U.S. Machine Tools Prosper. *WARD'S Auto World, 24*(10), 85.

Winter, R. E. 1987. In 1990s, U.S. Will Have Fewer Shops, More Foreign Names in Machine Tools. *Wall Street Journal,* 17 August, p. 8.

Winter, R. E. 1988. Cincinnati Milacron Starts Third Revamp. *Wall Street Journal,* 8 April, p. 4.

Winter, R. E., & Stricharchuk, G. 1987. Ground Down: U.S. Machine-Tool

Makers Lose Out to Imports Due to Price, Quality. *Wall Street Journal,* 17 August, pp. 1, 8.

Wrigley, A. 1988a. Ford's "Partners" on Engines Must Compete for Build Order. *Metalworking News,* 16 May, pp. 1, 33.

Wrigley, A. 1988b. Hueller Sells First US System. *Metalworking News,* 30 May, pp. 1, 25.

Wrigley, A. 1988c. Latest Supplier Partnership Pushes Limits. *Metalworking News,* 9 May, pp. 1, 36.

5

Scale and Regulation Shapes an Innovative Sector: Jockeying for Position in the World Pharmaceuticals Industry

HELZI NOPONEN

In an era of national concern over lagging competitiveness in manufacturing and slipping performance in high-tech export sectors in particular, the U.S. pharmaceutical industry remains a global leader. While most U.S. industries were hit hard by the negative effects of lagging export sales and surging imports in the early 1980s, the pharmaceutical industry performed better than other high-tech sectors, increasing its share of the U.S. high technology trade surplus from 7% in 1980 to 21% in 1985 (Dixon, 1987, p. ix). While other U.S. industries were suffering major loss of market share to Japan and to European producers such as West Germany, pharmaceuticals bucked the tide. Japan became the single-largest foreign market for U.S. drugs, accounting for over 20% of all U.S. exports to that country in 1981. The United States replaced West Germany as world leader in trade surplus in 1981 (Dixon, 1987, p. 14).

Pharmaceuticals are also one of the most lucrative of U.S. industries. In 1990 returns on sales were 19% and returns on equity were 32%, compared with sales and equity returns for the Standard and Poors 400 industrials of 4% and 16%, respectively (Standard and Poors Corporation, 1992, p. H1). Pharmaceutical industry performance has consistently exceeded that of other U.S. manufacturing industries (U.S. Industrial Outlook, 1990, pp. 50–51). Pharmaceuticals have consistently ranked first in profitability among 26 industries, first in sales every year since 1982, first in equity since 1986, and first in investors for 1990 (U.S. Industrial Outlook, 1990, p. 18). One U.S. company, Merck, the world's largest drug multinational, ranks fifth in market value ahead of such U.S. giants as AT&T, Ford, Coca-Cola, Mobil, American Express, and General Motors (*Business Week*, 1991, p. 100).

Despite its strong performance, the pharmaceutical industry receives less attention than autos, steel, or electronics because its employment base is relatively small and spatially concentrated. However, it plays a key role in the economic base of certain states in the Northeast and the Midwest. Furthermore, jobs in this innovation-based industry are of good quality. The industry employed about 175,700 workers in 1989, 82,000 or 42% of whom were production workers earning an average of $12.88 per hour, higher than the manufacturing average of $10.47 (U.S. Industrial Outlook, 1990, pp. 50–51). The balance of the work force is made up of well-paid scientific and technical workers engaged in drug research and development, trained salespersons engaged in intensive marketing of products to physicians, clerical staff managing the mountains of paperwork involved in drug testing and approval, and legal and administrative personnel managing global corporate operations.

At the international level the United States is the world leader in drug production. Total U.S. shipments in 1989 were $46.8 billion in a worldwide market of $150 billion (U.S. Industrial Outlook, 1990, pp. 50–51).[1] In addition, of the world's 20 largest drug makers, 11 are U.S.-based, compared with 3 each for Germany and Switzerland and 1 each for France, the United Kingdom, and Japan. In the postwar period the United States has led the world in drug discoveries, originating 61% of total new chemical entities (NCE) introduced between 1940 and 1988 (Pharmaceutical Manufacturers Association, 1989, p. 19). Today it also leads in biotechnology breakthroughs which promise to be the wonder drugs of the future. Pharmaceuticals, therefore, are a stunning example of American competitive advantage. However, the pharmaceutical industry may be facing hard times ahead. Changes in industry structure are likely.

For consumers, demand for medicine is relatively price inelastic because most are covered by third-party reimbursements. Competition in the research-based pharmaceutical industry hinges on successfully commercializing drug innovations. The cost of drug research and development has increased dramatically, rising over 80% in real terms over the past 7 years (*Economist*, 14 February 1989, p. 64). Companies must have the resources to spend upwards of $125 million over 7 to 10 years in order to bring just one new drug onto the market (*Business Week*, January 8, 1990, p. 102). Rapid technological change and short product lifetimes (in terms of the time period before improved versions and generics cut into once-protected sales) require that the maximum return on this investment be sought in as many markets as possible. In addition to R&D resources, therefore, marketing resources on a grand scale are needed. In the 1990s the skyrocketing cost of drug development and marketing coincides with rising costs of health care and increasing pressures on government to contain costs. Governments around the world have considered the pharmaceutical industry to be an essential part of a nation's health care system, and since early on they have tried both to foster it and to regulate it. Significant government regulation, in the form of approval processes, import restrictions, licensing arrangements, and pricing controls among nations, was responsible for the industry becoming one of the first to go multinational.

In order to successfully finance R&D and marketing activities today, some firms claim they need over $1 billion in annual sales (*Economist*, 22 July 1989, p. 61). This is one factor in the recent changes in the structure of the pharmaceutical industry. Over the last 3 years there have been several acquisitions of smaller firms by larger ones, mergers between U.S. multinationals, and mergers between profitable U.S. firms and foreign multinational firms, all creating truly global business operations (*Wall Street Journal*, 13 April 1989, p. A8). In addition, a variety of strategic interindustry alliances have occurred in pharmaceuticals similar to those occurring in other high-tech industries, such as computing and telecommunications.[2] Examples include interfirm consolidations of resources through cooperative marketing agreements, interorganizational research and technical links, cross-licensing deals and joint ventures, reciprocal development and clinical work, and equity holdings (Howells, 1990a, 1990b).

The recent wave of corporate mergers and strategic alliances provides a snapshot of predicted industry realignments. In 1989 alone, over 130 mergers, acquisitions, joint ventures, and agreements were undertaken in the health care industry (U.S. Industrial Outlook, 1990, pp. 50–51). A troubled Smith-Kline Beckman, with sluggish sales in its leading drug and few new drug developments coming on line in the near future, merged with Beecham of the United Kingdom, making it the second-largest drug firm behind Merck. It quickly lost this position with the merger of two strong U.S. companies, Bristol Meyers and Squibb. Other mergers involved Dow Chemical's acquisition of Marion Labs and Eastman Kodak's acquisition of Sterling Drug.

Foreign firms are consolidating as well, as evidenced by the acquisition of Connaught BioSciences of Toronto by Institut Merieux S.A. of Lyons, France. European and Japanese firms have had their eye on acquiring U.S. firms, especially traditional drug houses with a strong marketing sales force, in order to increase U.S. sales of their existing products. They have also sought to acquire holding interests or outright ownership of U.S. biotechnology start-ups, in order to strengthen their position in new technological innovations. For instance, Chugai, a Japanese firm, acquired Gene-Probe, a leading U.S. biotech firm. In another instance, Rhone-Prolenc, a French chemical and drug company, acquired the Rorer Group based in Pennsylvania.

How will the U.S. pharmaceutical industry fare in the era of consolidation, strategic alliances, and heightened global competition? Will it continue to thrive despite rising costs, increasing government regulation, and health care cost-containment pressures? Or will it lose out to foreign firms whose home-base governments are more actively supporting drug innovation, such as France and Japan, or to regional market blocks, such as the creation of a single unified European Economic Community (EEC) market after 1992? How is the industry positioned to take advantage of the next frontier in drug discovery, gene-spliced drugs and other biotech breakthroughs? If U.S. firms manage to maintain their wide lead over other pharmaceutical producers in other nations, will it be accompanied by growth of the industry and employment in the United States or by increased R&D activity and production overseas? Which regions and communities, both here and abroad, stand to gain in this next period of growth for the global pharmaceutical industry?

HISTORICAL LOCATION OF
THE PHARMACEUTICAL INDUSTRY

The Classical Period

The modern drug industry dates from the early-to-mid-19th century with the manufacture of alkaloids such as quinine and morphine in France and Germany (Redwood, 1987, p. 27). Apart from these few alkaloids, up until 1910 most of the drugs in existence were single-source botanical, mineral, or animal extracts that were used as simple purgatives, emetics, and narcotics; these were produced by individual pharmacists on a small scale (James, 1977, p. 1). The U.S. pharmaceutical industry has its origins in this period of apothecaries, local druggists, and traveling medicine venders. It was then a very dispersed and artisan-based activity. Many of the firms known today developed from retail suppliers to producers of these simple compounds.

Philadelphia, the site of the nation's first college of pharmacy, was also home to some of the first notable American apothecaries which later developed into profitable U.S. pharmaceutical companies such as Smith Kline and Wyeth. A founder of another old pharmaceutical house, Edward R. Squibb, also got his training in Philadelphia, although he first set up business in Brooklyn. These companies gained the respect of leading hospitals and physicians for the purity and reliability of their compounds in an era of adulterated and fraudulent medicines. Purchases of quinine by the federal government during the Mexican War and of other drugs during the Civil War were a boon to the early pharmaceutical firms on the East Coast. Many of these early houses such as Warner-Lambert, Merck, and Squibb have since moved most of their operations to New Jersey locations. The major pharmaceutical firms in the north central states, such as Abbott in the Chicago area, Upjohn in Kalamazoo, Michigan, and Eli Lilly in Indianapolis, Indiana, also started as family-owned drug retailers serving the needs of the booming industrial heartland and later expanded into drug production with the discovery of methods of machine pill manufacture. Upjohn's founder was granted a patent on the first "friable" pill, one that dissolved easily in the body.

In contrast to the U.S. experience, most of the major European drug firms began as divisions of existing chemical or textile companies.[3] In Europe in the late 1800s the groundwork for the coming chemotherapy revolution of the 1930s was being laid with research into chemical compounds and dyes within the laboratories of the coal tar dyestuff industry in Germany, Switzerland, and France. Aniline dyes proved useful as a method to stain and track infectious disease-causing germs newly discovered by Pasteur in France and Koch in Germany (Tucker, 1985, p. 7). The first chemical synthetic drugs, aspirin, phenacetin, and barbitone, were developed in Germany by 1900 (James, 1977, p. 1). In 1909, also in Germany, the first "magic bullet", arsphenamine (Salvarson), a treatment for syphillis, was discovered by Ehrlich. It was not until the 1930s that other magic bullets, so named because of their ability to attack the cause of the infection and not kill the patient, were developed. This period was the beginning of the chemotherapy revolution and of the modern pharmaceutical industry.

The Chemotherapy Revolution

The research teams involved in the penicillin production race, fielded by the small and medium chemical and drug companies in several countries, were the beginnings of the research-based pharmaceutical industry. However, after the discovery of the first synthetic compounds, progress was slow in coming, as it proved difficult to mass-produce the active substances (Tucker, 1985, p. 11). German, British, and American efforts were prominent. The first of the bacterial infection-fighting sulfa drugs was discovered by Domagk in a German dye laboratory in 1935. Penicillin was first discovered in Britain by Fleming in 1929, but not tested on humans until 1941.

Pharmaceutical firms raced to find a method of mass-producing penicillin, sulfa drugs, and broad-spectra antibiotics being developed because of the prestige and anticipated high profits that would come with cornering the market on these lifesaving compounds. Governments aided in the search because of the pressing need to treat the millions of wounded during World War II (Tucker, 1985, p. 12). Pfizer, an American firm, won the penicillin production race using the deep vat fermentation process it had pioneered to produce citric acid, a common ingredient in medicines of the day (Pratt, 1985, pp. 8–10).[4] Yet, because of over supply (there were 21 other producers besides Pfizer), the cost of penicillin dropped drastically, from $20 a dose to 2 cents in only a few years, cutting deeply into profits (Pratt, 1985, p. 11).

The penicillin saga alerted firms to the necessity of acquiring proprietary rights over their drugs. Corporate strategy began to focus on developing drugs and securing patents for them in order to capture the market for an extended period and thereby recoup high and risky R&D costs by being able to charge prices significantly higher than production costs. Pfizer was noted for its new and aggressive approach to marketing. The company was primarily a supplier of refined chemicals to other drug companies, and it lacked the reputation in the industry to successfully market its new drug oxytetracycline (Terramycin) over competing drugs of longer established firms (Tucker, 1985, p. 13). Pfizer spent enormous amounts of money on advertising and directly approached doctors with hard-sell promotional incentives and giveaways. These practices set the standard for the postwar era of heightened drug-marketing competition (Tucker, 1985, p. 14).

Most of the U.S. firms, located in the Midwest and the Northeast, also experienced a boom in R&D activity and production in the war periods. Firms began to turn out the wonder sulfa drugs or "wound tablets" carried by soldiers to combat infection. These firms remain highly profitable today, having been geared up by war demand for further expansion in the postwar period.

The Golden Age

Prior to World War II most industrialized countries were self-sufficient in pharmaceutical production, with their needs served by local manufacturers of unsophisticated products in simply administered forms: pills, liquids, and the like. What little trade occurred was dominated by Germany, the lead innovator of magic bullets of the early period (James, 1977, p. 17). But the German industry suffered greatly during the war with the destruction of capacity, loss of export markets, and isolation from research into technological developments, especially antibiotic breakthroughs, taking place in the United States and the United Kingdom (Jones, 1977, p. 17). In contrast, Switzerland, one of the first countries to establish subsidiaries in the United States, was able to continue to develop its multinational networks during the war years. Today Switzerland has a large pharmaceutical industry greatly exceeding the size of its small home market.

The German setback served the budding U.S. industry particularly well. The U.S. pharmaceutical industry was the best situated of the major producers in the postwar period to expand into global markets. The war itself had provided the impetus for intensive research efforts into lifesaving antibiotics, aided by government funds. And the U.S. economy, unlike the devastated European economies, was poised for new business opportunities. The United States had unused technology, scientific talent, and pent-up demand from the Depression era and the war years. Hundreds of new chemical drug compounds were discovered during the postwar period, initiating what has been called "the golden age" of the pharmaceutical industry (Redwood, 1987, p. 6). These included lifesaving or life-enhancing cardiovasculars, antihypertensives, and central nervous system drugs, as well as newer antibiotics effective on a broader range of the bacteria spectrum. Many of the Midwest firms, in particular, also diversified into agricultural and animal health lines in addition to their global pharmaceutical operations.

The Government and Generic Industry Challenges

The golden age of drug innovation was winding down by the 1970s as the industry as a whole began to face the limits of the chemotherapy revolution. The previous decade also brought new challenges in the form of increased government drug regulation and consumer discontent. At the same time firms faced rising costs of R&D in a world inflationary period. There was a marked decline in truly innovative drug introductions and an increase in "copycat" drugs, or known drugs improved in terms of delivery or dosage forms.

In 1959 the Kefauver congressional committee investigated the monopoly power of the U.S. industry, citing excessive prices and profits. These debates together with a health scare resulting from the thalidomide disaster led to the 1962 drug amendments.[5] The FDA now required firms to show not only the nontoxicity but also the increased effectiveness of new drugs. This requirement raised costs and slowed the drug approval process.

In addition, as the patents on previous drug discoveries began to expire, firms experienced stiff competition from generic drug producers. The government was blamed for costly delays in the drug approval process and the resulting shrinkage of effective patent protection. Generic producers were also dissatisfied with having to operate under the strictures of the same approval process. The debate over regulation resumed in the early 1980s with the government now perceived as being part of the problem rather than the solution to industry performance (Comanor, 1986, p. 1179). In 1984, after several years of congressional debate, patent protection was extended for up to 5 years to offset approval delays. Generic producers only had to prove bioequivalence of their products for previously approved drugs whose patents had expired.

Biotechnology Threshold

Today the pharmaceutical industry may be on the threshold of the next frontier in drug discovery, biotechnology, which analyst Akihiro Yoshikawa claims will be the "core technology for the next industrial revolution" (*New York Times*, 13 July 1988, p. 34). Advances in molecular biology and related sciences have changed old ideas about living organisms, whether they be plants, animals, or humans, thus creating new ideas for agriculture, veterinary sciences, medicine, and drug innovation. Protein-based drugs developed from genetic engineering using recombinant DNA techniques and monoclonal antibodies were the first biotechnical areas of interest to the pharmaceutical industry. But research on carbohydrates has also proved promising for the role they play in regulating processes in the body (*New York Times*, 20 August 1990, p. D2). The biotechnology field offers the possibility of more-accurate "magic bullet" drugs, developed from genetically engineered substances that are able to penetrate and destroy diseased cells while avoiding healthy cells and the body's own defense mechanisms. The most notable biotechnology products include the leukemia and cancer treatment interferon, human growth hormone, human insulin, and the anticlotting drug called tissue plasminogen activator. In 1987 there were over 65 biotechnology-based drugs undergoing human trials and today there are an estimated 8,000 backlogged patent applications for biotechnology discoveries at the U.S. Patent and Trademark Office (*Wall Street Journal*, 6 July 1989, p. B1).

INTERNATIONAL LOCATION OF
THE PHARMACEUTICAL INDUSTRY

The main ingredients of a modern drug industry are (1) materials in the form of botanicals, biologicals, animals, refined pharmaceutical chemicals, and crude chemicals; (2) labor in the form of skilled scientific, medical, marketing, legal, administrative/managerial workers, and both skilled (fine chemicals) and semiskilled (finished drugs) production workers; and (3) plants and equipment in the form of high tech chemical refineries, manufacturing plants, research labs, computer facilities, technical libraries, research farms, and so forth. Given these requirements for a modern drug industry, it is not surprising that the market is dominated by firms based in advanced industrialized countries.

Developing nations have also fostered domestic drug industries, and some, such as Brazil and India, have progressed quite far, serving a large portion, 65%, of their domestic market (*New York Times*, 20 June 1988, p. B1). India, which accounts for only 2% of the world market, has recently begun exporting generic drugs overseas to other third world nations, ignoring product patents and selling at one-tenth the price of Western firms (*Economist*, 20 August 1988). Mexico currently serves 90% of its domestic market, aided by high tariff barriers. Mexican producers now worry about their future if the North American Free Trade Agreement is ratified and barriers fall.

A small group of industrialized nations, however, still dominate the industry worldwide. Five countries lead the global market in pharmaceuticals: the United States, the United Kingdom, Germany, France, and Switzerland. These are the countries in which the earliest and most significant drug developments occurred and where the modern drug industry was born. In 1988 Germany, the largest drug exporter, led the world in positive balance of trade, followed by Switzerland, the United Kingdom, France, and the United States (see Figure 5.1).

In 1990 U.S. manufacturers, however, accounted for more than half the world's shipments of drugs (Standard and Poors Corporation, 1991, p. H18). Besides having the greatest number of top pharmaceutical firms, the United States is also first in R&D activity, easily edging out the nearest competitor, France, with over 399 new drug introductions since 1963 (see Figure 5.2). Japan has been the rising star in drug innovation lately, surpassing West Germany with 257 introductions compared to 206 over the same period.

The United States is also the largest drug market. The next-largest national market for pharmaceuticals is Japan, followed by Germany. All three countries have large and aging populations with high levels of personal income. Japanese have the highest per capita consumption of medicine. In addition, Japan has a unique system whereby doctors prescribe and supply medicine directly to the patient, pocketing the difference between government reimbursed price and manufacturer discounts. This arrangement will likely be phased out in the near future as the Japanese government tries to control prices. Medicines account for 17% of the health budget in Japan compared with only 7% in the United States. Japan has the largest negative trade balance in pharmaceuticals. Other large net importers include Italy, Canada, Egypt, Australia, and Austria (see Figure 5.3).

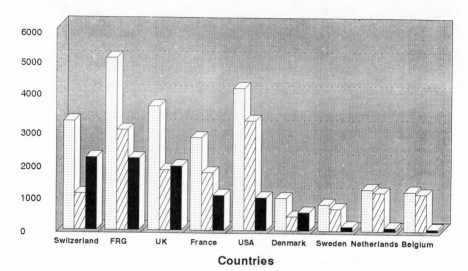

FIGURE 5.1. World trade medical and pharmaceutical products leading net exporters, 1988 (Millions of Dollars). *Source: 1988 International Trade Statistics Yearbook*, U.N., vol. 2, as cited in *PMA Statistical Factbook*, September 1991.

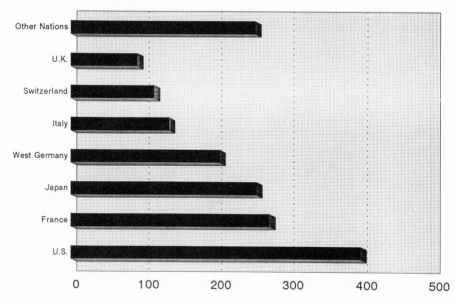

FIGURE 5.2. Total new drug introductions by country 1963–1990. *Source:* E. Reis-Arndt, *Medical Marketing & Media*, August 1983, p. 12 (1961–1980 figures); and "World Drug Introductions," *Scrip*, various issues (1982–1990 figures). No 1981 figures were available, as cited in *PMA Statistical Factbook*, September 1991.

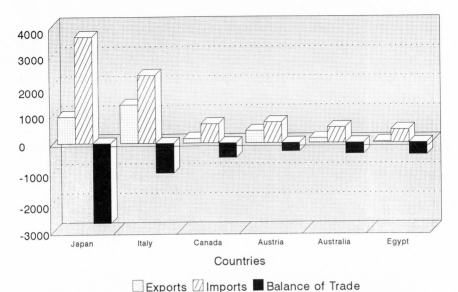

Countries

☐ Exports ⧄ Imports ■ Balance of Trade

FIGURE 5.3. World trade in medicinal and pharmaceutical products leading net importers, 1988 (in $million). *Source*: *1988 International Trade Statistics Yearbook*, U.N., vol. 2, as cited in *PMA Statistical Factbook*, September 1991.

U.S. performance in the global pharmaceutical industry is linked less to exports and more to sales by U.S. subsidiaries overseas (see Figure 5.4). Overseas operations account for 40% of sales and earnings (Standard and Poors Corporation, 22 July 1991, p. H23). After serving the needs of the U.S. market, U.S. firms as a whole have located foreign operations mostly in Latin America, followed by Europe, Asia, and Africa. More than one-third of all sales in Western Europe are made by U.S. drug companies (Standard and Poors Corporation, 1992, p H3). Firms from the United Kingdom, France, Germany, and Switzerland have also located subsidiaries in the United States.

U.S. PHARMACEUTICAL INDUSTRY LOCATION

In the United States the drug industry is located in all states except Alaska and the District of Columbia, but it is concentrated in the original centers of innovation in the northeast and in the north central region and has expanded in recent periods in California and Puerto Rico. The indus-

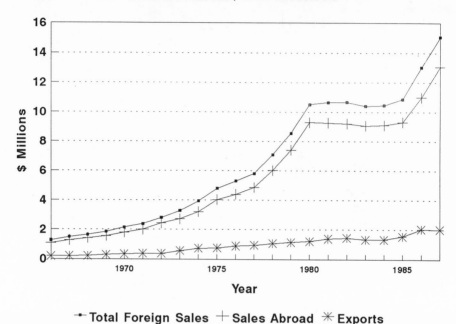

FIGURE 5.4. Foreign sales of ethical pharmaceuticals by U.S.-owned PMA firms (in $million). *Source*: *PMA Annual Survey*, various years.

try locational pattern is consistent with the patterns of innovation-based industries whose locational imperative is to remain near resources of skilled labor in original centers of innovation (Markusen, 1985, p. 149). In the Northeast, New York, New Jersey, and Pennsylvania have the greatest number of pharmaceutical facilities and the highest employment levels. In the central region, Illinois and Indiana have the next-largest concentration of facilities and employment in the industry. In the West and the Southwest, California and Texas stand out as the favored sites for pharmaceutical location and employment. In the South, pharmaceutical employment has been rising in North Carolina where foreign pharmaceutical firms have set up branch plants and subsidiary R&D facilities in the high-tech Research Triangle Park of the Raleigh-Durham area.

Compared with U.S. mainland locations, Puerto Rico is an attractive location for manufacturing plant location due to its special tax breaks designed to stimulate employment in the territory. Pharmaceutical firms can use transfer pricing to report a large portion of their total profits as emanating from their Puerto Rican subsidiaries, which are exempt from taxes (Gordon & Fowler, 1981, p. 153).

Data on employment in the pharmaceutical industry by state in the postwar period show a boom in employment for all the states where the industry is concentrated up until 1972. New Jersey showed the most dramatic employment gains in the period 1958 to 1972, leveling off in the most recent period, yet maintaining its wide lead over all other states (see Figure 5.5). In contrast, neighboring New York had either stable or moderate employment gains up to 1967, and declining employment thereafter. By 1972 New Jersey had surpassed New York as the top state pharmaceutical employer, benefiting in part from decentralization of firms from New York. New York may also be slipping in its locational advantage for biomedical research. A state study showed that New York with its internationally famous medical centers once dominated federal grants for biomedical research, but that it has recently lost out to places like Boston and San Francisco which have been strong competitors in the biotechnology field (*New York Times*, 17 October 1988, p. 15). The major factors cited for the decline of New York were the cost of living,

FIGURE 5.5. Pharmaceutical employment by state 1947–1987 (1987 gives estimated values). *Source*: U.S. Department of Commerce, Bureau of the Census, *Census of Manufactures*, 1947–1987. Industry Series, Drugs.

the cost of constructing and modernizing laboratories, and the deteriorating quality of life.

Overall, the northern and central New Jersey area seems to be the
favored location for the research-based pharmaceutical industry with over
a dozen major research-based pharmaceutical firms, including the largest drug multinational, Merck, which is located in Rahway, New Jersey. Several subsidiaries of foreign firms, such as Hoffman-LaRoche,
Hoescht, and Ciba-Geigy have also set up operations in the New Jersey
area. Considerable economies of scale operate, especially for the research-
based portion of the ethical (available by doctor's prescription only)
pharmaceutical industry.[6] Drug innovation requires an interdisciplinary
team of highly trained and well-paid professionals from medicine, biology, chemistry, and biochemistry, and expensive laboratories, equipment,
and support services. The cost of starting up a research-based pharmaceutical firm is extremely high. Research laboratories are very expensive in terms of the necessary scientific talent and sophisticated equipment and technical support services (libraries, computers, animal/plant
testing facilities). In addition, there are nonscale cost advantages inhib-
iting entry of new firms, such as significant learning curves in accumu-
lating knowledge in certain disease processes. These factors have resulted
in the agglomeration of the research-based segment of the industry in
the original centers of innovation.

There does not appear to be any threat to the continuing locational
advantage of this area. The New York–New Jersey area offers the industry proximity to a highly skilled labor force, major centers of medicine
and education, major air and water port facilities, rail and interstate
linkages, a supplier chemical industry, and a large segment of the American market along the Northeast Corridor. In addition, the region encompasses the world's premier center of global finance, communications,
public relations, advertising, and marketing which is a key locational
concern for oligopolist industries (Markusen, 1985, p. 149). Recent
mergers and strategic alliances among firms headquartered just a few
towns away from each other further enhance the agglomerative inertia
of the central New Jersey area.

The Philadelphia metropolitan area, another early center of drug
manufacture, today remains an attractive location for the research-based
pharmaceutical industry. It shares many of the locational attributes of
the central New Jersey area, and it is also a major center of medical
research and training. Employment has remained steady in the tristate
region of New York, New Jersey, and Pennsylvania, which together
accounted for over a third of total U.S. employment in the industry in
1987.

There has been declining employment in the north central region, especially in Illinois, Indiana, and Michigan, and rising employment in southern and western states such as California, Texas, and North Carolina. North Carolina, which had insignificant employment before 1977, has showed strong gains over the most recent period. The Research Triangle Park area of Raleigh, Durham, and Chapel Hill has recently attracted research-based pharmaceutical firms, such as branch plants of the United Kingdom's Glaxo and Burroughs Wellcome. This is an attractive location because of its proximity to major medical research and teaching hospitals and its highly skilled labor pool, and because of a number of favorable firm locational factors (low-cost housing, many amenities, the prestige of a high-tech campuslike industrial park setting, and so forth).

FACTORS AFFECTING LOCATION OF THE GLOBAL PHARMACEUTICAL INDUSTRY

Technological Requirements of Pharmaceutical Functions

Within the pharmaceutical industry there are differences in the degree of decentralization to foreign location by functions that will influence location of pharmaceutical establishments engaged in marketing, production, and R&D.

Marketing

Marketing is a labor-intensive and local function, so this is often the first step in overseas activity of a drug firm. Marketing operations exist in almost every country in which a firm markets products. Knowledge of local customs and promotional tactics is the key to marketing success.

Production of Final Product

The formulation and packaging of active ingredients into finished products are also common foreign activities of multinational drug firms. Beginning in the late 1950s the larger drug companies in different countries began to set up overseas subsidiaries to market products for local markets or to produce finished products directly for the local market.[7] Many countries had established nontariff barriers, banning the import of finished pharmaceutical products in order to stimulate employment, technological development, and other economic spillovers. Subsidiaries were set up to manufacture the active ingredients into final administered form and to package and label it according to local language and government specifications. The manufacturing process, although technically intricate, can be broken down into routine steps and requires unskilled and semiskilled workers in a modern plant facility. Multinational firms, however, usually do not locate production overseas in the absence of restrictions on imports unless the market is large and lucrative (Dunning, Burstall, & Lake, 1981, p. 68).

Production of Active Ingredients

While employment in the production of finished ethical drugs was moving away from the home country, the export of the intermediate active ingredients to subsidiaries overseas increased. The production of active ingredients, a technically more complex process, requiring skilled labor and a fully developed technical and economic infrastructure, is usually carried out in the home nation, less commonly in off shore sites having low taxes, such as Puerto Rico in the case of the U.S. industry.

Research and Development

Traditionally R&D functions have favored a single domestic location. As mentioned previously, the multi-disciplinary aspect of research, the combining of biology, chemistry, bio-chemistry, and medicine sciences, leads to economies of scale. Support services such as specialized libraries, computer facilities, farms, etc. further strengthens this tendency. In 1976, one analyst estimated that 80% of firm R&D was done in one facility in the parent country (Dunning et al., 1981, p. 69).

Today, this location pattern is changing for both U.S. and foreign producers. For U.S. firms, drug testing is easier and less expensive overseas. In addition, the FDA is relaxing some regulations on the acceptance of overseas test trials for approval of drugs marketed in the United States. The delay in approving a drug for market in the United States has also led U.S. firms to carry out R&D activity and drug approval overseas first, so that they can get their drug to the market as fast as possible in order to recoup investment sooner and capture a greater market share over therapeutic competitors. The percentage of R&D expenditures of U.S. firms spent overseas has increased significantly from only 10% in 1972 to 15% in 1983 and 20% in 1990 (Standard and Poors Corporation, 22 August 1991, p. H21).

For firms in general, regardless of national base, the rising complexity and cost of R&D, the increase in drug development times, and the decrease in product lifespans has led them to undertake interfirm strategic alliances in R&D, often across national boundaries. For small firms, in particular, mounting costs have driven many to seek links with larger firms, either at the R&D stage or later at the marketing stage, in order to recoup the monumental expenses they have incurred in developing the new drug (Howells, 1990b, p. 500). This is particularly true for small biotechnology firms who have often "bet the company" on a promising bioengineered drug, but who lack the resources to successfully market it.

Another example of the use of strategic R&D alliances is the case of the Japanese pharmaceutical industry trying to catch up with foreign competitors and globalize their operations. Takeda, the largest Japanese firm, has undertaken research links with the United States (via joint ventures with Abbott/Tap Pharmaceuticals and Cyanamid, and licensing deals with Upjohn) and with Europe (via joint ventures with Grunnenthal and licensing deals with Ciba-Geigy, Roche, and Glaxo). Howells (1990b, p. 507) indicates that commercial links can influence the choice of a country for eventual R&D center investment, as was the case with Takeda's selection of Frankfurt, Germany, for its European R&D headquarters. Today many firms, recognizing no exclusive American superiority in scientific talent, have located R&D operations in several countries. One firm, Eli Lilly, which already has an R&D facility in Britain, is constructing a $100 million R&D facility in Japan. The use of and rapid improvements in information and communication technologies will facilitate coordination of more decentralized and internationalized patterns of pharmaceutical R&D in the future (Howells, 1990b, p. 509).

Market Structure

In the global pharmaceutical industry there are many submarkets by therapeutic class such as antibiotics, antidepressives, antihypertensives, vaccines, digestives, analgesics, and so forth. Not all firms participate in all therapeutic class markets to the same extent. Because patterns of disease vary by world region, that is, by countries' climatic, cultural, demographic, and development situation, the size of particular submarkets also vary by country. For example, diseases of affluence result in large markets for cardiovascular, central nervous system, and ulcer drugs in developed countries, especially the United States, while diseases of poverty stimulate demand in vaccines, anti-infectives, and respiratory drug submarkets in lesser developed countries.

The overall size of the market depends on population size, income levels, and the characteristics of the health care system. The market for ulcer drugs is perhaps the world's most lucrative; the top ulcer drug in

1991 sales was Glaxo's Zantac at $916 million. Other top-selling drugs in the world include cardiovascular drugs, especially clot dissolvers and antihypertensives or blood pressure drugs.[8] To the extent that disease patterns vary by geographic region, there will be a similar pattern of firm activity by geographic region. Here a single firm may capture up to 40% or more of market sales. Glaxo's Zantac for example, accounts for 58% of the world ulcer market, recently knocking out the nearest competitor, Smith Kline's Tagamet and thereby contributing to that company's recent crisis and merger with Beecham of the United Kingdom. This is an example of how rapid technological change and short product lifetime can rapidly change the fortunes of companies. A single block-buster drug can sky-rocket a firm into the top ranks and just as easily cause it to be eclipsed by a similar winning product of a rival firm. This has led analysts to describe the industry as one characterized by dynamic oligopoly (Dunning et al., 1981, p. 60). The rankings of the top multi-national drug firms can vary widely from year to year.

It is not surprising that ulcer and cardiovascular drugs are the hottest sellers. The aging of affluent populations in industrialized nations and the increase in the incidences of degenerative diseases insure that these will be strong markets in the future. A significant learning curve in these disease processes have resulted in successful research teams tending over time to concentrate their efforts in certain areas. The costs of R&D activity are so high that it is not possible for a single firm to have on-going projects in every single therapeutic class. [9] These degenerative disease classes of drugs require greater R&D effort beginning with basic research and more involved testing and efficacy trials.[10] This type of R&D activity is more risky but provides greater profit margins. It will, however, be carried out by a decreasing number of much larger firms, mostly based in the United States and United Kingdom, who currently hold a strong market lead and who can afford the huge and risky investment (James, 1987, pp. 81–82).

Industry Structure

Most of the major multi-nationals in this industry are vertically integrated producing pharmaceutical chemical products as well as finished drug preparations. Like the chemical industry, production of fine pharmaceutical chemicals, which are the active ingredients into pharmaceutical preparations, is a complex multi-stage synthesis process. As such there are significant economies of scale and production requires costly overhead and working capital in inputs, equipment and technical staff. Pharmaceutical chemical production is usually carried out only by the largest multinational companies. Smaller companies are involved in the production of finished drug products, a more standard manufacturing process that is less difficult, transforming the complex active ingredients into its packaged administered form, such as tablets, capsules, liquid, injectables, and creams, through processes of compounding, dispersion, granulation, formulation, and the like (James, 1977, pp. 14–16).

Similar processes involved in finished pharmaceutical manufacture and cosmetic, food, and drink production have enabled companies in these latter product areas to enter the pharmaceutical industry through transfer of manufacturing technology. Examples of this type of entry include Beechams and Revlon (James, 1977, p. 16).

Because chemical production and pharmaceutical fine chemical production are similar technical processes, some chemical firms have diversified into pharmaceuticals, often to escape the cyclicity of the chemical industry (*Wall Street Journal*, 18 July 1989, p. A3). Pharmaceuticals tend to be recession-proof, for people cannot forego illness in bad times and most rely on third party reimbursements for their drug purchases. Examples of U.S. chemical company diversification into pharmaceuticals include DuPont, Dow, and Cynamid. This pattern is much more common in Europe, however, and the German giants of Hoescht, Bayer, and BASF, France's Rhone Proulenc, and the United Kingdom's ICI have as much as 25% of their sales in pharmaceuticals (Tucker, 1985, p. 26). The German chemical giants with their pharmaceutical divisions have been very successful in the global market compared with other firms in their pharmaceutical industry. The success of these chemical firms is certainly linked to the traditional chemical-synthesis approach to drug discovery that marked the golden age; it remains to be seen if these giants can succeed in the new bio-engineered drug developments. In contrast, in the United States, the most successful firms have been more narrowly focused research-based pharmaceutical firms with the greatest portion of their total sales coming from drugs.

Firm Strategy

Many pharmaceutical firms, in order to reduce reliance on risky R&D costs, diversified during the 1970's and 1980's into cosmetics, health care equipment, household, and other consumer products. These ventures were often less profitable for the drug firms because of management problems, lack of expertise and inferior financial performance compared with drug products (Redwood, 1987, p. 12).

In the late 1980's and early 1990's, competition within the industry has changed as firms urgently seek a critical mass in sales and R&D

activity in order to remain competitive in the rapidly consolidating global drug industry. Some analysts have even referred to the recent "mergermania" as the "global drug wars" of the 1990's.

Over the last few years the most successful firms have begun to reconcentrate their efforts on drug research and development and divested their non-drug divisions. The number of new drug introductions promising real therapeutic breakthroughs has begun to rise sharply, and the stakes in drug research have risen dramatically. For instance, Merck, the world's largest and most successful drug multi-national, on its way to the top position divested itself of its many of its non-pharmaceutical subsidiaries acquired in the 1960's and 1970's, in order to concentrate its resources on drug innovation. Today it has 15 major drugs on the market with sales of over $100 million for each one and one drug with sales of $1 billion. Merck does not glide along on its top standing; it has recently negotiated a strategic alliance with DuPont to develop OTC drugs. This joint venture, combined with promising drugs in the Merck research pipeline, will further strengthen the position of the world's largest drug firm. Merck's competitive firm strategy has set the standard in the industry.[11]

Other firms have begun to follow Merck's strategy, divesting non-pharmaceutical units and seeking ways to enhance their R&D effort, especially in the biotech field, or their marketing power via mergers with other firms with strengths in these areas. This strategy has been behind some of the 1989 corporate mergers. Smith Kline Beecham benefits from Beecham's success in consumer products and OTC drugs, thereby helping to fill its gap in the research pipeline, while Beecham gains Smith Kline's R&D capacity in the prescription drug field. In another merger, Squibb benefits from Bristol Meyer's global sales force and fills Bristol Meyers shortcoming in prescription drugs (*New York Times*, 28 July 1989, p. 1).[12] In yet another marriage of a superior drug innovator and a formidable drug marketer, Merck and Johnson and Johnson have agreed to a joint venture in the OTC market. Brand name producers are seeking strategic alliances with OTC drug firms having marketing expertise selling directly to consumers.

Some firms have adopted an aggressive R&D strategy, while others have been more cautious and their innovation has lagged as a result. One type of strategic alliance has been for successful marketers to license the drug discoveries of successful innovators, especially foreign firms lacking the capacity to produce or market in the huge American market. Marion Labs, with annual sales of $752 million in 1988, has been the most successful in this strategy, licensing drugs from Sweden, West Germany, Switzerland, and Japan and marketing them in the United States. Its superior pharmaceutical sales force was a factor in its recent acquisition by Dow Chemical, yet another example of the recent consolidation in the industry.[13]

Another strategy to surmount the rising costs of R&D has been adopted by small start-up firms that are attempting to develop and commercialize passed-over drugs. These chemical entities, called "Lazarus" or raised-from-the-dead drugs, were abandoned in the testing stage because they were too risky, problematic, or potentially unprofitable at the time. The small firms license the drug from the innovator firm and develop it for a smaller market or for new uses, such as topical use or dermatologics. They do not incur heavy investment in R&D because most of the research work is at an advanced applied stage.[14]

As in many high-tech industries, the United States has been a pioneer in the new biotechnology field and currently controls about three-quarters of global research. The biotech industry has been characterized by start-up of small firms attracting significant venture capital. While some biotech firms are struggling to stay independent, others are being bred to be sold to larger pharmaceutical firms seeking a biotech partner (*Wall Street Journal*, 19 July 1989, p. B2). Still others are not able to take their innovations through testing and approval, or to market them on a global scale. Japanese and European firms have sought strategic alliances with prime U.S. biotech firms. Switzerland's Roche Holding startled the industry by acquiring the largest and most successful biotechnology firm, Genentech, in 1990. Some analysts argue that the U.S. pharmaceutical industry stands to gain the most in the coming decade since it has the largest multinationals, many currently flush with super profits from billion-dollar-a-year drug sales. Other analysts worry that without a long-term coordinated strategy involving government, industry, and academia, the U.S. stands to loose its competitive lead in yet another high-tech field to countries like Japan whose governments are more aggressively promoting their infant biotech industry.

Government Policy

The global pharmaceutical industry is highly regulated by national governments. In the United States, regulation is primarily concerned with issues of product safety and to a lesser extent with industry profits as they affect health care cost containment. In Europe regulation centers primarily around pricing. Japan has moved from a situation of government restriction on marketing and foreign investment to opening of markets cost containment, and promotion of biotechnology.

The U.S. pharmaceutical industry as a whole appears to have a united voice in government regulatory policy issues. The Pharmaceutical Manufacturers Association (PMA), the umbrella organization for the research-based end of the industry, is mainly concerned with preserving the incentives for R&D activity and limiting government regulation that adversely affects industry profits and markets. Based on these two broad concerns, the PMA is particularly concerned with preserving patent protection, speeding the pace of the drug-approval process, minimizing generic competition, opposing changes in marketing practices, and resisting price controls. While the industry has a clearly defined policy toward long-term competitiveness, it does not necessarily focus on the preservation of American pharmaceutical jobs or the economic base of pharmaceutical-dependent communities. In contrast, the U.S. government's focus has been on consumer welfare with regards to product safety, efficacy, and affordability. The federal government devotes little attention to the beneficial economic spillover effects of preservation of American high-tech jobs or the American technological lead in the industry.

Other governments, such as France with drug innovation and Japan with biotechnology promotion, have consciously aided their national industry as part of an overall industrial policy toward high-tech sectors. France, for example, bases the price it will allow a firm to charge on its products on the extent of the firm's investment in R&D facilities in the country (Howells, 1990, p. 500). In general, European governments are currently being forced to consider the long-run viability of their industries with respect to the changes being negotiated to bring about a unified market in pharmaceuticals after 1992. The position of various industries and governments in regulatory issues of patent approval, drug approvals, markets and marketing practices, price control, and industry promotion are examined below as they affect global industry performance and location.

Patent Protection

The pharmaceutical industry is interested in obtaining the greatest return on the huge sums of money invested in R&D activity and also in preserving the incentives for R&D investment in the future. Perhaps the most important issue in preserving the incentives for R&D investment is improving protection of patents and intellectual property rights. There are two types of patent protection on pharmaceuticals: a stronger form, the product patent, and a weaker form, the process patent. There is a wide range of patent protection across countries on pharmaceutical products, with more protection found in developed countries, especially the large producers such as the United States, and relatively less protection among developing countries, especially those trying to develop an indigenous industry such as Brazil, Mexico, and India. Italy up until 1978 had no patent protection. Its domestic pharmaceutical industry developed very rapidly as a result of imitating patented products. Today, among EEC members, Portugal, Spain, and Greece currently have no patent protection, a situation that will change with market unification. Among the developed countries, 17 to 20 years of patent protection is the norm.

Patent protection where it does exist in developing nations is difficult to enforce. Countries such as Brazil and India have taken the Italian route to building up their domestic drug industry by imitating patented Western products. These countries tend to have no patents or only weak process patents of a few years. The PMA lobbied for tougher standards on process patents in the 1987 trade bill discussions in Congress in order to make it a violation of U.S law, with liability for damages, to sell or import products made abroad that violate U.S. patent law.

At the international level the PMA has worked with the U.S. Patent and Trademark Office and the World Intellectual Property Organization to preserve protection on intellectual property rights and to help set minimum standards to be added to the General Agreements on Tariffs and Trade (GATT). It has assisted the European pharmaceutical associations, especially in the United Kingdom, in seeking longer patent protection. The PMA has been successful in extending the patent protection period in Canada, thereby undercutting the booming and largely Canadian-owned generic drug industry there. In more forceful steps, it has filed a Section 301 petition of the 1984 Trade Law against Brazil and Chile in order to persuade these countries to adopt patent protection on drugs. Its Section 301 petition against Thailand resulted in that country's loss of $140 million in trade preferences with the United States and ultimately in an agreement to institute patent protection on drugs. The industry was also instrumental in urging the United States to obtain concessions on patent rights from Taiwan and South Korea.

The U.S. industry policy toward patent protection does not conflict greatly with overall government policy toward the issue of intellectual property rights. The United States is interested in protecting its new technologies from illegal copying, although at times it may not wish to pursue punitive measures against specific violating countries because of other geopolitical or economic development goals.

Other patent-related issues designed to improve incentives for R&D activity in the United States for both domestic and foreign subsidiary firms include opposing amendments to the Orphan Drug Act. An orphan drug is one targeted at a rare disease, that is, one affecting fewer than 200,000 people. In 1987 the pharmaceutical industry spent $54.6 million in R&D activity into rare diseases (U.S. Industrial Outlook, 1990, pp. 50–51). The amendments would have reduced the 7-year exclusivity in marketing for the 14 companies that have spent $183 million on orphan drug research and development and produced 45 drugs affecting 20 million Americans. The act has come under fire from government officials who cite the extremely high costs of the drugs and enormous profits for the firms as a result of blocked competition. Amgen's drug Epogen, which costs between $4,000 to $8,000 for a year's treatment, has yielded upwards of $200 million in sales. This same drug, which is effective for multiple uses (treating anemia in kidney patients, in AIDS patients, in premature infants, and so on) has an orphan drug designation for each use. The total number of people using the drug greatly exceeds the 200,000 level, but since separate clinical trials were required for each intended use, Amgen can use these trials to justify separate market monopolies (*New York Times*, 30 April 1990, p. D7).

Some biotech firms assert that the marketing exclusivity granted by the law is essential to attracting investors since biotech patents are uncertain. Others, however, counter that the law is unfair to those firms whose competing products are just a few months behind in the approval process. There are about 350 drugs with FDA-approved orphan drug status currently under development. If they come to market with annual treatment prices ranging from $5,000 to $15,000 and above, there will likely be a revolt by government and other drug reimbursers.[15] This policy currently favors R&D location and employment of the United States in general, and the biotech innovation centers in California in particular. If amended it may have a dampening affect on employment growth of firms in the bioengineered segment of the industry within the United States.

Drug Approval Process

One factor in the rise of the cost of drug development is the lengthy and elaborate drug approval process in the United States. The average number of months taken by the FDA to approve a new drug entity (NDA) has risen steadily to an average of 31 months in 1987. This contrasts with an average foreign drug approval time of only 15 months. In the race to market a drug, this costly and lengthy delay may seriously disadvantage U.S drug firms. The delay and added expense of the drug approval process in the United States has led many U.S. firms to carry out R&D activity, clinical trials, and drug approval abroad, with a resulting loss of high-paying U.S. jobs. Other spillover effects are lost as well, including financing for universities, a shrinking pool of critical scientific talent, and lost manufacturing opportunities of new products typically granted to nearby producers (*New York Times*, 22 February 1989, p. 30). The approval process on bioengineered drug products is even more seriously backlogged and could drive the biotech industry overseas as well.

The pharmaceutical industry has responded to this situation by trying to make the approval process more efficient. They have lobbied aggressively for increased funding of the FDA to hire more reviewers. But at the same time they have also fought against recurring proposals to charge the drug firms user fees to have their NDA applications processed. Other efforts at increasing efficiency in the approval process include efforts to computerize some of the data review process. Exchange programs between the FDA and the research-based firms have been created to increase understanding of the drug discovery and drug approval processes for FDA reviewers and drug developers. The complexity of the drug approval process itself and the lack of scientifically qualified reviewers is a major problem, especially in the more complex biotechnology field. Progress in these policy areas would boost the competitive position and employment levels of all U.S. firms and their subsidiaries regardless of domestic or foreign location. States with large concentrations of biotech firms, however, such as California and Massachusetts, would likely gain even more employment.

Regulation of Markets and Marketing Practices

Because of the extraordinary cost of drug research and development, the global pharmaceutical industry is interested in recouping this investment by penetrating every conceivable market and resisting any encroachments into those markets for as long as possible. Regulation affecting drug markets and marketing practices therefore are of particular concern to the industry.

The market for prescription drugs is unique because first, there is a protected monopoly of the market for the 17-year period granted by the patent, and second, the product is not sold directly to the consumer, but to intermediate agents such as physicians, pharmacies, hospitals, HMO's, and government health clinics.[16] Sales are carried out by a large and aggressive traveling sales force armed with free samples and other promotional gimmicks, literature, and in-depth knowledge of the individual drug products. Also, the intermediate buyer and the ultimate consumer do not always make payment for the product, but he or she is reimbursed by a third party, either the government or group health insurers for those with private health insurance.

After expiration of a patent, other firms that have not invested any R&D in the development of a drug can begin to manufacture that drug at a higher profit margin under its generic or scientific name after they have demonstrated the bioequivalence of their product. The drug will continue to be sold under its original brand name, but now it faces stiff price competition from the generic substitutes.

U.S. government policy can promote the market for generics versus brand names in several ways, with the resulting effect of promoting employment in more dispersed generic production locations that do not have the R&D agglomeration anchors of the research-based end of the industry. With the goal of reducing mounting health care costs, it can set prescription policy for doctors by requiring a generic substitution option, and it can promote substitution in its own facilities and in its regulation of third party reimbursements. Over time, the percentage of drugs sold directly to private pharmacies has declined, as has the ability of the industry to control prescribing practices (see Figure 5.6). Pressures to contain the spiraling cost of health care have led to battles within the industry over prescription practices, such as allowing generic substitutions and therapeutic class substitutions (therapeutic classes are drugs with different active ingredients but effective on the same condition). The industry resists both types of substitutions, the former, by contesting the design and wording of doctor prescription forms discouraging generic substitution, and the latter, by trying to limit the setting for therapeutic substitutions to in-patients in hospitals.

These government regulatory policies have directly affected competition in the industry. In 1982 generics accounted for only 2% of the prescription drug market. By 1989 their share had risen to 33% (*Business World*, 2 October 1989, p. 87). Increasingly, research-based pharmaceutical firms are switching their prescription drugs to over-the-counter (OTC) versions as they near patent expiration in order to lock in consumer loyalty in the OTC market before generic firms can produce their versions of the drug. The strategy is designed to maintain market share over generic producers whose substitutes can cause a decrease in annual sales by up to 40% after expiration. The FDA has 46 prescription drugs under consideration for declassification. In general, the FDA has more than 25 drugs classified as prescription-only that are available in overseas OTC markets (U.S. Industrial Outlook, 1990, pp. 50–53). This gap will favor foreign firms if they are able to maintain sales on their products in foreign OTC markets to a greater extent than U.S.–research-based firms are able to do so in the U.S. market.

The generic drug industry in the United States suffered a major setback in 1989 when the illegal activities of generic producers and some FDA officials were uncovered. The FDA approval status was revoked on 30 products and 141 other compounds were suspended (*Wall Street Journal*, 6 September 1989, p. B1). Data were falsified in FDA documents, and in several cases the branded product was submitted for the bioequivalence test. Several major HMOs, worried about the safety and efficacy of the generic doses, pulled the generic drugs from their approved

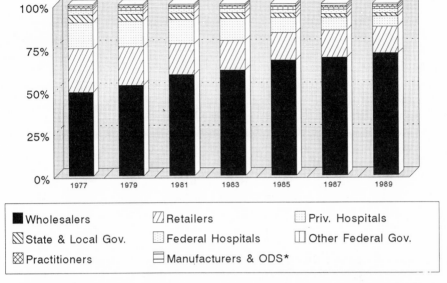

FIGURE 5.6. Percentage distribution of U.S. ethical pharmaceutical sales by class of customer; years between 1977 and 1989. *Source*: *PMA Annual Survey*, various years, as cited in *PMA Statistical Factbook*, September 1991. *Other direct sales.

list and substituted the branded drugs. The timing of the scandal caused some states, urged on by brand name producers who widely circulated warning letters, to delay consideration of changes in prescription practices designed to promote generic substitution. As a result of the scandal, the FDA has hired more reviewers and clamped down on the testing process, a move that has increased approval times and development costs and which ultimately may raise the prices of generics. Several firms are expected to fail or to sell out by 1992, further lessening competition between generics and branded drugs (*Business Week*, 2 October 1989, p. 87). The woes of generic producers become a windfall to the research-based branded producers who already make 60% of the generic drugs. These producers will benefit from the consolidation in the generic industry. Dramatic reductions in price for generics will cease to exist, and the health bill will rise accordingly (*Business Week*, 2 October 1989, p. 87).

Pharmaceutical firms have also resisted attempts by individual states and the national government in the Prescription Drug Marketing Act to change the way they market their product directly to physicians, specifically the giving away of free samples and expensive promotional gifts. The stakes in marketing are great, especially for high-margin drugs for chronic conditions and degenerative diseases. Such prescriptions can account for thousands of dollars in sales over the lifetime of the individual, thereby justifying the armies of detail men offering expensive marketing ploys to physicians (*Fortune*, 29 July 1991, p. 54). In the most extreme example, American Home Products was forced to end its free airline tickets incentive gimmick, which came to be known as the Frequent Prescriber program, after Massachusetts state Medicaid program began an investigation. Other criticism brought out in congressional testimony, resulted in the American Medical Association issuing guidelines discouraging doctors from accepting such gifts in exchange for prescriptions.

At the state level, the U.S. industry has argued for increased spending on Medicaid, especially the drug budget portion. At the national level, they have lobbied for increased spending on outpatient drug coverage, on medicare for the elderly, and on passage of catastrophic health insurance. At the international level, they have opposed the World Health Organization (WHO) attempts to adopt an international ethical marketing code, succeeding in getting a non-binding guidelines rather than a binding code. The PMA has also criticized WHO for its Revised Drug Strategy which they claim unfavorably regulates the supply of drugs in developing countries.

At state, national, and international levels the U.S. industry has lobbied against restrictive drug lists. The aim of restricted drug lists in developing countries is to ensure that essential drugs, desperately needed by the population, such as vaccines, antibiotics, and anti-infectives, are widely available at an affordable price. Scarce foreign exchange and development funds are not then wasted on nonessential drugs such as analgesics, cold remedies, vitamins, and the like. Industrialized nations also limit markets by setting an approved drug list for government reimbursement. The aim is to provide a supply of essential drugs for which governments will reimburse the costs, often at government-approved price levels, thereby reducing the health care bill for the country.

Import Tariffs and Export Restrictions

There are few tariffs on pharmaceutical chemicals or products. However, there are import restrictions on finished pharmaceutical products in many countries. Among developed nations, Japan and France had been the most restrictive on import of pharmaceutical products. Japan until 1981 required that testing of the product be carried out in Japan. France required that a visa be issued for each product, an approval process that had been manipulated in favor of French firms.

The United States until 1986 banned the export from the United States of drugs not approved by the FDA. This law was changed after biotechnology firms argued that, as a result of the long FDA approval and export restriction, they would be forced to set up plants overseas, or export their technology through licensing arrangement with foreign producers, and thus lose their competitive edge in the new biotechnology field. The revised law now permits export of drugs that are pending FDA approval to selected countries, as long as they have been approved by the importing country. As a result of the change, several U.S. firms canceled overseas plant construction plans and expanded their U.S. facilities. At the time of the change some analysts predicted that this regulatory change would add 10,000 jobs to the economy (*Business Week*, 22 December 1986, p. 46). Jobs have likely been saved or added in all states with significant drug production, but more so in areas with biotechnology employment.

Price Controls and Cost Containment Measures

Price controls on pharmaceutical products are commonplace. The United States is the rare exception among nations in not controlling either the price of drugs or profits of drug makers in the economy. It does not, however, pay unusually high prices for its pharmaceuticals compared with countries that do control prices, although it does have the highest per capita expenditure on health care, with the drug portion accounting for about 7% (Pharmaceutical Manufacturers Association, 1989, p. 29). The U.S. government, however, spurred on by deficit reduction pressures, has succeeded in reducing the national drug bill spent on the Medicaid program for the poor. In 1990 the U.S. Congress passed a law requiring that discounts from drug producers that are currently available to large hospitals, HMO's, the Veterans Administration, and the Defense Department also be made available to the Medicaid program.[17] While the industry, through the PMA, had been fighting the Medicaid discount, individual firms broke ranks. Merck has offered Medicaid and individual state programs their best discounts, in return for keeping all of Merck's product on the approved drug list. This did not necessarily mean savings for individual states. For example, Medi-Cal drug negotiator Jim Parks estimated that California would save $2.8 million in Merck rebates, but would have a net cost of $4.5 million with the inclusion of two previously unapproved Merck drugs (*New York Times*, 31 July 1990, p. D2).

With continuing U.S. government debt pressures, the increased lobbying by elderly groups, who are not as well covered by third party reimbursements as employees (Medicare, as opposed to Medicaid, only pays in-hospital drug costs), and more increased production of expensive "miracle" drugs, the government offensive on prices is likely to continue. This slide into managed drug pricing has made the U.S. bio-technology field particularly nervous. The cost of developing bio-engineered drugs is even more staggering than the cost of developing more traditional drugs. The cost of producing Amgen's kidney treatment drug Epogen was $300 million. At $6,000 for an annual supply, the government, as the largest customer via Medicaid reimbursements, has hotly debated the issue of the drug's price. Yet the industry counters that the drug produces other savings in decreased need for costly and risky blood transfusions. It is also argued that the drug maker, Amgen, has mortgaged its future on this single product and needs not only to recoup its cost, but to make enough profit to continue R&D in the biotech field (*Washington Post*, 19 June 1989, p. 31). Yet, as more applications are approved worldwide, annual sales could reach $3 billion.[18]

The outcry against the high cost of AIDS treatment has come not only from government critics of the industry but also from vocal AIDS activists and patients. Burroughs Wellcome, the producer of AZT, had resisted attempts to lower the price, citing the costs of R&D and doubts about the projected product lifetime of the drug. But in the face of continuing public opposition and a rapidly expanding market for AZT, the company reduced the price of the drug from $8,000 to $6,400 within 2 years (*Wall Street Journal*, 19 September 1989, p. A3).

The U.S. pharmaceutical industry is also outspoken on regulatory matters at the international level. It has closely monitored the negotiations for the 1992 European Community Unification dealing with harmonization of policies regarding drug registration, pricing, reimbursement, and labeling. Some of the provisions controlling transfer prices and therapeutic classification for reimbursement have been eliminated. At the individual country level, the industry association has opposed cost containment measures that would reduce the government drug bill in Italy, the Netherlands, and West Germany, which they claim would weaken the incentive for therapeutic innovation. They have also lobbied against a single drug approval authority for the EEC and promoted the alternative of separate national authorities with a central body guidelines and oversight.

Industry Promotion

Governments engage in few direct incentives to promote the pharmaceutical industry. The industry is small in terms of sales and employment, in comparison to the total economy and to specific sectors such as autos or the chemical industry in general. It is also generally self-financing from its super profits. The exceptions are the French, who promote their industry through fiscal incentives and tax concessions. Surprisingly, Japan, a strong supporter of export industries, failed to create a global drug industry because the industry came under the Health and Welfare Ministry rather than the dynamic Ministry of International Trade and Industry (MITI) (*Economist*, 24 March 1990, p. 74). Japan did promote a strong national pharmaceutical industry through severe controls over foreign competition. With substantial profits from huge domestic sales (Japan has the highest per capita consumption of drugs), the Japanese industry had little incentive to export. But lately, as the Japanese population began to age, bureaucrats lifted restrictions on foreign competition and also began to make annual cuts in drug prices. Japan, spurred by generous R&D tax treatment, has became a formidable drug innovator, as indicated by the fact that half of the new drug introductions in the United States since 1981 have been of Japanese origin. But the Japanese industry is unlikely to become a major exporter. The complexity of the drug approval and marketing process in the United States has led the Japanese to go directly to offshore production, initially through licensing and joint venture agreements overseas in America and Europe.

More recently, however, the Japanese have become more aggressive, undertaking strategic alliances to build R&D centers, academic research labs, and manufacturing plants, and acquiring small firms. Hitachi has funded a controversial $15 million biotechnology research center at the University of California at Irvine. Although all research work results will be published, Hitachi will fill several professorships with its own people and will hold all patents rights on the work produced by students working with the Hitachi employees. Close proximity to the research underway means they will enjoy a considerable head start in commercializing any breakthroughs, with the risk that technology and production employment may be transferred to Japan (*Business Week*, 7 August 1989, p. 73). Is the United States once more allowing its competitive edge in new technologies be eroded by foreign competition? Unlike the U.S. government, the Japanese government has targeted biotechnology as a priority sector in the 1990s. It is aggressively promoting the Japanese industry through favorable tax treatments, heavy government R&D expenditures, and active support for industry consortiums, which worked so well in computing, telecommunications, and other high-tech sectors.

CONCLUSION

The U.S. pharmaceutical industry faces tough challenges ahead as the pace of globalization within the industry increases dramatically. All producers, foreign and domestic, are facing increased competition, rising costs, and worldwide pressure to lower drug prices. As profits become squeezed, firms are looking to foreign markets in order to increase sales and reach the break-even point on the financial curve. European firms, facing easing trade barriers with the completion of the European Economic Community, will be vulnerable in their home markets from low-cost EEC countries like Greece and Spain. They will be looking to the lucrative U.S. market to increase their sales. In turn, U.S. companies are looking toward Japan, the Far East, and the European market in order to increase their global sales.

But companies, both here and abroad, are no longer satisfied with licensing agreements with foreign firms in return for royalties. They are intent on building up an international sales force of their own so as not to dilute profits. American firms have ended many joint marketing agreements with Japanese firms and vice versa. Japanese and European firms are stalking midsize U.S. drug houses with expertise in marketing. Second-tier U.S. firms may be swallowed up if they cannot grow large enough to compete in today's global markets. This will have a negative affect on U.S. jobs, as mergers and takeovers often bring huge layoffs and plant closures when the operations of two companies are streamlined and redundant functions eliminated.

Top-ranked U.S. companies, meanwhile, will invest heavily in R&D in search of the next billion-dollar drug, but increasingly this investment will occur overseas. Clinical safety and efficacy trials and drug approval processes are often cheaper and swifter to carry out overseas because both medical and drug regulatory systems are less bureaucratic and more efficient. The shorter the approval process, the longer firms can enjoy the monopoly profits granted by the patent. This competitive edge in drug testing and approval for Europe may not unduly hurt the profits of U.S. firms that have a global reach and can easily transfer functions. But it will create a drug lag for U.S. consumers, and will also cost U.S. jobs directly through the loss of R&D personnel and indirectly through the loss of valuable spillovers in production and scientific capacity.

U.S. multinational firms, however, are well established in Europe and in a better position to benefit from falling trade barriers in the EEC in 1992. The major benefits from market integration will come from rationalizing existing operations, and especially by concentrating secondary production in a smaller number of larger centers (Howells, 1991, p. 46). This improvement is not of major importance since production costs are less significant than R&D and marketing activities for the research-based pharmaceutical industry. Smaller national firms within the EEC, however, will not only lose their protected markets, but will also find entry costs of serving the larger common market with larger sales forces quite high. Other firms operating in low-cost environments will have to make costly upgrades in their operations to meet higher EEC standards (Howells, 1991, pp. 45–46).

Cost containment pressures on governments will surely increase in the future with the aging of populations in industrialized nations and the complicated nature of degenerative disease processes. As technology changes and more-expensive bioengineered drugs reach the market, the cost of national drug bills will be a hotly debated issues. The U.S. industry enjoys one of the last open drug markets of any leading producer nation. While managed prices through government reimbursement, prescription regulation, and promotion of alternative generics will steadily increase, it is unlikely to cripple an industry that has historically enjoyed super profits. It will also not disadvantage the U.S. industry in relation to its foreign competitors who face the same restrictions in the American market as well as stricter cost controls in their home markets.

The key question affecting the industry regarding price and marketing controls is whether it will harm the incentives for R&D activity in the long run. The industry spends about 15–17% of sales on R&D, but spends about twice that much on marketing. Too often, this involves the aggressive marketing of expensive "me-too" drugs with little therapeutic advantage over existing, lower-cost preparations. Governments' increasing control over runaway prices and marketing excesses are overdue and unlikely to destroy the incentives for R&D for those firms that are able to efficiently manage R&D activity.

Only about a quarter of R&D expenditures are spend on original research into drug innovation; the remainder is spent on safety, efficacy, and FDA approval phases (*Fortune*, 29 July 1991, p. 55). Improving the efficiency of the drug approval process, especially as the industry crosses over the new threshold of biotechnology, is perhaps a better path for preserving the incentives for R&D than allowing the industry to continue to boost prices far in excess of the consumer price index.[19] Drug innovations can then enjoy a quick diffusion in many markets at an affordable price for the consumer and an acceptable rate of return for the firm over the life of the drug.

The FDA, however, is understaffed, inefficient, and mired in bureaucracy. It is not clear that it delivers a higher level of consumer protection than its European counterparts who are able to approve drug applications in half the time. Likewise, if the murkiness surrounding patents on bioengineered drugs are cleared away and the patent approval backlog cleared, U.S. investors will not abandon this promising field. Improving the patent and drug approval process will go a long way toward keeping valuable basic and applied research functions in the United States. If the government could clean up and improve its regulatory house to match or surpass its European and Japanese counterparts, it could pursue its cost containment and health care agenda, while also benefiting the industry, both foreign- and domestic-owned in the United States. American jobs would be protected and the competitive lead in one of the few remaining U.S. high-tech sectors would be preserved.

The U.S. pharmaceutical industry is a global winner. Its firms are highly profitable, aggressive innovators and marketers, and strategic multinational players who are likely to maintain their top position in the coming decade. U.S. pharmaceutical workers and industry-based communities, however, are more vulnerable. It is not the lure of low-wage overseas production sites, but rather low-cost development and approval sites that threatens the stability of American jobs and the local economic base. A coordinated U.S. industrial development policy for pharmaceuticals and bioengineered health products focusing on improving government regulation and scientific capacity would maintain the competitiveness of the industry and reaffirm its U.S. locational pattern.

ACKNOWLEDGMENTS

I wish to acknowledge the able research assistance provided by Stephanie Jones, Meera Viswanathan, and Arturio Barrios. Meric Gertler, Peter Dicken, Ann Markusen, and Julie Graham provided excellent comments on earlier drafts of this chapter.

NOTES

1. This includes shipments made by branches of U.S. companies abroad.

2. See Cooke and Wells (1990) for an analysis of strategic alliances within the computing and communication industries.

3. The British pharmaceutical industry has a mixed origin with some companies evolving in the same manner as U.S. firms from retailers and manufacturers of pharmaceutical compounds, one from a dye company as in the German and Swiss pattern, and others from medical supply or consumer goods manufacturers into full-fledged research-based pharmaceutical firms (Tucker, 1985).

4. Pfizer was founded by two German immigrant brothers in New York City in 1849.

5. Thalidomide, a drug licensed in the United Kingdom and Europe but rejected in the United States, caused severe deformities in children born to mothers who had taken the drug. The drug was rejected, despite pressure to approve, by a conscientious FDA official who was concerned about reported numbness in the finger joints.

6. This is compared to the other main components to the industry, the nonprescription or over-the-counter market and the generic drug market.

7. The exception to this trend toward global operations was Japan, which, preoccupied with fulfilling its large domestic demand, did not move overseas. Until 1967, as with other industries, Japan also restricted entry of foreign companies into their market (James, 1977, p. 20).

8. Examples include Pfizer's Procardia, a cardiovascular drug with $510 million in 1991 sales; Merck's Vasotec an antihypertensive drug with $404 million in 1991 sales; and Merck's Mervacor, a cholesterol reducer with $505 million in 1991 sales (Standard and Poors Corporation, 1992, p. H5).

9. A notable exception is Merck which already fields a broad range of products and has set itself the goal of penetrating every therapeutic and geographic market.

10. It takes much more time to demonstrate efficacy for a slow degenerative disease than for an acute disease. This problem has led to much controversy and pressure on the FDA to release experimental drugs for such conditions as AIDS and Altzheimers.

11. In contrast, Johnson and Johnson remains one of the few large diversified drug companies.

12. Competitive pressures were directly responsible for the merger, according to internal merger documents obtained by *Business Week* (17 April 1989, p. 22): "Virtually all firms are seeking marketing partners to expand their penetration."

13. Dow had been dissatisfied with its earlier acquisition of Merrell Drug company and sought Marion to shore up its position in the pharmaceutical industry (*Economist*, 22 July 1989, p. 61.)

14. The Lazarus drug makers are satisfied with dominating a niche market, with $10–50 million in annual sales; although small in comparison to what a research-based firm would consider worthwhile, this amount is not insignificant given their size (*Business Week*, 19 December 1988, p. 90).

15. The industry association has also joined efforts of other high-tech industries in making permanent the R&D tax credit and increasing it to 25%.

16. The patent is applied for quite early, at the point at which it shows promising pharmacological activity rather that at the point of its approval for distribution. The many years of development, clinical testing, and the drug approval process seriously erodes this 17-year market exclusivity.

17. The legislation, introduced by Senator Pryor, is estimated to save Medicaid $1.9 billion over the 1991–1995 period (Standard and Poors Corporation, 1991, p. H19).

18. Because the drug boosts the production of oxygen-carrying red blood cells, it also boosts athletic performance in healthy individuals and is undetectable in drug checks. It may well replace the reliance on steroids for those athletes seeking an artificial edge in performance.

19. For example, between 1981 and 1988 prices on 80% of the drugs sold to the elderly increased by 8.6% *a year*, more than twice the average for the consumer price index. In contrast, generics rose only 2.7% for the same period (*Fortune*, 29 July 1991, p. 54).

REFERENCES

Comanor, W. S. 1986. The Political Economy of the Pharmaceutical Industry. *Journal of Economic Literature*, 24, 1178–1217.

Cooke, P., & Wells, P. 1990. Uneasy Alliances: The Spatial Development of Computing and Communication Markets. *Regional Studies*, 25(4), 345–354.

Cooper, J. D. 1978. *The Economics of Drug Innovation: The Proceedings of the First Seminar on Economics of Pharmaceutical Innovation*. Washington, DC: John Wiley and Sons.

Cooper, J. D., ed. 1976. *Regulation, Economics, and Pharmaceutical Innovation: The Proceedings of the Second Seminary on Pharmaceutical Public Policy Issues*. Washington, DC: American Enterprise Institute for Public Policy Research.

Cooper, M. H. 1980. *Prices and Profits in the Pharmaceutical Industry*. Oxford, England: Macmillan.

Dixon, B. 1987. *Beyond the Magic Bullet*. New York: Data Resources.

Dunning, J. H., Burstall, M. L., & Lake, A. 1981. *Multinational Enterprises, Governments and Technology: A Study of the Impact of Multinational Enterprises on National Science and Technical Capacities in the Pharmaceutical Industry*. Paris: OECD.

Gordon, M. J., & Fowler, D. J. 1981. Performance of the Multinational Drug Industry in Home and Host Countries: A Canadian Case Study. In *The Drug Industry: A Case Study in Foreign Control*. Toronto: James Lorrimer/ Canadian Institute for Economic Policy.

Howells, J. 1990a. The Internationalization of R&D and the Development of Global Research Networks. *Regional Studies*, 24(6), 495–512.

Howells, J. 1990b. The Location and Organization of Research and Development: New Horizons. *Research Policy*, 19(2), 133–146.

Howells, J. 1991. Pharmaceuticals and Europe 1992: The Dynamics of Industrial Change. *Environment and Planning A*, 24, 33–48.

James, B. G. 1977. *The Future of the Multi-national Pharmaceutical Industry to 1990*. New York: John Wiley and Sons.

Jorde, T. M., & Teece, D. J. 1989. Competition and Cooperation: Striking the Right Balance. *California Management Review*, 31(3), 25–37.

Kogan, H. 1984. *The Long White Line: The Story of Abbott Laboratories*. New York: Euromonitor Publications.

Lall, S. 1973. *The Multinational Corporation*. London: Pharmaceutical Manufacturers Association.

Liebenau, J. 1987. *Medical Science and Medical Industry: The Formation of the American Pharmaceutical Industry*. Baltimore: Johns Hopkins University Press.

Markusen, A. 1985. *Profit Cycles, Oligopoly, and Regional Development*. Cambridge: MIT Press.

O'Reilly, B. 1991. Drugmakers under Attack. *Fortune*, 29 July, pp. 48–63.

Pharmaceutical Manufacturers Association. 1975. *Prescription Drug Industry*

Factbook. Washington, DC: American Enterprise Institute for Public Policy Research.

Pharmaceutical Manufacturers Association. 1989. *Facts at a Glance.* Washington, DC: Pharmaceutical Manufacturers Association.

Pharmaceutical Manufacturers Association. *U.S. Trade in Drugs and Medicinal Chemicals: Analysis of Trends and Forecasts to 1990.* Washington, DC: Pharmaceutical Manufacturers Association.

Pharmaceutical Manufacturers Association. 1991. *PMA Statistical Factbook,* September, Washington, DC: Pharmaceutical Manufacturers Association.

Pratt Jr., E. T. 1985. *Pfizer: Bringing Science to Life.* New York: The Newcomen Society of the United States.

Redwood, H. 1987. *The Pharmaceutical Industry: Trends and Forecasts for 1990.* Washington, DC: Pharmaceutical Manufacturers Association.

Redwood, H. 1987. *The Pharmaceutical Industry: Trends, Problems and Achievements.* Suffolk, England: Oldwicks Press.

Reich, M. R. 1990. Why the Japanese Don't Export More Pharmaceuticals: Health Policy as Industrial Policy. *California Management Review,* Winter, 124–150.

Reis-Arndt, E. 1983. *Medical Marketing and Media,* as cited in *PMA Statistical Factbook,* September, 1991.

Schwartz, H. 1988. *An Essay on Drug Discovery and Development.* Princeton, NJ: Squibb Corporation.

Standard and Poors Corporation. 1991. Prescription Drugs, Industry Faces New Competitive Pressures. *Standard and Poor's Industry Surveys,* 22 August 1991, pp. H18–H29.

Standard and Poors Corporation. 1992. Health Care, Hospitals, Drugs and Cosmetics—Current Analysis. *Standard and Poor's Industry Surveys,* 30 April 1992 (Section 2), pp. H1–H5.

Tucker, D. 1985. *The World Health Market: The Future of the Pharmaceutical Industry.* New York: St. Martin's Press.

United Nations. 1988. *International Trade Statistics Yearbook,* Vol. 2, U.N. as cited in *PMA Statistical Factbook,* September, 1991.

U.S. Industrial Outlook. 1989. Washington, DC: U.S. Department of Commerce, Bureau of Industrial Economics.

U.S. Industrial Outlook. 1990. Washington, DC: U.S. Department of Commerce, Bureau of Industrial Economics.

U.S. Industrial Outlook. 1991. Washington, DC: U.S. Department of Commerce, Bureau of Industrial Economics.

World Drug Introductions, *Scrip,* various issues as cited in *PMA Statistical Factbook,* September, 1991.

Wells, N., ed. 1978. *Pharmaceuticals among the Sunrise Industries.* New York: St. Martin's Press.

6

Increasing Trade, Declining Port Cities: Port Containerization and the Regional Diffusion of Economic Benefits

SCOTT CAMPBELL

Most of the contributors to this book have examined changes in international trade for individual industrial sectors. This chapter takes a distinctly different view. I examine how changes in international trade have transformed seaports, which in turn have dramatically altered the economic role that ports play for cities and regions. Modern North American seaports of the 1990s bear stunningly little resemblance to the classic teeming docks of the 1950s' movie *On the Waterfront*. In their modern guise, ports reveal a fundamental change in how international trade shapes port cities and penetrates national economies.

There are at least four crucial changes behind this transformation of American ports: the volume of international trade, shipping routes, cargo type, and shipping technology. First, there has been a tremendous increase in international trade over the past 30 years, reflecting the rise of the global economy. This trade has not only grown, but has also shifted its orientation from Europe toward Asia, altering both transoceanic and domestic cargo flows. This reorientation has been accompanied by a change in the nature of goods shipped into and out of North America, with great emphasis placed on speedy delivery of high-value goods.

Perhaps the most dramatic—and certainly the most visible—change, however, has been in the area of shipping technology, both at the docks themselves, and in the rail and road access to the ports. Traditional "break-bulk" methods (discussed below) for the movement and handling of general, oceangoing cargo have been almost completely replaced by automated containerization. These changes in the methods of shipping and cargo handling have not only affected port landscapes and the economies of shipping, they have fundamentally altered the relationship between port and city. Ports have traditionally been centers of economic and cultural activity in cities, if not the raison d'être of the city's initial development. The introduction of new technology and operating methods in ports, combined with changes in the volume and destination of international trade, has transformed this traditional developmental function, and consequently requires a new conception of the port's role in a city and region.

Ports have traditionally served many functions: sources of employment, revenues, and taxes; major attractors of industries; a cause of lower prices and greater availability of consumer goods for port residents; centers of militant labor activity; and communications nodes. Each function has changed in response to containerization. This chapter examines how one particular function of ports has changed: the role of the port in economic development. The emphasis is on employment and on firms that are either related to or dependent on port activity. I use the San Francisco Bay Area as a test case, although the economic changes to be described here have been repeated in other port regions. Oakland, once a relatively insignificant harbor, has become the largest port in the region and one of the leading container ports on the West Coast. Meanwhile, the once thriving break-bulk piers of the Port of San Francisco are now largely abandoned.

I will begin with a description of the nature of traditional or "break-bulk" shipping and cargo handling, including port technology, labor requirements, the nature of the labor process, land requirements, and port layout. I will then outline the development of container technology, the innovation on the traditional form of shipping and cargo handling. I next describe how the pattern of shipping in the United States has changed in the postwar period. After discussing concepts necessary to understand port economic impacts, I then turn to a case study of San Francisco Bay Area shipping, first reviewing past and present cargo flows in and out of the region. I analyze the effects of this transformation on port activity, concentrating on three types of employment activity: direct port jobs (primarily longshoring), port-related employment (in maritime services such as ship chandleries and freight forwarders), and port-dependent employment (in firms receiving materials or shipping products by sea). Finally, I offer some conclusions concerning the changing roles of ports in cities, and in doing so expand the scale of the analysis to consider some of the national and international implications of these changes.

TRADITIONAL SHIPPING AND CARGO HANDLING

Until the 1960s the primary means of handling oceangoing cargo was the break-bulk method. Cargo was divided or "broken" into units small enough for human labor to handle with only modest mechanical assistance. (Bulk cargoes, such as grain, lumber, iron ore, and oil are usually handled at private, specialized ports, and thus receive less consideration in this chapter.) The particular nature of break-bulk cargo and shipping determined the form of the port, the labor process, and the relationship between port and city.

The most distinct characteristic of break-bulk cargo handling was its labor-intensive nature: large "gangs" of longshoremen were required to labor for a week or more to unload and load a ship, often working around the clock. The limits of human strength, as well as the constant need for ingenuity to handle and compactly stow cargo of disparate sizes, shapes, and fragility imposed significant limits on the speed of cargo handling.

Storms at sea, irregularity of demand, seasonal surpluses, and ice-bound seasons were only a few of the numerous causes of fluctuations in ship arrivals, and hence in the need for dock work. This led to the creation of a casual labor system, whereby work was secured only for the duration of a ship's stay in port. Originally obtained in the morning's shape-up (whereby employers choose from prospective longshoremen gathered on the pier), as of 1934 the longshoremen on the Pacific Coast obtained jobs through the union hiring hall. (East Coast longshore workers continued to be hired through the shape-up many years after the practice was abolished on the West Coast.) Bird (1971) explained the traditionally militant stance of longshoremen's unions (as well as seamen's and miner's unions) by citing the close link with the union rather than the employer, along with the lack of skill transferability (longshoremen learned few skills that could be used in other types of jobs), minimal occupational stratification, and the unpleasantness and physical demands of the work. The frequent strikes and other "job actions" were seen as necessary steps to combat the numerous abuses that casual longshoremen were particularly vulnerable to, such as speedups, noxious cargo, excessive sling loads (a unit of cargo suspended by a crane), discrimination, and unjustified firings.

The lengthy stays of ships required a large number of berths, leading to the development of numerous small "finger piers," so named because they were closely spaced and radiated out from the shore. A pier consisted of a large transit shed for the temporary storage of goods, surrounded by a narrow "apron" (a flat loading and unloading surface between the transit shed and the water), and was usually served directly by rail lines. The technology used at dockside was relatively simple and inexpensive, and its interchangeable nature conceivably allowed a ship to dock anywhere in the world or a longshoreman to work any pier. This latter characteristic also encouraged the use of casual labor.

The port itself was usually located upriver and as close as possible to the city center. This location reduced the more costly transport of goods by land and also facilitated access to a large, urban, dockworker labor force.

MODERN CONTAINER SHIPPING

The impetus to redesign the method of cargo handling came after World War II. Costs while in ports (primarily labor costs) had risen to over 40% of all costs for shippers; frequent strikes had led to greater labor supply uncertainty; and pilferage and damages were causing losses of up to 24% of cargo (Wilson, 1982). Congressional committees and the U.S. Maritime Administration pressured the shipping industry to become more competitive and to discipline labor, or else face possible state intervention in shipping operations. In addition, the Department of Defense, along with other federal departments, began studying ways to improve civilian cargo-handling efficiency (Maritime Cargo Transportation Conference, 1964). All these factors, taking place in an atmosphere in which American shippers were losing business to foreign lines, accelerated the push toward a major change in shipping. Containerization offered solutions to all these problems. The first use of containers in 1956 was a shipment of 58 boxes between New York and Houston. This shipment was organized by Malcolm McLean of the McLean Trucking Company, which later became the massive Sea-Land Service, Inc.

It is important to realize that the steamship companies, rather than the ports themselves, have been the major catalysts in international container development. They play this role because they have the most to gain or lose through the success or failure of container shipping. Bird (1971, p. 194) referred to the link between shipping companies and ports as a master–servant relationship, in which "traffic demand is served by ships which in turn make demands that ports struggle to fulfill." This relationship is important to keep in mind when I address the role of the port in economic development later in this chapter. Since the port is dependent on shipping companies, which in turn are directly dependent on world trade, the port has less freedom in development, and certainty in long-term business, as compared to industrial sectors. A port may make decisions about the scale and type of facilities (e.g., whether to invest in a new container crane or a bulk loader), and on marketing its services to attract more shipping lines, but it is ultimately susceptible to the fluctuations and unpredictability of world trade.

Essentially, containerization is a transportation system in which the shape and size of cargo is standardized or "unitized" through the use of containers, greatly facilitating the use of rapid mechanical means of cargo handling and stowage. Containerization has made possible the dramatic streamlining of old shipping methods, which were traditionally intricate, labor-intensive, and time consuming, involving multiple handling, packing, and repacking of cargo. A typical procedure for modern container shipping is as follows:

1. A shipper contacts his or her agent, freight forwarder, or steamship company.
2. The steamship company arranges to have a container delivered to the shipper's plant by contacting a local cartage agent, a motor carrier, or a railroad.
3. The shipper loads the container which is then sealed and moved by truck or train to shipside.
4. The container is inspected.
5. The container is loaded aboard the ship by a portainer, a crane designed specifically for containers.
6. The ship sails to the port of destination.
7. The container is transferred by crane to the chassis of a truck or a railcar.
8. The container is again inspected.
9. The container is delivered, still sealed, via truck or rail to its final destination.

Technically, containerization is simply the loading of cargo into a uniform-sized package, whose dimensions are generally 8 feet wide, 8 feet tall, and either 20, 30, or 40 feet long. Yet containerization also has made possible the development of a "through concept" of shipping, in which the journey from overseas by ship to port and then by rail or truck to inland market is considered a single trip. The container is loaded by the exporter and is not opened again until it reaches its final destination. Consequently, the effects of containerization have gone beyond shipping to change the trucking and rail industries, in which ships, trucks, and trains are integrated in a comprehensive container transport system. One example of this is the growing use of trucks and trains to ship containers across the continent, known as overland common point cargo

(OCP) or "land-bridge" cargo, which will be discussed later in this chapter. This practice has increased cargo-carrying levels on transcontinental highways and rail lines, and is seen by some as a key factor in the recent revitalization of the nation's railroads.

There is a temptation to relate this maritime technological transformation to the recent perception of fordism giving way to flexible specialization. A first view might suggest that the traditional break-bulk method has the inefficiency and variability of craft work, while the standardization of container boxes, cranes, ships, and trucks reflects fordist mass production. Yet this interpretation has two problems. The first is timing: if containerization represents a fordist revolution, then its rise in the 1960s and 1970s came just at the time when fordist industries were apparently on the *decline*. The second is functional: container boxes may superficially look like symbols of mass production, yet seen in context high-speed container shipping plays an admittedly unromantic but nevertheless necessary role in a flexible and specialized global industrial economy. The moral of this story is that not every element of the modern economy must be specialized and fragmented; rather, flexible specialization requires a massive, highly standardized distribution system to link markets and producers.

Cost Savings from Containerization

Containerization results in substantial cost savings for several reasons. First, less longshore labor is needed. Second, larger ships can take advantage of lower labor costs per ton at sea since, above a given size ship, the crew size remains constant. (Such large ships were not advantageous with break-bulk technology, since the time delays at port increased proportionally with ship size.) Third, the substantially faster turnaround time in ports (usually 1 day or less) leaves more time for sailing, and consequently increases the amount of cargo a ship can carry per year. Fourth, containers virtually eliminate theft and damages, thus reducing insurance costs and eliminating the old practice of allowing for such losses by sending a larger (and consequently more costly) shipment. Fifth, the "through concept" allows the cargo to leave the port area by rail or truck almost immediately, lowering local warehousing costs. Sixth, faster shipment means that less capital is tied up in goods inventory, thereby lowering the cost of capital.

It should also be noted that the extent of cost saving varies with the amount of cargo. A manufacturer or exporter, having enough cargo to fill an entire container, can send the full container directly to the port. A smaller business, however, one that has only a modest amount of cargo, must send the export goods to a freight consolidator. The freight consolidator in turn combines the cargo of several exporters into one container, which is then sent to the port. These two conditions are referred to as FCL (full container load) and LCL (less than full container load), respectively. The advantages of shipping large amounts of cargo are thus readily apparent: one eliminates the expense of paying an intermediary (the consolidator), and also avoids potentially costly damages and time delays by bypassing an additional handling of the cargo before it is containerized. Cost advantages for large shipments already existed with break-bulk cargo, yet the operating network and inherent dimensions of container shipping have exacerbated these cost differentials.

Yet containerization did not bring down the cost of shipping as much as expected, primarily owing to the massive capital costs involved in converting ports and shipping fleets. It may seem curious that shippers bypassed a relatively inexpensive innovation with significant productivity increases, palletization, for a very costly innovation with greater productivity increases. Palletization is an alternative to containerization, whereby cargo is unitized on pallets. It is more labor-intensive than containers, partially because pallet loads are smaller than container loads, and more time consuming, since greater care is needed in handling the exposed cargo. Yet the use of pallets would have had a relatively modest impact on the existing waterfront labor force, and required a significantly smaller investment in new technology. Bird (1971, p. 100) has interpreted this decision to bypass palletization in favor of containerization as a deliberate attempt by the newly formed U.S. shipping consortia to regain their prominence in world trade, knowing that smaller shipping groups (such as the Scandinavians, who supported palletization) could not as easily afford the massive capital costs required to containerize.

Despite its high costs, containerization occurred at a surprisingly rapid rate, with many companies containerizing more out of fear of competition than from intrinsic confidence in containers. The nature of container shipping also contributed to this rapid conversion, since a container ship or port is of value only within a comprehensive network of container ships and ports. At first, no one wanted to be the only container shipper (with nowhere else to dock and unload), but quickly this logic was reversed, and no one wanted to be left out of the game. By the late 1960s the momentum of this technical conversion became self-sustaining, and a return to break-bulk shipping became doubtful. Today, even small third world countries have begun to containerize, for they recognize that they must conform to the new world shipping standards if they are to compete in international markets.

Containerization's Impact on Port Design and Operation

The introduction of container technology dramatically changed the form of the port, the labor process, and the relationship of the port to the city. The most significant change has been the reduction of labor requirements: a ship that once would have required 160 workers 1 week to unload now requires only 50 workers for 20 hours to unload (Bird, 1971, p. 146). This represents a productivity increase from approximately 30 to 600 cargo tons per worker per week.

The traditional casual system has also largely disappeared, and the remaining longshoremen usually have permanent positions with one firm. Port activity now entails a stratification of the work force through skill differentiation. It generates transferable skills, and is less physically demanding, reducing the key explanatory factors behind a strike-prone labor force.

The port itself has been dramatically transformed. The ideal layout involves a simple, linear quayage, with 20 to 30 acres of land per berth for container handling and storage. The port landscape is dominated by multimillion-dollar container cranes and ancillary container-moving vehicles, and is distinctly void of the bustling human activity that once characterized the waterfront. The worldwide standardization of container-port machinery (a prerequisite of unitized cargo) has, somewhat paradoxically, been simultaneously accompanied by specialization, so that the old practice of common-user piers has been replaced by programmed-tied user terminals: the operator of the terminal is the operator of the ship.

The modern container port works best with uncongested access to highways, as well as massive areas of flat, undeveloped land. The relative speed of inland transportation vis-à-vis ocean travel encourages the placement of container ports as close to open water as possible to reduce shipping distances. The net result of these three requirements is the relocation of port facilities from an upriver city location to a downriver peripheral location.

The structures of the existing break-bulk port generally serve as a liability rather than as an asset for container service, since the pier aprons are often too narrow for truck access, the berths are too small, and the ancient brick warehouses are not appropriate for container shipping. The cost of completely converting the piers, demolishing unneeded structures, developing truck access, and providing 20 to 30 acres per container berth (often requiring expensive fill) is often simply prohibitive. For the existing break-bulk port, these new locational and site requirements have usually meant abandonment and decay, unless the city is able to convert the piers to nonmaritime uses.

THE CHANGING DISTRIBUTION
OF PORT ACTIVITY IN THE UNITED STATES

In 1962, when the eastern United States was still the center of the American economy and Asian trade was still modest, Atlantic Coast ports handled 61% of all cargo value entering and leaving the country (see Table 6.1). By 1987 their share dropped to 40%. Gulf Coast ports also dropped from 20% to 13% of all cargo value. Worst off were the Great Lakes ports, which not only dropped from 6% down to a meager 1.3%, but actually handled less cargo value, adjusted for inflation, in 1987 than they had 25 years earlier. The industrial decline of the Midwest has also devastated the region's marine ports.

The big winners were the Pacific Coast ports, which increased their share from 13.2% in 1962 to a leading 46.4% in 1987. In real (1987 dollar) terms, these western ports went from moving $10.5 billion worth of cargo in 1962 to $146.8 billion in 1987.

There have also been dramatic—and troubling—changes in import–export trade balances in the regional port areas. In 1962 exports of dry, nontanker goods exceeded imports by $2.8 billion (in 1962 dollars), and this trade surplus was reflected in all four U.S. port regions. Twenty-five years later, only Gulf Coast ports showed a significant surplus, although Great Lakes ports also showed a slight surplus. In stark contrast, Atlantic Coast ports imported nearly $50 billion more than they exported. But Pacific ports were the largest "contributor" to the national trade deficit, with imports exceeding exports by more than $86 billion. Over half of all imports into the United States enter Pacific Coast ports, with Los Angeles and Seattle area ports alone receiving 45% of all U.S. imports. These two regions have now surpassed San Francisco's traditional role as the "gateway to Asia," or more accurately, as Asia's gateway into American markets.

The allocation of shipping activity around the United States has been affected not only by the changing location of industries and consumers, but also by a new form of shipping: "land-bridge" or overland common point cargo. The economics of cargo transport have created a situation in which shipment of goods from Asia to the East Coast of the United States is now potentially faster and consequently less expensive by a combination of ship and rail rather than by ship alone (via the Panama Canal). This system, which transfers containers from ship to a transcontinental train (referred to as a "unit train") at a Pacific Coast port, in effect uses the continent as a bridge between two distant ports. This bridge concept is also used for shorter journeys, such as those from Asia to the Gulf Coast via the Pacific Coast ports, or for longer journeys, such as those from Asia to Europe. (This concept has also been

TABLE 6.1. Waterborne Exports and Imports, by U.S. Region, 1987 and 1962 (Dry, Nontanker cargo)[a]

	1987			1962			
Exports	Weight (million lb)	Value ($million)	Value to weight ($/lb)	Weight (million lb)	Value ($million)	Value in 1987 dollars ($million)	Value to weight ($/lb)
U.S. Total	642,511	96,281	0.15	241,956	13,206	40,018	0.17
Atlantic Coast	149,970	37,755	0.25	92,695	7,397	22,415	0.24
Gulf Coast	268,221	24,149	0.10	70,394	3,320	10,061	0.14
Pacific Coast	161,603	30,249	0.19	29,334	1,621	4,912	0.17
Great Lakes	62,717	2,128	0.03	49,533	868	2,630	0.05
Imports							
U.S. Total	331,320	219,712	0.66	198,065	10,360	40,311	0.20
Atlantic Coast	143,702	87,554	0.61	101,536	6,919	26,922	0.27
Gulf Coast[b]	79,569	13,699	0.17	48,963	1,402	5,455	0.11
Pacific Coast[c]	81,688	116,514	1.43	16,489	1,483	5,770	0.35
Great Lakes	26,364	1,947	0.07	31,077	556	2,163	0.07

[a]Deflator calculated from export and import GNP implicit price deflators.
[b]The Gulf Coast includes Puerto Rico.
[c]The Pacific Coast includes Hawaii and Alaska.
Source: United States Dept. of Commerce, 1987, Tables E-1 and I-1.

applied in Eurasia, where cargo is shipped between Asia and Europe via the U.S.S.R., rather than through the Suez Canal.)

The effect of this service is to introduce interregional port competition between ports. Until recently, cargo passing through a port would primarily be bound for somewhere in the port's region, limiting competition for this cargo to ports within that particular region. But the current situation allows a shipper to send cargo through a choice of ports in several different regions. Such competition is exacerbated by the scale economies of container ports, in which individual ports are strongly encouraged by the massive fixed costs of container facilities to aggressively attract new business.

This situation is particularly significant on the Pacific Coast, where a shipper may send bridge cargo through Seattle, Portland, San Francisco–Oakland, Los Angeles–Long Beach, or Vancouver, B.C. Seattle (as well as Vancouver) benefits from having the shortest sailing distance to Asia, whereas Los Angeles is closer to many inland markets, and does not need to send bridge cargo by rail over the Sierra Nevada. San Francisco-Oakland, once the West Coast's leading port area, consequently finds itself in a precarious middle ground between Seattle and Los Angeles. Portland is in a similar situation, to the point where many shippers send cargo to Seattle by ship, and then to Portland by truck or rail.

This change in the geographic logic and scale economies of international shipping has led to the rise of Los Angeles and Seattle, and the resulting "squeeze" of Portland and San Francisco into smaller shares of Pacific trade, especially with imports. Even the export trade, traditionally dominated by the Bay Area, has been partially rerouted through Los Angeles.

It is difficult to predict the long-range outcome of this interregional port competition, yet it does appear that San Francisco and Oakland will continue to lose their share of Pacific trade. Consequently, forecasts of economic benefits due to Bay Area ports, based on the assumption of a constant share of the rapidly growing Far East trade (as in the Seaport Planning Advisory Committee *Seaport Plan* [1982]), will overestimate the actual benefits to be obtained.

The development of bridge cargo is thus a further step in the isolation and alienation of the port from its surroundings. The growing percentage of cargo that never enters the port's regional markets or factories, but is just "passing through," is transforming the role of the port from a center of local economic activity to a single link in a complex transportation network that readily crosses geographical as well as economic boundaries. In a sense this represents the continued functional separation of a port from the economic networks within a port city, and the reintegration of these various ports into a worldwide network of trade.

PORTS AND ECONOMIC DEVELOPMENT

Ports have traditionally played a central role in their associated cities' economic development. Their benefits to the local community were easily identifiable, thus readily justifying local fiscal support of the port through subsidies, tax exemptions, infrastructure provision, and issuance of bonds. These benefits included thousands of jobs for longshoremen and other port workers, and other jobs generated by port-related businesses that provided services to the port and industries attracted to the port to take advantage of lower import and export transportation costs. In addition, development of these industries and services, as well as the extensive port-related infrastructure, attracted other businesses to the port city that had no direct business with the port itself (economies of agglomeration). Finally, the city benefited from lower prices and greater availability of consumer goods, since locally consumed imported goods had lower transport costs and a lower rate of spoilage and/or damage as compared to these goods consumed inland These various benefits tended to be quite localized, with most of the businesses located within the port city or on port land itself.

The transformation of shipping through containerization has changed the structure of the industry, and consequently redistributed the economic benefits due to maritime trade. The most apparent change is the dramatic decline of longshoring employment through the substitution of machinery for labor. The "through concept" of containerization, by diminishing the significance of the port as a transshipment point and also lowering inland transportation costs, has had two major effects. For producers, it has decreased the relative advantage of locating industry near the port. For consumers, it has decreased the relative purchasing power advantages of living in a port city. The general result of containerization thus appears to be the shift of port benefits from a local to regional and national scales.

These changes in the role and dynamic of ports have also made more difficult the task of evaluating the benefits of seaports, and so taxes the traditional methods of economic impact analysis. As a result, analyzing the economic role of modern ports presents somewhat of a dilemma.

THE RESULTING PARADOX OF RISING PACIFIC TRADE AND DECLINING PORTS

Amid all the discussion of world trade imbalances, the new international division of labor, and the flood of Asian manufactured goods into the United States, the port presents the most tangible landscape for reading these changes. Through these terminals, across the quays, and inside the containers pass the Japanese automobiles, Korean steel, and Chinese clothes, as well as the wheat, wood, and coal bound in the opposite direction.

To observe these massive flows of cargo impresses one with the absolute importance of the port in the world economy. There is no doubt that the role of the port in the world economy has increased with the rise of transoceanic industrial interdependence. Yet this global importance does not necessarily imply an equivalent importance in terms of benefits for the locality and region. It is paradoxical that the modern port does not provide the region with many of the traditional port benefits, and yet is absolutely essential for the larger economy. The stark contrast between the sparsity of direct employment and revenues it generates, and the tremendous value of its cargo, creates an attitude in which massive local port investment often appears not worth the expense, particularly when compared to alternative uses of valuable waterfront land. And yet eliminating the port seems to be out of the question.

This ambiguity concerning the value of a port has been greatly exacerbated by the mechanization and integration of port terminals and their inland feeder networks. The traditional benefits of a port—crudely visible in the form of waterfront factories, warehouses, and grain mills, a fabulous array of international consumer goods in the port town shops, and thousands of longshore workers teeming to and from the docks— have been replaced by the more ubiquitous and imperceptible networks of truck lines, unit trains, land-bridge service, inland container consolidators, and dispersed industry; and the resulting benefits are more difficult to account for and to place boundaries around.

It is thus more difficult to analyze the value of a port by means of a traditional benefit–cost analysis, because the benefits are so difficult to trace and measure and because they often do not accrue to those who bear the costs. Development of the modern semiautonomous port authority, whose model is that of New York and New Jersey, has removed port investment policy from general city budget considerations and may have prevented port benefits from becoming an issue of public scrutiny and debate. Traditional spatial analysis has also proven somewhat inadequate, since the once-tight port economic area has given way to a diffuse, nonconcentric, and even nonspatial pattern of port benefits. The consequence is often a vague and resigned faith in the belief that modern ports provide nonquantifiable benefits for the region by improving trade linkages, attracting industry, maintaining a city's position as an economic nodal point, and generally "lubricating" the economy. The faith also holds that although these benefits cannot be accurately measured, the alternative of eliminating the port would surely have grave and destructive consequences.

Later in this chapter I will use the case of the San Francisco Bay Area to isolate port benefits into three categories: direct, port-related (backward linkages), and port-dependent (forward linkages). Whereas most port economic impact studies are concerned with tabulating costs and benefits of ports, my focus will be on how these three types of port activity influence the pattern of regional economic development.

CHARACTERISTICS OF CARGO AND THEIR REGIONAL ECONOMIC IMPACTS

A few generalizations should be made here on how various types of cargo have different impacts on the region. There are at least six distinct ways to categorize cargo: its method of measure, form, comparability, end use, direction, and origin/destination. I will discuss each briefly.

Method of Measure

There are two primary ways of measuring cargo: by weight and by value. These two reflect the method of shipment (which is affected by weight) and the contents of shipment (value). (By volume is a third approach, though in its application it is fairly similar to weight.) The use of one or the other measure significantly changes the ranking of ports. Cargo weight is a more important measure of port activity, since weight determines the port charges and size of shipment, and in turn the level of maritime services and employment. Value, on the other hand, is a more important measure of the role of maritime activity in trade and industry, since its reflects the level of sales and purchases of businesses and consumers. The traditional preference for cargo-weight statistics may reflect an orientation toward concern with port use capacity rather than concern with port–city economic relationships.

Form

Though the level of port activity increases with cargo weight, it is also affected by the form of shipment. Heavier cargoes, such as wood, coal, iron ore, steel, and grain, are usually sent as bulk cargo, which involves a highly mechanized loading system and no individual packaging. Lighter cargoes, such as clothes, electronics, or footwear, are usually sent as general cargo, which—despite the advances of containers—still requires more individualized handling and packaging. Consequently, general cargo shipments generate more port activity (and port employment) than does bulk cargo. A study of the Port of Milwaukee in 1967 found that break-bulk cargo generated seven times greater direct income for maritime services than bulk cargo (Schenker, 1967, p. 131). It is not clear how much this difference has since declined due to containerization.

End Use

The form of shipment often reflects the third variable of cargo: its end use. Bulk cargoes are generally raw material inputs for production, whereas general cargoes are more often consumer goods. This distinction generally determines whether the cargo will increase industrial production or directly contribute to greater availability (and perhaps lower cost) of consumer goods.

Direction

The direction of cargo, that is, whether it is being imported or exported, is often neglected in port impact studies. Indeed, for the port itself, there is little apparent difference between cargo moving in one or the other direction. Imports must be unloaded from the ship, inspected, and placed on trucks or trains; to export, one merely reverses the process. This symmetry, most clearly evident in the loading and unloading of containers, where it is difficult at any one moment to determine the direction of the cargo, creates a situation in which the same amount of port activity is generated, regardless of cargo direction. Yet for the port region the direction is significant. (Indeed for the national economy's balance of trade, this distinction is crucial.)

Substitutability

To analyze the regional employment impact of imports, one must introduce a fifth variable: whether there is an alternative source (substitute) for the import. Certain industries may be dependent on materials shipped through a local port, yet that does not mean that the industry is wholly dependent on that port. If the second-best substitute is shipping the foreign materials via another port or airport, then the marginal regional employment benefit of the port in question is not simply the value of the cargo; rather, it is equal to the marginal increase in final goods production employment due to the production cost savings of using the local (cheaper) port facilities rather than the more expensive airport or other seaports. One may thus generalize that ports have particularly high employment impacts when the cargo is an intermediate good that has no domestic substitute, and particularly when the next-best transport alternative (which for most shipments to the Bay Area is air cargo or Los Angeles ports) is prohibitively expensive.

Origin/Destination

The origin of exports and the destination of imports are of increasing significance for determining the economic impact within the port region. Given the growth in OCP or land-bridge cargo—in which the cargo's origin and final destination are both outside the region—one cannot assume that all cargo passing through a region also passes through the region's economy.

The regional benefits of this type of cargo are reduced to its use of maritime services, without any perceptible direct impact on regional consumers or industries. In addition, the wharfage charges (a charge assessed against the cargo, based on weight or volume) for OCP cargo are often lower than for local cargo. For example, in 1984 OCP cargo at Bay Area ports was charged at $2.90 per 1000 kilograms or per cubic meter (as manifested by vessel), whereas local cargo was charged at $3.90 (Marine Exchange of the San Francisco Area, 1984, p. 61).

Though the OCP/local cargo balance can greatly fluctuate from month to month, and data on this breakdown are not easily obtained, rough estimates of OCP percentages of total cargo in the mid-1980s were 30% for San Francisco, 40% for Oakland, 40% for Los Angeles/Long Beach (though they receive a tremendous amount of OCP cargo, it is counterbalanced by a large regional market), and roughly 75% for Seattle (Peters, 1983).

How has the rise of OCP cargo affected the economic impacts of ports? Since regional industrial and consumer benefits are generated only by cargo with an origin or a destination within the region, the rise of bridge cargo suggests that these benefits have not increased proportionately over time with cargo levels. For example, one can guess that the regional benefits per dollar of cargo value due to the Port of Oakland (which has a large percentage of bridge cargo) are not as great as the benefits per dollar of cargo value for the Port of San Francisco 20 years ago (which had less bridge cargo), if all other factors are held constant. Also, a bridge-cargo-oriented port (such as Seattle, with an estimated 75% of cargo bound for east of the Rockies) generates less regional benefit per unit of cargo than a port with a lower percentage of bridge cargo (such as Oakland).

CASE STUDY: THE SAN FRANCISCO BAY AREA

I now turn to the Bay Area to illustrate these changes in ports and regional economies. Though some of the general tendencies of recent port development have taken on a different form in the Bay Area due to the geopolitical uniqueness of the area (for example, the presence of twin cities, and the particular geography of the area, combining river, bay, and central, peninsular city), the Bay Area case nevertheless reflects the universal changes in port cities.

The early history of Bay Area shipping (1848–1880s) was characterized by the dominance of the Port of San Francisco. Virtually all cargo, including grain, initially passed over the San Francisco docks. By the 1880s, however, the grain and lumber trade began moving to other Bay Area ports, primarily along Carquinez Strait in northern Contra Costa County (from Crockett to Antioch). Industrial ports also developed in this area, including those for explosives (Hercules), sugar refining (Crockett), steel (Pittsburg), and oil (Richmond). In addition, cargo ports developed in Oakland and Alameda (Encinal Terminals), and later in Richmond. Yet these East Bay cargo ports remained quite small and mostly functioned as feeder service to San Francisco. San Francisco thus remained the dominant port, especially for general cargo, up to the 1950s.

How Did San Francisco "Lose Out" to Oakland?

The rise of containerized shipping and the shift of cargo handling from San Francisco to Oakland are two parallel and linked events. There are several explanations of why Oakland successfully converted to containerization and San Francisco did not, and it appears that each city self-consciously contributed to this technological and spatial transition. In a larger context, this shift is part of a general worldwide tendency to relocate port terminals away from central city locations to peripheral, "greenfield" sites, as typified by such port relocations as those from Manhattan to Port Elizabeth, New Jersey, from Antwerp to Zeebrugge, and from London to Tilbury (and further downstream). Oakland contained a rather large expanse of tidewater land, suitable for the construction of simple linear quays with several hundred inexpensive acres of hinterland for container storage and handling. San Francisco's port, particularly its Northern Waterfront, consisted of antiquated finger piers, which would require major conversion and demolition to be suitable for container handling. In addition, land use along the San Francisco waterfront is fairly dense, making difficult the task of assembling the requisite 20 to 30 acres per container berth. Also, San Francisco's piers, designed for railcar loading, were generally too small to allow direct truck access. Truck traffic was further hindered by inner-city traffic congestion. Oakland's port is well isolated from the city's traffic and could offer direct truck access to the piers.

San Francisco's location at the tip of a peninsula was also a major disadvantage, requiring trucks to use the congested trans-bay bridges, and rail cars to either circumnavigate the bay via San Jose or to be ferried across the bay by boat. Oakland's location, on the other hand, was ideal for container cargo, for it was situated near three transcontinental rail termini and well connected with the interstate highway system. The significance of the Port of Oakland's access to the increasingly important trucking business was recognized even before the rise of containerization, as is made evident in this 1950 statement by Frank M. Chandler, traffic director of the Truck Owners Association of California: "I think perhaps the East Shore Highway and the San Leandro Freeway have done more probably to attract the traffic from the valleys into the Oakland port facilities than almost anything else that has been done, or could be done" (California State Legislature, 1951).

Other factors, including their differing institutional settings, help to explain Oakland's rise and San Francisco's decline. Oakland has a fairly aggressive and autonomous port authority that was relatively free from local government constraints, and hence could pursue expensive and risky containerization development in the early 1960s without much public resistance. Oakland also received major federal assistance for port development, including a rather controversial grant from the Economic Development Administration in the 1960s of more than $10 million (Pressman & Wildavsky, 1973). The Port of San Francisco was controlled by the State of California until 1968, and this more-removed administrative structure may partly explain San Francisco's sluggishness in responding to containerization. (A legislative act of 1968, known as the "Burton Act," transferred the port from the state back to the City and County of San Francisco, yet placed significant restrictions on investment and land development.) In addition, older and traditionally successful ports, like industries, tend to be conservative regarding new technology, initially refusing to accept the need to change existing practices. Attempts by San Francisco to "catch up" were made more difficult by two other factors: shipping lines tended to sign long-term (20–30 year) leases with Oakland, and the higher interest rates of the 1970s dramatically increased the cost of capital-intensive container technology investment.

The development of containerization in Oakland as a means of breaking the strength of organized longshore labor has also been suggested as an explanatory factor. However, this argument better explains the general worldwide shift to containers than the particular shift of port activity from San Francisco to Oakland. Since dockworkers in both Oakland and San Francisco belonged to the same union local, shifting cargo handling to Oakland in itself would not necessarily weaken the International Longshoremen's and Warehousemen's Union (ILWU).

A final explanation of San Francisco's hindered port development is that the city in part implicitly did not want to containerize extensively. As I previously mentioned, conversion to container terminals requires hundreds of acres of hinterland. Consequently, the conversion of particularly the Northern Waterfront to container handling would have either required massive bayfill (which would have been politically as well as technically unfeasible) or major land acquisitions (which would have been very expensive). The increasing commercial value of waterfront property (for offices, residences, restaurants, and tourism) may have discouraged an aggressive program of container terminal development in the Northern Waterfront.[1]

The Distribution of Port Activity in the Bay Area

If the shift of cargo flows across U.S. regions reflects changes in the national and international economies, then the shift of cargo flows within the Bay Area reflects the changing relationship between a regional economy and its local ports. Oakland is now the area's major port, through which 67% of northern California's nontanker imports and 80% of nontanker exports (in value) passed in 1987.[2] (See Table 6.2.) San Francisco, which is still the area's leading break-bulk port, had three container terminals in the 1980s and handled 14% of Bay Area non-tanker imports and 12% of exports in 1987. Richmond is the leading oil terminal and has recently started container operations. In 1987 it handled 8% of dry (nontanker) imports and 1% of dry exports. The smaller Bay Area, Delta, and coastal ports of northern California handled the remaining 10.3% of imports and 7.0% of exports. The Carquinez Strait area continues to be the site of several specialized industrial ports, such as auto importing at Benecia and oil at Martinez.

The three large Bay Area ports—Oakland, San Francisco, and Richmond—all experienced "trade deficits" in 1987, as the value of their imports exceeded their exports. This was true for total shipments to and from all northern California ports in 1987 ($13.4 billion in imports versus $6.2 billion in exports). This deficit represents a departure from the past; unlike Seattle and Los Angeles, which have generally been net importers, the Bay Area was until recently a net exporter. (Only in terms of weight do exports still exceed imports, which reflects the unenviable American position of buying more valuable goods than it sells abroad.)

Oakland has not always dominated Bay Area shipping. Through

TABLE 6.2. Waterborne Exports and Imports, by West Coast Customs Districts and Individual Northern California Ports, 1987 (Dry, Nontanker cargo)

Exports	Weight (million lb)	% of northern CA	Value ($million)	% of northern CA	Value/ weight ($/lb)
U.S. Total	642,511	—	96,281	—	$0.15
Los Angeles region	31,412	—	11,576	—	$0.37
Northern California	15,879	100.0%	6,158	100.0%	$0.39
San Francisco	1,332	8.4%	764	12.4%	$0.57
Oakland	6,732	42.4%	4,902	79.6%	$0.73
Richmond	976	6.1%	61	1.0%	$0.06
Portland, Oregon, Columbia River	59,877	—	3,622	—	$0.06
Seattle region	45,451	—	7,760	—	$0.17
Imports					
U.S. Total	331,320	—	219,712	—	$0.66
Los Angeles region	38,344	—	63,594	—	$1.66
Northern California	10,971	100.0%	13,352	100.0%	$1.22
San Francisco	1,629	14.8%	1,884	14.1%	$1.16
Oakland	5,405	49.3%	8,995	67.4%	$1.66
Richmond	1,526	13.9%	1,099	8.2%	$0.72
Portland, Oregon, Columbia River	7,538	—	4,139	—	$0.55
Seattle region	21,798	—	34,631	—	$1.59

Source: United States Dept. of Commerce, 1987, Tables E-1 and I-1.

1965 San Francisco was the clear leader in the value of general cargo handled, particularly in imports. The late 1960s was a period of transition, during which Oakland dramatically increased its cargo activity due to its new container terminals (the first terminal was built in 1962), while San Francisco cargo activity began to level off. Oakland rapidly overtook San Francisco during the early 1970s, more than quadrupling the value of both imports and exports from 1970 to 1980. During the same period the value of exported goods crossing San Francisco docks dropped 32%, and imports declined by 42%. These changes occurred in a setting of overall growth for Pacific shipping, in which northern California cargo more than doubled from 1970 to 1980.[3]

The relative value and weight of cargo offer a crude measure of the type of cargo, assuming that cargos with a higher value-to-weight ratio reflect more-"sophisticated" or higher value-added goods. For exports, San Francisco and Oakland had similar value-to-weight ratios during 1987 ($0.57/pound and $0.73/pound, respectively). Richmond exported low-value bulk cargo ($0.06/ton). In contrast, Oakland imports particularly high-value cargo ($1.66/pound), whereas San Francisco (at

$1.16/pound) imports a mix of both lower-value general cargo and dry bulk cargo (such as newsprint). Richmond again has the lowest relative value ($0.72/pound).

Cargo by Country

This rise of Pacific ports is reflected in the recent surpassing of the Atlantic by the Pacific Ocean as the leading trading route for the United States as a whole. This trade reorientation is particularly apparent in the Bay Area: 80% of the $14.0 billion worth of cargo shipped to and from the San Francisco-Oakland Customs District (which includes all northern California ports) during 1982 was Asian imports and exports (Port of Oakland, 1983).

Japan is the Bay Area's most important trading partner among the Asian countries, to and from which over one-third of all cargo value is shipped. Europe remains the second-most-important trading partner, though it is being challenged by Korea and Taiwan, with significant trade with the Philippines, Thailand, Indonesia, and elsewhere in the Far East. An example of the relative scale of Bay Area–Asia trade is that nearly as much cargo value is exported to Singapore (a country of several million) as to Europe (a continent of several hundred million). The remaining regions of the world are modest trading partners in comparison, with the exception of heavy imports from Central America (primarily low-value crude fertilizers and minerals) and North America (primarily paper and paper board from Canada), and high-value exports to Australia (primarily vehicles and machinery).

Asian countries are the clear leaders in terms of exporting high-value cargo, with Hong Kong's exports the most valuable cargo per ton (clothing and electronics). Europe's cargo is significantly less valuable per ton (the leading imports are vehicles and beverages). Cargo to and from the Americas and Africa has the lowest value-to-weight ratio of all.

Of particular interest is the relationship between import and export cargo value-to-weight ratios. With the exception of Central America and Australia, the per-ton value of imports into the Bay Area greatly exceeds the per-ton value of exports. For example, imports from Hong Kong in 1982 were valued at over $3.00/pound, whereas exports to Hong Kong were worth only $0.86/pound. This initially surprising situation is classically associated with a resource-extraction region, where heavy raw materials are shipped out and valuable industrial products are received.

Cargo by Commodity

The ports within the San Francisco-Oakland Customs District handle a tremendous variety of goods, from pharmaceuticals to fertilizers, textiles to telecommunications equipment. Some 7.5 million tons of goods, with a value of $7.0 billion, were exported from these ports in 1982; 3.4 million tons of goods, at a value of $7.0 billion, were imported during the same period.

The low value-to-weight ratios for exports from Bay Area ports reflect the traditional role of the region as the shipment point for California agricultural and forest products. Cereals and cereal preparations (including wheat, corn, rice, and the like) were the leading export by weight, comprising nearly 1.5 million tons in 1982. Petroleum and petroleum-based products (such as synthetics, resins, plastics, and fertilizers) and metals are the only nonagricultural/forest products among the top 10. When measured by value, industrial exports play a more significant role, with industrial machinery, textiles and raw cotton, fruits and vegetables, general machinery, and cereals the top-five export products. Though the Bay Area does export many high-tech products, such as computers, they are overwhelmed in the export statistics by these lower value-added products.

Industrial goods dominate Bay Area imports. By weight, nearly 20% of all imports were iron and steel products (623,000 tons). The most valuable import was vehicles ($1.3 billion), followed by clothing, coffee, tea and spices, telecommunication and sound equipment, footwear, office machines, electrical machinery, and metals.[4] Again, the Bay Area trade figures seem to reflect almost a third world pattern of exporting low-value raw materials and importing sophisticated industrial products.

ECONOMIC IMPACTS OF BAY AREA PORTS: DIRECT PORT EMPLOYMENT

Direct employment includes jobs that are involved in handling and moving cargo at the port site and engage primarily longshoremen, clerks, and foremen. This has traditionally been a key benefit of maritime activity and the most easily measured, since most employment is located directly within the port area.

There has been a massive decline in longshoremen registration over the past 40 years.[5] This decline was constant between 1951 and 1958, followed by fluctuations during the next 10 years and then by a pattern of steady decline from 1969 to the present (see Figure 6.1). The number of hours worked has also fallen dramatically, declining even faster than the number of registered workers since the 1970s. This indicates that the average amount of time a registered longshoreman works per year has declined (in 1983 the average was equivalent to twenty-two 40-hour work weeks). This decline is initially surprising given the decasualization of longshoring employment and the transition to stable, permanent dock

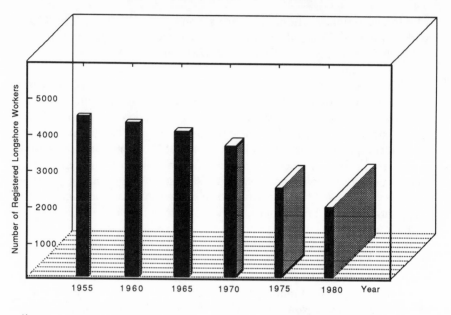

Key:

Height: Number of Registered Longshore
         Workers for the given year

Width: Hours worked per worker per year
         (1525 in 1955; 1008 in 1980)

Depth: Value of Dry Cargo per Worker-Hour (each
         dotted line represents $250 in 1967 dollars)

Front Surface Area (black shaded): Total
         Hours Worked

Volume of Cube: Total Value of Cargo.

FIGURE 6.1. Number of registered longshore workers, hours worked, and value of cargo per worker-hour (in constant dollars). San Francisco Bay area ports, 1955–1980. The declining height over time represents the declining number of longshore workers in the Bay Area. The narrowing width of the front surface reflects the decline in the average number of hours worked in a year. The greatly increasing depth over time reflects the dramatic impact of mechanization on worker-hour/cargo value rations. Finally, the five fold increase in volume represents the great increase in cargo value over time. *Sources*: Pacific Maritime Association, 1973; Pacific Maritime Association, 1983; U.S. Customs Department, 1955–1980.

employment. However, this pattern probably reflects the development of a two-tiered employment situation, in which some longshore workers put in 40 hours per week, while others are idle yet remain registered.

Productivity, as measured by value of cargo handled per work hour (adjusted to 1967 dollars), has consistently increased since 1955, with dramatic increases since the introduction of container facilities during the mid-1960s. Had containerization not been introduced, and therefore had productivity remained constant at the 1955 level, over 39 million longshore hours would have been required in 1980 rather than the 2.1 million actually employed (assuming the same amount of cargo).

The cargo value/worker-hour productivity ratio should continue to increase as more break-bulk facilities are replaced by container terminals. For example, the percentage of general cargo that was handled as break-bulk at the Port of San Francisco dropped from 48% to 29% between 1981 and 1983, with a corresponding decline in labor requirements (Peters, 1983, p. 1). It is difficult at this time to predict the extent to which break-bulk cargo will be replaced by containers; yet even if some cargos continue to be in break-bulk form, they will be a minor percentage of the total.

The net result of these changes is that the ports in the Bay Area contribute only a modest amount of direct employment opportunity, particularly when compared to the value of maritime cargo and the scale of port operations. Consequently, the indirect impacts of maritime trade are becoming increasingly significant for economic development as the traditional direct benefits recede in importance. These indirect impacts are discussed in the next two sections.

PORT-RELATED EMPLOYMENT IN THE BAY AREA

This group encompasses businesses that sell their services to the ports and shippers. It includes a variety of maritime services, such as ship agents, maritime attorneys, ship chandlers (suppliers of ship equipment), truckers, and stevedores (dockside cargo handlers).

Traditional employment statistics sources do not provide adequate detail on maritime-related employment, for there is no one standard industrial classification for this sector. However, there are three general categories that best reflect maritime employment: SIC 42, Trucking and Warehousing; Standard Industrial Classification (SIC) 44, Water Transport; and SIC 47, Transportation Services. Though these do not include all employment in question and, more importantly, do include jobs that are *not* maritime-related (most likely the latter is greater than the former, so that these figures overestimate maritime-related employment), they do provide an indication of employment location and change over time. These three categories will be analyzed for the three major port counties in the Bay Area—Alameda (Port of Oakland), Contra Costa (Port of Richmond), and San Francisco (Port of San Francisco)—from 1947 to 1987. (See Table 6.3.)

Overall, three-county employment in the trucking and warehousing (SIC 42) sector is growing, with a total of over 22,000 jobs in 1987. San Francisco was once the leading employer, but was surpassed by Alameda County in the 1950s. Employment has also been steadily growing in Contra Costa County. This shift from San Francisco to the East Bay reflects the locational shift in shipping, as well as the general shift in food storage, processing, and general wholesaling to this part of the region.

Total employment in the water transportation sector (SIC 44) has declined since World War II, especially in San Francisco. This decline reflects the significant reduction in longshore employment (which is included in this 2-digit sector, and hence overlaps with the employment figures in Figure 6.1). In contrast, Alameda County has generally increased its employment since the mid-1960s, corresponding to the growth of the Port of Oakland (though it declined during the 1980s). Of interest, however, is the continued dominance by San Francisco of this sector, even though it has long since lost its position as the leading port city.

The transportation services sector (SIC 47) includes such services as freight forwarders, ship brokers, ship agents, customhouse brokers, packers, craters, and railroad-car renters. Overall employment for this sector has been steadily increasing. San Francisco, with over 5000 of 9000 jobs in 1981, continues to grow and dominate this sector in the region.

The total three-county employment for these sectors in 1987 was 37,391, up from 33,940 in 1981. San Francisco has 47.5%, Alameda County 41%, and Contra Costa County the remaining 11.5%. Though this is certainly an overestimate of maritime-related services (since it includes such jobs as non-water-related trucking, as well as double counting longshore employment—already included in Figure 6.1), it suggests that although Alameda and Contra Costa are gaining employment related to the port, San Francisco still appears to be the largest center of maritime-related employment.

To better understand the historical change in port–city interactions in maritime services, I needed more precise data on the location and, particularly, the function of maritime businesses. Consequently, I developed an alternative approach that, despite certain inherent limitations,

TABLE 6.3. Employment in Maritime and Maritime-Related Sectors in the Three Bay Area Counties with Major Port Facilities

Year	Trucking and warehousing (SIC 42) (U.S. Total in 1987: 1,428,571)			Water transportation (SIC 44) (U.S. Total in 1987: 165,956)			Transportation services (SIC 47) (U.S. Total in 1987: 315,316)		
	San Francisco	Contra Costa	Alameda	San Francisco	Contra Costa	Alameda	San Francisco	Contra Costa	Alameda
1987	7,922	3,176	11,228	4,608	187	1,273	5,248	919	2,830
1981	5,723	2,109	9,496	6,974	355	2,237	4,833	463	1,750
1976	10,145	1,761	8,506	15,551	252	1,111	3,750	180	534
1971	6,244	1,556	8,654	7,910	138	837	2,920	71	663
1966	6,353	1,394	9,215	8,669	94	278	3,099	36	649
1962	6,192	1,211	7,720	9,095	292	650+	1,870	—	380
1956	5,940	996	5,595	7,976	204	805	1,148		688
1951	5,716	636	4,401	11,202	203	649	1,188	24	190
1947	6,604	413	3,646	25,723	350	153	1,920	153	777

Source: United States Bureau of the Census, County Business Patterns: California.

illustrates changes in maritime services in detail. This method involved the tabulation of maritime-related businesses by type of service and by city from a maritime services directory (Marine Exchange of the San Francisco Bay Region, 1969, 1974, 1984.).[6] The three different years, 1969, 1974, and 1984, for the directory cover the period during which the locus of port activity shifted from San Francisco to Oakland.

I posed several basic questions: Have the number of firms grown or declined over time? Have the locations of the firms changed? Are there sector changes in numbers and patterns, that is, can the divergent locational patterns of different maritime services be explained by the natures of their businesses?

Several trends are readily apparent: the total number of maritime service firms increased from 1969 to 1984, from 525 to 715; the absolute number and growth rate of firms varies greatly by type of maritime service; and numerous cities in the Bay Area have some sort of maritime-related business. The most distinct (and initially surprising) feature, however, is San Francisco's continued dominance of maritime services. A concentration of these firms in San Francisco during a time when it was the leading cargo-handling port (1969) is not surprising. However, one would expect that many of these firms would have relocated to the Oakland area, and to a lesser extent, to the recently developing Port of Richmond area, during the 1970s and early 1980s. Yet this was not the case. San Francisco continues to have the most firms from each maritime service category (with the exceptions of "containers," "cargo," "bunker fuel and lubrication," and "stevedoring"), and has virtually all the firms in several categories (including admiralty attorneys, export packing, and railroad offices).

The location of selected maritime services within the Bay Area in 1969 and 1984 is graphically indicated by Figures 6.2 and 6.3. Though some decentralization is apparent during the 15-year period, most firms are still located in San Francisco. It is also interesting to note the development of maritime services south of both major ports, particularly in south San Francisco and Burlingame, 6 miles further south (see Figure 6.3). This development may be related to the nearby San Francisco airport, located in San Mateo County.

Within the wide range of "maritime services" different types of services have quite different locational requirements. These differences are reflected in patterns of decentralization from San Francisco over time. To systematize these differences, I combined 21 different service categories into four basic groups based on their type of relationship to maritime activity: firms that provide financial, legal, administrative, and related services ("business services"); firms that directly serve shippers ("ship services"); firms that are related to the movement of freight; and

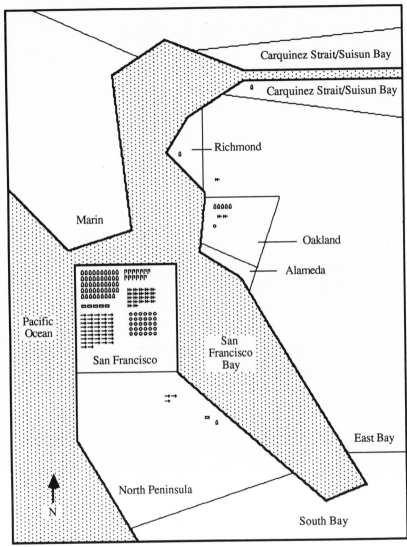

FIGURE 6.2. Location of selected maritime services, 1969. Each symbol represents one firm. *Source*: Marine Exchange, 1984.

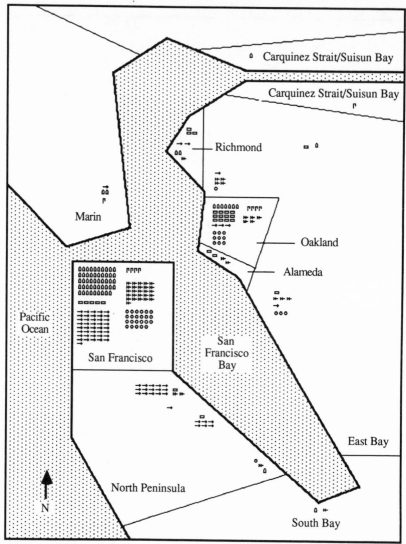

FIGURE 6.3. Location of selected maritime services, 1984. Each symbol represents one firm. *Source*: Marine Exchange, 1984.

firms that supply equipment and supplies. These four groups of firms are then indicated by their location, which for simplicity have been grouped into the four major general-cargo port cities (San Francisco, Oakland, Richmond, and Alameda), and five subregional areas (See Table 6.4).

Maritime firms that have remained most concentrated in San Francisco are those that provide business services to ports and shippers. San Francisco's share of the region's maritime business-services firms has only dropped from 93% in 1969 to 90% in 1984. This sustained concentration can be explained by two possible factors. First, these firms do not require immediate physical proximity to the ports. Since their primary transactions involve information and finances (itself a form of information), modern banking and communication technology allow these businesses to be removed from the port area. Second, these firms benefit from locating in a large, advanced, service-oriented central city, which provides important agglomeration economies for banking, legal, and administrative firms. These firms are also particularly susceptible to the prestige associated with a San Francisco address, as well as to the advantages of the San Francisco working environment for employee attraction. (One San Francisco port official commented that many ship agents would lose some of their best employees if the firm moved to Oakland.)

Ship services exhibit the next-highest concentration in San Francisco, which had 65% of all such firms in 1984. This sustained concentration may be due in part to the spatial inertia of ship repair shops, towing services, and chandleries. The major transformations in cargo-handling technology, which accelerated the shift of port activity from San Francisco to Oakland, may not have equally affected the technology of ship services, allowing the existing firms in San Francisco to maintain much of their competitiveness.

Equipment and supplies is the third-most concentrated of the group, still maintaining 55% of its firms in San Francisco, though this is a major decline from 95% in 1969. The high proportion of these firms in the East Bay may be due to the general presence of machine and related industries in this area.

The final group of firms, those related to the movement of freight, demonstrate the greatest degree of spatial decentralization from San Francisco. Both Oakland (16%) and Richmond (5%) have the highest percentage of these firms compared to the other three maritime service groups. This group demonstrates the strongest locational dependency to be near general-cargo port activity. These firms handle nonstandardized and short-notice orders for items such as pallets, containers, and stevedoring work, where proximity to the port is a plus.

In summary, the general characteristic of maritime services is that, despite a trend of decentralization in some types of firms, San Francisco

TABLE 6.4. Number of Bay Area Maritime-Related Firms by Type and Location, 1969-1984

Location	Business services[a]			Ship services[b]			Related to movement of freight[c]			Equipment and supplies[d]		
	1969	1974	1984	1969	1974	1984	1969	1974	1984	1969	1974	1984
San Francisco	103	110	180	82	72	81	193	146	141	90	74	71
Oakland	6	6	8	3	6	11	22	30	46	3	4	15
Richmond	1	4	3	1	5	1	2	4	15	—	2	4
Alameda City	—	—	1	—	1	4	2	2	4	—	1	3
Other East Bay	—	—	1	—	2	8	1	8	29	2	5	21
Carquinez Strait/ Suisun Bay	—	1	1	—	2	1	—	—	6	—	—	1
North Peninsula	1	1	2	—	2	9	6	40	35	—	3	7
South Bay	—	—	1	—	—	1	—	—	1	—	—	2
Marin	—	—	2	—	—	8	—	—	4	—	1	4
TOTAL	111	122	199	86	90	124	226	230	281	95	90	128

[a]Includes ship agents, admiralty attorneys, commercial banks, and railroad offices.
[b]Includes barging/towing and water taxi, bunker fuel and lubrication, chandlers, shipbuilders and repairs.
[c]Includes carloaders, containers (leasing, cargo), customs brokers (leasing, cargo), customs brokers, freight forwarders, export packing, pallets, stevedoring, trucking, warehousing (note: customs brokers and freight forwarders classifications changed over time).
[d]Includes cranes, electric (marine), electronics (marine), equipment, supplies, and service (marine).
Source: Marine Exchange, 1969, 1974, 1984.

is still the location of most maritime-related firms. This sustained concentration has various explanations, including inertia; the prestige of a San Francisco address; the advantages of proximity to its diverse, advanced-service, central city; and its more attractive working environment. Put simply, when the center of port activity shifted from San Francisco to Oakland, most maritime services did not move with it.

These data lend evidence to the hypothesis that ports no longer need to be very close to either the central city or related maritime services. This spatial separation of the various aspects of shipping, cargo handling, and maritime services is consistent with the more general trend within manufacturing industries to spatially separate the various levels of production. As in manufacturing, it appears that the "production"-oriented maritime services (such as stevedoring, containers-cargo, and the like) are located near the active port centers, whereas the management-oriented maritime services (such as ship agents and maritime attorneys) are located in the central city. An even more apt comparison is the service industries, where prestige-laden front offices are separated from both back-office clerical sweatshops and retail offices.

This tendency has implications for the role of port activity in local economic development in the Bay Area. The traditional multiplier used to calculate how many local jobs will be generated in maritime services due to increased cargo handling in Oakland may exaggerate the actual job increases, since much of the new employment may go to San Francisco. However, if Oakland continues to gain a larger share of the region's maritime services, then the local employment impacts of increased cargo through its port will increase. It is too early to tell how far this shift of maritime services to Oakland and the East Bay will proceed, and whether Oakland will ever surpass San Francisco in the number of financial, legal, and administrative maritime services.

PORT-DEPENDENT EMPLOYMENT
IN THE BAY AREA

The third economic impact to be explored are businesses that buy services from the port to export their products or to import raw materials (as distinguished from port-related businesses, which sell services to the port). There are four basic types of port terminals that ship and receive industrial materials and goods. Some businesses have their own private port terminals with specialized, bulk-loading equipment, such as the C & H Sugar terminal in Crockett and the petroleum refinery terminals in Richmond. A second type of port facility is a bulk terminal within a larger, combined general cargo/bulk cargo public port. Examples are the steel import terminal within the Port of Oakland and the paper terminal within the Port of San Francisco. A third type is the standard breakbulk or container terminal, which is used to ship final goods or higher value, nonbulk production materials. A fourth type is the Ro/Ro terminal (roll-on/roll-off), used to load and unload vehicle carriers. An example is the auto import terminal upriver from San Francisco in Benecia.

Several difficulties arise when one estimates port-dependent employment. First, the mere location of a business on port land does not imply port dependency, since many such businesses might well function at current levels even if the port were completely closed. Such a business may be located on port land for other reasons, such as inexpensive land costs, availability of land, less-stringent environmental restrictions, view (for example, for a restaurant or office complex), and access to water (for industrial cooling). Some businesses are indeed located in waterfront areas to take advantage of good transportation access, but with rail and truck lines, rather than with water transport. (Stauffer Chemicals in Richmond is an example of such an industry.) Though these good rail and road networks may have their origins in the nearby port, they are now autonomous transit networks, rather than feeder services for the port. Even those businesses that originally located on port land so as to use the port may now ship and receive via truck, rail, or air; and consequently they cannot be classified as port-dependent. (The U.S. Steel plant in Pittsburg, California, is such a case, since the use of deep-water shipping via Suisun Bay has been greatly replaced by rail and truck shipments.) Though no recent estimates are available, a 1966 Association of Bay Area Governments study found that nearly half of all the shoreline industrial use was occupied by non-water-oriented industries (Muncy, 1968, p. 31).

Second, an industry's use of port facilities does not necessarily imply complete port-dependency, since there are usually substitute means and paths of shipment. The value of the port is clearly not equal to the value of the cargo passing through it, but rather to the value of the service. As a result, the value of the port must be measured in reference to its alternatives. The net benefit of a port is equal to the amount of business activity that would disappear were the port to close. (A maritime strike, depending on its length and prior announcement, offers a unique and nontheoretical opportunity to examine the short-term effect of ports on the economy.)

The ideal analysis of this industrial port-dependency would entail a comprehensive survey of all manufacturers and other businesses, asking: What do you ship and/or receive through the ports? What method of transport would you use instead of the port? How much would this nonport shipment cost you? How would these costs affect your production, sales, and employment?[7]

Conducting such a survey is obviously a difficult task, and there is a frustrating lack of adequate data to know the exact economic impacts caused by port users. One study, commissioned by the Pacific Merchant Shipping Association (PMSA) in 1982, estimated the increased production and employment due to Bay Area ports at $4.4 billion, with 35,000 port-dependent jobs (Pacific Merchant Shipping Association, 1982; Recht, Hausrath and Associates, and Temple, Barker and Sloane, Inc., 1981). This represented approximately 1 in every 70 jobs, and 1 in every 14 manufacturing jobs, in the region (see Table 6.5).

Port dependency in the Bay Area economy, suggested by the percentage of the industry benefiting from maritime trade, varies across sectors. Metals, chemicals, and petroleum are highly dependent; their low value/weight ratio increases the cost advantage of shipping by water versus rail or truck. High-technology goods, textiles and apparel, and food products are less port-dependent; their higher value–weight ratios and greater need for rapid delivery (particularly with perishable foods), make truck, rail, and air-cargo shipping more appealing.

The PMSA study did not address the location of these industries, but by comparing county-level industrial employment to the types of port-dependent employment, we can make some a simple estimate of the regional employment distribution.[8] Do Bay Area counties with port facilities have larger shares of port-dependent employment?

Santa Clara County, now better known unpoetically as "Silicon Valley," has a huge high-tech sector that is less dependent on regional

TABLE 6.5. Benefits Attributable to Maritime Trade in the Bay Area in 1980

Selected industry	Sales ($million)	Jobs	% of industry
High technology	$1,120	17,940	9%
Metals	$630	7,440	18%
Petroleum	$1,770	1,050	17%
Chemicals	$350	2,500	16%
Food products	$340	2,040	6%
Textiles and apparel	$60	1,350	10%
Subtotal of selected industries	$4,270	32,320	
Total of all industries	$4,400	35,000	

Source: PMSA, 1982.

ports than industries in general. By contrast, Alameda County and Contra Costa Counties are apparently more port-dependent, primarily in metals, petroleum, and chemicals.

On balance, however, the distribution of port-dependent sectors versus all sectors seems surprisingly similar. Santa Clara dominates both categories about equally (55.2% and 55.3%, respectively), and the differences are less than 5% in all five counties. This similarity arguably reflects increased dispersion of port-dependent industries from their traditional waterfront locations. The development of inexpensive truck and rail service to ports (particularly for containers) means that port accessibility no longer requires port proximity, with the exception of such heavy industries as steel and oil refining. Port-dependency thus no longer necessarily implies waterfront-dependency.

This regional decentralization of port-dependent industry is particularly interesting when compared to the locational pattern of port-related (maritime service) businesses, which are unusually concentrated in or near San Francisco. This difference suggests that technological and operational changes in shipping have affected the relationship between ports and their users in different ways from the relationship between ports and their service suppliers. Most port-dependent industries are increasingly influenced by locational factors unrelated to ocean transportation, and these influences tend to have a *decentralizing* effect (such as the desire for lower land costs, lower housing costs for employees, nonunion labor, and availability of land). Similarly, most maritime-related services no longer need to be directly adjacent to the port, yet the remaining locational factors generally have a *centralizing* effect (such as the advantages of being near other financial, legal, and administrative services). One may thus see the difference between footloose port-dependent industries and locationally inertial port-related services as an indication that it is easier to relocate machines, factories, and employees than to relocate business ties and networks.

The implications of these locational tendencies for economic development are complex, yet one can make the following generalization. An increase in maritime trade through a given Bay Area port will have at least three major spatial effects on the location of employment: a localizing effect, a centralizing effect, and a decentralizing effect. The increased direct employment (in, for example, longshoring) will be located at the port in question, hence either in Oakland, San Francisco, or Richmond. The increased port-related (maritime service) employment will tend to be located in San Francisco, and to a lesser extent in Oakland and adjacent cities. The increased port-dependent industrial employment will tend to be located in Santa Clara County and other traditionally peripheral Bay Area locations. This latter effect is not because the port dependency necessitates a peripheral location, but rather because other locational factors stimulate industrial growth in these areas. The resulting causal structure of this decentralization can be stated as follows: increased maritime activity leads to the expansion of new manufacturing businesses in the region, which in turn make locational decisions based primarily on non-maritime-related criteria (with the exception of certain heavy industries).

Consequently, (1) the expansion of port employment contributes primarily to local economic development; (2) the expansion of maritime services contributes to both local and central city economic development; and (3) the expansion of port-dependent industries contributes to a more ubiquitous regional (and even transregional) economic development. Since there are approximately twice as many port-dependent jobs as compared to direct and port-related jobs combined (35,000 versus 17,230), one may assume that the decentralizing effect resulting from increased maritime trade will be stronger than either the local or centralizing effects.

LESSONS FROM SAN FRANCISCO AND OAKLAND: THE PORT CITY IN A SYSTEM OF CITIES

The nagging paradox from the Bay Area is that San Francisco is a thriving city with a struggling port, while Oakland is a struggling city with a thriving port. Apparently, the relationship between ports and local economies is neither simple nor constant. To answer this puzzle, I took a step backward and looked at the historical development of port cities and the role of the port in the system of cities.

This perspective sees the economic role of ports not just as the sum of the various costs and benefits at a given moment, but rather as the unique function of port cities as compared to other cities, particularly as this function changes over time. To isolate this particular function of port cities, I have borrowed two different typologies of city regions (standard metropolitan statistical areas, or SMSAs) in the United States: the first is by the city's function in the modern economy (Noyelle, 1983), and the second is by its type of port (Corro, 1980). A comparison or cross-tabulation of these two typologies reveals a striking predominance of port cities with national or regional diversified service functions, and the predominance of nonport cities with specialized services and manufacturing functions (see Figure 6.4).

Urbanists have recently noted that diversified-service cities are adjusting significantly better than the specialized-service and manufacturing cities to the demands of the new national and international eco-

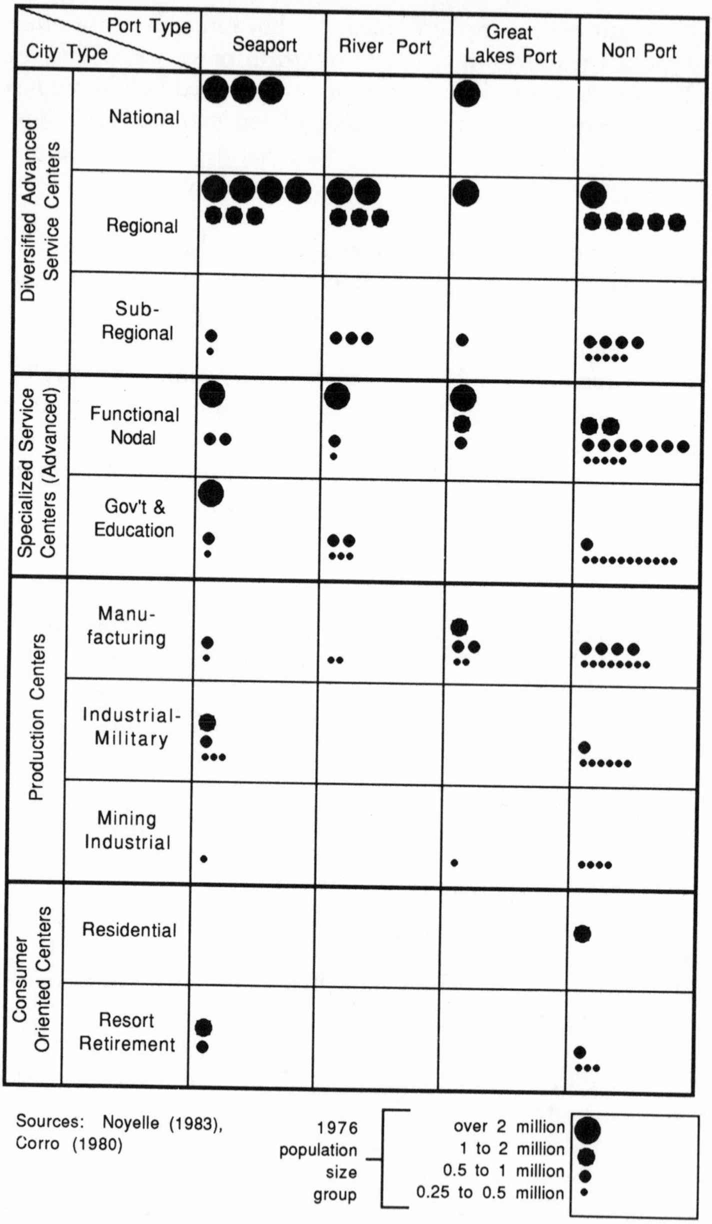

City Type ＼ Port Type	Seaport	River Port	Great Lakes Port	Non Port
Diversified Advanced Service Centers — National	●●● ●		●	
Regional	●●●● ●●●	●● ●●	●	● ●●●●
Sub-Regional	● ●	●●●	●	●●●● ●●●●●
Specialized Service Centers (Advanced) — Functional Nodal	● ●●	● ● ●	● ●	●● ●●●●●● ●●●●●
Gov't & Education	● ● ●	●● ●●●		● ●●●●●●●●●●●
Production Centers — Manufacturing	● ●	●●	●● ● ●●	●●●● ●●●●●●●●
Industrial-Military	● ● ●●●			● ●●●●●●
Mining Industrial	●		●	●●●●
Consumer Oriented Centers — Residential				●
Resort Retirement	● ●			● ●●●

Sources: Noyelle (1983), Corro (1980)

1976 population size group — over 2 million ● / 1 to 2 million ● / 0.5 to 1 million ● / 0.25 to 0.5 million ●

FIGURE 6.4. SMSAs classified by economic type, port type, and size (each circle represents one metropolitan area)

nomic situation (which entails the new international division of labor, the rise of information systems, and the decline of traditional manufacturing employment). If this pattern is real, and if these diversified-service centers are disproportionately port cities, what does this suggest about the role of ports in this transformation? The first possible explanation is based on the traditional benefits of a port town: that greater access to raw materials and markets creates greater productivity, productive flexibility, higher employment, and greater purchasing power. Yet the validity of these argument has been put into question by the development of containerization, which has reduced many of these traditional benefits.

I have a second and more speculative explanation. One may refer to it as a "pathways" hypothesis, since it is an explicitly historical explanation of the evolving role of ports in local economies. Port cities have been more flexible and better prepared to convert to the needs of a service economy than the nonport cities. The past presence of an active port helped to attract and develop a wide and sophisticated array of businesses that served the maritime trade business in the port city. These businesses included extensive financial, legal, communications, and administrative services, which were adept with international trade. These firms were initially dependent on international maritime trade for their business. Eventually, however, they began to diversify into other areas of business, business that still took advantage of their international experience and networks, but that was no longer directly dependent on cargo passing through the port. Consequently, when the crisis of American manufacturing struck in the 1960s and 1970s, these cities were better able to adjust to the new economic structure through the presence of these established international and national business networks. Manufacturing and specialized service cities, lacking these networks and established business communities, were much more entrenched in their old economic patterns and could not adjust as easily.

San Francisco may be a good example of this transition. The existence of port activity encouraged the early development of an extensive system of supporting banks, legal offices, accountants, freight forwarders, and the like. These businesses eventually diversified into nonmaritime activities. Consequently, when the city's port business began to decline in the 1960s, these businesses were able to remain in the city and continue to thrive. The presence of these businesses is seen as a key factor in San Francisco's unusually smooth and successful transition from a manufacturing center to a leading world corporate city. Los Angeles may be an even better example.

The above discussion raises a second issue concerning the role of the port in the city's development: did the modern advanced service city arise primarily from the port-related (maritime service) firms or from the port-dependent industries? Here is a situation where the historical pathway analysis may offer an explanation of economic development where the ahistorical economic-base model has proven inadequate.

One would expect that port-dependent industries, which provide the greatest economic benefits of the various port economic impacts, are the source of port cities' greater ability to innovate and adjust to new economic necessities. According to traditional economic-base theory, demand for exports drives the system by stimulating production of goods and materials (basic sector), and the maritime services (nonbasic sector) merely respond to this exogenous force.

Yet observing the actual development of modern port city economies, this traditional model does not seem to completely apply. Instead, it appears that the modern port city service economy has arisen from the maritime services, which are no longer the endogenous follower of the economic-base model. The demand for these services is no longer intermediated through the manufacturers by way of the port; rather, these services are directly demanded for by the national and international corporate economy.

To simplify this concept, one may speak of an economic cycle, consisting of two dynamics: intraperiodic and interperiodic. The intraperiodic is characterized by stability, productive efficiency, and the lack of innovation or structural change. Demand is the key factor, which drives the port through port-dependent industries. The economic-base model applies well here, and describes a given period of port technology, where the concern of the port city is the greater efficiency of the port to accommodate the demand placed by industries on its services.

In contrast, the interperiodic is characterized by structural change, instability, the crisis of existing institutions, and innovation. Supply (of services) is the key factor, which determines the direction of innovation and structural change. The pathway model applies well here, and describes the transition between two periods of port technology, where the port city is confronted with the crisis of the existing economic structure and is concerned with what direction to take the economy.

The third issue concerns the continued role of ports in urban economic development and innovation. If the traditional port was fertile in terms of new work being added to old work—whereby maritime businesses expanded, diversified, and became autonomous—can the same be true for the modern container port? I would argue that the modern port lacks this regenerative ability for several reasons: First, the work of a container port is fairly repetitive and efficient, which does not usually lead to innovation, compared to the "valuable inefficiencies" of breakbulk ports—a term Jane Jacobs used to describe the innovative power of cities. Second, the development of containerization was promoted by shipping companies, rather than by ports, so that most ports never benefited from learning how to innovatively develop a container system. Instead, they usually received the container cranes and systems as an already developed technology. Third, the spatial and functional separation between maritime services and the port may also hinder their interaction to generate innovations or "spin-offs." Relating this hypothesis to the Bay Area, can it be seen as a factor in San Francisco's greater success than Oakland in developing a service economy?

The role of the port in economic development is thus in part a historical one, in which it establishes certain patterns of business which continue on by virtue of their own momentum even after the port itself has receded in prominence. For port policy analysis, however, one must ask the question, Does the port continue to play this catalytic and innovative function? It is too early to conclude, yet clearly as the technology of the port changes, so too will its role in laying a "pathway" for future economic development and innovation. The differences in the port–city interactions in San Francisco and Oakland may offer evidence of this changing role of the port.

The implication of this discussion is that two essential questions must be asked when analyzing the role of the port in economic development. The first is, How many benefits are currently generated by the port, as measured by direct, related, and dependent employment? The second is, How will the port of today shape the economy of tomorrow? The first is one of scale (How many jobs?); the second is one of direction (What new work will arise from the old?).

CONCLUSION

The modern port plays a different role in a city and region than that of its traditional predecessor's role. The obvious port–city interaction of the past—with factories, warehouses, wholesalers, and maritime services surrounding the port land, and thousands of longshoremen teeming between the piers, the union hall, and the adjacent bars, pool halls, and boardinghouses—has been replaced by a less perceptible and identifiable interaction. The link between the port and the city is no longer obvious in the land-use patterns near the wharfs. There appears to be a growing separation of port and city on many levels: politically, with the rise of autonomous port authorities; economically, with the dispersal of port-related and port-dependent businesses throughout the region; and physically, with the relocation of central-city port terminals to peripheral sites.

This chapter has focused on one aspect of the port's changing role in the city: the direct and indirect employment that it generates and sustains. Direct port employment, was once the most visible economic benefit of port activity, is now dramatically diminished in importance. In addition, the traditional casual system of labor has been replaced by a much smaller, formal labor force. In contrast, port-related employment has grown, yet is not as close or spatially dependent on the port as it once was. Finally, port-dependent employment is the largest benefit of all, and its locational pattern is the most ubiquitous. Perhaps the most important long-term role of the port, however, is its stimulation of nonmaritime economic development, even after the port itself has declined in significance. This may help to explain why traditional port cities often develop into advanced, diversified, service centers. Yet this key role may have declined in recent years: modern container ports probably no longer serve this function as well as traditional ports. In addition, the economic decline of cities such as Buffalo suggest that bulk-cargo ports also did not lay the foundations for a future service industry, for they lacked the necessary linkages with such services.

Beyond the regional economy lies interregional port competition. The development of land-bridge cargo shipments, and the increasing scale economies of containerization, have concentrated cargo handling in fewer, but larger ports. In the coming years fewer cities will be able to successfully use maritime ports as a foundation of economic development. The port cities that will be squeezed out in this interregional shipping competition will be lucky if their past trading activities germinated an advanced service sector, and will turn to large developers to convert their abandoned waterfront real estate (along the lines of New York's Battery Park City and the London Docklands).

The Bay Area dramatically reflects these changes in port development. Indeed, the question that underlies much of this regional analysis of shifting port activity from San Francisco to Oakland is whether this shift has really benefited Oakland at the expense of San Francisco. Certainly in terms of port revenues this is true; in the larger context, however, the paradox of a thriving port in a struggling city opposite a decaying port in a thriving city cannot be seen as merely coincidental. This observation makes one question the traditional belief in ports as a vital cornerstone of economic growth in a city, and points to a new and more complex port–city interaction. This review has been a first step to define this new relationship.

ACKNOWLEDGMENTS

An earlier version of this chapter appeared as a working paper (see Campbell, 1986). I would like to thank Ann Markusen, Michael Teitz, Michael Wiseman,

Peter Hall, and Melvin Webber, as well as an anonymous reviewer, for comments on earlier versions of this chapter.

NOTES

1. It must be pointed out that this argument would not be as relevant for the more-remote and industrial Southern Waterfront (the location of San Francisco's three container terminals during the 1980s), where there has been little commercial development. (Southern Pacific's long-planned "Mission Bay" project may introduce such a commercial orientation to the Southern Waterfront, though the container terminals are not directly adjacent to Mission Bay.)

2. Compare this to regional shares in 1980: Oakland (65% of imports and 70% of exports); San Francisco (15% and 15%); Richmond (4% and 2%); Alameda (5% and 1%). The inclusion of tanker shipments (primarily petroleum) often distorts cargo figures, particularly weight statistics, due to its extremely low value-to-weight ratio, and are consequently removed (U.S. Department of Commerce, 1980, 1987).

3. The city of Richmond, a key center of World War II shipbuilding, tried to compete with Oakland, 10 miles to the south, for the booming container business. Despite initial great hopes, it has not succeeded in gaining even 10% of northern California shipping activity.

4. In general, one sees a greater consistency among import products than export products, both in product type percentages and in value-to-weight ratios. This suggests that a region's exports are more specific to a region's local raw materials and industrial capacity, whereas its imports reflect more the national trend in business and personal consumption.

5. Nonlongshoring employment (such as clerks and foremen) has not been included due to lack of data. These port occupations have traditionally added about 15–25% to the total employment figure. While the following employment figures cannot consequently be seen as representing all port employment, changes in longshoring employment generally represent a corresponding change in total employment.

6. The most apparent limitation of this method is that business activity is counted by firm and not by employees, so that a large firm is not distinguished from a small one. Consequently, one cannot assume that a change in the number of firms over time, between places, or across businesses, represents a proportional change in employment. Also, the business address of a firm may not necessarily be its only location. Finally, the percentages of the firm's sales that go to maritime activity vary, ranging from only a small percentage (for example, banks) to virtually all sales (for example, ship repairs). However, if one does assume that a change in the number of firms over time in general represents a change in the activity of this type of service, then such an analysis can reveal some basic tendencies in San Francisco Bay Area maritime-service businesses during the past 15 years.

7. A prototype questionnaire for port-dependent businesses is offered in the 1979 *Port Economic Impact Kit*, published by the U.S. Department of Commerce.

8. For a detailed discussion of these estimates, see Campbell (1986).

REFERENCES

Bird, J. 1971. *Seaports and Seaport Terminals*. London: Hutchinson.

Bureau of the Census, U.S. Department of Commerce. 1951, 1956, 1962, 1966, 1971, 1976, 1981. *County Business Patterns. California*. Washington, DC: U.S. Goverment Printing Office.

California State Legislature. 1951. *Final Report of the Senate Fact-Finding Committee on the San Francisco Bay Area Ports*. Sacramento: California State Legislature.

Campbell, S. 1986. *Transformation of the San Francisco Bay Area Shipping Industry and Its Regional Impacts*. Working Paper no. 454. Berkeley: Institute of Urban and Regional Development, University of California.

Corro, P. 1980. "Regional Affects of Containerization." Unpublished Ph.D. dissertation, City and Regional Planning, University of California, Berkeley.

Gruen, Gruen and Associates. 1970. *Report on Waterfront Committee*. San Francisco: Gruen, Gruen and Associates.

Marine Exchange of the San Francisco Bay Region. 1969, 1974, 1984. *Golden Gate Atlas*. San Francisco: Marine Exhange of the San Francisco Bay Region.

Maritime Administration, U.S. Department of Commerce. 1979. *Port Economic Impact Kit*. (Prepared by Arthur D. Little.) Washington, DC: Government Printing Office.

Maritime Cargo Transportation Conference. 1964. *San Francisco Port Study*, Vol. 1. *Description and Analysis of Maritime Cargo Operations in a U.S. Port*. Washington, DC: National Academy of Sciences/National Research Council.

Muncy, D. 1968. *Waterfront Industry around San Francisco Bay*. (Prepared for the San Francisco Bay Conservation and Development Commission.)

Noyelle, T. 1983. The Rise of Advanced Services. *Journal of the American Panning Association*, 49(3) 280–290.

Pacific Merchant Shipping Association. 1982. *Maritime Industry: A $2.1 Billion Benefit to the San Francisco-Oakland Bay Area Economy*. (Prepared by Temple, Barker & Sloan Inc., and Recht, Hausrath and Associates.) San Francisco: Pacific Merchant Shipping Association.

Peters, R. L. 1983. "Fiscal Year 1982/83 Tonnage Statistics." Memo, Port of San Francisco (10/5/83).

Port of Oakland. 1983. *Foreign Trade: Oakland-San Francisco Customs District & U.S. West Coast, January–December 1982*.

Pressman, J. L., & Wildavsky, A. 1973. *Implementation: How Great Expec-

tations in Washington Are Dashed in Oakland; or, Why It's Amazing that Federal Programs Work at All. Berkeley and Los Angeles: University of California Press.

Recht, Hausrath and Associates, and Temple, Barker, and Sloan, Inc. 1981. *San Francisco Bay Cargo Forecast*. (Prepared for the Army Corps of Engineers, San Francisco District.)

Regional Science Research Institute. 1980. *Conjoining an Input–Output Model and a Policy Analysis Model: A Case Study of the Regional Economic Effects of Expanding a Port Facility*. RSRI Discussion Paper no. 117. (Written by B. H. Stevens, G. I. Treyz, and J. K. Kindahl.) Amherst, MA: Regional Science Research Institute.

Schenker, E. 1967. *The Port of Milwaukee*. Milwaukee: University of Wisconsin Press.

Seaport Planning Advisory Committee. 1982. *The San Francisco Bay Area Seaport Plan*. (Prepared for the Metropolitan Transportation Commission and the Bay Conservation and Development Commission.)

U.S. Department of Commerce. 1955, 1960, 1965, 1970, 1975, 1980, 1987. *Waterborne Exports and General Imports*. Washington, DC: Government Printing Office.

Wilson, R. P. 1982. "The Containerization of Ports." Unpublished manuscript, University of California, Santa Cruz.

7

Restructuring and Internationalizing: Domestic Shifts in the Insurance Industry

PETER WISSOKER

JULIE GRAHAM

As one of the so-called producer services, the insurance industry was endowed in the 1970s and 1980s with a particular kind of development potential. Producer services, including finance, insurance, and real estate (FIRE), have been distinguished from other services as constituting an element of the export base of cities and regions. In particular, these industries have been credited with the spectacular revitalization of world cities such as Los Angeles, Tokyo, and London, where talented and educated young people flocked to work and live (often indistinguishable activities) during the boom years of the 1980s. In contrast to the older industrial regions of the United States and the United Kingdom, the world cities glitter and pulsate with continued or renewed prosperity. They thrive rather than suffer by virtue of their integration into the international economy.

Examining the insurance industry in terms of its regional development potential, and more specifically its potential to increase its international exports and thereby enhance the development of insurance-producing regions, we are immediately confronted with a less-rosy picture. Like other financial sectors, this massive industry participated actively in—and suffered passively from—the speculative frenzy of the 1980s, with consequent deleterious effects on employment in its primary functions of producing and marketing insurance. Rationalization during this period involved the closing of a number of large insurance "plants," the relocation of back office work away from inner city locations, and the incorporation of an increased percentage of women (that is, low-wage workers) in the labor force. For a sector that is an element of the "healthy" part of the U.S. economy, the social and economic implications of these employer strategies do not seem promising.

Moreover, the expansion of insurance firms' foreign markets seems to promise little for U.S. workers and communities. Most markets of any size are saturated and slow growing, and both large and small markets tend to be heavily regulated. Foreign markets are also likely to be served by overseas branches employing foreign workers. Perhaps worst of all, entry into foreign insurance markets is often a first step for insurers in internationalizing their investments. For these major institutional investors to increase their international orientation, even by a few percentage points, means that potentially hundreds of thousands of jobs will be created outside rather than inside U.S. borders. Insurers, then, are a major potential channel of capital export and it is this form of internationalization that has the greatest potential to affect U.S. workers and communities.

In this chapter we will first examine the changing geography of employment in the U.S. insurance industry. We then set U.S. insurers in their historical and international contexts, focusing in particular on the upheavals of the 1980s. Examining restructuring during the 1970s and 1980s, we will emphasize the impacts of diversification, technological change, and cost cutting on the nature and location of employment. Finally, we will consider the various forms of internationalization taking place in the industry. We conclude with a brief discussion of the policy implications of increased international investment.

THE CHANGING DOMESTIC LOCATION
OF INSURANCE EMPLOYMENT:
SUNBELT AND SUBURBAN SHIFTS

The insurance industry includes SIC 63 (insurance carriers), which will be the focus of this chapter, and SIC 64 (insurance agents, brokers, and services). Discussions of SIC 63 usually treat the industry as producing three different types of insurance: life/health (L/H), property/casualty (P/C), and reinsurance. The former two are known as direct insurance and the latter as indirect, since it usually involves the sale of insurance to other insurance companies to spread the risks of large policies over a greater number of people. Life/health accounts for approximately 60% of direct insurance premiums, with health insurance making up a little over one-fifth of that share (American Council of Life Insurance, 1991). Very often, then, the L/H industry is just called "life."

U.S. employment in SIC 63 has traditionally been concentrated in roughly a dozen states, all but three of which are in the industrialized North (see Table 7.1). In 1948 New York had more than twice as many insurance workers as any other state. Since that time employment has shifted proportionally to the Sunbelt rim, with California displacing New York as the leading insurance state in 1987, Texas ranked fourth, and Florida edging into the top 10. Despite these shifts, insurance employment on the state level has been relatively stable during the post–World War II period. As Table 7.1 indicates, only Florida is a newcomer to the top-10 states. This relative stability in the national distribution of employment belies the changing locational structure of the industry, in which employment has become increasingly decentralized from its traditional location in the inner cities of major urban areas. In 1986 Ross documented the movement of back office employment out of larger cities during the 1970s. She found that counties containing large cities had the largest decreases in insurance employment. Of the 15 counties with the largest absolute loss in insurance employment, 11 were home to major cities (see Table 7.2). Of the 20 counties with the largest absolute gains in employment, only 6 were home to cities of more than 500,000 (see Table 7.3). Five of the growth areas were small cities, led by Hartford, which was the number one city in terms of absolute gain in insurance employment, and seven were first ring or suburban counties. According to Ross, these data reflect—among other things—the relocation of back office functions away from major urban centers.

Ross's hypothesis is further borne out by an examination of changes

TABLE 7.1. Top 10 States in Insurance Employment, 1948 and 1989

1948		1989		Rank in 1948
New York	91,399	California	144,713	3
Illinois	40,054	New York	123,166	1
California	36,458	Illinois	98,073	2
Pennsylvania	35,399	Texas	81,319	7
New Jersey	35,233	Pennsylvania	77,059	4
Massachusetts	26,098	Massachusetts	62,836	6
Texas	22,303	Ohio	62,335	9
Connecticut	20,676	New Jersey	60,035	5
Ohio	20,478	Florida	56,281	—
Michigan	13,212	Connecticut	51,988	8
U.S. total	504,578	U.S. Total	1,449,000	

TABLE 7.2. Fifteen Counties with the Largest Absolute Loss in SIC 63
Employment: 1970–1981

	County type	Employment SIC 63		Employment change 1970–1981	
		1970	1981	Total	%
New York, NY	CC	76,655	67,145	−9,510	−12.4
Wayne, MI	CC	16,609	8,904	−7,705	−46.4
Suffolk, MA	CC	33,248	25,784	−7,464	−22.4
Essex, NJ	MC	22,084	15,511	−6,573	−29.8
San Francisco, CA	CC	19,391	13,696	−5,695	−29.4
St. Louis, MO	MC	7,522	4,538	−2,984	−39.7
Philadelphia, PA	CC	24,494	21,578	−2,916	−11.9
Bronx, NY	CC	3,409	867	−2,542	−74.6
Kings, NY	CC	4,080	2,030	−2,050	−50.2
Baltimore City, MD	CC	6,094	4,113	−1,981	−32.5
Washington, DC	CC	7,701	5,936	−1,765	−22.9
Richmond, VA	SC	5,935	4,325	−1,610	−27.1
Orleans, LA	CC	6,958	5,361	−1,597	−23.0
Queens, NY	CC	3,200	1,898	−1,302	−40.7
Alameda, CA	FR	4,976	3,743	−1,233	−24.8

CC—Central cities/Counties with primary cities > 500,000 population in 1980.
MC—Middle cities/Counties with primary cities of 250,000–500,000 population in 1980.
SC—Small cities/Counties with primary cities of 50,000–250,000 population in 1980.
FR—First ring/Counties next to or in the same SMSA as central or middle cities.
NM—Nonmetropolitan/Counties with no city > 50,000 population in 1980.
Source: Ross, 1986, p. 57.

in urban employment in insurance between 1981 and 1989. During that period the three large cities (Chicago, Dallas, and Houston) that had grown the most over the period studied by Ross, as well as some smaller cities (including Hartford), lost insurance employment, while job growth continued in a number of smaller cities and suburban areas included in the survey (see Table 7.4). Furthermore, many of the large cities, including New York, Boston, Philadelphia, San Francisco and New Orleans, continued to lose insurance jobs (see Table 7.5). Thus, in an industry in which employment grew by 187% over the period 1948 to 1989, there was substantial job loss in central cities. In addition, job growth in smaller urban and suburban areas took place to some extent at the expense of workers in large urban centers. This industry which has experienced growth in each of 10 or so major states (see Table 7.1) has at the same time been shedding workers in the cities, disrupting the labor market in those centers just as certainly as have suburbanizing and internationalizing manufacturing industries experiencing market contraction.

TABLE 7.3. Twenty Counties with the Largest Absolute Gain in SIC 63
Employment: 1970–1981

	County type	Employment SIC 63		Employment change 1970–1981	
		1970	1981	Total	%
Hartford, CN	SC	29,449	48,984	19,535	66.3
Cook, IL	CC	45,318	58,718	13,400	29.6
Dallas, TX	CC	22,343	32,745	10,402	46.6
Orange, CA	FR	5,136	14,666	9,530	185.6
Harris, TX	CC	11,595	18,732	7,132	61.6
Oakland, MI	FR	2,287	9,413	7,126	311.6
Franklin, OH	CC	10,539	17,120	6,581	62.4
King, WA	MC	9,424	14,660	5,236	55.6
Morris, NJ	FR	497	5,722	5,225	1051.3
Polk, IA	SC	7,710	12,653	4,943	64.1
Dane, WI	SC	2,279	7,212	4,933	216.5
Hampden, MA	SC	4,649	9,578	4,929	106.0
Maricopa, AR	CC	4,912	9,788	4,876	99.3
DeKalb, GA	FR	915	5,736	4,821	526.9
Johnson, KS	FR	1,018	5,565	4,547	446.7
Douglas, NB	SC	7,956	12,500	4,544	57.1
St. Louis, MO	FR	2,771	7,163	4,392	158.5
Marion, IN	CC	12,250	16,588	4,338	35.4
Norfolk, MA	FR	1,023	4,840	3,817	373.1
Cumberland, PA	NM	257	3,803	3,546	1379.8
U.S. Total		1,058,000	1,229,375	171,375	16.2

CC—Central cities/Counties with primary cities > 500,000 population in 1980.
MC—Middle cities/Counties with primary cities of 250,000–500,000 population in 1980.
SC—Small cities/Counties with primary cities of 50,000–250,000 population in 1980.
FR—First ring/Counties next to or in the same SMSA as central or middle cities.
NM—Nonmetropolitan/Counties with no city > 50,000 population in 1980.
Source: Ross, 1986, p. 54.

THE WORLD INSURANCE INDUSTRY

The modern practice of risk sharing in the form of insurance appears to
be a European invention, recorded as early as the 13th century in Spain.
In Britain, the first statute dealing with insurance was written in 1601.
Not surprisingly, it had to do with marine insurance, the form most
commonly sold in Britain during the 16th and 17th centuries. Other forms
of property insurance emerged at about the same time. After the Great
Fire of London in 1666, for example, a number of companies formed
to sell fire insurance. A century later Benjamin Franklin formed the first
fire insurance company in the American colonies. By the 19th century

Germany, France, and Russia also had fire insurance firms (*Encyclopedia Britannica*, 1929).

Though the payment of benefits at the time of death goes back to the Roman collegia and was familiar to members of medieval guilds as a way of covering burial costs, life insurance in the modern sense did not begin until the 16th century. It was first associated with marine insurance, covering the lives of those going on ocean voyages. Life insurance did not become an important product in the United States until the mid-19th century, when the number of firms selling life insurance went from 15 to 243 and the value of insurance in force increased 40 times over a 20-year period (Zelizer, 1979).

The British insurance industry was the first to internationalize, as it followed British investment abroad (Lee, 1986, p. 66). At the end of

TABLE 7.4. Changes in SIC 63 Employment 1981–1989 in the Twenty Counties with the Largest Absolute Job Gain 1970–1981

	County type	Employment SIC 63		Employment change 1981–1989	
		1981	1989	Total	%
Hartford, CN	SC	48,984	36,622	−12,362	−25.2
Cook, IL	CC	58,718	58,119	−599	−1.0
Dallas, TX	CC	32,745	25,813	−6,932	−21.2
Orange, CA	FR	14,666	22,396	7,730	52.7
Harris, TX	CC	18,732	14,824	−3,908	−20.9
Oakland, MI	FR	9,413	12,283	2,870	30.5
Franklin, OH	CC	17,120	19,170	2,050	12.0
King, WA	MC	14,660	15,042	382	2.6
Morris, NJ	FR	5,722	9,308	3,586	62.7
Polk, IA	SC	12,653	19,072	6,419	50.7
Dane, WI	SC	7,212	9,859	2,647	36.7
Hampden, MA	SC	9,578	14,473	4,895	51.1
Maricopa, AZ	CC	9,788	11,969	2,181	22.3
DeKalb, GA	FR	5,736	7,489	1,753	30.6
Johnson, KS	FR	5,565	6,646	1,081	19.4
Douglas, NB	SC	12,500	8,315	−4,185	−33.5
St. Louis, MO	FR	7,163	9,066	1,903	26.6
Marion, IN	CC	16,588	16,111	−477	−2.9
Norfolk, MA	FR	4,840	7,225	2,385	49.3
Cumberland, PA	NM	3,803	7,530	3,727	98.0

CC—Central cities/Counties with primary cities > 500,000 population in 1980.
MC—Middle cities/Counties with primary cities of 250,000–500,000 population in 1980.
SC—Small cities/Counties with primary cities of 50,000–250,000 population in 1980.
FR—First ring/Counties next to or in the same SMSA as central or middle cities.
NM—Nonmetropolitan/Counties with no city > 50,000 population in 1980.
Source: County Business Patterns, 1970, 1981, and 1989; Update of Ross, 1986.

TABLE 7.5. Changes in SIC 63 Employment 1981–1989 in the 15 Counties with the Largest Absolute Job Loss 1970–1981

	County type	Employment SIC 63		Employment change 1981–1989	
		1981	1989	Total	%
New York, NY	CC	67,145	54,733	−12,412	−18.5
Wayne, MI	CC	8,904	11,066	2,162	24.3
Suffolk, MA	CC	25,784	19,265	−6,519	−25.3
Essex, NJ	MC	15,511	12,982	−2,529	−16.3
San Francisco, CA	CC	13,696	9,616	−4,080	−29.8
St. Louis, MO	MC	4,538	4,087	−451	−9.9
Philadelphia, PA	CC	21,578	18,051	−3,527	−16.3
Bronx, NY	CC	867	437	−430	−49.6
Kings, NY	CC	2,030	1,738	−292	−14.4
Baltimore City, MD	CC	4,113	7,935	3,822	92.9
Washington, D.C.	CC	5,936	7,197	1,261	21.2
Richmond, VA	SC	4,325	3,713	−612	−14.2
Orleans, LA	CC	5,361	3,065	−2,296	−42.8
Queens, NY	CC	1,898	3,161	1,263	66.5
Alameda, CA	FR	3,743	4,561	818	21.9

CC—Central cities/Counties with primary cities > 500,000 population in 1980.
MC—Middle cities/Counties with primary cities of 250,000–500,000 population in 1980.
SC—Small cities/Counties with primary cities of 50,000–250,000 population in 1980.
FR—First ring/Counties next to or in the same SMSA as central or middle cities.
NM—Nonmetropolitan/Counties with no city > 50,000 population in 1980.
Source: County Business Patterns, 1970, 1981, and 1989; Update of Ross, 1986.

the 19th century some British firms opened offices abroad while others, following a practice still common with internationalizing insurance firms today, simply bought established firms in the host country. The London and Lancashire Insurance Company, for example, acquired two U.S. firms in the 1880s and a third during the 1890s. Over this same time period it also acquired companies in Australia, Canada, South Africa, and South America.

Before World War I, British firms not only sold insurance outside Britain but invested the premiums in foreign markets as well. After the war, however, investment remained for the most part within the British Isles, in part because of government restrictions on investment overseas (Lee, 1986, p. 173).

In all the industrial economies insurance has grown as industrial wealth has increased. As a growing segment of the population has had access to disposable income in the 20th century, the life insurance industry grew. And between the two world wars, which themselves gave the insurance industry an enormous boost, automobile insurance increased dramatically. The growth of this form of insurance continued after World War II, as increasing numbers of automobiles were sold. In addition, pension funds increased as more and more employers offered pension plans as part of an enlarged benefits package.

Since then, of course, the industry has become truly gargantuan, accounting for nearly 9% of U.S. and nearly 10% of Japanese GDP (*Sigma*, February 1992). In 1986 total premium volume was $858.5 billion worldwide, and grew about five and a half times as fast as world GNP; in 1987 and 1988 premium volume grew twice as fast as world GNP (*Sigma*, May 1988). Five countries—the United States, Japan, Germany, Britain, and France—accounted for 77% of the world market in 1989 (see Figure 7.1), with Japan growing at the fastest rate.[1]

Perhaps the most notable thing about the geography of world insurance production and sales is its concentration in the developed market economies. In 1989 Central and South America, Africa, and Asia (excluding Japan) accounted for only 6.1% of total world premiums. According to *Sigma* (May 1988), the insurance gap between rich and poor countries is widening. Switzerland leads the world in density (per capita insurance expenditures) at $2376 in 1989 while premiums for most Third World countries average under $200 per capita, with South Korea and South Africa standing out as exceptions. These two countries are also exceptional with regard to insurance penetration (premiums as a percent of GDP). With Ireland, they have the highest penetrations in the

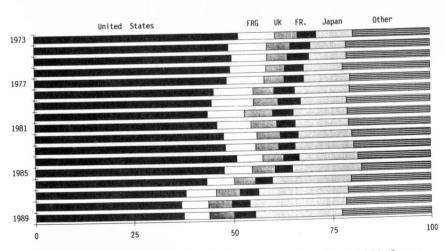

FIGURE 7.1. Percentage of total world insurance premium, 1973–1989. *Source:* *Sigma*, various dates.

world, over 10%, while Japan, the United Kingdom, and the United States are all slightly under 10% (*Sigma*, 2/92).

Another important characteristic of the international insurance industry is the degree to which the major markets are closed. Most governments are intensely worried about the financial power of these massive institutional investors and are reluctant to hand over a large fraction of domestic "savings" to foreign firms. This accounts in part for the restrictions on the entry of foreign firms into the major national markets that have made it difficult for U.S. firms to export or produce insurance products outside their national boundaries.

HARD TIMES FOR U.S. INSURERS: THE 1970S AND 1980S

To understand changes in the nature and location of insurance employment over the past few decades, one must be aware of the rather turbulent recent experience of insurers and their attempts to adjust to difficult times. Many companies changed their orientation to the insurance market during this period, or changed their investment strategies, or both. When such adjustments failed, or produced additional unanticipated difficulties, rationalization and cost cutting ensued—facilitated by computer technology and the availability of a large pool of educated women workers. Closures, relocations, and related layoffs became a familiar experience for insurance employees, despite the slow but steady overall growth in industry employment.

Insurance firms are engaged in two basic revenue-generating activities, the provision of insurance and the management of investment. Over the past two decades insurers have experienced serious problems in both areas. These difficulties have differed for the L/H and P/C subsectors though their attempts to adjust have been remarkably similar, with similar implications for the nature and location of employment.

Life Has Its Problems

Life insurers make their money by selling three basic products—life insurance, health insurance, and pensions and annuities—and by investing the premiums they receive as payment for these products. Revenue is generated from the first activity by taking in a premium that is higher than the benefits paid out, or by obtaining a fee to manage these services from a corporation. They hold the premium until they must pay benefits, using it as an investment vehicle to accrue earnings that will presumably exceed the benefits (including interest) that they will eventually pay out.

Life insurers have experienced serious difficulties since the 1970s, when competition from alternative forms of investment such as individual retirement accounts (IRAs) cut into their market. Runaway inflation at the end of the decade, and the high interest rates that attempted to slow it, lowered the value of life insurance policies, most of which had a yield of around 4%. The declining market prompted the industry to introduce a number of higher yield products, and to offer their existing policyholders the opportunity to replace their outmoded policies with newer, more competitive forms of insurance. While these actions helped to build up slumping demand, by the 1980s the long-term effects of increased competition were reflected in falling profit margins as the combination of higher interest payments and lower premiums cut into net revenues (*National Underwriter Life/Health*, 16 March 1987, p. 14; *Best's Review Life/Health*, September 1987, p. 18).

The competitive predicament of life insurers was exacerbated by the existing structure of regulation. Policyholders took advantage of policy loans[2] at the 6% interest rate set by government regulators to invest elsewhere at a higher rate of return. By 1981 9.3% of life insurers' assets were tied up in low-interest policy loans, double the percentage of 20 years earlier. Insurers had to rearrange their portfolios to meet this new demand for cash, often cashing in bonds and other long-term instruments before they had matured or borrowing money at unfavorable rates.

At the same time, and for related reasons, hundreds of new firms entered the industry in the late 1970s and early 1980s (American Council of Life Insurers, 1989, p. 50). These firms competed with existing companies on the basis of a specialized product or on price and benefits. They were able to offer higher returns on their policies because they were not holding a large portfolio of long-term, low-yield investments as most older insurers were. Compounding the problem, a number of P/C insurers developed life insurance subsidiaries as part of a strategy of diversification. P/C firms already had short-term investment portfolios and so were similarly poised to take advantage of the higher yields.

Despite the development of new, higher yield life products, life insurers' share of consumer savings fell from 5.2% to 2.5% between 1970 and 1987. Consumers were shifting their long-term savings into pension funds,[3] which offered a higher guaranteed yield than life insurance, as well as into treasury bonds, tax-exempt bonds, and money market funds (*Statistical Abstract of the United States*, 1989, p. 487). This change in the market is reflected in the fact that life insurance now accounts for only a third of life insurers' premium income. By the mid-

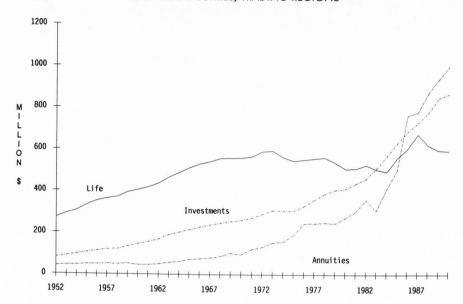

FIGURE 7.2. Life insurers' CPI-adjusted revenues by type, 1952–1990. *Source*: American Council of Life Insurers.

1980s annuities and pension funds had supplanted life insurance as the primary source of revenue in the life insurance business (U.S. Department of Commerce, 1988) (see Figure 7.2).

In addition to the problems of the life insurance market, problems related to risk and regulation also face the life industry. The spread of AIDS has presented a new and consequential dimension of risk. Banks are currently lobbying Congress for the right to sell all types of insurance and, though their efforts to date have been relatively unsuccessful, they could potentially cut deeply into the insurance companies' market. Finally, insurance companies are concerned about fallout from court cases relating to the issue of gender-based rate setting (U.S. Department of Commerce, 1988).[4]

P/C Has Its Woes

While life insurers tend to suffer competition from banks and investment companies, competition in the property/casualty industry is basically an internal phenomenon. The P/C industry is crowded and highly competitive. Roughly 3500 companies write P/C policies, of which 900 write the majority. No firm controls more than 10% of the market. With so many firms competing for premiums, the market is highly susceptible to price wars. In fact, price wars are so common in the P/C line that they have been given a name: underwriting cycles.

These cycles are marked by periods of reckless price cutting and the underwriting of less-than-acceptable risks (a process known as cash flow underwriting), followed by periods of unusually high rates to compensate for the losses of the previous years. When a number of companies feel that they can once more begin to lower their rates the cycle begins again.

In the 1980s the industry experienced a particularly interesting version of this cycle. Early in the decade many companies began to underwrite at a loss to generate funds for investment at the high interest rates that prevailed at that time. At the time reinsurance was also available at very competitive rates, giving them an added margin of safety.

This period of underwriting bad risks at low premiums to take advantage of high rates of return might not have been problematic were it not for changes in the size, frequency, and breadth of legal decisions concerning malpractice and liability. The size of personal liability lawsuit settlements increased at a rate of at least 10% annually between 1980 and 1986, with more than 1600 "million dollar verdicts" between 1983 and 1986 (Insurance Information Institute, 1990). In the United States insurees were making claims for things that had never been considered when the policies were sold—bars, for instance, were being sued for traffic deaths involving individuals they had served.

As the number of suits increased, draining insurers' resources both for settlements and for legal fees, investment returns slowed with the lowering of interest rates. Resources were further drained by a series of lawsuits involving environmental and other hazards, such as toxic wastes, that had not been calculated into the cost of coverage.

In response to this crisis, insurers raised their rates on many coverages and reassessed their notions of "acceptable" risk, leading to record profits in 1986 and 1987. But while the "crisis" may have subsided, the market, particularly for commercial risks, had changed. P/C companies had lost commercial customers, cities and towns and others who left the market voluntarily or were pushed out. Many companies had tired of paying into a pool to support the environmental malpractice of others. Fed up with unstable and sometimes outrageous prices, they began to look for alternative ways to insure themselves, including the formation of captive insurance companies—wholly owned insurance subsidiaries usually located offshore and managed by a captive management firm. At the same time a number of different groups, including cities, bars, and day care centers, were unable to procure liability insurance because of increasing costs. The government has attempted to insure some of these groups, while others have set up their own self-insurance mechanisms, such as risk-retention groups in which several parties set aside a portion of their resources to cover their potential liabilities. Captives, risk-retention groups, and other forms of self-insurance now make up between 30 and 40% of the commercial market. The continuing entrance of new firms into the market compounded the effects of the shrinking commercial market, and all insurers had to subsidize the increasing bankruptcy rate of the late 1980s.[5]

Restructuring as a Response

For both L/H and P/C the 1970s and 1980s created the conditions for some relatively radical changes. In particular, both types of insurers developed strategies to avoid a continuation of the losses of the first half of the 1980s. Life insurers had developed a new and diverse line of products (with, however, lower premiums and higher interest rates than earlier products), while both types of insurers took on the administration of corporate self-insurance programs. In general, insurers have put more emphasis on customer service, which has often involved automation to speed up processing of policies and claims.

The profitability of life insurance firms, like their P/C counterparts, is increasingly dependent on their investments rather than their underwriting, where competition has forced them to offer high yields at low prices, courting actual losses on the insuring end of the business (*National Underwriter Life/Health*, 16 March 1987, p. 16). In the 1970s and 1980s, for a variety of reasons, life insurers pursued a shift away from a long-term focus and toward shorter term, more easily liquidated investments. This meant a decrease in the proportion of their investments in mortgages on farms and one-to-four family houses, and a corresponding increase in the amounts devoted to commercial loans and mortgages. Insurers in general were avid purchasers of junk bonds, of which they held 30% in February 1990 (*New York Times*, 13 February 1990, p. D24), and their holdings of nonpaper assets showed a marked increase. Commercial real estate investments (shopping malls and office parks were popular) and firm acquisitions (especially real estate and securities and investment firms) escalated during the 1980s. In general, life insurers moved away from their "buy and hold" investment strategy and toward portfolio switching, shorter average maturity, and greater liquidity as well as toward the purchase of real assets (Gart, 1989, p. 264). P/C insurers had far fewer options in the movement of their assets but they tended to shift out of stocks and into bonds—both state and municipal tax-exempt and private—and also out of long-term bonds into shorter maturity bonds and money market funds (Ernst & Whinney, 1980, p. 33).

Like other investors, many insurers found their investments of the 1980s—and especially their increased exposure to the vagaries of the real estate market—to be problematic. Insurers felt that rent increases were more likely to earn them money in a time of inflation than mortgages valued at a low fixed rate, but the real estate market failed to meet their expectations. In November 1991 Aetna announced that it was expecting mortgage and loan defaults to reach as high as $1.3 billion (5% of its assets in these types of holdings) (Connolly, 1991). When the bottom fell out of the real estate market, The Travelers had to add $415 million to its reserves for real estate operations because of the high rate of default on properties it was developing in both the Southeast and Texas, an expense many smaller insurers could certainly not afford (*Journal of Commerce*, 29 July 1988, p. 9A). As of October 1990 22% of The Travelers's real estate holdings were "in trouble," and real estate made up 20% of The Travelers's assets, as opposed to the industry average of 10% (*New York Times*, 9 October 1990, p. D10). Similarly, by the end of the 1980s Prudential had become nervous about leveraged buyouts, especially when they were being leveraged at 10–12 times earnings before interest and taxes (EBIT) rather than 3–4 times EBIT (Lahart, 1988).

At this moment, insurers in both L/H and P/C face more options and more dangers than at any period in the history of the industry. Cycles are worse now, markets are no longer characterized by slow but steady growth, and investments are more risky. Many insurance firms are huge, diversified financial institutions operating in a variety of product and national markets. But they face a storm of competition in the insurance field, and a highly unstable global financial system as a field for their investments. Junk bonds, leveraged buyouts, and real estate speculation, the ruin of many an individual and institutional investor, are part of the world of the average insurer, promising huge losses as well as huge profits. Rationalization, cost cutting, and other forms of restructuring have become a recurrent reality for this industry, with an impact on the labor force and on communities and regions that rivals that of major manufacturers.

DOMESTIC EMPLOYMENT IMPACTS
OF INSURER RESTRUCTURING

The ups and downs of the 1970s and 1980s, as well as insurers' strategies for coping with them, have had a substantial impact on insurance workers, many of whom have borne the brunt of industry restructuring. As insurers have diversified their business focus, workers in the insurance end of the business have often experienced rationalization prompted by losses in an entirely different sector; and as competition has heated up for both subsectors, cost cutting in the form of automation, relocation, and reorientation to the labor market has hit insurance workers hard.

Automation and Feminization

A labor-intensive industry with many standardized production tasks, insurance was easily adapted to computers.[6] The early use of computers in the industry involved the computerization of discrete tasks—for example, record keeping, accounting, billing, and payroll—within a stable organizational context. The second wave of computerization began in the late 1970s with more far-reaching effects. Systems were designed to perform insurance production processes, including underwriting, rating, claims processing, and policy production. A number of discrete, Taylorized tasks were combined into a single process and automated. The initiator of a policy, for example, could now enter the necessary information into a central data base, rather than sending it to be entered at a central data processing office.

The second wave of computerization presented insurers "with a variety of solutions to questions of job design, work organization and structure" (Applebaum & Albin, 1989, p. 250). Many firms automated a number of "skilled" jobs, reducing their skill levels and their pay. Personal lines underwriting, for example, has been automated at a number of firms, reducing the need for professional underwriters and shifting the task to clerical workers. Some automated underwriting programs can process over 80% of P/C lines such as automobile insurance. The rest are evaluated by human or "exceptions" underwriters.

With automation, not only has the labor process changed but the work force has changed as well. As of 1982, women made up more than 60% of the insurance labor force, up from 54% in 1970. This change reflects an increase in professional as well as clerical employment, particularly in computer-oriented departments where women are being hired at all levels, reflecting what insurance companies feel is their greater adaptability to a computer environment (Baran, 1987, p. 50). In one firm undergoing automation, the underwriting department went from being over 60% male to being entirely female (Baran, Ross, Van Meurs, & Cohen, 1985, p. 50). As so often happens when women move into traditionally male jobs, the status of the departments where this takes place has slipped as has the occupational mobility and pay level of the workers. Insurance firms traditionally pay low average wages as a trade-off for supposed lifetime job security. Women in the insurance industry are generally paid at least 20% less than their male counterparts. In higher level jobs women make about 56% of what men make (Ross, 1986, p. 27).

The upgrading of the skill level of clerical positions has been accompanied by the elimination of many lower-level underwriting jobs such as rater or underwriter's assistant. Many of these jobs were formerly a way for women to move out of a clerical position into the professional occupations. Now there are very few women who can make the jump to the position of "exceptions" underwriter. Increased responsibility and skill demands are thus being placed upon women whose mobility on the organizational ladder has decreased. Some companies recognize this and try to compensate by hiring more women into entry-level professional positions. Nevertheless, the difference between what is achievable by entry-level professionals and women who enter as clericals, no matter how skilled or educated they are, is growing. A further consequence of the "skilling" of clerical work is the elimination of a number of jobs that were formerly available to women of relatively low educational attainment, so that the insurance industry is less accessible to women of color in the inner cities (Baran & Teegarden, 1987; Applebaum & Albin, 1989).

Rationalization and Relocation

Coincident with changes in the labor process and labor force have been the changes in the geography of insurers described above. Traditionally, insurance firms have located their home offices in major cities like New York or Chicago and their regional branch offices in secondary cities. Until about 20 years ago the back office where clerical work is performed was located in the major city with the home office. In recent years, however, back office functions have been increasingly relocated to small cities, suburbs, and even nonmetropolitan areas. Insurers cite labor and real estate costs and labor quality as the major reasons for their relocation (Ross, 1986). Many feel that inner-city high school graduates do not have the basic literacy skills necessary to fill the new upgraded clerical positions, especially since quality control has become an integral part of these positions. In moving to small cities and suburban locations, insurers are moving into labor markets with large numbers of relatively well-educated women who are looking for a second family income close to home and who will not demand high wages or take advantage of the benefits package (Ross, 1986; Nelson, 1986).

At the same time that they are relocating back offices out of the central city, insurers are retreating from the large-scale network of branch offices that was developed in the 1970s primarily to provide a support system for agents. This often involves closing branch offices and consolidating the work in regional offices. When Continental restructured, for example, the number of fully staffed branch offices dropped from

33 to 12, which became regional offices (*Insurance Review*, September 1989, p. 33). But while firms are consolidating support functions they are also decentralizing in a number of ways. The point of data entry, for example, has in many cases shifted from a back office to the agent's office. The automation of fairly simple underwriting and claims adjusting is also leading to a shift of some of that work into the field. High volume agents are being given terminals that feed directly into a company's computer from which they can underwrite, rate, and print out a policy. Life insurance agents can use the computer to get fast estimates on prices and yields for their new, more complex policies. Thus, a new form of decentralization is taking the place of the old. Large branch offices are being eliminated in favor of a more diffuse set of smaller offices. Underwriters are being dispersed from central underwriting facilities to smaller regional or district offices. Where there used to be an office of 50 people, there now may be one underwriter, or a team consisting of an underwriter, some claims adjusters, and a few marketing employees.

In the 1980s these shifts in the deployment and location of workers have occasioned a number of plant closings and major layoffs in the insurance industry. The closing of back offices in the inner cities left large numbers of minority women unemployed. In the closing and streamlining of branch offices, major layoffs were often combined with offers of early retirement.

One concomitant of the downsizing of offices is that a smaller office is more mobile and implies less of a commitment to a region. Insurance corporation real estate managers are now trying to maintain greater flexibility in their operations so that relocation or closure is possible on short notice. This has led to a reduction in the average lease for office properties from 10 years to 3 and at most 5 years (*Site Selection*, August 1989, p. 938).

During the period of restructuring in the late 1970s and 1980s there were incredible gains in productivity within some of the largest firms. Prudential, for example, increased its revenues by 40% (in real terms) between 1976 and 1986 while only increasing its work force of 61,700 by 700. Some insurers, including John Hancock and New York Life, experienced a net shedding of employees during those years. On the other hand, Aetna Life and Casualty increased its work force by 65% while increasing its real revenues by just 58% (United Nations Centre on Transnational Corporations, 1989, pp. 184–186). It is likely that a good part of this employment growth, like the employment growth during the 1970s, was due to mergers and acquisitions.

Overall, employment has grown slowly in the insurance industry since the mid-1970s (see Figures 7.3 and 7.4), while premiums have

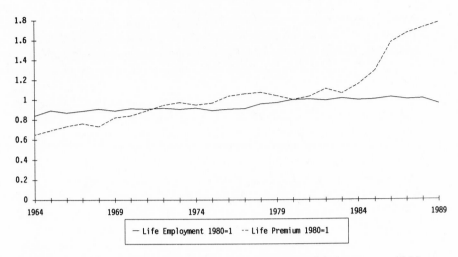

FIGURE 7.3. Real premium income and employment, life insurance, 1964–1989.

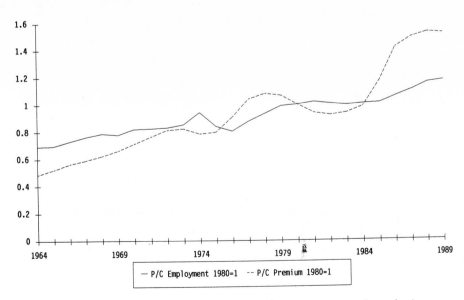

FIGURE 7.4. Real premium income and employment, property/casualty insurance, 1964–1989.

grown more rapidly. The quality of employment, on the other hand, has gone down. Clerical jobs have been automated and "reskilled" to incorporate many of the tasks of professionals, without corresponding increases in wages. The internal labor market has been segmented, so that workers who come in at the bottom can no longer climb to the top. The labor force has been feminized, continuing and reinforcing the industry tradition of providing low wage employment. Despite insurers' reputation for offering lifetime employment as a trade-off for low wages, job security has been severely reduced, and many employees have faced layoffs and plant closings due to rationalization and relocation. In terms of employment, then, the industry's recent record does not really accord with the glowing images of economic development that are associated with producer services.

THE INTERNATIONALIZATION
OF U.S. INSURANCE

Until the 1980s all but a handful of U.S.–based insurers shaped their international business around the needs of their multinational commercial clients. This involved either opening a branch office abroad, participating in a network that wrote insurance overseas, or making agreements in foreign countries to reinsure a client's risks, which a foreign insurer would then underwrite. Very recently, however, insurers have moved to expand their international marketing and to internationalize in a variety of other ways. The implications of these moves for domestic employment and development cannot yet be assessed, but they do not seem particularly encouraging.

At the same time that U.S. insurers have internationalized their operations, the U.S. market has become the target of foreign firms. In 1985 foreign insurers wrote approximately 4% of U.S. premiums; by 1989 they were writing 11%. Many firms selling insurance in the U.S. market have established themselves by acquiring U.S. firms. Some of the largest acquisitions include General Casualty (purchased by Swiss-based Winterthur), Fireman's Fund (purchased by the German firm, Allianz), and Businessmen's Assurance of Kansas (purchased by Generali of Italy) (Decaminada, 1991).

Acquiring a local firm is probably the easiest way to enter the U.S. market. Foreign firms attempting to set up entirely new subsidiaries in the United States encounter a mind-boggling array of state regulations, as has been pointed out in the GATT negotiations. Since each state has a different set of insurance regulations, firms must in essence establish

50 companies, most requiring local reserves, in order to cover the 50 states.

The Europeans have always been more interested in the U.S. market than have the Japanese, and British firms have operated in the United States for more than a century. Although the United Kingdom is still the preeminent foreign insurer in the United States, its share of total inward foreign direct investment (FDI) shrank from 40% in 1980 to 28% in 1990. Dutch, Swiss, and Canadian firms account for a growing share of FDI (*Survey of Current Business*, August 1982, p. 36; August 1991, pp. 5, 78) (see Figure 7.5).

Some foreign firms operate in the United States primarily to insure plants established there by corporations based in their home countries. Thus Japanese insurers are primarily interested in insuring Japanese

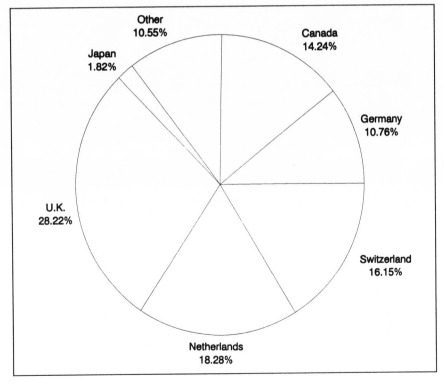

FIGURE 7.5. National shares of foreign direct investment in the U.S. insurance industry, 1990. *Source*: *Survey of Current Business*, 1991.

"transplants." Nippon Life, for example, has been "operating in the U.S. since 1984 through its wholly-owned subsidiary, NLI Insurance Agency Inc., which markets group life, health, pension and long-term disability products to Japanese-American companies with whom Nippon has a relationship" (*National Underwriter Life/Health*, 2 December 1991, p. 4). Recently, however, they have decided to start a second company to market these types of products to U.S. companies, with The Travelers providing "sales support, billing, claims and management of a managed care network . . . and Principal Mutual supporting the Japanese insurer's group pension products" (*National Underwriter Life/Health*, 2 December 1991, p. 4).

Given that foreign direct investment in the United States considerably exceeds FDI by U.S. insurance carriers, it is unlikely that FDI has had a negative net effect on employment. But insurance companies are complex entities that are internationalizing in a variety of ways. Below we examine the various types of international activity in which U.S. insurers are currently engaged, considering possible impacts on domestic employment and development.

Foreign Employment by U.S. Firms

While some banks and airlines have flown their clerical work to the Caribbean for processing throughout the 1980s, insurers have until very recently kept their data processing in the United States. Since 1988, however, they have begun to establish facilities overseas to engage in production for reexport.

Between 1988 and 1991 seven insurers established data processing facilities in Ireland. These facilities are relatively large, involving 50–500 employees and an initial investment of as much as one million pounds. Wilson (1991) cites labor cost and quality, transport and communications, and public policy as the three major factors influencing the choice of Ireland as a back office location. Irish workers require no health benefits and are typically paid less than two-thirds of what a U.S. clerical worker makes (Wilson, 1991, p. 10). The labor force is very well educated, with few employment alternatives and a consequent low turnover rate compared to the United States. Excellent communications facilities (upgraded by the Irish in the early 1980s at a cost of 1.3 billion pounds) and proximity to the Shannon airport allow for overnight turnaround of processed information (Wilson, 1991, pp. 12–13). Finally, the Irish Development Authority offers tax breaks and financial incentives, training grants, construction subsidies, and site development, and the government places few restrictions on capital flows (Wilson, 1991, pp. 15–16).

In addition to moving clerical work overseas to engage in production for reexport, insurers are shifting professional jobs to foreign markets. Since 1986, for example, Continental International has stationed underwriters in London and Hong Kong who have the power to write large commercial policies for firms operating in those countries without approval from the home office in New York. Other insurance companies have also moved the responsibility for underwriting large foreign commercial contracts out of the home office and into the foreign office (*Business Insurance*, 24 November 1986, p. 23; personal interview with Don Meyer and Richard Ryti, AIG, 26 January 1990). AIU (an AIG subsidiary) now has only one manager and one assistant working in New York for its entire European operation (personal interview with Meyer and Ryti).

International Marketing and Insurance Provision

International "trade" in insurance is relatively limited, and the largest insurance markets are almost always dominated by domestic insurers. In 1987 only Austria, Canada, and Spain had greater than 12% foreign penetration. Slightly more than 40% of the Canadian market, which is the seventh largest in the world (*Sigma*, February 1991), is controlled by foreign firms, predominantly from the United States and the United Kingdom (*Sigma*, February 1989). Usually, sales by foreign insurers are generated and administered by representatives located in the country of sale, so that "international" transactions do not have significant employment implications for the country of "origin."

There was little movement by U.S. carriers to sell insurance in foreign markets until the late 1980s. In 1990 roughly 55 of the approximately 6000 insurers doing business in the United States had internationalized their product sales beyond North America and less than a dozen had "any significant international interests" (Powers, 1990, p. 19). The sales of these firms comprised approximately 3% of total sales.

Two companies, AIG and CIGNA, wrote more than 60% of foreign premiums in 1988 (*National Underwriter Property/Casualty*, 11 July 1988, p. 9). These companies have the ability to write policies without using an intermediary in over 130 countries. Other U.S. firms, which are now entering overseas markets, are concentrating on markets in Europe and Asia. While some firms are targeting the larger markets such as those of Japan and the United Kingdom, a number of companies are focusing on smaller but faster growing markets such as those in Italy, Spain, South Korea, and Taiwan. Many firms see the Japanese market as relatively saturated and entering it as analogous to "reinventing the Toyota and trying to sell it there" (*Journal of Commerce*, 7 July 1988, p. 11A).

As we noted above, opening foreign subsidiaries may involve relocating underwriting that is currently done in the United States. Sometimes, however, firms will purchase existing firms and the production and sales capacity that goes with them. Prudential and Continental both acquired firms in Brazil; many companies including Metropolitan, Continental, and St. Paul have purchased insurers in the United Kingdom. Such acquisitions are often the best entry into markets where language differences and lack of familiarity with a complex tangle of regulations and customs often effectively bar foreigners from operation.

Many governments, of course, restrict the entry of foreign insurers into their markets, or restrict the repatriation of premiums, in order to retain domestic control over the investment of domestic insurance premiums. (This reflects the tremendous development potential that invested premiums represent.) Such restrictions were the target of the "financial services" negotiations of the Uruguay Round of GATT talks, until they broke down in late 1990 (Block, 1991). The United States was intent on reducing or eliminating barriers to trade in services, including insurance, banking, and securities, and was pressing strongly for a Services Agreement that would "impose obligations for governments to maintain transparent, predictable and non-restrictive rules for foreign services and foreign service providers" (Powers, 1990, p. 3). In pushing for "liberalization," the United States strongly opposed unequal treatment of domestic and foreign insurers (except in cases where the latter were favored), and government-owned or government-sanctioned monopolies in insurance provision. In the case of India, which is the largest insurance market in the world dominated by a government monopoly, U.S. negotiators met with intransigence and countered with threats of retaliation (on which the United States did not follow through) (Powers, 1990, pp. 11–12). In other cases, however, the talks have met with greater success and U.S. insurers are looking forward to increased liberalization when the talks resume.

As compared to the U.S. industry, the industry in certain other countries is more outward looking. Sixty-five percent of Swiss insurers' premium volume comes from abroad, as does 23% of French and 10% of German (compared to 3% of U.S. volume in 1990). The United Kingdom is the largest exporter of insurance in the European Community (EC), mainly to the United States, and the three largest Dutch firms do 45–65% of their business outside the country (*Economist/Arthur Anderson*, 1990). As of 1992 the European insurance market promises to become more internationalized, both because of the wave of mergers and acquisitions accompanying increased regional integration and because of the lowering of international barriers.

Financial Services and Other Noninsurance Activities

While U.S.-based insurers are looking to sell insurance in the Asian and European markets, they are also carrying out some of their financial and real estate activities in foreign markets. Most of the large life insurers are involved in such international dealings. Prudential has a large multinational presence in the securities field through its Bache subsidiary. The St. Paul purchased one of the largest insurance brokerages in the world, not simply for the purpose of marketing insurance but also as a way of investigating and monitoring overseas investments. Aetna expanded its overseas presence into the Australian market as a fund manager in 1990 after selling its life business there in 1989 (*Journal of Commerce*, 10 April 1990, p. 9A). AIG is very active in foreign real estate markets, particularly in countries that limit the export of capital where they must find creative ways to invest their funds domestically. AIG also provides a variety of financial services including venture capital and letters of credit for international transactions.

A number of companies have established financial service subsidiaries in Japan. Prudential has several Japanese subsidiaries of which the most recently established is designed to manage Japanese pension funds and investment trusts by investing in Japan, Germany, the United States, and the United Kingdom (*Journal of Commerce*, 29 March 1990, p. 9A). They have also entered into an arrangement with three large Japanese life insurance companies and Jones Lang Wootton International of the United Kingdom to invest in overseas (relative to Japan) real estate (*Journal of Commerce*, 22 February 1990, p. 9A). Other firms with subsidiaries in Japan include Metropolitan Life and Equitable.

Several insurers have used direct investment in noninsurance businesses as a means to gain access to insurance markets in foreign countries. Equitable and Prudential purchased financial service firms that do business internationally. AIG purchased an interest in a London-based brokerage with an international clientele. Through purchasing preexisting businesses and by setting up new enterprises, U.S.-based insurers have begun to diversify internationally, establishing a presence in financial and real estate markets in countries where they may have limited access to the insurance market.

Foreign Investment of Insurance and Pension Funds

Another international activity of insurance companies is portfolio investment. In the late 1980s and early 1990s insurance companies began to expand their investment subsidiaries in foreign countries. Prudential bought international investment experience when it purchased Bache Halsey Stuart Shields, which had offices in many more countries than Prudential did. Prudential also formed its own European investment subsidiary in Luxembourg to trade in securities. Metropolitan Life had been investing internationally for a number of years before it decided in 1990 to form a joint venture with CS First Boston to oversee the investment of the $200 million it had set aside for its international portfolio.

Although the available information is sketchy, it is clear that there has been an increase in insurers' foreign portfolio investments, particularly in long-term corporate bonds and, to a lesser extent, in foreign government bonds and short-term corporate bonds. These three types of foreign bonds represented 3.4% of all life insurer assets in 1988 (American Council of Life Insurers, 1990).

While no separate data are available, it appears that investment in foreign stocks is increasing as well. Though it does not specify which portions are invested by insurers, data on pension funds allows us to estimate the foreign investments of insurance companies, since life insurers manage approximately 30% of pension fund assets. In 1990 international portfolio investment represented 3.6% of the assets of the top 200 pension funds (*Pensions & Investments Weekly*, 21 January 1991, p. 17). Pension funds had at least $125 billion invested overseas by the end of 1990,[7] which represents an increase of $40 billion over 1989. Approximately 85% of the $125 billion is invested in equities. Although most of the remaining foreign investment is in bonds, pension fund managers are also beginning to invest in "foreign real estate, venture capital, and leveraged buy-out opportunities" (*Pensions & Investments Weekly*, 22 January 1990, p. 18).

International investment by pension funds companies is expected to increase from 4 to 20% of total assets by the year 2000 (*Pensions & Investments Weekly*, 11 July 1988, p. 1). Opinion is divided as to whether these will be in international financial markets or whether they will simply target global corporations.

Even though the current percentages of total investment invested overseas appear small, the foreign investments of pension fund investors are large in absolute terms.[8] The total assets of pension funds invested abroad would be equivalent to the assets of the fourth-largest corporation in the world. IBM employs 383,000 people with assets equal to roughly three-quarters of the amount pension funds have invested overseas. The combined foreign investment of life insurance and pension funds is large enough to be the third largest corporation in the world, behind General Motors and Ford (*Fortune Global 500*, 1990).

Though portfolio investment has no direct or easily quantified implications for U.S. employment, it is one of the conditions that makes employment possible. Insurance companies, like other financial institutions, allocate capital to different activities and regions and in the process participate in the creation and movement of employment. Given the massive financial assets of insurance firms, their greatest impact on employment is indirect—through their financial activities. The movement of several thousand data entry jobs overseas seems relatively inconsequential in comparison to the potential jobs foregone on account of foreign portfolio investment.

CONCLUSION

In the 1970s and 1980s employment growth in the insurance industry came to a near standstill because of automation and rationalization, the latter often prompted by losses in the noninsurance end of the business. At the same time large numbers of urban workers have been displaced by the relocation of back offices to suburban areas. Job quality has declined, with the truncation of job ladders and an increase in the proportion of low-wage jobs (that is, jobs held by women).

Insurance appears to be a "basic" industry with major regional development potential; its back office processing centers create massive regional concentrations of employment. Yet those centers are subject to huge fluctuations in numbers of employees. Hartford, the "insurance capital of the world," is a case in point. The city (and region) lost approximately 15,000 jobs between 1986 and 1989, dropping Connecticut from sixth to tenth place in state insurance employment. The promise of the producer service sector, which was to propel us into post-industrial prosperity, certainly has not been realized in the case of insurance.

Insurers not only produce and sell insurance, thereby directly creating jobs for insurance workers, they also invest the premiums they generate and the pension funds they manage, thereby indirectly creating jobs for workers in the full range of private industries. For this reason, the increasingly international orientation of insurance company investment is a matter of some concern. Historically, union pension funds (also known as Taft-Hartley pension funds) have been intensely resistant to overseas investment strategies for fear of exporting jobs and of risking pension funds in unsafe investment environments. Now, however, this constraint seems to be loosening, in part because of union interest in and support for the changes in Eastern Europe and in part because of increased acceptance of the global economy as the appropriate field for investment (*Pensions & Investments Weekly*, 24 December 1990, p. 1). Without sharing the domestic priorities of the Taft-Hartley pension funds, insurers are even more likely to turn to overseas investment opportunities, often with the blessing of the pension beneficiaries interested in high rates of return.

Insurance firms represent an enormous potential conduit for the export of capital. While the United States is attempting, by pursuing openness in foreign markets through GATT, to enhance the competitive position of U.S. firms overseas and to redress the trade deficit in goods through the export of services (Powers, 1990), it is ironically at the same time creating the conditions for major outflows of capital. It is clear that as insurers become more adept and entrenched in foreign markets they will increase their proportion of overseas investments. If the U.S. government is really concerned about the implications for domestic development of foreign transactions, it should perhaps consider the capital allocation role of insurers as well as their access to product markets.

ACKNOWLEDGMENTS

The authors would like to thank Peter Dicken, Meric Gertler, Ann Markusen, and Helzi Noponen for their helpful comments on an earlier draft of this chapter.

NOTES

1. Western Europe tends more than any other world region to specialize in reinsurance.

2. Loans in which policyholders borrow on the savings they have accrued through payments on their policies.

3. Though life insurers had themselves diversified into pension funds, they only managed to take on roughly 30% of the available business.

4. Opponents of gender- (or age-) based rate setting argue that evaluating the life expectancy, driving behavior, and so on, of individuals by placing them in a social category violates their individual rights (Bernstein & Green, 1988, p. 77).

5. Almost all insurers pay into funds set up to guarantee claims that need to be paid after an insurer becomes insolvent. These funds are established at the state level. The amount insurers have had to pay into these funds has increased substantially in the past few years. Out of the $2.2 billion paid in insurer assessments to state funds between 1969 and 1987, 40% or $900 million was paid in 1987 alone (U.S. House of Representatives, 1990, p. 2).

6. Having a large supply of money didn't hurt. Insurance companies were among the first to utilize computer equipment.

7. This figure comes from InterSec Research Corporation of Stamford, CT.
8. The figures on international investment probably underestimate it. They do not include, for example, the purchase of bonds issued by multinational corporations to finance their overseas investments.

REFERENCES

American Council of Life Insurance. Various dates. *Life Insurance Fact Book.* Washington, DC: American Council of Life Insurance.

Applebaum, E., & Albin, P. 1989. Computer Rationalization and the Transformation of Work: Lessons from the Insurance Industry. In S. Wood, ed., *The Transformation of Work*, pp. 247–265. Boston: Unwin Hyman.

Baran, B. 1987. The Technological Transformation of White-Collar Work: A Case Study of the Insurance Industry. In H. Hartmann, ed., *Computer Chips and Paper Clips*, vol 2, pp. 25–62. Washington, DC: National Academy Press.

Baran, B., Ross, J., Van Meurs, A., & Cohen, S. 1985. "Technological Innovation and Regulation: The Transformation of the Labor Process in the Insurance Industry." Working Paper no. 9. Berkeley Roundtable on the International Economy, University of California, Berkeley.

Baran, B., & Teegarden, S. 1987. Women's Labor in the Office of the Future: A Case Study of the Insurance Industry. In L. Beneria & C. Stimpson, eds., *Women, Households and the Economy*, pp. 201–224. New Brunswick, NJ: Rutgers University Press.

Bernstein, J., & Green, R. 1988. *The Insurance Industry in Canada.* Vancouver, BC: Fraser Institute.

Block, L. 1991. Insurers Await Result of GATT Talks. *Business Insurance*, 25(49), 16–20.

Connolly, J. 1991. Aetna Says Problem Real Estate Loans Could Reach $1.3 Billion. *National Underwriter Life/Health*, 95(47), 23.

Decaminada, J. 1991. The United States Insurance Market—Significant Developments. *International Insurance Monitor*, November, p. 13.

Economist/Arthur Anderson. 1990. "Insurance in a Changing Europe 1990–1995" Special Report no. 2068. London: Economist/Arthur Anderson.

Ernst & Whinney. 1980. *Ernst & Whinney Financial Reporting Trends Property/Casualty Insurance.* Cleveland, OH: Ernst & Whinney.

Gart, A. 1989. *An Analysis of the New Financial Institutions.* New York: Quorum.

Insurance Information Institute. 1990. *1990 Property/Casualty Insurance Facts.* New York: Insurance Information Institute.

Lahart, K. 1988. The View from the Rock. *Financial World*, 157, 18.

Kunreuther, H., & Pauly, M. 1987. "International Trade in Insurance." Unpublished manuscript, Wharton School, University of Pennsylvania.

Lee, C. H. 1986. *The British Economy since 1700.* Cambridge: Cambridge University Press.

Nelson, K. 1986. Labor Demand, Labor Supply and the Suburbanization of Low-Wage Office Work. In A. J. Scott & M. Storper, eds., *Production, Work, Territory*, pp. 149–171. Boston: Allen & Unwin.

Powers, L. 1990. "Current Negotiations in Financial Services and Financial Dumping." Testimony before the Task Force on the International Competitiveness of U.S. Financial Institutions, Committee on Banking, Finance and Urban Affairs, U.S. House of Representatives, July 17.

Rennie, R. 1987. Investment Strategy for the Life Insurance Company. In J. D. Cummins, ed., *Investment Activities of Life Insurance Companies*, pp. 1–37. Homewood, IL: Irwin.

Ross, J. M. 1986. "Technology and the Relocation of Employment in the Insurance Industry." Working Paper no. 16. Berkeley Roundtable on the International Economy, University of California, Berkeley.

United Nations Centre on Transnational Corporations. 1989. *Foreign Direct Investment and Transnational Corporations in Services*. New York: United Nations.

U.S. House of Representatives, Committee on Energy and Commerce, Subcommittee on Oversight and Investigations. 1990. *Failed Promises: Insurance Company Insolvencies*. Washington, DC: U.S. Government Printing Office.

U.S. Department of Commerce. 1988. *1988 U.S. Industrial Outlook*. Washington, DC: U.S. Government Printing Office.

Wilson, M. 1991. "Offshore Relocation of Producer Services: The Irish Back Office." Paper presented at the annual meeting of the Association of American Geographers, Miami, April.

Wissoker, P. 1992. "Internationalization and the Firm: A Critique of Productionism Using the Case of the Insurance Industry." Unpublished M.S. thesis, University of Massachusetts at Amherst.

Zelizer, V. 1979. *Morals and Markets*. New York: Columbia University Press.

8

Trade as a Regional Development Issue: Policies for Job and Community Preservation

ANN R. MARKUSEN

The studies in this book demonstrate great volatility in patterns of international industry location and show how thoroughly policy-based those patterns have often been. In addition, numerous studies of steel, auto, textile, and machining regions that have experienced plant closings have found that the adjustment process is long and often irreversibly negative. Many unemployed workers never find steady work, and many who do must accept permanent pay cuts and jobs with no benefits or job security. Contrary to the picture of instant adjustment implicit in free trade models, where freed-up resources are immediately devoted to higher and better uses, workers and their host communities often find their labor power and public infrastructure wasted for long periods of time, if not permanently. In addition to incurring psychic costs of major proportions, an unemployed worker's move to a region where new jobs are more accessible requires a substantial net loss in wealth, as houses are sold at depressed prices and migration costs draw down on savings. And in the aggregate, the reshuffling of auto or electronics or insurance jobs around the nation and around the world entails a net lowering of the standard of living, as wages and environmental and health standards are pushed down to the lowest common denominator.

The industry studies suggest that economic development, be it in Detroit or Los Angeles, eastern Kentucky or western Montana, is increasingly the product of international, rather than strictly national, forces. Many more industries are organized internationally now, and firms' choices of sites to produce and trade are made across international borders as easily as they once crossed state lines. (This openness of the domestic economy is new for the United States and Canada; many smaller countries [Australia, New Zealand] and developing countries have traditionally had much higher rates of gross national product [GNP] dedicated to world markets. Although exports from the United States are still relatively small as a percent of GNP [7%], they often loom much larger from the point of view of the country importing them.) As markets have internationalized, the number of decision-making actors has grown, in the guise of both giant corporations and national governments. Where once an analysis of the American auto industry could be fashioned out of the behavior of the Big Three with some reference to the U.S. Congress and trade agreements with Canada, now an analysis of its prospects, especially for subregions such as Detroit or eastern Tennessee, must encompass the behavior of Japanese, European, and Latin American firms as well as Ford, General Motors (GM), and Chrysler. Furthermore, the actions of Japanese, Brazilian, Canadian, and European governments bear upon the final division of labor among nations, and within them, among regions.

Together, the authors of the case studies in this book demonstrate powerfully that specialization and the ability to compete in any one industry is not simply, or even principally, the result of some innate comparative advantage that inures in site-specific natural resources, topography, or received culture. They reveal that the actual distribution of production and complementary trading patterns can develop along one or several paths, depending upon an industry's maturity, its position—forward or backward—in the chain of production, and the role played by the overall development designs of its leading firms and host governments. The policy prescriptions they offer are designed to initiate a less-disruptive process than the one presently in place. In this chapter a number of conclusions are drawn from a comparative assessment of the industry profiles.

WORLD OLIGOPOLISTS AND THEIR COMPETING STRATEGIES

It used to be, up through the 1960s, that the American auto industry was the *American* auto industry: its output was produced in domestic plants and its producers were domestically based firms. Only small numbers of autos were exported, and imports were minimal as well, with the single exception of growing trade with Canada, which accelerated in the 1960s. As domestic demand grew, it was served by domestic (and Canadian) plants. Studies of the location of the American industry accepted the contiguous 48 states as the universe within which auto firms competed, and geographic shifts in the industry could be studied by watching these firms' behavior. Indeed, several interesting studies were done of the unique locational preferences of the cartel known popularly as the Big Three, or more bluntly, simply "Detroit," since these preferences resulted in the reinforcing of auto industry concentration in that city.

Today an analysis of the location and number of American auto jobs can no longer be studied by looking at the Big Three. The decline in auto jobs and their shift toward a new axis of domestic production in the Southeast are the products of competition among an expanded set of firms, including those based in Japan, Europe, Latin America, and Canada. Because each of these foreign firms enjoys greater or lesser support from its home government, the levels and sites of domestic auto jobs are also a function of the interplay between governments, between foreign firms and the American government, and between American firms and foreign governments.

The same is true for many other key industries: for steel, for machine tools, for pharmaceuticals, even for service industries like shipping and insurance. Industries not scrutinized in this book, like aerospace, farm machinery, computers, oil, and textiles, exhibit the same complicated multinational complexion. Most important internationally trading industries are now multinucleated, with large national firms thrust into more-spirited competition with similarly sized and politically well-endowed firms from other nations. To make matters even more complex, partnerships of more or less intimacy and longevity are being forged across national lines, with governments as well as firms.

Although the playing field is more crowded, and the teams harder to distinguish from each other, there is not necessarily more competition in the neoclassical sense of the term. The number of players is still relatively small, their sizes and clout are varied, and none of them is unaware of the behavior of its neighbors. These are characteristics of oligopolized markets, not perfectly competitive ones. A fascinating shake-up in industrial structure is taking place, where small and medium-sized domestic firms are disappearing or being swallowed up while the big multinational firms are finding their markets more crowded and less profitable (Harrison, 1989; Mowery, 1987). But since they remain oligopolists, their energies are directed in large part to the continued management of markets via schemes for consolidation of position, including plant shutdowns, mergers with competitors, and appeals to governments for interventionist policies. Some firms have been more successful than others, and geographical shifts in the locus of production are the outcome. The big firms, however, are pursuing profits, not sites per se.

On a nation-by-nation basis, industries have in the past chosen quite distinctive postures toward the international arena in choosing both markets to compete in and sites for production. For instance, the American steel industry chose consistently to restrict its production facilities to the domestic market, serving markets abroad from that base rather than building plants elsewhere. For steel, the enormous size of the domestic market matched or exceeded the minimum necessary scale of production and grew rapidly enough to absorb new capacity additions. In contrast, the machine tools industry in the various European nations, and to a lesser extent in the United States, had to seek external markets to allow them to reach a minimum efficient scale of production, as did the youthful Japanese steel industry.

These choices vary by decade as well. At times, worldwide or domestic economic circumstances have intervened to dictate key choices that would not have been made at a later date or in another era. The U.S. steel industry in the 1930s was on the brink of going international, following autos' lead, when the Great Depression cut deeply into domestic demand. At that critical juncture companies like U.S. Steel scrapped plans to build mills in places like Brazil, hoping to employ excess domestic capacity by exporting steel from Pittsburgh. In another example, key and ultimately growth-limiting decisions about technology and markets were made by American machine tools companies who in the 1950s and subsequent decades enjoyed consistent and highly profitable cold war sales to the Pentagon and its prime contractors. As hostilities melted in the late 1980s, these firms found themselves poorly equipped to compete in international civilian markets.

These differences in behavior do not fall neatly along national lines. Not all Japanese industries are export-oriented and not all American industries are preoccupied with domestic markets. Within the United States some industries have chosen to aggressively market internationally and/or to locate a sizable share of capacity abroad, while others have remained insular. While steel remained an industry of American plants serving American steel users, the big American auto firms built plants abroad to serve overseas markets, and the big pharmaceutical companies marketed drugs, made in domestic plants, aggressively abroad. Scale imperatives and the innovative character of some industries explain much of this variation. In order to cover the extraordinary costs of new drug development, pharmaceutical companies were impelled to seek markets as broadly as possible, an impetus also present in other innovation-based industries such as aerospace and computers. For somewhat different reasons, economies of scale have also encouraged insurance companies to go multinational, albeit only a few have to date.

The corporate and industry-wide strategies that ultimately create or destroy jobs at the regional-community level are not always explicitly spatial ones. The industry studies show that choices about technology, often mediated by the nature of industry structure or the ambitions of dominant firms, often radically restructure the geography of an industry. The American steel industry, comfortably reaping oligopolistic profits in its insulated market of the 1950s, chose not to invest in the newer, riskier basic oxygen furnace. Their European and Japanese neighbors, reindustrializing after the war's devastation, did take the risk. As a result, the locus of steel production shifted internationally in favor of those countries. The American shipping industry, in order to maintain and heighten its oligopolistic power, pushed for expensive investments in containerization that would disadvantage its competitors from smaller nations who preferred the more labor-intensive and less-expensive palletization. The result was a wrenching substitution of capital for labor and a dispersion of employment away from materials-handling ports.

Sometimes, however, the strategy is deliberately spatial. For multinational auto firms locating in the United States, for instance, the choice of new greenfield sites in the upper South reflects a cold, cash calculus. Such siting enables them to restrict recruitment to mainly white, rural, young people who will work harder for less money and tend to eschew unions, thereby enabling the employer to escape the burden of pension and health insurance costs for older workers whose benefits have been tied to existing plants through collective bargaining contracts. Furthermore, a well-publicized site selection process wins the foreign auto firms lucrative subsidies from state and local governments in the bidding war for jobs. Often, states with existing auto plants will not participate in the bidding war because such offers are seen clearly as unfair advantages given to incoming firms over existing ones, who are after all their competitors.

NATION-STATES AS COACHES, MANAGERS, AND BANKROLLERS

If large national firms are the players and team members, then their national governments do the coaching, managing, and even bankrolling of the matches. Just as in the worlds of baseball, soccer, and cricket, some coaches and managers do better than others, sometimes because they are more skilled, and often because they have better resources. Some teams can end up staying in the basement for years, while others can rise to the top with new management and strategy as yet others slide down from the top ranks, unable to reverse their fortunes.

As the case studies show, no industry is free from dramatic differentials in the presence, endowment, and skill with which their governments support the private, and public, enterprises within their borders.

In the United States stiff tariff barriers permitted the late-19th-century development of the early steel and machining industries, who with autos gained world leadership by the early decades of the 20th century. Since then, government sponsorship has been restricted to arbitrating among domestic firms, both mitigating the worst of oligopolistic practices but also helping them consolidate their power over markets, on the one hand, and labor force, on the other. Laissez-faire attitudes toward both trade and industrial policies suited well the young upstart nation in its 20th-century bid to become the dominant world power.

Once that power began to wane, financial rather than industrial interests prevailed in government circles to prolong the laissez-faire stance. Banks, investment houses, financial exchanges, and business services all benefited from the internationalization of capital and commodities. Every movement of capital abroad, every foreign direct investment in the United States, and all expansions in trade require their cash and services. Despite the weakening of domestic manufacturing, the financial sector thrived on the restructuring of the 1980s and used the Treasury and Commerce Departments to pursue their free trade and deregulatory goals. Only in the early 1990s, when the underlying weakness of the entire economy caught up with the financial sector, did the American laissez-faire posture begin to be seriously questioned by large segments of industry and the public.

Other industrialized countries, with the exception perhaps of Great Britain and Canada, were more cautious in their stance toward trade. Especially wary of the negative impact unrestrained trade could have on domestic jobs and regions, they effectively limited the penetration of their markets by foreign producers—Europe's control of its domestic auto market is an example. Japan vigorously protected its nascent auto industry in the postwar period, with tariffs as high as 40%. It accommodated its rice farmers, computer makers, steel mills, and construction firms with similar effective barriers to imports. Developing countries were even more adamant: they clamped down on imports by erecting tariff walls too high to scale, such as Latin American auto tariffs of 200%.

It is not simply trade practice that distinguishes American governmental coaching from those of its trading partners. Concerted programs, often ensconced in permanent large bureaucracies, help the branches of industry to promote exports, finance new investments in plant and equipment, extend research and development monies, and manage macroeconomic aggregates like interest rates and exchange rates in favor of domestic producers. Often such aid includes barely disguised nationalist policies that take the shape of bureaucratic regulation, red tape, or other noneconomic barriers to entry into domestic markets. Often too the governments involved are willing to step in to ameliorate short-term adversities, through special loans or compensation for currency exchange rates manipulated for other ends.

That Japan has been the master of these strategies, engaging in targeted industrial policy, is well known. The variants in other developed as well as developing countries are less celebrated. Not all of them succeed. Brazilian efforts to develop an internationally competitive steel industry, for instance, have been disappointing, with the exception of a new coastally sited joint venture with multinational corporations. The Indian strategy of investing in production for an internal market under relatively high protective walls has met with mixed success: while India's steel industry is not very competitive, its insurance industry has flourished.

What seems to work best are national government-industry strategies where close partnerships between big firms and nation states evolve complex, integrated, and cooperative plans that minimize the power of foreign governments or foreign firms to extract monopoly profits or impose market management while enhancing the ability to export and ensuring at least modest domestic market growth. When such strategies are supported by long-term subsidization of the industry, in terms of technical expertise as well as sheer financial aid, they often do produce highly productive, state-of-the-art industries. The steel industry study demonstrates the differences across countries. Brazil's steel industry was badly hurt by its need to sell to multinational auto firms who had an upper hand in the market and who therefore depressed prices, while Japan's steel industry flourished under the domestic partnership between Japanese steel and auto firms, both cooperating to achieve increasing returns to scale by exporting. Korea's increasingly formidable steel industry focused on coastally produced semifinished steel to be shipped to U.S. partners as well as on serving its indigenous and export-oriented auto industry.

Of course, other attributes of such partnerships are necessary conditions for their success. Rewards for entrepreneurship and performance, and control of graft and corruption, help to explain why some countries do it better than others. From Brazil to the former Soviet Union corruption has sabotaged efforts to promote industrialization and competitiveness. Cultural homogeneity or, in multicultural regions or nations, equal opportunity, access, and mutual respect among disparate groups, helps to promote a cooperative growth strategy. The net effect of political stability, although much touted in the development literature, is less clear. Although industrial policies have flourished under stable, if repressive, regimes such as those in South Korea and China, many other countries with political stability are not doing so well—one might include the United States here. Conversely, countries like Italy have done quite well despite turbulent national politics.

Ironically, the geography-altering impact of these concerted industrial policies reaches far beyond their effect on their domestic industries. Nontariff barriers and export subsidies in the United States make it difficult for many developing countries to compete in agricultural and other sectors. Similarly, American corporations find they must respond to trade barriers erected by foreign governments or to demands for domestic content. As a result, they make decisions to forego certain markets and to serve others by locating plants abroad. To the extent that the U.S. government threatens to manage access to domestic markets, foreign corporations may do the same, as they have done with autos. As a result, how many U.S. jobs there will be, and where they will be located, is determined through a complex process of deliberation, negotiation, and cooperation between large multinational corporations and the various states they must deal with around the globe.

SUPRANATIONAL STATE INSTITUTIONS AND NEGOTIATIONS

The shaping of the international trade and production system also takes place in international forums and organizations. Trade negotiations under the umbrella of GATT (General Agreement on Trade and Tariffs) are designed to eliminate barriers to trade and to "level the playing field" among potential trading partners. Efforts to form the European Community (EC) and free-trade zones like that proposed for Canada, the United States, and Mexico are theoretically designed to create trading blocs within which greater specialization can take place, increasing efficiency, and increasing returns to scale can be achieved. Institutions like the World Bank and the International Monetary Fund (IMF) pursue currency and lending policies that channel developing countries' strategies in certain directions.

Nowhere are the differing strategies concerning industrial policy and postures toward trade clearer than when the nations involved gather at the international bargaining table. Largely due to the leadership of the United States and Great Britain, several rounds of trade talks in the postwar period have pushed toward the lowering of trade barriers and the liberalization of trade internationally. In previous rounds many tariff barriers were lowered, but various nations have continued to press for the elimination of nontariff barriers and various subsidies which they claim constitute unfair trade practices. In recent years the protection of agriculture has proven a stubborn stumbling bloc, both in multilateral and bilateral trade. Japan and Korea are anxious to protect their aging, small rice farmers, while France and other European countries fight for the survival of small cheesemakers and against the importation of beef with high levels of hormones. The U.S. criticizes public-sector investments in the European Airbus consortium as constituting an unfair trade practice, while the Europeans decry the massive Pentagon subsidies to the American aircraft industry.

Issues of jobs, environmental protection, and community stability also emerge in the formation of trading blocs and supranational integrated economies. In the debate over the North American Free Trade Agreement American and Canadian opponents point to the potential loss of jobs in manufacturing, not just from heightened competition from lower priced Mexico commodities but also from accelerated migration of capital and plants to Mexico. Canadians worry that inferior social welfare programs south of their borders will erode their own fine health and welfare systems, while environmentalists worry that Mexico's lower standards for pollution, pesticides, and air quality will undermine U.S. and Canadian achievements. Mexicans worry that large numbers of poorer farmers will be wiped out by U.S. and Canadian agribusiness exports. In Europe, similar concerns have been the subject of long negotiations creating the EC. However, the reunification of Germany and the challenge of eastern European and North African underdevelopment have evoked new opposition to the EC from those who fear economic disruption and the lowering of living standards.

Trade negotiations and trading blocs, even their potential formation, form an inducement to industrial location in other ways too. Japanese auto producers made a strategic decision in the early 1980s to locate auto assembly plants in the United States for fear that growing protectionist sentiment would close off the lucrative American market to them. The emergence of the EC has spurred American and Japanese firms to locate plants in Europe to gain treatment comparable to what European firms will have within the wider EC market. The decision to export from the home base versus siting plants abroad is thus a function of anticipated trade policy and in turn shapes the distribution of industries internationally.

In shaping developmental patterns, institutions like the World Bank and the IMF have also played a significant role, especially in developing countries' policies over the decades. Since they arbitrate currency questions, control vast sums for development lending, and deal with debt repayment, their advice to and requirements imposed on third world countries have dramatically altered development paths. In the past two decades two tenets of international financial agency practice have been paramount here: the counseling of export promotion, instead of import substitution or domestic market development policies; and the austerity policies forced on countries whose debt burden has become large and often unmanageable. The former accelerated the rate of specialization in the world economy, adding to the disruption in developed countries' industries. It also kept the lid on wages in developing countries, since penetrating developed countries' markets relied upon the low-wage advantage, thereby retarding internal market growth. While the strategy has provided substantial export earnings and growth for a handful of countries (for example, Taiwan, South Korea, and Malaysia), it has increased indebtedness, export dependency, and narrow specialization for many others. The austerity prescriptions of the IMF compounded this poor performance, plunging large parts of Latin America into negative growth and rapidly declining living standards in the 1980s.

In short, then, these international organizations and arenas also shape world industrial growth, location, and specialization processes. Although states are the major actors in them—the United States has long dominated the World Bank, for instance, and has played a lead role in the GATT talks—multinational corporations, banks, industrial and trade associations, farmers, and environmentalists all work through their national delegations for their own particular interests. The map of world production and trade might be remarkably different today if development assistance and trade negotiations had followed other paths.

HOW MANY JOBS, AND WHERE?

The canvasses painted by these industrial scholars suggest a process of strategic mapping of production onto space that differs dramatically from that depicted in the elaborate graphs of international trade theory. Assuming some overall level of global demand, the interaction of the agents in this process allocates production units and jobs across international and subnational borders. To interpret, then, the level, stability, and quality of jobs in any one location, one must inquire into both historical and contemporary corporate and state behavior, transcending political boundaries. Instead of analyzing steel or insurance employment in Pittsburgh or Manhattan as the outcome of a struggle between Gary, Detroit, and dispersed American minimills, or between suburban and small-town back-office sites and traditional city skyscrapers, each is derived from an international, and highly political, allocative process.

U.S. consumers of steel and steel products can be served by domestic plants, either producing locally or across the continent, or purchase products directly from overseas plants, or indirectly consume foreign-made steel embodied in domestically made or assembled goods. U.S. steelworkers may make steel chiefly for the U.S. market, but employment can be expanded or contracted depending upon how much is sold abroad—directly or embodied in steel-using products like autos, farm and construction machinery, or machine tools—and also depending upon the penetration of foreign producers in the domestic market, both in raw steel and in steel-using imports. The same options hold for all other American industries, be they manufacturing or service sectors.

From the point of view of any single community, then, surviving in the world economy is first a function of the size and growth of the world market and the market share maintained by the nation as a whole, and second, a function of the location of production units within the nation. Corporate and state actors collude and compete to determine the former, while multinational corporations, both domestic and international, and the various levels of the government collude and compete to determine where, regionally, production will take place. The alterations that have taken place in American regional economic activity are the joint outcome of these two aspects of internationalization.

Multiple outcomes are therefore possible. Heightened trade and internationalization may enhance the prospects for production, and therefore jobs, in those communities that host industries with a comparative advantage, however constructed, but only if jobs can be anchored there rather than migrating to other domestic or foreign sites. Job loss in a region can be attributed to absolute loss of market share, either through the collapse of export markets or the successful penetration of imports, or it can be caused by producer shifts to new domestic sites or by preferences for greenfield sites by foreign direct investors. When output levels decline, the associated job loss may be spread relatively evenly across regions, or it may fall disproportionately on a region with a concentration of relatively older or less-efficient facilities. Each of the industries scrutinized in this book exhibits a rather unique outcome for U.S. regions.

In steel, the bulk of internationally related job losses since the late 1970s were linked to the direct reduction of domestic sales as steel imports from Japanese, European, and increasingly South Korean and Brazilian steel companies increased their market share. Since landlocked sites like Pittsburgh; Youngstown; northern Alabama; Geneva, Utah; and Fontana, California, suffered a locational cost disadvantage, and in the case of the first three, also suffered from relatively antiquated and less auto-oriented mills, job losses were much heavier there than in the greater Chicago area. Although some large new investments in electrogalvanizing cold rolling mills were initiated by Japanese steel multinationals, these tended to be located at or nearby existing steel mills along the Chicago-Detroit axis, since they were all joint ventures with American steel firms and targeted at the auto industry.

Autos are a very different story. Here, absolute declines in domestic jobs were also attributable to import penetration, but they were spread relatively more evenly across the regions, with perhaps a slight tendency toward net reconcentration of domestic employment in the greater Midwest. However, in response to perceived threats of protection and as part of a longer term oligopolistic strategy, Japanese firms created new jobs within the United States by building large new assembly plants. Although a couple of these were built in or nearby to American auto plant centers, most were deliberately placed outside the commuting sheds of existing autoworkers, recruiting an auto-inexperienced labor force. The center of gravity of this new capacity is in the upper South: Tennessee and Kentucky. Japanese success, as Howes shows, has wiped out jobs at other American sites, particularly in the greater Detroit region.

Perhaps of all the industries studied, the economic activities arrayed around ports have experienced the most disruptive changes with internationalization. Changes in shipping technology, embodied in containerization, reinforced the concentration of related service-sector jobs—in transportation, finance, marine insurance, and the like—in major central cities like San Francisco and New York while dispersing blue-collar jobs—unloading, unpacking, warehousing, and wholesaling—to suburbanized or interior locations. Jobs evaporated from the actual point of transfer, the ports' docks themselves, totally mechanized out of existence. Downtown office buildings added jobs in Seattle and Manhattan, while cities like Reno and Minneapolis benefited from new jobs in unbundling and distributing imported goods from containers.

In all these industries net geographical shifts in the locus of production have had significant international causes, and in each the mix of forces has differed. Of course, not all shifts in domestic production patterns are caused by international forces. The insurance industry, for instance, has redistributed itself across American domestic territory by following populations south and west, by exiting central cities for suburbia, and by favoring small and medium-sized towns as sites for back-office functions. Most of this is attributable to radical changes introduced by computing technologies and to intensified competitive pressures introduced by deregulation and the entrance of new domestic competitors into the business. If anything, the internationalization of the insurance industry, through its attraction of foreign firms and its concentration of international operations in big cities, has retarded this dispersion. Technological change and profit-motivated cost-cutting behavior explains some of the redistribution of jobs in industries like steel, especially in the minimill phenomenon, and in autos as well, where profit-squeezed suppliers have also shifted toward lower cost southern sites.

In other industries, particularly machine tools and pharmaceuticals, internationalization has not apparently contributed to net shifts in the location of production, although it has affected the level of domestic economic activity. In both these industries the significance of innovation, a relatively higher degree of small-batch and tailor-made output, and the need for a more skilled labor force has helped to anchor employment in existing centers. Moreover, the rise of larger and larger firms in these industries, a counterpart of internationalization, reinforces certain host centers. In pharmaceuticals, the arrival of foreign firms in the United States, as part of their market share strategy, has not affected the general pattern of location, because they tend to locate their operations close to existing high-tech labor pools and the specialized services that have grown up around drug regions like northern New Jersey and the northern suburbs of Chicago.

Overall, it appears that internationally induced job change is apt to be more disruptive in older, mature industries than in newer ones with a relative comparative advantage. In the more mature industries, like steel, autos, and machine tools, the magnitude of employment loss due to loss of international market share as well as decisions by American multinationals to produce abroad has been much greater. In steel, these losses were differentially distributed, causing considerable hardship in some regions. In autos, the shift southward in the center of gravity of domestic production due to new Japanese plants compounded import-related job loss with devastating results for cities like Detroit. The emphasis on more-innovative and craftlike production in both machine tools and pharmaceuticals, as well as the consolidation of production in fewer domestic firms, helped to sustain existing production centers, even when, as in machine tools, total employment fell.

The case studies also show that there are limits to the degree of internationalization introduced by distance, culture, and political practices. One striking characteristic of all these industries is the degree to which its domestic mix of output is tailored to the particularities of each national, and even subnational, market. The atomization of the American population, through the diffusion of auto ownership, familial dispersion, and the relative absence of either formal state or informal community social safety nets, has created a relatively unique and extensive market for insurance. High levels of auto ownership, extensive public investment in highways, and dispersed living patterns shape the American steel and auto industries. The enormous $300 billion-a-year defense budget places its peculiar demands on steel, auto (trucks and tanks), and machine tools, and accounts for the prosperity and geographical concentration in the aerospace industry. The American diet, exacerbated by relative prosperity, has created a distinctive domestic market for cardiovascular and ulcer drugs. In all these cases, such peculiarities help to anchor and protect domestic jobs. The same will be true of production complexes in many other countries. This "market pull" will, however, encourage domestic companies to set up production sites abroad instead of shipping from domestic plants to serve foreign markets.

TRADE POLICY, INDUSTRIAL POLICY

The case studies restrict themselves to probing the difference between what used to be and what now is. Their depiction of domestic U.S. job loss and net job shifts does not reveal the true magnitude of the international dimension because they do not try to imagine what would have happened had American trade and industrial policies actually nurtured domestic industries and implemented practices used elsewhere, like domestic content requirements, effective limits on the pace and level of importation, and promotion of export-oriented industries. It is impossible to judge the degree to which lost jobs might have been saved and new jobs created had corporate and government strategies been different. But surely there would be more jobs in some industries, and these jobs would have been preserved and/or added to the stock of jobs in many communities and regions. Indeed, those industries like aerospace enjoying de facto industrial policy through the aegis of the Department of Defense's enormous procurements, subsidized R & D programs, and Buy America policies, have added thousands of jobs to the economies of Los Angeles, Seattle, and Colorado Springs, while helping to retard decline in older high-cost regions such as Boston and Long Island.

Job loss, and the more invisible foregone production and employment owed to yielding of market share in internationally expanding industries, is a thoroughly political phenomenon. No one viewing the remarkable Japanese success in recent years can argue that it is a function of adherence to laissez-fare competitive practices. In contrast, the clinging of top American advisers and policymakers to the laissez-faire posture has wreaked havoc on many sectors and the regions that host them. Over and over, the case studies show how U.S. government practices shape, hinder, or nurture industries. Ineffective trade restraints in the face of grossly "unfair," or at least different, trade practices abroad have contributed to severe losses in steel and autos. Indifference to technological and financial constraints, except when serving Pentagon missions, have handicapped industries like machine tools and steel. While patent management has promoted pharmaceutical industry profits, and regulations have aided consumers, no overall concern with American pharmaceutical industry preeminence or retention of jobs has guided development policy in that sector.

Often the strategies of firms, even multinational ones, are counteracted by those of the state. This appears to occur more often in the United

States than in European or Asian countries. American firms' attempts to cartelize, through mergers or collusion, are often stymied by antitrust practices. While antitrust law does protect the consumer from predatory competition, it also handicaps U.S. firms in their oligopolistic struggle with large foreign multinationals. Efforts to secure trade protection are less apt to be effective in the United States than in most other countries, as are effective controls on foreign direct investment. One major reason for the lack of effective cooperation between U.S. industrial corporations and the national government is the extraordinary hold that dominant international financial corporations and institutions like banks have over national economic policymaking, at least since 1980. Moreover, the ubiquity of foreign imports and foreign-built plants, coupled with democratic access to Congress and that institution's major role in economic policymaking, means that international corporations and domestic companies thriving off imports work at political cross-purposes to industrialists trying to forge favorable industrial policies.

All this may be coming to an end. The lagging performance of the American economy, and the spread of the U.S. recession abroad through its depressing effects on export markets for Japan, Europe, South Korea, and the developing countries, puts U.S. trade and industrial policy, or lack of it, back in the spotlight. In the new debate a mixed chorus of voices can be heard contending with the neoclassical "free trade" position, which is still the predominant one among economists and in the federal government. Since the empirical evidence appears to be going against the free traders—liberalized trade is not creating more jobs for Americans or reducing the trade deficit, and workers displaced by imports are not easily finding work in new sectors—greater credence is being given publicly to the dissenting theories and trade prescriptions outlined in Chapter 1.

The new international division of labor (NIDL) position lends itself to two different policy prescriptions, each rather diametrically opposed. One, some industrialists and some but by no means all of the labor unions favor the restoration of tariff barriers and other trade protections that will protect domestic market shares and stop the flow of low-wage jobs to other nations and maintain the United States as a relatively diversified economy, spanning the low to high wage industries. One innovative twist on this position is the demand by the labor movement in the United States that imports not be allowed from countries with repressive labor policies. This was codified in watered-down form in recent trade legislation, which specified that the president may enact trade sanctions on countries that deny workers the right to organize. The other policy spinoff of the NIDL position, a more radical view, counsels that not much can be done to stem the tide and that international organization of labor is the only possible response to the deterioration of world wage levels and living standards that will result.

The flexible specialization school disagrees with the NIDL position that migration of industrial work to low-wage countries is inevitable. They argue that the emergence of more-fickle, differentiated market niches and the development of computerized technologies make smaller batch and vertically disintegrated production possible and profitable. Firms competing on this basis will tend to agglomerate near business suppliers and customers, creating the possibility for reconcentration of production within advanced industrial countries. Trade and industrial policies are less important, then, than policies that encourage flexible specialization in production, including business assistance and human capital formation. Whether this prescription can work for the majority of communities in industrialized countries is dubious. Empirically, the number of flexibly specialized production districts remains small, and their origins and nature a matter of controversy (Markusen & Park, 1993).

The revisionist trade theorists, working with a dynamic strategic trade theory, call for a managed trade policy to slow the pace of disruptive change and complement a broader industrial policy. They are proposing, in essence, national economic development strategies where each country would anticipate future sectoral specializations and seek to enhance job creation and stabilization. In a world where some countries do practice strategic trade and industrial policy and others don't, severe trade imbalances and relatively large differential growth rates can result, which are ultimately destabilizing for the entire system. Instead, the revisionists point to the crucial link between trade and growth strategies, pointing out accurately that trade alone will not guarantee either national or international net trade, especially if much of it is based on downward pressure on wages.

The revisionists, although by no means a homogeneous group when it comes to policy, favor targeting industries on the basis of growth potential, job preservation, and strategic importance on economic or foreign policy grounds. They call for a coordinated package of financial, trade, training, and R & D incentives to engender the development of the targeted industries (Thurow, 1992). Not all nations are equally well positioned to conduct such strategic trade and industrial policies, especially when aimed at industries with increasing returns to scale or those that require sophisticated technologies and human capital. Critics worry that expanded competition among nations, based on the emergence of the Japan/North America/European triad, will command the lion's share of resources and deepen the rift between developed and developing (including the former USSR) nations. How growth and stability will be achieved and distributed in the coming world of heightened trade and industrial policy consciousness is as yet unclear.

The authors in this volume each offer prescriptions for their industries designed to enhance the number or at least the stability of domestic jobs. Each focuses on a different set of factors, aimed at both corporate and state arenas, contingent on the unique histories and contemporary situations of each industry. This diversity justifies, in our view, the methodology chosen here. In a multinational, multinucleated world, each industry is like a stage with a unique set of actors engaging upon it. Each industry has a different number of top corporate competitors, spread differentially across the major trading nations, with different degrees of financial power, market share, and cooperation enjoyed by each. Although each nation state has a distinctive trade and industrial policy posture that it brings to each industrial forum, in actual practice its promotion and restrictions for that industry will reflect the political clout and complexion of industrial leaders domestically, political inroads made by importers and foreign firms, and crosscutting foreign policy concerns.

It is unlikely that the postwar American policy regime, committed to free trade and adamantly opposed to industrial policy, will succeed in reversing the recent decline in American industry and living standards. The real value of these case studies is the systematic way they reveal the international nature of the playing field and the far-from-impersonal way in which companies and governments vie for position. If they succeed in demonstrating that markets are made by the interaction of corporate and political agents, exposing the notion that firms are dictated to by markets as a fraud, they have performed a great service. If they successfully show that persistent unemployment and waste of infrastructure and industrial base are a product of free trade and laissez-faire strategies, they will contribute to the growing pressure for a reassessment of national economic development policy. Perhaps then the United States might engage more effectively in an international discussion about how to manage trade and industrialization to maximize community stability, living standards, and environmental quality in a way that is fair and progressive for all peoples.

REFERENCES

Harrison, B. 1989. The Big Firms Are Coming Out of the Corner: The Resurgence of Economic Scale and Industrial Power in the Age of "Flexibility." Paper presented at International Conference on Industrial Transformation and Regional Development in an Age of Global Interdependence, Nagoya, Japan, September 21.

Markusen, A., & Park, S. O. 1993. "New Industrial Districts: A Critique and Extension from the Developing World." Working Paper. Project on Regional and Industrial Economics, Rutgers University.

Mowery, David. 1987. *Alliance Politics and Economics: Multinational Joint Ventures in Commercial Aircraft.* Cambridge, MA: Ballinger.

Thurow, L. 1992. Head to Head: The Coming Economic Battle Among Japan, Europe and America. New York: William Morrow.

Index

Abbott pharmaceuticals, 179
Aerospace firms
  machine tool demand, 155, 156
  subsidies, 293
Aetna Life & Casualty, 269, 272
Agglomeration economies, 79
Agricultural industries, 27
AIG company, 277
Aircraft technology, 23
American Motors, 66
Amgen's Epogen, 198, 204
Antibiotics, 179–181
Antihypertensive drugs, 192
ARMCO, 133
Arms sales, 27
Atlantic Coast seaports, 220, 221
Automation, insurance industry, 270, 271
Automobile assembly plant closings, 69–71
Automobile industry, 45–87, 286, 287
  employment, 82–85, 295, 296
  export-led growth, 58–64
  geography in U.S., 64–74
  global production patterns, 51–64
  Japanese transplant production, 71–85
    and social dumping, 74–83
  joint ventures, and steel, 116, 117
  location theories, 48–51
  machine tool demand, 155, 156
  orthodox economic theory, 48, 49
  and steelmaking facilities, 114, 116, 117
  as strategic industry, 45, 46
Automobile parts suppliers
  Japanese production system, 76
  shakeout, 69
  transplanted Japanese companies, 81
Automotive Products Trade Act, 66

Basic oxygen furnace, 105, 106, 130, 289
Benefit costs (see Fringe benefits)
Bidding wars, assembly plants, 79, 80

Big Three automakers, 287
Biomedical research, 187–189
Biotechnology
  and drug approval, 199, 203
  Japan's activity in, 205
  Merck's strategy, 194
  mergers, 195
  patent protection, 198
  price control threat, 204
  strategic alliances, 177, 178
  as threshold industry, 182
  and U.S. export policy, 203
Blacks, assembly plants, 79, 87
Brand name drugs, 200, 201
Brazil
  automobile production, 56
  debt crisis, and steel, 111, 112, 125, 126, 132
  integrated steel plants, 107
  joint ventures, 115, 116, 130
  machine tool industry, 150, 151
  pharmaceuticals, 183, 197
    patent regulations, 197
  state-sponsored steel production, 103, 291
  steel imports to U.S., 97
  steel production, 96, 111, 112, 122
  U.S. policy toward, 125, 126
Break-bulk cargo method, 214, 217, 235
Bridge cargo (see Land-bridge cargo)
Bristol Meyers, 177, 194
Britain (see United Kingdom)
Bulk cargo, 225, 226, 231, 232
Burroughs Wellcome, 204
"Burton Act," 229
Businessmen's Assurance of Kansas, 274

California
  insurance industry, 258
  machine tool industry, 153

303